The Definitive

THE DEFINITIVE SIMON GRAY I

faber and faber

LONDON · BOSTON

This collection first published in 1992
by Faber and Faber Limited
3 Queen Square London WC1N 3AU

Photoset by Parker Typesetting Service, Leicester
Printed in England by Cox & Wyman Ltd, Reading, Berkshire

Butley was first published in 1971 by Methuen and Co. Ltd. The lines from T. S. Eliot's *Collected Poems 1909–1962* are reprinted by permission of Faber and Faber Ltd. The lines by Beatrix Potter, from *Cecily Parsley's Nursery Rhymes* and *Appley Dappley's Nursery Rhymes*, are reprinted by permission of Frederick Warne and Co. Ltd.
Wise Child was first published in 1968 by Faber and Faber Limited.
Dutch Uncle was first published in 1969 by Faber and Faber Limited.
Spoiled was first published in 1972 by Methuen and Co. Ltd.
Sleeping Dog was first published in 1968 by Faber and Faber Limited.

A CIP record for this book is available from the British Library

ISBN 0–571–16223–1

CONTENTS

Butley

To the staff and students, past, present and future, of the English Department, Queen Mary College, London.

Butley was first presented by Michael Codron on 14 July 1971 at the Criterion Theatre, London. The cast was as follows:

BEN BUTLEY	Alan Bates
JOSEPH KEYSTON	Richard O'Callaghan
MISS HEASMAN	Brenda Cavendish
EDNA SHAFT	Mary Wimbush
ANNE BUTLEY	Colette O'Neil
REG NUTTALL	Michael Byrne
MR GARDNER	George Fenton
Director	Harold Pinter

ACT ONE

An office in a College of London University. About 10 in the morning.
The office is badly decorated (white walls, greying, plasterboards)
with strip lighting. There are two desks opposite each other, each with
a swivel chair. Ben's desk, left, is a chaos of papers, books, detritus.
Joey's desk, right, is almost bare. Behind each desk is a bookcase.
Again, Ben's is chaotic with old essays and mimeographed sheets
scattered among the books, while Joey's is neat, not many books on the
shelves. On each desk there is a table lamp and in front of each desk a
hard chair. There is one telephone, on Ben's desk, the flex of which is
long enough to reach Joey's desk. There are a few hard-backed chairs
around the walls, and one armchair, in Ben's corner of the room. On
the wall is a blown-up picture (photograph) of T. S. Eliot, with a
smear across it and one of its corners curled. The panels to the office
door are frosted glass, behind which people, when they approach, are
dimly seen.

BEN is a heavy smoker, and should smoke more frequently than the text
indicates. JOEY does not smoke.

As the curtain rises, BEN enters, in a plastic raincoat, which he takes
off and throws into his chair. He has a lump of cotton wool on his
chin, from a particularly nasty shaving-cut. He goes to his chair, sits
down, looks around as if searching for something, shifts
uncomfortably, pulls the plastic mac out from under him, searches
through its pockets, takes out half a banana, a bit squashed, then
throws the raincoat over to Joey's desk. He takes a bite from the
banana, removes it from the peel and drops the last piece onto his desk.
Then he throws the peel onto Joey's desk. He slumps into his chair – a
long pause – the telephone rings.

BEN: Butley, English. Hello, James, have a nice break? (*A pause –*
he mouths a curse.) Sorry, James, I can't talk now – I'm right
in the middle of a tutorial – bye.
(*Then he touches the cotton wool and tries to pull it off. He lets*
out an exclamation. Touches his chin, looks at his finger.)
(*In an undertone*) Bugger!

(*He gets up, looks under his desk, drags out a bulging briefcase from which he pulls an opened bag of cotton wool. He delves into his briefcase again and takes out a tin of Nescafé. He shines the base on his sleeve, then holds it to his chin as if it were a mirror. He tries to put the cotton wool on, then switches on the light. It doesn't come on. He sticks the cotton wool on. He shoves the Nescafé tin back into his briefcase and stuffs the cotton wool into his jacket pocket. He goes across to the main switch and flicks it on. The strip lighting flickers into brilliance. He checks the cotton wool using the glass door of his bookcase as a mirror, then, unable to bear the striplight, flicks it off again. He goes across to Joey's desk and tries the lamp. It comes on. He wipes stray wisps of cotton wool from his fingers with the banana skin, then drops it into the clean ashtray on Joey's desk. He switches off Joey's lamp and carries it across to his desk. There is a shape at the door, then a knock.*)

Bugger! Just a minute!

(*He carries his lamp across to Joey's. The door opens cautiously.*)

A minute I said. (*He goes to the door and checks it with his hand.*) Hello.

STUDENT: (*Off*) Hello.

BEN: (*After a pause*) Can I help you?

STUDENT: (*Off*) Well, it's my tutorial. On Wordsworth. The Prelude.

BEN: Oh. No, I can't give tutorials during the first week after the break I'm afraid. Too much administration.

STUDENT: (*Off*) Oh? When should I come then?

BEN: Come at the same hour of the same day of next week.

STUDENT: (*Off*) Next week?

BEN: Next week. If we keep to our timetable we'll know where we are, won't we? All right? (*He closes the door.*)

(*He goes back to his desk, sits down and takes out of his pocket a copy of 'Cecily Parsley'.*

'The Prelude'.

(*He shudders, then turns a page, reaches for the light, clicks it. Nothing happens. He gets up and goes over to Joey's desk, tries the light, it comes on. He sighs. He sits down in Joey's chair, opens*

one of his drawers, props his feet in it, and settles down to read.
JOEY *comes in with a briefcase. He puts it down on his desk,*
clears the banana peel into the waste-paper basket, picks Ben's
raincoat up, carries it over to the peg, puts the desk lamps back on
their respective desks. He turns on his table light – it comes on.)
Good morning.

JOEY: Good morning.

BEN: Nice to see you.

JOEY: Nice to be seen. What's the matter with your chin?

BEN: I'm trying to cultivate cotton wool on it. Your own is
shining pleasantly, what did you have to work with, a razor?

JOEY: What did *you* use?

BEN: Anne left one behind. Behind the fridge, to be exact. So
either mice have taken up shaving, or that stubble was
sheared from her calves. I thought of mounting a tuft in a
locket. You needn't have taken the only one we have.

JOEY: It also happens to be the only one I have.

BEN: Couldn't you have shared Ted's? It's no pleasure slicing
open my chin with my estranged wife's razor blade. The
symbolism may be deft, but the memory still smarts.

JOEY: I didn't mean to take it, in point of fact. I put it in the bag
without thinking.

BEN: Lust is no excuse for thoughtlessness. And where is your
bag? (*He stands up and peers round for it.*)

JOEY: What? Oh, I left it with Reg.

BEN: Reg? Who's Reg? (*He perches on the front of his own desk with
his feet up on a chair and lights a cigarette.* JOEY *hastily occupies
the vacated desk chair.*)

JOEY: Reg is his name.

BEN: Whose name?

JOEY: Ted's.

BEN: Reg is Ted's name?

JOEY: The one you call Ted is the one I call Reg. He calls himself
Reg too.

BEN: How sweet.

JOEY: In fact, everybody calls him Reg except you. You call him
Ted.

7

BEN: Why do I do that, I wonder.

JOEY: To embarrass me.

BEN: Oh yes, that must be it. (*Pause.*) Did you have a good
weekend?

JOEY: It was all right. (*Pause.*) Have you seen James this
morning?

BEN: Ah! Our Professor! He's just been hounding me on the
telephone. He and Hazel spent most of the break in bed
recovering from one of Hazel's gastric goulashes.

JOEY: Did he say anything? I mean, are there any details yet?

BEN: You want details of James' diarrhoea?

JOEY: You know what I mean. About my board.

BEN: Ah. About your board. Now when is that, exactly?

JOEY: A fortnight tomorrow.

BEN: Indeed? A fortnight tomorrow? Mmmm. Where the hell is
it? (*He begins to search in his desk drawers – JOEY comes over to
him.*)

JOEY: What?

BEN: It's no real advance. (*Sits.*) But it's got some interesting
things in it. Damn! Anyway –

'How do you do, Mistress Pussy?
Mistress Pussy, how do you do?'
'I thank you kindly little dog,
I fare as well as you!'

JOEY: Did he say anything?

BEN: You're genuinely interested in this promotion of yours,
aren't you? Why? (*Little pause.*) No, he didn't say anything.
Your name didn't come up, and there's no reason that it
should until, in the normal course of events and strictly
according to the rules, the board is rigged, the strings are
pulled, and it's passed over to that of someone more closely
related to the Principal, or with more distinguished
qualifications. I should warn you that there are almost as
many of the latter as of the former.

Cecily Parsley lived in a pen,
And brewed good ale for gentlemen;
Gentlemen came every day.

(JOEY *goes to his shelves and takes down a book*.)
Till Cecily Parsley ran away.
Why? (BEN *crosses to* JOEY.) Why has he got your bag?
JOEY: He happened to pick it up for me when we got off the train.
BEN: Not many young men are as gallant these days. You haven't
been home yet then?
JOEY: To the flat. No? (*He sits at his desk.*)
BEN: Ah. Why not?
JOEY: Because I didn't have time, obviously. (*He begins to correct
a set of essays from his briefcase.*)
BEN: I waited for you.
JOEY: Did you? Sorry.
BEN: (*Watches him*) You had a nice little mid-term break then, did
you?
JOEY: It was all right.
BEN: Well, are you going to tell me about it, or shall I probe and
pry?
JOEY: I'd rather let it slip out naturally, if I may?
BEN: But you're much more charming under interrogation. My
natural force plays excitingly with your natural
submissiveness. Or has your holiday changed you, as we say
in the trade, radically? (*He opens Joey's briefcase.*) Ah-hah! I
thought so! (*As* JOEY *looks up.*) Blake! Why is your briefcase
bulging with Blake! (*He opens one of the books and takes out a
piece of paper.*) What's this?
JOEY: I happen to be lecturing on him this half. (*He tries to take
the book and notes from him.*) Kindly don't mess my notes up.
Can I have it back, please?
BEN: Notes to whom? Reg?
What immortal hand or eye
Could frame thy fearful symmetry?
Ted is certainly quite symmetrical – in a burly sort of way.
Did he who made the lamb make thee?
(*Laughs.*)
JOEY: All right, all right, let's *be* infantile. (*He goes across to Ben's
desk and picks up his briefcase.*)
BEN: (*Drops Joey's book and notes, lunges across and grabs his own

9

briefcase) No, bags first go. I haven't unpacked it for weeks.
(*He opens it, as* JOEY *returns to his marking. He pulls out an empty scotch bottle, then a red-covered manuscript.*)
It's laid out like a film script. It must be an American MA thesis – Ah – 'Henry James and the Crucified Consciousness' –aaah.
(BEN *wanders over to Joey's desk, pulls out a blue sock, puts the thesis down on Joey's desk, along with a few more papers, files, crumpled newspaper, the Nescafé tin and the briefcase itself.*)
Now where's the other – there must be a pair –

JOEY: (*Picks up the thesis*) You mean you forgot to give his thesis back?

BEN: Not yet. So far I've forgotten to read it. Forgetting to give it back will come later. Failing Americans is a slow and intricate ritual and that's what they come here for – the ritual – aaah, here it is. (*He takes out another sock. It is red. He picks up the blue. Looks at them.*)

JOEY: Those are mine. Naturally.

BEN: Naturally you're very welcome. (*He tosses the socks at* JOEY.) Personally I wouldn't be caught dead wearing a pair like that. (*He lifts up his trousers, studies his socks.*)

JOEY: Those happen to be mine, too.

BEN: You really must give up buying cheap socks. I can feel a hole growing around the toe.

JOEY: (*Savagely*) Perhaps if you bothered to cut your toe-nails – (*He picks up the thesis and essays* BEN *has dropped.*)

BEN: Are we going to have a tantrum?

JOEY: The thing is to stop your rubbish creeping across to my side of the room. (*He makes as if to stack them neatly, then crams them savagely into Ben's shelves.*) Here, anyway. (*He goes back to his desk and continues marking.*)

BEN: *Are* we? I'd quite enjoy one.

JOEY: Would you?

BEN: Then I'll know you're back, you see. You've been a little thin on presence so far.

JOEY: There's not enough room.
(BEN *sits down cross-legged on the top of Joey's desk and watches*

JOEY. *He clears his throat delicately. He smiles genteelly.*)

BEN: (*Genteel*) I was just wondering if I might enquire as to how your friend is, may I?

(JOEY *smiles.*)

Hoh, h'I'm so glad.

(JOEY *continues transcribing marks.*)

May h'I hask, done all those, 'ave we?

(*He takes the essay* JOEY *is holding.*)

Ho, but you 'adn't done them last week 'ad you? Did you do them on the train, going h'up with your friend?

(*Shape at the door,* BEN *doesn't notice.*)

H'I h'always say that h'if h'a job's worth doing h'it's worth h'ignoring.

(*Knock on the door.* BEN *turns, starts to move rapidly to it. When it opens,* MISS HEASMAN, *a pretty, competent-looking girl steps in.*)

MISS HEASMAN: Oh, sorry, I was just wondering when my tutorials are.

BEN: Same as last term, except of course for this week.

MISS HEASMAN: You didn't take me last term. My name is Heasman, Carol Heasman. I'm replacing Mrs Grainger.

BEN: Mrs Grainger?

MISS HEASMAN: Yes. She said she didn't get to see you often, owing to administrative tangles.

BEN: Mrs Grainger got into administrative tangles?

MISS HEASMAN: No, you were busy with them.

BEN: If only they'd let us get on with it and teach. (*Laughs.*) Anyway, you'd better come at the same hours as Mrs Grainger, all right?

MISS HEASMAN: I expect so. What were they?

BEN: Could you find out from Mrs Grainger, please?

MISS HEASMAN: I'll try.

BEN: Thank you. (*He holds the door wider.* MISS HEASMAN *goes out.* BEN *returns to his desk.*) I didn't care for that one at all, there was an air of mad devotion about her that reminds me of my wife's mother, the mad monk. (*Looking at* JOEY, *who is still transcribing marks.* JOEY *tries to go on working. In a normal tone after a pause.*) You're in trouble, Joey.

JOEY: What? (*He looks up.*)

BEN: I'm sorry. I've been wondering how to tell you. But as you've still got a fortnight before the board. (*Sits. Pause.*) A member of the department has his knife out.

JOEY: Who?

BEN: That pre-break meeting we had – the one you had to leave early – to meet Reg?

JOEY: Yes. Well?

BEN: The contemporary books list?

JOEY: Yes. Well, go on.

BEN: On the face of it, you were very adroit. You didn't actually support me, but you indicated a certain, attitude shall we say? By coughing into my speeches with dialectical authority. You wouldn't have thought that so genteel a rhetorical device could give offence. On the face of it. Eh?

JOEY: But who – who did I offend?

BEN: (*Gets up and perches on the front of his desk again*) First of all who proposed that a contemporary novels list – Burroughs, Genet, Roth, etc. – be added to our syllabus?

JOEY: You did.

BEN: And who opposed it?

JOEY: Everybody else. Except – me.

BEN: Who won?

JOEY: We – you did. They gave way in the end – didn't they?

BEN: (*Sinisterly*) Oh yes, it was passed unanimously – but I happen to know that one person – one powerful person there – resented *our* victory and blamed you – yes, you – for it.

JOEY: But this is ridiculous! It's absolutely – I scarcely said anything anyway.

BEN: Exactly. But this person was hoping – was *relying* – on you to oppose that book list with every cell in your body.

JOEY: Ben, please – eh?

BEN: Think, child, think! Who had most to lose by that list being passed? Who is *most* affected?

JOEY: Nobody. Nobody at all. You're the one who's going to

teach it, they'll be *your* lectures, *your* seminars, *your* tutorials . . .

BEN: (*After a long pause, as* JOEY *realizing, looks at him*) Exactly. Precisely. Absolutely. Fool! Imbecile! Traitor! Lackey! – I wouldn't be caught dead reading those books. And you know how it exhausts me to teach books I haven't read. Why didn't you oppose me?

JOEY: It's your fault. Your instructions were quite clear.

BEN: Haven't you heard of a sub-text? It's very fashionable now. In fact, I remember advising you to use the word twice in every paper when I was guiding you through your finals. (*He goes to examine him.*) But what's the matter, dear? You're looking a little peaky around the gills, wherever they are? Were you frightened, a trifle? You needn't be – you played the toad to perfection. (*He returns to his desk.*)

JOEY: Is there a sub-text to that? Or can I take it as straight abuse?

BEN: It's straight abuse. Can you take it?

JOEY: (*Trembling slightly*) No, not any longer. (*He gets up, and begins to pack his briefcase.*)

BEN: Where are you going?

JOEY: To the library.

BEN: Why?

JOEY: I've got a lecture at twelve.

BEN: But you're not running away from me so soon?

JOEY: And there are a few things on my Herrick I've got to dig up. (*He goes to the door –* BEN *cuts him off.*)

BEN: Dig up! (*Laughs.*)

    Diggory, diggory Delvet

    Little old man in black velvet

    He digs and he delves

    You can see for yourselves

    The holes dug by Diggory Delvet.

It is velvet, isn't it, this jacket? (*Fingering it.*)

(JOEY *tugs his sleeve away.*)

No, don't flounce.

(*They stand staring at each other.*)

13

You were due back last night, remember?

JOEY: Did it make any difference?

BEN: In that I spent the evening expecting you.

JOEY: In point of fact, I said I'd be back either last night or this morning.

BEN: Also you didn't phone.

JOEY: I was only in Leeds for four days. Of course I didn't phone.

BEN: Why not? Language difficulties? I reserved a table at Bianchi's. I was going to take us out.

JOEY: (*After a pause*) I'm sorry.

(BEN *shrugs. They each return to their desks.*)

It just didn't occur to me –

BEN: It doesn't matter.

JOEY: I'm sure I said –

BEN: Yes, yes, I expect you did. I assumed you were coming back, that's all. And as I spent four days on the phone to people who weren't there – bugger! (*He sits down at his desk.*) I'm sorry. All right? And if that doesn't satisfy you, Edna thinks well of you, and James is more than happy.

JOEY: How do you know?

BEN: These things slip out. Under my persistent questionings.

JOEY: Edna's actually very important, isn't she? (*He goes across to* BEN *and sits on the hard chair in front of Ben's desk.*)

BEN: It depends rather on the context.

JOEY: I mean in terms of influence –

BEN: You mean in terms of promotion?

JOEY: Well – (*Grins.*)

BEN: She'll certainly sit on your board, yes. Don't worry. You'll get your lectureship. Then you'll be safe for ever.

JOEY: I like Edna, in point of fact. No, really. We came in on the tube together this morning. She was telling me about her Byron –

BEN: Can we actually – do you mind? – not discuss either Edna or Byron but most of all Edna on Byron, for purely private reasons just at the moment. The thought of them weighs on my spirit. (*Pause.*) Tell me, while you were amusing yourselves in Leeds, I saw a film on television about a publisher who hates himself. I've been meaning to ask you – does Ted hate himself?

JOEY: He quite likes himself, actually.

BEN: I don't blame him. He seemed an amiable sort of chap the one time I met him, even though his mouth was full of symbolic sausage and his fist around a tankard of something foaming symbolically. I had the impression that most people would like him. And as he seemed exactly like most people, only from the North, ergo, he'd be favourably disposed towards himself only more so, or not? (*Smiles*.)

(JOEY *also smiles*.)

Tell me, does he ever discuss his work with you? Or does he leave it behind him at the office? When you go around for one of those little dinners, does he put his feet up, perhaps, while you slave away over a hot stove, or does he do the cooking? No, I don't mean to probe – or am I prying? For instance, in our Professor's ménage Hazel rips the meat apart with saw-edged knives while James brews up sauces from *Guardian* headlines. In my ménage, when I had one – remember? – Anne under-grilled the chops and over-boiled the peas while I drank the wine and charted my dropping sugar count. Now that you and I are sharing my life again I open the tins and you stir the Nescafé again, just as we always used to do, those evenings, at least, when you're not cooking for Reg or Reg isn't cooking for you – which, arriving where we began, does it happen to be? and if it's the former, why, now I think of it, have you never cooked for me, do you think?

JOEY: He does the cooking, in point of fact.

BEN: Christ I feel awful. (*Pause*.) Do you know, all the time you were away, I didn't have one telephone call. I consider that very frightening. Not even from Tom.

JOEY: Oh. (*Pause*.) I thought you found his company intolerable.

BEN: But one likes, as they say, to be asked. Also one likes people to be consistent, otherwise one will start coming adrift. At least this one will. (*Stands up*.) Also how does one know whether Tom is still the most boring man in London unless he phones in regularly to confirm it. This is the fourth week running he's kept me in suspense. He and Reg have a lot in common, haven't they? (*Pause. He sits on the desk.*)

JOEY: (*Drily*) Really?

BEN: Didn't Ted do his National Service with the Gurkhas?

JOEY: I really can't remember. I've never been very interested in Ted's – Reg's – military career, which was anyway about a decade ago. (*He goes back to his own desk.* BEN *follows him.*)

BEN: Oh, but the experience lives on for us through our born raconteurs – and Ted is something of a raconteur, isn't he? That magnificent anecdote of his – surely you remember?

JOEY: No. (*He picks up his briefcase and moves towards the door.*) I really must get to the library –

BEN: No, wait. (*Blocks his way.*) You repeated it to me. About the Gurkha and the bowl of soup. (*He holds up two fists.*) I don't know if I can do your imitation of his accent – woon day Chef was in ta kitchen – is that close? – stirring ta soup wi' his elbows – wan in coom a little tyke –

JOEY: I remember.

BEN: I was sure you would. Your imitation of Reg made me laugh so much that I was prepared to overlook its cruelty. Anyway my point was simply that Tom's a great National Service bore, too. There's that six-volume novel he's writing about it – that's something else. Yes. He's stopped showing me his drafts. (*He goes back to his desk.*)

JOEY: The last time he brought one around you dropped it in the bath.

BEN: It! He brought around seventeen exercise books, of which I dropped a mere three into the bath. No, I don't like his silence. It's sinister.

JOEY: Well, you could always phone him up. (*He starts for the door again.*)

BEN: I haven't finished. (*He comes over, takes Joey's briefcase from him and sits in Joey's desk chair.*)

JOEY: I must do something on this bloody lecture.

BEN: Why? You're looking furtive. Why are you looking furtive?

JOEY: I'm not looking at all furtive.

BEN: Have you seen Tom recently?

JOEY: No. No I haven't.

BEN: When did you last hear from him?

JOEY: (*Shrugs*) Perhaps he's busy.

BEN: Of course he's busy. He's too dull to be anything else, the
question is, why has he stopped being busy with me? (*He
returns to his own desk and sits on the hard chair.*) Do you think
he's dropped me? His attentions have been slackening since
my marriage broke up, now I come to think of it.

JOEY: (*Carefully*) He's very fond of Anne, isn't he?

BEN: (*Laughs*) That's an idea. I must find out whether he's been
hounding her.

JOEY: But Anne – (*Stops.*) She likes him, doesn't she? I mean, I
always thought – had the impression that she was fond of
him?

BEN: Oh, I expect she became addicted. She took up all my vices
except drinking, smoking and you. She never cared for you.
Did you know that?

JOEY: I had my suspicions. Thank you for confirming them.

BEN: She said that Tom became a school teacher because he had
to prove, after three years of being taught by me at
Cambridge, that education was still a serious affair. Whereas
you wanted to get back to your old college here and with me
because you were incapable of outgrowing your early
influences. Nursery dependence. This analysis was based
crudely on the fact that you are homosexual. She also said
you were sly and pushing, and that she didn't trust you an
inch.

JOEY: You never told me this before.

BEN: You never asked me before.

JOEY: I didn't ask you now, either.

BEN: I know. But I got tired of waiting. (*Pause.*) Do *you* like *her*?

JOEY: I thought we were friends.

BEN: I'm sure you still are. (*He sits in the armchair, Joey's briefcase
tucked under his arm.*) She just can't stand you, that's all.
Something about you gives her the creeps, was her word.
Creeps. (*Laughs.*) What's the matter? Are you upset?

(JOEY *shakes his head*.)

You shouldn't be. It was just her way of getting at me. Don't you see how I emerge? As someone whose protégé is a creep? But *I* didn't take offence. I don't see why you should.

(*Pause.* JOEY *tries to take his case –* BEN *clutches it to him.*) Tell me, what does he do, Reg's dad?

(JOEY *looks at him.*)

(*Smiles.*) But we're not ashamed, are we?

JOEY: (*Pause*) He owns a shop.

BEN: What sort of shop?

JOEY: Just a shop. (*He walks away from him.*)

BEN: Just a shop? Just a shop like Harrods, for example. What does he sell?

JOEY: (*After a pause*) Meat, I think.

BEN: You think. Did you ever see the shop?

JOEY: Of course. Why?

BEN: Was there meat on display?

JOEY: Yes.

BEN: In that case he either owns a meat museum or if it was for sale you're quite right, he owns a shop that sells meat. He's what's called a butcher.

JOEY: (*Sits on the hard chair in front of Ben's desk*) That's right, he's a butcher.

BEN: Mmm-huh. And do they live over their shop?

JOEY: (*Hesitates*) No. They live in um, in a place just outside Leeds, in point of fact.

BEN: In Point of Fact? And what sort of place is it, a Georgian terraced house, a Chippendale-style flat, a dug-out, a rural cottage; a bungalow!

JOEY: Yes. A bungalow.

BEN: A bungalow, eh? Now let's see, starting with the garden, do they have, say, plaster gnomes in the garden?

JOEY: And also much to your satisfaction, say, an electric fire with coals in it, and a sofa decorated with doilies and a revolving bookcase with the collected works of Mazo de la Roche –

BEN: In the garden? How witty!

JOEY: And their front door-bell plays a tune, can you believe that? (*Pause*.) They happen to be very nice people, nevertheless.

BEN: Nevertheless what?

JOEY: (*Emphatically*) Nevertheless they happen to be very nice people.

BEN: (*Sits on the edge of his desk, leaving Joey's briefcase in the armchair*) What tune? (*Pause*.) Does Reg's mother work in the shop too?

JOEY: No.

BEN: Oh. Where is she then, in the day-time?

JOEY: Out.

BEN: Out where?

JOEY: Just out.

BEN: She has a job then?

JOEY: Yes.

BEN: And where does she do this job? On the streets?

JOEY: You could put it like that, yes.

BEN: What does she do? Sweep them?

JOEY: No.

BEN: She walks them?

JOEY: Yes, in point of fact.

BEN: The precise suburb is irrelevant. (*Pause*.) So Reg's mother is a prostitute.

(JOEY *giggles, checks himself.*)

JOEY: No, she's a – traffic warden.

BEN: She isn't! But what on earth did you do?

JOEY: Nothing in particular.

BEN: You went to a football match?

JOEY: Football match?

BEN: Hasn't it caught on there? Here in the South we place it slightly below music and well above theatre, in the cultural scale. Did you?

JOEY: What?

BEN: Go to any football matches?

JOEY: Well done. Yes we did. We went to a football match – and furthermore we wore rosettes, coloured scarves and special hats and carried rattles.

BEN: You didn't! (*Laughs.*) Rattles and rosettes? You didn't! You poor old sod. Why in Christ did you stay? (*Pause.*) All right then, why did he take you there? Is it like bringing one's latest girl back to the folks –?

JOEY: His friends back. He doesn't like people to know he's queer. A lot of the time he doesn't like me to know. But I suppose he probably took me there as a kind of compliment – and perhaps as a test.

BEN: To see if you could take him *au naturel*?

JOEY: That sounds reasonable, yes.

BEN: And could you?

JOEY: He's much more natural as a London publisher who knows all about food, and cooks marvellously. Much more natural and much more convincing.

BEN: But tell me – the butcher and the traffic warden – do they *know* –

JOEY: Know what?

(*A shape appears at the door.* BEN *charges out as* MISS HEASMAN *knocks.*)

BEN: Oops! Sorry!

MISS HEASMAN: Sorry!

BEN: (*Off*) Just dashing up to the Registrar's – some administrative tangle. Mrs Grainger isn't it?

MISS HEASMAN: (*Off*) Miss Heasman! I can't find Mrs Grainger but I'm very anxious for a session on *A Winter's Tale*.

BEN: Good God! Are you really? Well keep trying and perhaps by next week . . . I go up here. Goodbye.

(BEN *dodges back and surprises* JOEY *as he tries to leave.*)

. . . that you and Reg have it off together?

JOEY: Of course not. (*Shuts the door.*) And now I think I'd like to stop talking about it if you don't mind. I'm beginning to feel queasy.

BEN: Recollections of tripe and stout?

　　Guilt Lord, I pray
　　Answer thy servant's question!
　　Is it guilt I feel
　　Or is it indigestion?

Don't worry, *rognons au vin* at Bianchi's will calm the
unsettled soul. (*He sits on his desk – lights a cigarette.*)

JOEY: Tonight you mean? For dinner?

BEN: I hardly fancy them for tea.

JOEY: Um, the thing is, I'm um going around to Reg's tonight.
(*Pause.*) I – I didn't – I'm sorry, it just seemed impossible
not to go, under the circumstances.

BEN: Mmm huh. (*Little pause.*) I'm willing to treat Reg if
necessary.

JOEY: Well, you see Reg has already got our dinner.

BEN: Oh? And what's he got for your dinner?

JOEY: (*Laughs*) Well, kidneys, as a matter of fact. His father gave
him some special – English kidneys. As a treat. Lamb's
kidneys.

BEN: Mmm huh. (*Little pause.*)

JOEY: Sorry.

BEN: There's no problem. I'll get some more and Ted can cook
them for me. (JOEY *goes back to his desk. Pause.*) What's the
matter?

JOEY: I'd rather you didn't.

BEN: Mmm huh. May one ask why?

JOEY: It might be awkward.

BEN: Oh? May one wonder why?

JOEY: Perhaps he doesn't like you very much.

BEN: You surprise me. I thought he'd taken rather a fancy, on our
one meeting.

JOEY: (*Sits*) On your one meeting you pretended you thought he
was an Australian and addressed him as 'Cobber'. You also
pretended you thought he was an interior decorator, in order
to remind him of Ted, whom he knew to be his predecessor.
You were also sick over his shoes. It was a terrible evening.
He hated you.

BEN: You never told me this before.

JOEY: You never asked me before.

BEN: *That* was creepy. (*Pause.*) Anyway you exaggerate. The
confusion over his national identity and profession lasted a
mere twenty minutes at the beginning of the evening. It took

21

me some twenty seconds to be sick over his shoes at the evening's end. The intervening hour was an unqualified success, in spite of the odd misunderstanding that developed into the occasional quarrel. Also you know very well that I'd taken up drinking again because I was still brooding over Anne's departure. I had what is called a drinking problem. I no longer have it.

JOEY: Let's face it Ben, you drink every night. Very heavily.

BEN: Exactly. There's no problem. I'm used to it again. (*Pause.*) Well, Joey?

(JOEY *shrugs awkwardly.*)

I might also be glad of a chance to make it up. I enjoy being on terms with your chaps. (*Pause.*) Also I don't fancy a fifth night of eating alone. (*Pause.*) Well?

JOEY: He won't want you to come.

BEN: Have you asked him?

JOEY: No.

BEN: Then why don't you? Come on. Let's find out. (*He picks up the telephone, and hands it to him.*) Well?

JOEY: He's not there.

BEN: How do you know, unless you try?

JOEY: He said he wouldn't be there until after lunch.

(BEN *stares at him.*)

He told me he had some things to do.

(*There is a shape at the door, not noticed by* BEN *and* JOEY, *followed by a knock, and simultaneously* EDNA *comes in. She is in her late forties and carries a small pile of folders.*)

EDNA: Hello, Ben. Joey.

BEN: Hello, Edna.

JOEY: Hello.

EDNA: Am I barging in on something?

JOEY: No, not at all, in fact I was just on my way to the library. (*He picks up his briefcase and stands up.*)

EDNA: Oh, it's no good going there. It's closed while they install a new security device. It won't be opened until this evening.

JOEY: Oh. (*He sits down again.* BEN *goes to his desk.*)

EDNA: Isn't that a comment on our times? Do you know I found a couple of students in the canteen. They actually pretended to have heard from some source or another that there were no tutorials during the first week of the half. What do you think of that?

BEN: (*Sits at his desk*) *Folie de grandeur*. They must learn to leave such decisions to us.

EDNA: Exactly. I wonder what they'd have to say if we started putting them off for any nonsensical reason that came into our heads.

BEN: Yes, I often wonder that. There's so much about them one never finds out. I mean they come, they go away –

EDNA: (*Sits opposite* BEN) Do you know anything about my particular black sheep, by the way? His name's Gardner.

BEN: Gardner? Gardner, Gardner.

JOEY: Yes, he comes to the odd lecture, aloof in feathers.

BEN: Feathers?

JOEY: He wears a kind of hat with feathers in it.

EDNA: Yes, that dreadful hat. I wish there was some action we could take about that, too. You don't remember him, Ben?

BEN: I certainly can't place the hat.

JOEY: Isn't Gardner the one you had a conversation with just before the break? In a pub? You mentioned –

BEN: A feathered youth? In a public house? Certainly not.

EDNA: Actually, the reason I asked whether you remember him, Ben, is that you interviewed him for his place here. I've just looked him up in the files. (*She hands* BEN *Gardner's open file*.)

BEN: Possibly. I only remember the ones we manage to reject, like Father O'Couligan.

EDNA: I must say, Ben, his headmaster's report was very unfavourable.

BEN: I'm not surprised. Father O'Couligan was in his forties. The Headmaster must have had him in the sixth form for a couple of decades at least. And frankly five minutes of O'Couligan was as much as I –

EDNA: No, I was talking about Gardner. I simply can't help wondering what made you take him.

BEN: Well Edna, I suppose I must have decided he wasn't fit for anything else.

EDNA: A university isn't a charity, you know.
(*There is a silence.*)

BEN: Do you mean for me, Edna? Or for the students?

EDNA: I'm not in the mood to be flippant about the more loutish of our students today. Not with the committee's report on the Senate House fresh in my mind.

BEN: Sorry, what report?

EDNA: It was in *The Times* this morning.

JOEY: I read it. In *The Guardian*. It was very disturbing.
(BEN *looks at him.*)

EDNA: Disturbing! They completely destroyed the Velium Aristotle. Completely destroyed it. *That* was their way of protesting about South Africa.

JOEY: I thought it was about Rhodesia. The University maintaining relationships –

EDNA: Well, one excuse is as good as another, of course.

BEN: James said it was the Greek Colonels. But perhaps we're underestimating their capacity for direct logical connections. Perhaps they were protesting about the Velium Aristotle.

EDNA: It wouldn't surprise me. I had one or two last term who were mutinous about *The Faery Queen*.

BEN: You mean the Principal? He really should learn discretion.

EDNA: (*After a short pause, releases a burst of ghastly laughter*) No Ben, you mustn't say things like that. (*Laughs again.*) Besides the Velium Aristotle is no laughing matter. But I intend to nip Gardner in the bud before he gets completely out of hand. I'm not having any bomb-throwing hooligan skipping *my* seminars!

BEN: Any bomb-throwing hooligan has permission to skip mine.
(*He gets up and moves towards the door.*)

EDNA: (*Retrieves Gardner's file from Ben's desk*) Well there's no point in my haranguing you. I suppose I'd better take it to James.

BEN: To James?

EDNA: Certainly. Gardner is ripe for a Dean's Report. Oh, I

meant to say, you and Anne must come around soon, if you could bear an evening in my poky little flat. And Joey, of course.

BEN: Thanks.

JOEY: (*Enthusiastically*) I'd love to.

EDNA: How's the baby?

BEN: Oh, very well. As far as one can tell. With babies, I mean.

EDNA: Yes, they are indecipherable, aren't they? How old is he now?

BEN: He's (*thinks*) six or seven months about.

EDNA: It's wretched of me, but I've forgotten his name. Though I do remember him as a bonny little thing.

BEN: Miranda.

JOEY: Marina.

BEN: Yes. (*Laughs.*) Marina. He's called Marina.

EDNA: Oh dear, oh Ben, I'm sorry. I always think of babies as 'hims' or 'its'.

BEN: Well, it's probably safer these days. Our ends never know our beginnings.

EDNA: Any teeth yet?

BEN: Just the – uh – (*Wags his finger around his mouth*) – gums you know and a few wisdom . . . or whatever they're . . .

EDNA: That sounds most satisfactory. Are you all right for baby-sitters?

BEN: Baby-sitters. (*Laughs.*) Oh, no problem. Marina's mother is a marvellous baby-sitter. Anne has simply added a contemporary skill to Goethe's ideal woman. (*After a pause.*) I'm afraid we are going through what we professionals know as a sticky patch.

EDNA: Oh dear. Ben, I'm sorry. I don't know what to say. You must both be desperately unhappy. (*Pause.*) I do hope she's not in that flat all by herself.

BEN: Oh, we sorted that out. She told me that if I was half a man I'd leave. But on discovering that *she* was, she left herself. She's with her mother. Together they make up two pairs. I imagine Marina is the odd man out.

EDNA: I see. Oh dear. (*Pause.*) It's always so sad for the children.

BEN: Yes, we do suffer the most.

EDNA: Where are *you* now, Joey, are you still in that bedsitter?

JOEY: (*Little pause*) No. (*Another pause*.) I've moved back in with Ben again, in point of fact.

EDNA: Oh, so you're both back where you were then.

BEN: Exactly.

EDNA: By the way, did I mention that the little office next to mine's going begging at last? So if either of you wants a place of your own . . .

BEN: Thanks, Edna, but we're used to roughing it down here.

EDNA: It's up to you, of course . . . Well I must leave you two to get on with it. (*She goes to the door*.) If you should clap eyes on young Gardner, please send him straight up to me on pain of a Dean's report. (*She goes out*.)

(*There is a silence*.)

BEN: I enjoyed that. It was so graceful. In a little office next door to Edna. Christ. What does she want him for? (*He returns to his desk*.) She's got her own coterie – all those boys and girls that look as if they've got the curse permanently. (*Little pause*.) Her obsession with Byron is one of the more triste perversions. But she shouldn't be allowed to practise it with students. She's got her bloody book for therapy.

JOEY: She's finished her book. That's what she was telling me on the tube this morning.

BEN: Well done, Edna. I suppose it means another two decades while she finds a publisher.

JOEY: She's found one.

BEN: She never did understand her role. Which is not to finish an unpublishable book on Byron. Now the centre cannot hold. Mere Edna is loosed upon the world. (*Pause. Sits in the armchair*.) Bloody woman! (*Pause*.) Bugger! (*Pause*.) Bugger! The Dean's Report!

JOEY: It *was* Gardner you told me about then? The boy who complained about Edna's seminars in a pub.

BEN: Edna holds her seminars in a pub? I shall have to report this.

JOEY: The one you said was interesting.

26

BEN: I don't find anything interesting about a student who complains of Edna's seminars. You did it yourself years ago, and you're as dull as they come.

JOEY: Did you encourage him?

BEN: As far as I remember, which is frankly nothing, we had a perfectly respectable conversation about Edna's vagina, its length and width.

JOEY: Oh God!

BEN: You mustn't be jealous, Joseph. The young are entitled to the importunities that you once enjoyed.

JOEY: (*Gets up and walks towards* BEN) I can't afford to quarrel with Edna. Besides, I've got to like her.

BEN: Because you've got to, doesn't mean I've got to.

JOEY: She thinks of us as allies. If you upset her, she'll blame me too.

BEN: What the hell are you doing here anyway? You're not lecturing until later. You could have gone straight home and tidied up your room. It's in a disgusting state.

JOEY: The only room in the flat that isn't in a disgusting state is mine.

BEN: Really? Then can you explain why it looks as if a large, dignified and intelligent man has been going to seed in it?

JOEY: (*After a pause*) Did you have to use my room?

BEN: Do you think I could put up with the mess everywhere else? You're out most evenings, it's easy for you to keep your room clean. I don't see why you shouldn't learn what it's like to stay at home and fret your way into a drunken coma. (JOEY *after a moment, goes back to his desk and sits down.*) Is *that* your tantrum? How piffling.

JOEY: Look, Ben, I've got this lecture. Can I do some work, please? As I can't go to the library – Please?

BEN: (*Goes to him*) When will you phone Reg up then?

JOEY: I told you. After lunch.

BEN: Why are you lying about his being out? (*He points Joey's desk lamp directly into his face in interrogation.*)

JOEY: I don't make a habit of lying.

BEN: Which is why you go on being so bad at it.

27

(*There is a shape at the door.* BEN *looks towards it, hurries to his feet, as there is a knock. He goes over to the door, opens it a fraction.*)

(*Jovially*) Good morning, good morning, good morning.

STUDENT: (*Off*) I just wanted to find out about my tutorials.

BEN: Good. Good. Have you got an essay, please!

STUDENT: (*Off*) Well no, I mean you haven't set one.

BEN: Well do me one for next week, all right?

STUDENT: (*Off*) Well, what on?

BEN: You must decide for yourself, can't expect spoon feeding. Righto. (*He shuts the door, comes back rubbing his hands.*) I think that's the lot –

(*As a shape comes to the door, there is a knock. The door opens as* BEN *spins around.*)

MISS HEASMAN: I found Mrs Grainger, she says she would have come to you on Tuesdays at two if you'd been able to see her.

BEN: So be it. Tuesdays at two with our fingers crossed. (*He crosses them.*)

MISS HEASMAN: Today is Tuesday.

BEN: Ah well, I wouldn't have been able to see her again today, I'm afraid, as she would have needed a week in which to do me an essay.

MISS HEASMAN: Poor Mrs Grainger. But I'm all right as I've done one. (*She takes one out of her file, and hands it to* BEN, *who takes it reluctantly.*) I haven't put a title on, but I thought 'Hate and Redemption in *A Winter's Tale*'.

BEN: Needs work. (*He hands the essay back.*) That title.

MISS HEASMAN: Don't you want to read it before the tutorial?

BEN: No, you'll have to read it aloud to me. Unless, I tell you what, give it to me now and I'll do my damnedest to get it read before next week.

MISS HEASMAN: (*Her eyes go to Ben's desk*) No, I'll read it aloud. Two o'clock then. (*She turns and goes out.*)

BEN: (*Imitates her walk and slams the door*) Bugger! (*He comes back to his desk.*) 'Hate and Redemption' – I told you she was mad. She must be a secret agent, in Edna's employ . . . (*He picks up a handful of essays from the desk then drops them one by one on the floor.*) Hate and Redemption, Pity and Terror, Sin and Salvation. (*Dropping more essays onto the floor.*) Faith and Despair in *Pride and Prejudice*, *The Mill on the Floss*, Appley and Dappley, Cecily Parsley. (*Liturgically, as he is dropping essays. He looks at his desk.*) Why don't those cleaning women do their job properly? Standards are declining everywhere. Ruskin's char threw Carlyle's history of the French Revolution out with the other rubbish. But then they took a pride in their work in those days. (*He picks up another essay, looks at it, laughs and sits down.*) I should think Reg would enjoy cooking my kidneys. It sounds worse than settling my hash. Anne's mother the mad monk settles the hash of bus-conductors, milkmen, postmen, anyone stupid enough to waste their time insulting her. 'Oh, I settled his hash all right.' She probably got the taste for it after she killed off her husband. I wonder if there was any reference in the coroner's report to the state of his hash. This hash, my life . . . this long disease my . . . (*He begins to read, then lets it slip from his fingers, leans back, picks reflectively at the cotton wool.*) Why the hell did we call her Marina?

> I made this, I have forgotten
> And remember.
> The rigging weak and the canvas rotten
> Between one June and another September.

Born in June, May . . . April . . . February . . . November . . . Conceived in September . . . So sometime in early September there was what you might call a seminal fuck . . . Where? In the park once we . . . let me think, beneath the trees.

> Beneath the trees there is no ease.
> For the dull brain, the sharp desires
> And the quick eyes of Woolly Bear.

It must have been our last, we were already fallen into the sere, the yellow leaf, a flash of thigh in the yellow leaf,

> What seas what shores what granite islands towards my
>   timbers
> And woodthrush calling through the fog
> My daughter.

JOEY: You do miss her then?

BEN: (*Goes over to* JOEY) You know, what marks you out as a repressed as well as a practising pervert is your sentimentality over children. Marina doesn't need a mother or father, she needs a pair of hands, to pick her up, change her, put things to her mouth, put her down again.

JOEY: But later on she might need a father.

BEN: You generally have the taste to let *me* raise the subject of my ruined marriage.

JOEY: I can't help wondering whether you miss it.

BEN: Only the sex and violence. And these days one can get those anywhere.

JOEY: So there's absolutely no chance . . .

BEN: Chance of what?

JOEY: Of your marriage reviving. You don't want it to?

BEN: Reviving? It's never died. I consider it inviolate. I'm a one woman man and I've had mine, thank God.

JOEY: But things can't just go on as they are.

BEN: Can't they. Why not? (*He takes the telephone directory from his desk and begins to look up a number.*)

JOEY: But supposing she wants to marry again.

BEN: Good God! Who would want to marry *her*?

JOEY: You did.

BEN: That was before she'd been through the mill . . . (*He begins to run his finger down the column.*)

JOEY: (*Standing up*) Listen Ben, you could be making a mistake about Anne. If you really don't want to lose her –

BEN: (*Goes to the telephone on Joey's desk*). Your conversation is beginning to sound as if it's been stitched together from song titles of the fifties. (*He begins to sing.*) Making a mistake about Anne – . . . If you really don't want to lose her . . .

JOEY: Look Ben, I'm trying to tell you something.

BEN: Haylife and Forlings . . . (JOEY *looks at* BEN. BEN *sings as he dials.*) Three four eight – owe seven two owe.

JOEY: What are you doing?

BEN: (*Sits down and speaks into the telephone*) Ah hello – can I speak to Mr Nuttall, Reg Nuttall please.

JOEY: (*Hurrying over to the telephone*) He's not there.

BEN: Thank you. (*He waits, humming and smiling at* JOEY.)

(JOEY *seizes the telephone, they wrestle over it,* BEN *hangs on to it.*)

(*Into the phone, crouched away from* JOEY.) No, I'm waiting for Mr Nuttall please.

JOEY: All right. All right. I'll do it.

(BEN *hands him the receiver.* JOEY *puts the receiver down and holds onto telephone. There is a pause.*)

BEN: Well?

JOEY: Do you intend to stay in the room while I find out if he'll have you to dinner?

BEN: Certainly. But *you* needn't stay while I find out. (*He goes to pick up the telephone.*)

JOEY: (*Shouts*) I said I'd do it!

BEN: (*A long pause*) But what *are* you afraid of? He can only say no, in which case I'll only make your life a living hell.

JOEY: Perhaps I'm afraid he'll say yes.

BEN: Well, you do worry for him, don't you, dear?

JOEY: Why do you think it's him I'm worried for?

BEN: Oh, we all know how you worry for yourself. (*He reaches for the telephone.*)

(JOEY *holds it tight, and looks at* BEN. BEN *laughs and reaches for it.*)

JOEY: (*Runs away with it followed by* BEN) You're a fool, Ben. A bloody fool!

(BEN *stops. The telephone rings.*)

BEN: (*Takes the telephone and puts the base down on his desk.* JOEY *sits down at his desk*) Butley, Nursery. (*Laughs.*) Oh hello James, what? Ah, well I was just pondering those lines –

His rhythm was present in the nursery bedroom,

In the rank ailanthus of the April dooryard –

(*Pause.*) No, no, I'm quite free. (*Little pause. He mouths a curse.*) Gardner? Gardner, Gardner, Gardner. No I don't recall a student called Gardner – What year is she? Ah! *He!* (*He grimaces at* JOEY. *A shape appears at the door.*) Oh God, Poor Edna.

(*There is a knock on the door.*)

(*He claps his hand over the mouthpiece. To* JOEY) Block that
student! (*Into the receiver*) He says I *what*? No he must have
misunderstood me. I don't recall telling a student . . .

(JOEY *has gone to the door, opens it, then steps back.* ANNE
comes in. BEN *sees* ANNE, *gapes at her and turns back to the
telephone.*) Look, I appear to have miscalculated, I've got a
student after all, speak to you later, eh? Bye. (*He hangs up.
There is a silence.*) How are you?

ANNE: Thank you. And you?

BEN: Coping with Edna. Do you remember Edna? The one you
called a human contraceptive? Do you remember?

ANNE: Actually, I called her a pill.

BEN: Well, I updated you. (*He laughs.*)

(*Another silence.*)

ANNE: How are *you*, Joey?

JOEY: Oh. Um, very well thanks. Um, how's Miranda?

ANNE: Marina. She fills her belly and her nappy. She grows the
odd tooth. She cries.

BEN: How adult. Except for the odd tooth, one loses that.
(*Pause.*) Actually, I've been thinking of finding a new
dentist. I know you dote on Tonks, darling, but he's terribly
camp. One sits in that chair with one's whole body at his
mercy. (*To* JOEY) Who do you go to?

JOEY: A man in Pimlico.

ANNE: Joey's teeth are always in marvellous condition.

BEN: Are they? Let's see.

JOEY: What?

BEN: Let's see your teeth.

(JOEY *grimaces.* BEN *goes close, inspects them.*) You're quite
right. (*To* ANNE) They sparkle. Although from time to time
I've noticed – (*He hums 'Christ the Lord is risen today'.*)

ANNE: (*Laughs to* JOEY) One of Ben's marriage jokes. I'm
surprised you haven't heard it.

JOEY: Well, I haven't.

ANNE: How flattering for me.

JOEY: (*After a pause*) Well, I think it'd be better if I – I'd better get along. (*He picks up his briefcase.*)

BEN: Why?

ANNE: Because he's embarrassed.

BEN: Are you?

JOEY: I've got a lecture.

BEN: He has. On Blake.

ANNE: Ah. Then he'd better go.

(JOEY *goes out.*)

BEN: He's very sensitive. You frighten him.

ANNE: Because he's creepy, and he knows I know it.

BEN: Yes. I've told him. He took it surprisingly badly.

ANNE: (*Pause*) You've settled down nicely together again, then, have you?

BEN: We have our ups and downs.

ANNE: That's all right then. May I sit? (*She sits on the hard chair in front of Ben's desk.*)

BEN: I went to see you over the weekend, as arranged, but you were out.

ANNE: Yes, I'm sorry.

BEN: Grounds for a scene though, don't you think?

ANNE: Oh, I should wait. (*Little pause.*) I had to see Tom's headmaster about a job.

BEN: And did you get one?

ANNE: Yes.

BEN: Good. (*He stares at her.*) But you look a trifle peaky around the gills – wherever they are. I can never locate them on Joey. Are you all right?

ANNE: I'm fine.

BEN: Good. I saw Marina instead. I expect your mother the mad monk told you.

ANNE: She said it was very quick. Like a visit from the postman.

BEN: I was there for twenty minutes. You'd better check on the postman. Ah! (*He sits at Joey's desk.*) Well, this is almost as delightful as it's unexpected, to what is it owed?

ANNE: I came to find out whether you wanted us back.

BEN: (*After a pause*) Is that an offer?

33

ANNE: No. It's a question. I'd like the truth please. *Do* you want us back?

BEN: Frequently. (*Little pause.*) But not permanently. Do you want to come back?

ANNE: No.

BEN: We've cleared that up then. I think we're going to get on very well from this time forth, don't you?

ANNE: (*Pause*) Joey hasn't told you, then?

BEN: Told me what?

ANNE: He's known for weeks. His – what's his name – friend Reg must have told him.

BEN: Reg?

ANNE: Tom told him. At least, he told me he had.

BEN: Tom? Tom and Reg? What on earth have Tom and Reg got to do with us?

ANNE: He's asked me to marry him.

BEN: (*After a pause*) Which one? (*Pause.*) You're not. (*Laughs.*) You can't be.

ANNE: Yes I am. Do you mind?

BEN: Yes, yes, I mind very much. (*Pause, he pulls himself together.*) After all, a man's bound to be judged by his wife's husband. The most boring man in London – you said yourself he was the dullest man you'd ever spent an evening with.

ANNE: That was before I got to know him properly.

BEN: And what do you call him now?

ANNE: The dullest man I've ever spent the night with. But I don't mind. Why should you?

BEN: Because – because I shall miss old Tom, that's why. I'm too old to make mature new friendships with bores, far too impatient. (*He walks round to his own desk.*) They have to grow on you steadily, hours by hours through years on years, until they're actually doing their bit towards holding you together. Like ivy around crumbling walls. (*Little pause.*) Is that why you want him?

ANNE: Are you going to make difficulties?

BEN: What?

34

ANNE: About the divorce?

BEN: Divorce?

ANNE: You see, I'm not allowed to marry him until I'm divorced from you. It's the law of the land. Are you going to make difficulties?

BEN: This is humiliating.

ANNE: But deserved. By both of us.

BEN: (*Laughs*) I'll bloody make difficulties all right. After all, this is liable to be the only phase of our marriage that I shall enjoy. At least since the moment in the registry office when the clerk who handled our contract was under the impression that he was supposed to bind me for a year or two to the mad monk your mother. (*He gets up and faces her across his desk.*) I'll have to have my fun somewhere, won't I? Because after all one moment of pleasure isn't much out of a whole year, is it?

ANNE: It's a moment more than I had.

BEN: And how many moments do you expect from your next?

ANNE: I shan't count them. I'm not in it for fun, you see. I never was. And nor were you.

BEN: Oh. What *was* I in it for?

ANNE: Perhaps you wanted a break.

BEN: Well, I'm certainly getting one, aren't I?

ANNE: Or perhaps you were frightened. But it doesn't matter any more because you're not any more. And I suppose you needn't ever try again, now that you've found out whatever it is you were determined to learn. (*Pause.*) I don't care. Not at all.

BEN: Then you're half-way there. And Tom will certainly teach you to sit still. (*He walks round behind her and comes to face her.*) If you must get married again, surely we can do better for you than that. After six weeks you'll be the two most boring men in London. There are signs already. You're developing a new tone – a combination of the didactic and the enigmatically stoic – that's more than half-way towards Tom's prose style. By the way, does he know that you greet spring and its signs of life with wheezing and sneezes from your hay-fever? Tom endorses spring. He admires it for its moral exuberance. (*Pause.*) Do you still make little popping sounds when you drink your coffee? No, it's your nose – your nose I've always taken exception to, or is it your mouth? You can't marry Tom.

ANNE: I can.

BEN: All right, you probably can. You can probably do a lot of hideous things. You're tough, versatile and brutal. What I mean is, don't.

ANNE: Why not?

(*A shape appears at the door.*)

Well?

(*A pause.*)

EDNA: (*Knocks, steps in*) Can I have a word? (*She is obviously distraught.*)

BEN: By all means. (*He gestures to* ANNE.)

EDNA: Oh, I'm sorry, I didn't realize – I'll look back later, if I may. (*She goes out.*)

ANNE: He's asked me to live with him until we get married. Are you going to make trouble?

BEN: Tell me, when did we last have it off? Was it that time in the park, beneath the trees, or did we have a quick go subsequently, in bed or under the kitchen table, Joey and I were trying to work it out –

(ANNE *rises.*

He jumps away, as if expecting a blow, shields his face, then laughs, shakily.) You're going to live with him *until* you get married, did you say? At least that's a realistic prospectus. (*He calls out, as* ANNE *leaves.*) Bye, darling. Bye bye, sweet princess, goodbye . . . (*He closes the door behind her and stands pulling at the cotton wool on his chin. He pulls it off.*) Ahh, Butley is himself again. (*Hums 'Christ the Lord', then sings.*)

 Christ your breath is bad today

 Haa-aa-al-it-osis. Haa-aa-

(*He breaks off, trembling. He sits down at his desk, puts his hand to his face, takes it away, looks at it, touches his chin, inspects his fingers.*) Bloody woman! Bloody woman! (*He feels in his pocket and takes out more cotton wool. Curtain.*)

ACT TWO

The office as before. It is shortly after lunch. When the curtain rises
MISS HEASMAN *is sitting on the hard chair by Ben's desk, reading from*
her essay. BEN *is apparently asleep in the armchair a cigarette in his hand.*

MISS HEASMAN: (*A pause – she looks at* BEN) 'Hermione's
reawakening – the statue restored to life after a winter of
sixteen years' duration – is in reality Leontes's reawakening,
spiritually, and of course the most moving exemplification of
both the revitalization theme and thus of forgiveness on the
theological as well as the human level.'

BEN: Level?

MISS HEASMAN: Yes.

BEN: The human *level*?

MISS HEASMAN: Yes. Um, shall I go on?

BEN: Mmm.

MISS HEASMAN: 'The central image is drawn from nature, to
counterpoint the imagery of the first half of the play, with its
stress on sickness and deformity. Paradoxically, *A Winter's
Tale* of a frozen soul –'

BEN: Bit fish-mongery, that.

MISS HEASMAN: (*Laughs mirthlessly*) '– is therefore thematically
and symbolically about revitalization.'

BEN: Sorry. Re-whatalization?

MISS HEASMAN: Re-*vi*talization.

BEN: (*Gets up and goes to* MISS HEASMAN) Thematically and
symbolically so, eh?

MISS HEASMAN: Yes. (*She looks towards him challengingly*.) 'The
central image is drawn from' – no, we've had that – um. 'In
this context –'

BEN: Can you see?

MISS HEASMAN: What?

BEN: (*Aims his desk light at Miss Heasman's essay, forgets to turn it on,
goes to a hard chair in the corner of the room and sits down out of
view*) There.

37

(MISS HEASMAN *after a moment, leans over, turns on the light.*)
Sorry. No irony intended. (*Pause.*) 'Context.'

MISS HEASMAN: Um, yes. 'In this context it might be said that
Leontes represents the affliction that is a universal, and so
contingently human evil, and in this sense, the sense of a
shared blight . . .'

BEN: (*Lets out a noise like a laugh, pretends to be coughing*) Sorry.
Yes, a shared blight – yes, look, how much longer is it
exactly?

(MISS HEASMAN *fumbles through the pages* – BEN *goes over to
his desk.*)
I'll tell you what, as our time together's drawing to a close,
read the last two or three sentences, so we can get the feel of
your conclusion.

(MISS HEASMAN *looks pointedly at her watch, riffles through her
pages.* BEN *picks at the cotton wool on his chin, drums his fingers,
checks these movements, smiles attentively when* MISS HEASMAN
looks at him.)

MISS HEASMAN: Ready?

BEN: Please, please.

MISS HEASMAN: 'So just as the seasonal winter was the winter of
the soul, so is the seasonal spring the spring of the soul. The
imagery changes from disease to floral, the tone from mad
bitterness to joyfulness. As we reach the play's climax we feel
our own – spiritual – sap rising.'

BEN: (*After a long pause*) Sap?

MISS HEASMAN: Sap.

BEN: Sap. Sap. Yes, I think sap's a better word than some others
that spring rhymingly to mind. Good. Well, thank you very
much. What do you want to do – I mean, after your exams?
(*He sits on the hard chair apposite* MISS HEASMAN.)

MISS HEASMAN: Teach.

BEN: English?

MISS HEASMAN: Yes.

BEN: Well, I suppose that's more radical than being a teacher of
exams, for which I think you're already qualified, by the
way. I hope you'll take that as a compliment.

MISS HEASMAN: It isn't meant to be one, is it? But whatever you think of my essay, if I don't do well in the exams, I might not be able to be a teacher.

BEN: Teacher of whom?

MISS HEASMAN: Sixth forms, I hope.

BEN: Isn't it more exhilarating to get them earlier? Sixth-form teachers are something like firemen called in to quench flames that are already out. Although you can never tell – recently I've enjoyed reading almost as much as I did when I was twelve. I do hope I didn't slip through their net – it makes one lose confidence. But I'm sure *you'll* be all right. Perhaps books are just my *madeleines*, eh?

> Gravy and potatoes
> In a big brown pot
> Put them in the oven
> And cook them very hot.

MISS HEASMAN: I'm sorry?

BEN: And so am I. I'm not really myself this afternoon, what do you want to do next week?

MISS HEASMAN: We have to cover at least six Shakespeares.

BEN: From what I've heard already, Shakespeare's as good as covered. (*He opens the door.*)

MISS HEASMAN: (*Holds out her essay*) Could you please write some comments on this?

BEN: It's a good time to be merciless. (*Taking the essay.*) It comes in useful when dealing with the young.

MISS HEASMAN: Believe it or not, you can be as rude as you like. I don't take it personally.

BEN: That's another good way of taking the fun out of teaching. Good afternoon, Miss Heasman.

MISS HEASMAN: Thank you. (*She goes out.*)

(BEN *stands at the open door, gestures obscenely after her. Then, aware that he is holding her essay, pinches his nostrils, holds the essay at a distance, makes gagging sounds, pantomimes gas-poisoning as he goes back to his desk.* MISS HEASMAN *has come back to the door, stands watching him.* BEN *drops the essay onto his desk, stiffens, turns slowly. He and* MISS HEASMAN *stare at each other.* MISS HEASMAN *turns and goes quickly from the room.*)

BEN: (*Makes as if to hurry after her, stops*) Oh Christ! Bloody girl! (*He stands for a moment, then takes out an address book, looks up a name, goes over to his desk and dials the number.*) Hello, Kent Vale Comprehensive? Headmaster please. (*Little pause.*) Ben Butley. (*Aside.*) Friend to Education. (*Into the telephone.*) Thank you. (*He puts the telephone on the desk, runs over to a carrier bag, extracts a quarter of Scotch, runs back, clamps it under his chin, unscrews the cap as he talks in a Scottish accent.*) Ahh, hello Headmaster, sorry to trouble you on a trifling matter, but I've been trying to make contact with one of your staff, Tom Weatherley, and it's proving to be a tricky business. (*Pause.*) Ben Butley, Friend to Tom Weatherly, a member of your staff. Do you ken him? (*Little pause.*) Oh, naturally I don't want to disturb him if he's teaching, but I've got a rather delicate message for him, I'd rather entrust it to someone of authority like yourself, if I may? (*Listens.*) Thank you. It's just that could he and I have a little chin-wag – (*Little pause*) – chin-wag some time about the proceedings – solicitors, alimony, maintenance, custody, visiting rights – always so sad when there are wee bairns to consider – we always say – property, so on, so forth. (*Pause.*) Oh, I'm Tom's fiancée's husband. I've only just heard the news. By the way, HM, quite a coincidence, my wife that was, Tom's wife to be, Anne Butley that is, might be coming to teach in your school, I believe, do keep an eye out for her, I'd be most obliged. (*He takes the telephone away from his chin feels his chin, makes a face.*) Oh, and there is one other thing, could you tell Tom that he'll have to foot the bill for any ops this time unless he can get it on the National Health, I've got enough blood on my hands – (*Looks at his fingers*) – at the moment, and it's all my own, ha ha ha, if you see what I mean. (*Little pause.*) Oh you don't, well never mind, HM, I don't really think we educationalists should be expected to see anything but the clouds into which we thrust our heads eh? (*There is a shape at the door.* BEN *looks towards it.*)

Love to Tom and Anne when you see them, eh? Goodbye.
(*He puts down the telephone, stares towards the door, then takes
a swig of Scotch, goes to the door, peers through the frosted glass.
He drops the Scotch into his pocket and knocks gently against the
glass.*)

Tap tappit, tap tappit, he's heard it before.

But when he peeps out there is nobody there
(*Opens the door.*)

But packets and whimsey put down on the stair.
(*He walks over to his desk.*) Or is something frightening him
again? Is that why he's peeping through the frosted glass
with his whiskers twitching and his paws to his nose, eh?
(*JOEY after a pause, enters – goes to his desk, puts down his
briefcase and turns on the desk lamp.*)
If it's Anne you were hiding from, she's gone. If it's Edna,
she hasn't arrived.

JOEY: I heard voices. I thought perhaps you and Anne were still –

BEN: What? Thrashing it out? Having it off? What would Anne
and I still be doing, together in a small room, after two
hours? She was always succinct, even with her knickers down.

JOEY: I saw Edna in the common-room. She was just leaving
when I went in.

BEN: And how did she seem? Jovial?

JOEY: No, very upset.

BEN: Ah.

JOEY: Was that Miss Heasman I passed in the corridor?

BEN: How did she look? Jovial?

JOEY: She had her face averted. As if she were in tears.

BEN: Then that was certainly Miss Heasman, yes. Everything
seems to be running smoothly, doesn't it? (*He stares at
JOEY.*) Tell me, what did you make of old Anne turning up
in that enterprising fashion?

JOEY: I don't know.

BEN: You don't?

(*JOEY looks at him.*)

She was under the impression that you've known for some
time.

JOEY: (*A pause*) I did try to warn you.

BEN: Yes and thank you. But tell me, how come that you've known for some time?

JOEY: Well actually I got it from Reg.

BEN: From Reg? Yes? (*Pause.*) You know I think we're building up a case here for a conspiracy theory of personal relationships. Go on.

JOEY: (*Sits*) Tom's meeting Reg had nothing to do with me. It was something professional, I don't know what, but they got on very well and Tom told Reg and Reg told me, and then Tom phoned Reg and told Reg not to tell me or if he *had* told me to ask me not to tell you until he or Anne had told you.

BEN: Yes, I recognize Tom's delicate touch there in your sentence structure. It must have been amusing to hear me chatter mindlessly on about my marriage, eh?

JOEY: I tried to warn you.

BEN: But was it amusing? Was it fun? (*Pause.*) Are you going to answer me?

JOEY: Sorry. I took the question to be rhetorical.

BEN: (*Going over to him*) All right. Let me ask you, then, *why* you promised not to mention to your best friend – is that presuming? – that his wife was being screwed by, while contemplating marriage to, the most boring man in London? Is that question sufficiently unrhetorical?

JOEY: Because I didn't think it was my business.

BEN: Not your business? And how many personalities and dramas over which we've gossiped and whinnied in the past years have been our business? There have been some pretty sticky silences between us recently, and here you were, my dear, in possession of a piece of information that was guaranteed to raise at the very least an amused eyebrow?

JOEY: All right, because I'm a coward, that's why. I'm sorry. (*Pause.*) I *am* sorry, in point of fact.

BEN: Matters of fact and points of fact have been cluttering your syntax since you started going steady with that butcher's boy.

JOEY: I'm sorry because I hoped it wouldn't happen. Now it's a fact and I wish it weren't.

(BEN *laughs, tugs at the cotton wool on his chin and pulls it off. His hand is trembling.*)

I'm – I'm sure you could get her back.

BEN: How far back?

JOEY: To live with you. She and Marina.

BEN: That's too far back. Far too far back.

JOEY: Then what will you do?

BEN: Grab my quota of fun, that's all. (*He returns to the telephone.*) I'm working to a very tight schedule. I've given myself a mere week to get the most boring – and tenacious – man in London out of his job and home. I'm moving on to his landlady now.

JOEY: Fun?

BEN: Or trouble. I can't remember which I've promised myself.

JOEY: But what's the point of making trouble?

BEN: Fun. (*He dials again.*) Because hounding them from job and home is no trouble. Local councils, the police, whole governments do it. Why shouldn't a private citizen be allowed to join in? (*He waits, then slams down the phone –* JOEY *goes to the door.*) Where are you going? (*He dials another number.*)

JOEY: The library's open now. I thought I'd go up –

BEN: And hide again? Who from this time?

(JOEY *shrugs.*)

From Edna. Yes, it must be Edna.

JOEY: Well, I'm not going to be here when she comes to have it out with you.

(BEN *laughs.*)

I can't help it. *I'm* not going to antagonize her.

BEN: OK I'll do it for you. You run along.

(JOEY *looks at him, hesitates, then makes for the door.*)

(*Into the telephone*) Ah, Haylife and Forling, I must say you do drag out your lunch, some of which, by the way, appears still to be in your mouth, from the sound of you. (*As* JOEY *hurries to him from the door.*) This is Joseph Keyston, friend to Reg Nuttall, if you take my meaning, may I speak to him please? (*He hands the telephone to* JOEY.)

(JOEY *takes the telephone and puts it down. There is a pause.*)
You see how life repeats itself, with diminishing climaxes.
(*Little pause.*) Well? Is he still out, have you some more
moralizing to do, or are you simply welching on a promise?

JOEY: All right. If you want, I'll cancel Reg. We can go to
Bianchi's. Just the two of us.

BEN: (*In an American accent*) Cancel Reg? Cancel him? (*Laughs.*)
This is a human bean, you're talking about here, kid, not a
cheque, or an order of groceries, but a human *bean*! And
frankly dear, he's more of an attraction than your shy self, at
the moment. All our games together are going a trifle stale,
Reg and I may be able to find some new ones.

JOEY: Reg won't be very playful.

BEN: Don't worry. I shall get my fun. Besides, in this bag here,
kidneys! Yes, kid, kidneys! (*He waves the carrier bag at*
JOEY.)

JOEY: (*After a pause*) I'm sorry, Ben. Not tonight.

BEN: Mmm huh. So *you're* not inviting me.

JOEY: I'm not going. We can either eat at the flat or at Bianchi's.
It's up to you.

BEN: Well, if you're really not coming then there'll be all the
more kidneys for Reginald and myself. What do you think
he'll say to that, for an offer? (*A pause.*) Don't you care then?

JOEY: No. Not any more.

BEN: You're not breaking off with him, you competitive child
you? Is that what you're trying to tell me?

JOEY: No. I'm trying to tell you that it'll be much better if you
leave that side of my life alone. (*His voice shaking.*) I can't
stop you from phoning him up, you can do it any time, Ben,
I'm just advising you, because I don't think you'll get much
fun from him, I really don't. I know you've had a bad day
already, with Tom and Anne, but you're making it worse.

BEN: (*Makes as if to dial, hesitates, dials*) You're passing up a
chance for a Lawrentian-type wrestle. Can't I interest you?

JOEY: Just remember that I warned you. (*He sits quite still at his*
desk.)

BEN: Two warnings in one day.

(JOEY *watches tensely*.)

Haylife and Forlings? This is Ben Butley, friend to Joseph Keyston, friend to Reg Nuttall, with whom I'd like to speak, please. (*Little pause*.) Thank you. (*He looks at* JOEY, *grinning, is suddenly stopped by his expression*.) What is it? (*Little pause*.) Joey? (*He starts to put the telephone down, checks himself*.) Hello, is that Reg – (*Little pause*.) Ah, his secretary. (*He hesitates then makes up his mind*.) May I speak to him, please. (*Pause,* BEN *watches* JOEY, *then offers* JOEY *the telephone. He shakes his head.* BEN *listens again*.) I see. Thank you very much. (*He puts the telephone down, looks at* JOEY.) He's out. (*Smiles*.) Is that a relief?

JOEY: In a sense.

BEN: You'd better tell me about it.

JOEY: What?

BEN: Whatever it is you're warning me about.

JOEY: No. It's nothing.

BEN: Come on, Joey.

JOEY: It doesn't matter. Let it go.

(*There's a knock on the door.* BEN *drops the Scotch bottle into his pocket.* EDNA *puts her head in*.)

EDNA: Are you free now, please? (*She comes in.* BEN *sits down. Very calmly, smiling*) Now would you kindly tell me what transpired between yourself and this Gardner?

JOEY: (*Earnestly*) I don't know anything about it, Edna.

EDNA: (*Still calm*) My teaching, it appears, isn't up to his standard.

BEN: Indeed. Well, I can assure you, Edna, that it's more than up to mine. I know our society has become insolently egalitarian, but I refuse to believe that the gardener's verdict on your teaching will be given too much weight. I didn't know we had a garden – let alone –

EDNA: This is the first time in twenty years' teaching that I've been complained about.

JOEY: It's preposterous. You're a very good teacher, Edna.

BEN: All right. Well, let's get this sorted out. To whom did he complain?

45

EDNA: To James.

BEN: And what did James say?

EDNA: He said you'd promised Gardner he could have tutorials with you. This conversation apparently took place in a pub.

BEN: What? I've had no – well, there was a student, now I come to think of it, but my God I'd completely forgotten – I suppose it might have been Gardner, I scarcely took him in. He wasn't wearing feathers in his cap. (*Little pause.*) Previously you talked of a plumed youth, wasn't it? (*Laughs.*)

EDNA: And you said nothing to him about coming to you for Eliot?

BEN: I have an idea he told me he'd become keen on Eliot. That's all.

EDNA: Keen on Eliot.

BEN: Something of the sort. I suppose I assumed he was after a few tutorials – but really I haven't given him a thought.

EDNA: And did you discuss whether these tutorials are to replace his seminars with me?

BEN: Certainly not.

EDNA: And did you tell him to go to James and explain the circumstances – that he wasn't getting anything out of my seminars.

BEN: Is that what James said?

EDNA: He tried so hard not to tell me what Gardner had said that it was perfectly obvious. He had his diplomatic smile on – the one that makes him look exactly like a rabbit. But I suppose I should be grateful that he didn't encourage that lout to throw my furniture out of the window, or burn my notes. I work very hard for those seminars.

JOEY: We know you do, Edna.

EDNA: I don't expect gratitude, far from it. But I do expect a minimum of civilized behaviour. And I expect to be backed up by the Head of the Department and the other members of the staff when I'm unlucky enough to have a bolshy trouble-maker in my group.

JOEY: But of course we'll back you up.

EDNA: What happened at the Senate House – it's beginning here. The Aristotle is just the beginning. (*She sits down, fumbles in her handbag, closes it.*) But why did they pick on me?

BEN: I don't think anybody would want to pick on you, Edna.

EDNA: Because I'm a woman, that's why. It's always easier to get at a woman. They think we're more vulnerable. Well, in my case, they've got another think coming. I haven't finished with Gardner and like ilk. Not by a long shot. (*Pause.*) How dare he! How dare he complain!

BEN: (*Stands up*) Look, perhaps the best thing *is* to let me take him on.

EDNA: There's not the slightest question of that, Ben. Not the slightest. He stays in my seminars. That's all there is to it.

BEN: Of course. If that's the way you want it. The only trouble is, you may not see much of him.

EDNA: In that case, it will be my pleasure to get him suspended. I've already started a Dean's Report.

BEN: As you wish. It's certainly your privilege. I just don't see what'll be gained.

EDNA: The satisfaction of causing him trouble.

BEN: Yes, I can see that might be fun.

EDNA: I don't care. (*She opens her handbag, takes out a handkerchief.*) So you two *are* on his side then?
(BEN *looks at* JOEY – *they both go over to her.*)

JOEY: Certainly not. I think Edna's got every right –
(BEN *puts his hand on her shoulder.*)

EDNA: Leave me alone. (*She pulls her arm away.*)

BEN: Edna. (*Gently*) I'm sorry, Edna. It's my fault for not taking young Gardner seriously.

EDNA: Nobody takes anything seriously any more. But Universities were serious once, yes they were. But now they despise them, yes they do, just as they despise me. Just as you two despise me.

JOEY: Despise you!

BEN: I just didn't want you to be hurt – or worry too much.

EDNA: That's precisely what I mean.
(*The telephone rings.*)

47

BEN: Sorry – (*He answers the telephone.*) Butley, English. Oh, um, hello, actually no this isn't too good a time. I'm in the middle of something –

EDNA: (*Stands up*) If that's James, please tell him that I'm going home. As education has become optional in this College, I've chosen to cancel my classes for the rest of the day. (*She goes out.*)

BEN: Sorry, James. Could we talk later. (*He puts the telephone down, sits on the edge of the desk, has a swig of Scotch, stares at* JOEY.) Bloody woman!

JOEY: So you did agree to take Gardner in, then.

BEN: One of us took the other in, all right. I shall find out later which way around it is.

JOEY: You'll enjoy that, I'm sure.

BEN: I deserve it, after all this.

JOEY: And what about Edna?

BEN: Bloody woman, that's all about Edna. She's lucky to be rid of him. It's not my fault she's too vain to admit it.

JOEY: And all you had to do just now was to keep quiet, and then tell Gardner it couldn't be managed.

BEN: But I *am* managing it.

JOEY: Oh Christ! But what for? What the hell for?

BEN: Perhaps I had a sense of vacancies opening up in my life. I needed to fill them perhaps.

JOEY: Then why don't you do it from your legitimate students, instead of fobbling them off and refusing to teach them.

BEN: (*Sitting in armchair*) I haven't got any legitimate students. They're all bastards. Which is my term of endearment for bores. Gardner's interesting. He actually interests me. At least I think he does, I can't remember him clearly and I'll have to see the hat. You interested me once, dear, and look where it's got you. An Assistant Lectureship. Of course I don't know if my interest can carry you through your board –

JOEY: You mean he'll have a relationship with you, don't you? While all poor Edna can offer him is a relationship with Byron, in a properly conducted seminar.

BEN: (*Hums 'Christ the Lord has risen today'*) Well, Joseph, what

chance your lectureship now? Edna says you despise her.
And she's quite right. Toadying is the sincerest form of
contempt. (*Pause. They stare at each other.*) I remember when
you stood in this room, darkly dressed to colour up your
melancholy, and I had you read a little Eliot to me. Do you
remember? (*Little pause.*) Little did we know that a long time
away, far into the future, we would be worrying and fretting
together about your promotion. Our beginnings never know
our ends. They're always so sad, so sad.

(JOEY *turns to go.*)

Don't flounce, Dappley. It doesn't suit your mousey
hindquarters.

JOEY: It's not my fault you buggered everything up with Anne.
You don't have to bugger everything up for me, too.

BEN: No, I don't. I'm doing it as a favour and for fun.

JOEY: I'm sick to death of your fun! (*He goes to the door.*)

BEN: Bum-twitch, bum-twitch, bum-twitch, bum-twitch!

(*He laughs and* JOEY *slams the door. He runs after him and
shouts down the corridor:*)

Teacher's pet!

(*He comes back – has a swig of Scotch, takes the telephone over
to Joey's desk, starts to dial, changes his mind, takes another
drink. Little pause.*)

    Appley Dappley, little brown mouse
    Goes to the cupboard in somebody's house
    In somebody's cupboard there's everything nice
    Pot, scotch, french letters
    For middle-aged mice.

(*The telephone rings.* BEN *answers it.*)

Woolly Bear, English. (*Pause.*) What? (*Little pause.*) *Who*
would like to see Mr Keyston? (*Little pause.*) Indeed? Yes,
yes he's here, just a minute. (*He puts his hand over the
receiver, then speaks into it.*) Mr Keyston says kindly send him
along to the office. Thank you. (*He puts the telephone down,
puts the Scotch into a drawer, goes to the desk, sits down, takes
out a pen. Feels the cotton wool on his chin. There is a knock. He
pores over an essay as there is another knock.*) Come.

49

(The door opens. REG *enters.* BEN *goes on working at his essay.)*
Minute please. *(Then looks up.)*

REG: Is Joey here?

BEN: Good God, it's Reg, isn't it? Of course it is. *(He gets up, goes over, holds out his hand. As they shake hands.)* I'm terribly sorry, do come in.

REG: Your porter said he was here.

BEN: And so he will be. He just went off to have a brief word with a colleague in distress. How are you?

REG: Very well, thanks. And you?

BEN: *(Gestures towards his desk)* As you see. *(Laughs.)*

REG: Yes. *(He glances at the desk, appalled.)* Look, you're obviously very busy. If you just tell Joey I'm at the porter's desk –

BEN: Don't be silly. You sit yourself down over there – *(He offers him a chair)* – and I'll just finish this off, I won't be a minute. *(*REG *hesitates, glances at Joey's desk and bookshelves and lights a cigarette.)*
*(*BEN *pretends to go on marking, makes a few exclamations under his breath. Not looking up)* What brings you down here, anyway?

REG: I just thought I'd look in.

BEN: *(Writes furiously)* Have to make my script illegible so that they don't find out about my spelling. There. *(He pushes the essay away.)* To check up, eh?

REG: Check up?

BEN: Joey's always saying that if you got your hands on our little room, which is an everywhere, or rather on me, eh? as I'm responsible for the mess we're in – *(Laughs.)* But you should see our flat. Even Joey's room is like a pigsty – naturally, I'm the pig that made it that way. You really must come around and help us out. He says you've done wonders with your little kitchen.

REG: I'm in publishing.

BEN: *(Puzzled)* Yes?

REG: Not in interior decorating. *(He sits on the hard chair by Joey's desk.)*

BEN: Oh God yes. (*Laughs.*) I'm sorry about that. No, I don't get your job wrong any more. It would be inexcusable. I'm always making Joey tell me about it, in fact.

REG: I know. He's always telling me about having to tell you about it.

BEN: He says you're a marvellous cook.

REG: I'm glad he eats well.

BEN: And keeps his figure, lucky sod. (*Little pause. Gets up and sits on hard chair opposite* REG.) You know, Reg, I'm very glad to have the chance to speak to you privately – I behaved abominably the last time we met. I do hope – well, you've forgiven me for your shoes. I never apologized properly.

REG: It's all right. These things happen.

BEN: But your shoes survived, did they?

REG: They were suede.

BEN: Oh dear. Suede.
(*Pause.*)

REG: Look, you must want to get on. I'll go back to the porter –
(*He gets up.*)

BEN: No, you mustn't do that. (*He gets up.*)

REG: I don't mind. In point of fact we were doing a little business together. He's an Arsenal supporter.

BEN: Good God. Is he really? In point of fact?
(*There is a pause.*)

REG: So I can let you get on with –

BEN: Have a drink? (*He goes to his desk, opens the drawer.*)

REG: I don't think I ought to.

BEN: (*Coming back with the Scotch and two soiled glasses.*) You are lucky. Then you'll really enjoy it.
(*He pushes one of the glasses into* REG's *hand.* REG *peers down into the glass, winces at its condition.* BEN *dashes Scotch into it, then into his own.*)
I understand you've met my friend Tom. Tom Weatherley, by the way.

REG: I know Tom, yes.

BEN: You know all my domestic news, too, I gather. I only heard it myself today.

REG: Yes, I heard something about it. I'm sorry.

BEN: Do you detest warm Scotch? I don't know how you drink it in your part of the world?

REG: This is fine.

BEN: Good. Cheers.

REG: Cheers.

BEN: Thanks.

(*He drinks.* REG *goes to Joey's bookshelves.*)

It's nice to have some company. These last few hours I've felt quite like Antony at his close – the air is full of the God's departing musics. So do forgive any tendency to babble, eh?

REG: No, that's all right. I understand.

BEN: Cheers. (*He sits on the hard chair by his desk.*) Actually what this whole business has brought home to me is how dependent I am on my past.

REG: (*Turning to him*) But it was – excuse me – but it was quite a short marriage, wasn't it?

BEN: No, I was talking about Joey.

REG: Oh.

BEN: It's as if my marriage were an intermission, if you see. Now I'm catching up with my past again, which is where I suppose my future is also.

REG: Really?

BEN: Sorry. I'm being literary. But I always think of *you* as a born romantic. From Joey's descriptions of *your* past. A touch of the butterfly, eh?

REG: Really? And what does Joey say to make you think that?

BEN: Oh, I don't know – the way you've pulled up your roots in the North, what I imagine to be your emotional pattern, your love of the bizarre.

REG: (*Pause*) And how does that express itself?

BEN: Joe's always recounting your experiences – for example with the Gurkhas. You were with them, weren't you?

REG: I was stationed with them, yes. About ten years ago, during my National Service.

BEN: Exactly. And I scarcely knew what a Gurkha was – I still tend to think he's something you get with a cocktail.

REG: Do you?

BEN: They must be tough little towsers.

REG: They are. (*He sits at Joey's desk.*) You didn't do your
National Service I take it.

BEN: Oh Christ! Sorry, I mean no.

REG: How come?

BEN: I got took queer.
(*There is a pause.* REG *puts his glass down.*)
Oh! You're ready for another one.

REG: No, I – in point of fact, I'd rather not.

BEN: This is an altogether different suburb. (*He refills Reg's
glass.*)

REG: Sorry? What suburb?

BEN: Oh, it's little joke of Joey's. Almost impossible to explain
out of context. (*He pours himself a drink and leans on the front
of his desk.*) But how is the world of fiction?

REG: Can't complain.

BEN: Cheers. What have you got coming out at the moment?

REG: At the moment I'm doing two cookery books, an
authoritative guide to bird-watching in Lincolnshire, the
only intelligent account of the farce of El Alamein – by an
NCO needless to say – and a New Testament Commentary.

BEN: That's your *fiction* list?

REG: No, that's our list for next month.

BEN: No novels at all then?

REG: Well, just one of those historical romances where the hero
shoves his sword into assorted villains and his cock into
assorted ladies. It won't get the reviews but it'll make us
money.

BEN: If he did it the other way around you might get both.

REG: (*Laughs briefly*) But the point is, you see, by putting that one
through we can afford to do something worthwhile later. For
instance, I've just made a decision about a novel on National
Service life.

BEN: Oh, one of those. I thought that vogue was eight years dead.

REG: No, not one of those. This is something special, in my
opinion. Of course it mightn't interest you as you didn't do

53

National Service, but personally I found it moving, witty,
gracefully organized – genuinely poetic.

BEN: The National Service? Good God! Those qualities are hard
enough to come by in art. It's never occurred to me to look
for them in life, especially as run by the armed forces.
Cheers.

REG: Nevertheless I expect you *will* be curious in this case.
Theoretically I can't tell you our author's name as the board
doesn't meet until tomorrow, but if I just mention that he's a
comprehensive school teacher – (*He raises his glass slowly.*)
Cheers.

BEN: (*After a pause*) Well well, (*He sits in the armchair.*) The most
boring man in London strikes again.

REG: I'm sorry.

BEN: Why?

REG: It must be painful for you.

BEN: Why?

REG: Because of his relationship with you. It was wrong of me to
have mentioned it.

BEN: On the contrary. It was the correct move. Has Joey read it?

REG: Not yet. It was offered to me in strict secrecy – at least until
I'd made up my mind. But I can tell him about it now. I
think he'll like it.

BEN: That's because you don't know him very well, perhaps. He
may be something of a dilettante in personal relationships,
but he holds fast to standards on important matters. We once
drew up a list of the five most tedious literary subjects in the
world. National Service came fifth, just behind the Latin
poems of Milton.

REG: Really? And what occupied the other three places?

BEN: The English poems of Milton.

REG: When I was at Hull I chose Milton for my special subject.

BEN: That sounds an excellent arrangement. The thing is to
confine him to the North. Down here we can dally with
Suckling and Lovelace.

REG: And Beatrix Potter? Joey says you've got great admiration
for the middle-class nursery poets.

BEN: With reservations. I find some of the novellae a trifle heavy
    going. (*A pause.*) I call Joey Appley Dappley, did you know?

REG: Do you?

BEN: And he calls me Old Mr Prickle-pin. After

>   Old Mr Prickle-pin, with never a coat to
>   Put his pins in.

   Sometimes I call him Diggory Diggory Delvet, when he's
   burrowing away at his book.
   (*There is a pause.*)

REG: What did you mean by being took queer?

BEN: (*Coyly*) Oh, you know, I'm sure. (*Laughing.*) You do look
   shocked, Reg.

REG: That's surprising, because I'm not surprised even.

BEN: You don't think there's anything shameful in it, then?

REG: In what?

BEN: Dodging the draft.

REG: There are thousands of blokes from working-class homes
   who couldn't. They didn't know the tricks. Besides they'd
   rather have done ten years in uniform than get out of it that
   way.

BEN: Then you think there's something shameful in being taken
   queer?

REG: I'm talking about people pretending to be what they're not.

BEN: Not what?

REG: Not what they are.

BEN: But if people do get taken queer, it's nature we must blame
   or their bodies, mustn't we? Medicine's still got a long way to
   go, Reg.

REG: Why do you use that word?

BEN: What word?

REG: 'Queer.'

BEN: Does it offend you?

REG: It's beginning to.

BEN: Sorry. It's an old nursery habit. One of our chars used to say
   it. Whenever I came down with anything it would be, 'Our
   Ben's took queer again, poor little mite.'
   (*There is a silence.*)

Although I can see it's a trifle inappropriate for a touch of
TB –

REG: TB?

BEN: They found it just in time. At my board medical, in fact.
Why *do* you object to the phrase though?

REG: No, no, it doesn't matter. A misunderstanding. I'm sorry.

BEN: Oh, I *see*. *Queer!* – of course. Good God, you didn't think
I'd sink quite so low, did you? (*Laughs.*)

REG: I'm sorry.

BEN: It's all right.
(*There is a pause.*)
Cheers. (*He raises his glass.*)

REG: Cheers.
(*Another pause.*)

BEN: Homosexual.
(*Another pause.*)

REG: What?

BEN: Homosexual. I was just wondering – should one say that
instead of 'queer' – in your sense of the word. Homosexual.

REG: It doesn't really matter at all. I don't really care –

BEN: Do you feel the same about 'fairies' as you do about
'queers'?

REG: Yes, in point of fact. Since you ask.

BEN: Right, I've got that. (*He gets up and moves towards* REG.) Of
course they've almost vanished anyway, the old-style queens
and queers, the poofs, the fairies. The very words seem to
conjure up a magical world of naughty thrills, forbidden
fruits – sorry – you know, I always used to enjoy them
enjoying themselves. Their varied performances contributed
to my life's varieties. But now the law, in making them safe,
has made them drab. Just like the heterosexual rest of us.
Poor sods. (*Little pause.*) Don't you think?

REG: (*Stands up and puts his glass on the desk*) Oh, there's enough
affectation and bitchiness in heterosexuals to be getting on
with. (*He glances at his watch.*) Don't you think?

BEN: Oh don't worry. He'll be here in a minute. (*Pause.*) How are
things between you two, by the way?

56

REG: What things?

BEN: No complications?

REG: What kind of complications would there be?

BEN: In that our routine doesn't interfere with your – plural meaning – routine.

REG: Plural meaning? Meaning what?

BEN: Yours and his. Your routines together.

REG: Ah. Well, it has done, frankly, yes. Now you ask. But I don't think it will from now on.

BEN: (*Sits on the hard chair opposite* REG) Then you're beginning to get the hang of it? Good. Because sometimes I've suspected that our friendship – going back so far and including so much – so much of his history and so much of my history which has really become *our* history – singular meaning this time – must make it difficult for any new people we pick up on the side.

REG: Like your wife, do you mean?

BEN: Well done. Yes, like poor old Anne. She must have felt her share amounted to a minor infidelity, really. I speak metaphorically, of course but then I suppose marriage is the best metaphor for all our intense relationships. Except those we have with our husbands and wives. (*Laughs.*) Naturally.

REG: So you think of yourself as married to Joey, do you?

BEN: Metaphorically.

(*A pause. The telephone rings.* BEN *picks it up.*)

Butley, English. Oh, hello James – no, I'm afraid I still can't talk properly. I'm in the middle of a tutorial. (*He winks at* REG.) OK. Yes. Goodbye.

REG: What metaphor would you use when you learned that Joey was going to move in with someone else? Would that be divorce, metaphorically?

BEN: (*After a long pause*) What?

REG: (*Laughs*) Sorry. I shouldn't do that. But I was thinking that it must be odd getting news of two divorces in the same day.

BEN: (*Pause.*) Joey hasn't said anything.

REG: No. I'm giving the news. You might say that when he comes to me our Joey will be moving out of figures of speech into matters of fact. Ours will be too much like a marriage to be a metaphor.

BEN: (*Little pause*) I thought you didn't admit to being – what? – different?

REG: There are moments when frankness is necessary. No, our Joey's just been waiting for the right queen, fruit, fairy, poof or homosexual to come along. He's come.

BEN: (*After a pause*) Well, isn't he lucky.

REG: Time will tell. I hope so. But I'm tired of waiting to make a proper start with him. I'm tired of waiting for him to tell you. You know our Joey – a bit gutless. No, the truth of the matter is I've been trying to get Joey to bring you around to dinner one evening and tell you straight, so we could get it over with. I knew he'd never find the nerve to do it on his lonesome. But he's kept dodging about, pretending you were busy, one excuse after another. It's worked out quite well though, hasn't it?

(*The door opens.* JOEY *comes in. Sees* REG.)

Hello. We've just been sorting things out. Ben and I.

BEN: (*To* JOEY) Cheers.

(JOEY *stands staring from one to the other.*)

Yes, our Reg has just been giving me the second instalment of the day's news. But then traditionally, because metaphorically, I should be the last to hear.

JOEY: (*After a pause*) I wanted to tell you myself.

BEN: Wanted to, did you? And were you looking forward to a subsequent scene?

JOEY: No.

BEN: How unlike each other we are. I would have enjoyed it.

REG: (*After a pause*) How did your lecture go?

JOEY: All right.

REG: Grand. Any more teaching today?

JOEY: No.

REG: Come on then. (*He moves over to* JOEY.) Let's go move your things.

JOEY: No, I can't, until later.

REG: Why not?

JOEY: Because there's something I've got to do. (*He glances at* BEN.)

BEN: Oh, don't stay on my account.

JOEY: No. It's something I promised Edna I'd –

REG: Oh. Well, have you got time for a cup of tea?

JOEY: Yes.

(*They move towards the door.*)

BEN: Reg.

(REG *turns.*)

Are you coming back after tea?

REG: (*Looks at* JOEY) I don't see any reason to. Why?

BEN: I think you're pretty bloody good Reg. In your way. It's not my way, but it seems to get you what you want.

REG: So far. But thanks.

(BEN *goes across to the carrier bag, scrambles in it, comes back with a package, hands it to* REG.)

(REG *takes it.*) What's this? (*Opening the package.*)

BEN: My kidneys. Best English lamb.

REG: You've been done. They're New Zealand, thawed.

BEN: The small, dapper irony is that I've been trying to join you for supper all day – not to say for the last month. May I anyway?

JOEY: Of course.

REG: I'm sorry. We can't.

JOEY: Why not?

REG: Because I've just bought two tickets for the match tonight. From one of your porters. (*To* BEN) I'm sorry. Perhaps some other time. (*He passes the bag of kidneys to* JOEY *who passes them to* BEN.)

BEN: Thank you. (*He drops the kidneys on his desk.*)

JOEY: Do we have to go to the match?

REG: Yes. It's an important one. (*To* BEN) But some other time. Now I'd like that tea please.

(JOEY *looks at him and leads the way to the door.*)

BEN: (*Watches them*) Reg!

(REG *turns.*)

I didn't know you supported a London club too, Reg? (*He picks up the whisky bottle.*)

REG: Leeds are away to Arsenal.

BEN: Ah. Well, enjoy it.

REG: Thanks. (*He turns to the door.*)

BEN: Reg.

    (REG *turns again.*)

    Will you wear it all then?

REG: Sorry? What? Wear what?

BEN: Your gear and tackle and trim. Have you got it with you?

REG: What? (*Puzzled, he looks at* JOEY.)

BEN: Your scarf and cloth cap and rattle. Your rosettes and
    hobnail boots. Isn't that your road, any road, up your road?

REG: I'm parched. Can we compare customs some other time?
    (*He turns.*)

BEN: Reg! (*As* REG *seems to go on.*) Reg!

    (REG *steps back in.*)

    No, it's not customs, Reg, it's you old cheese. Personally I
    don't give a fuck that moom and dud live oop Leeds and all,
    or that the whole tribe of you go to football matches looking
    like the back page of the *Daily Mirror* and bellow 'Ooop ta
    Rovers' and 'Clobber busturds' or own a butcher's shop with
    cush on ta side from parking tickets.

    (JOEY *laughs* – REG *sees him.*)

    I really don't, old cheese. No, what's culturally entertaining
    is yourself. I'm talking about your hypocrisy, old darling.

REG: Is that what you're talking about?

BEN: (*Making a circle round Joey's desk through the speech*) Because
    you're only good at getting what you want because you're a
    fraction of a fake, old potato, you really are. You don't show
    yourself north except twice a year with your latest boy or
    sommat in tow, do you? And I bet you get all your football
    out of ta *Guardian* and television except when you flash a
    couple of tickets at some soft Southern bugger – do you
    object to that word, old fruit? – like me, to show some softer
    Southern bugger like him – (*Gestures at* JOEY) – how tough
    you are. Did you cling consciously onto funny vowels, or did
    you learn them all afresh? I ask, because you're not
    Yorkshire, you're not working class, you're just a lucky

parvenu fairy old fig, and to tell you the truth you make me want to throw up. Pardon, ooop! All over your characteristically suede shoes.

JOEY: (*Shuts the door*) Shut up, Ben!

BEN: (*Walking round* REG) Why, have I upset him? What's the matter, Reg? I thought you liked plain talk and straightforward blokes, brass tacks, hard dos and no bloody metaphors. *I* don't blame you for being ashamed of ta folks, except when you want to come the simple sod – sorry, homo – sorry, bloke. I'd feel ta same in thy clogs.

JOEY: Ben!

REG: Anything else?

BEN: Yes, tell me. (*Comes back to confront him.*) Have you had plain talk and brass tacks about thyself with moom, when she's back from pasting tickets on cars, lud, eh, or with dud while he's flogging offal, lud? Thou'd get fair dos all right then, wouldn't thee? From our dud with his strup? Or would he take thee down to local and introduce thee round to all t'oother cloth caps? 'This is our Reg. He's punsy. Ooop, pardon Reg lud. Omosexual. Noo, coom as right surprise to moother und me, thut it did, moother joost frying oop best tripe and garbuge and me settling down with gnomes to a good read of Mazo de la Roche.'

(*He laughs in* REG's *face. There is a pause. Then* JOEY *makes a spluttering sound, as with laughter.*)

REG: (*Turns, looks at* JOEY) Oh, I see. The information for all this drollery comes from you. Perhaps you'd better sort him out. (*He walks back to the door.*)

BEN: Reg! Coom 'ere lad! You coom and sort me out. Coom on, lud, it's mun's work!

(REG *stops, walks slowly towards* BEN.)

Cloomp, cloomp, cloomp, aye, tha's they moother's feet, Reg!

(JOEY *lets out another gasp. There is a silence,* REG *standing in front of* BEN.)

REG: I don't like these games, Joey. You know that.

JOEY: (*Spluttering*) I'm sorry, I didn't mean . . .

BEN: Going to cook my kidneys after all then?

REG: Is that what you want?

BEN: Ah coom on –

REG: No, I'm not playing with you. So don't say one more word, eh? Not a word. (*He turns to go.*)

BEN: (*Steels himself*) Ah Reg lud –

    (REG *turns around.*)

    Coom on then.

JOEY: Ben!

BEN: Owd sod, feery, punsy –

    (REG *hits* BEN *in the stomach, not very hard – he falls to the ground.*)

JOEY: Don't!

    (*There is a silence, then a shape at the door.*)

REG: There. Is that what you wanted?

    (EDNA *knocks, puts her head in.*)

EDNA: Oh sorry.

BEN: Living theatre. Next time around in Polish.

EDNA: Oh (*To* REG) I'll come back later. (*She goes out.*)

BEN: For a kick at my balls. Why should she be left out?

REG: (*Calmly*) But you're pitiful, pitiful. This man you've given me all the talk about. That you made me jealous of. (*He turns, goes to the door.*)

BEN: Still, couldn't take it, could you, butcher's boy!

REG: (*To* JOEY) It was silly. You'll have to outgrow that kind of thing Joey.

    (*He smiles at* BEN, *and goes out closing the door quietly. There is a long moment. Then* BEN *goes and leans on the edge of the desk, smiles at* JOEY.)

BEN: (*Touches his chin*) Your bugger's made me bleed again. (*Laughs.*) You're beginning to get little wrinkles around your eyes. Are they laughter wrinkles, or is it age, creeping up you on little crow's feet? (*Pause.*) You'll be one of those with a crêpe neck, I'll be one of the fat ones with a purple face, Reg will be . . . (*Pause.*) I was watching you while you were shaving the morning you were going to Leeds. If you'd moved your eyes half an inch you'd have seen me in the mirror. I was standing behind you studying your neck and my jowels.

JOEY: I saw you.

BEN: Ah! Well, what did you think of all that, with our Reg, eh?

JOEY: I thought it was creepy.

BEN: I wonder what your next will be like? Don't be afraid to bring him home, dear, will you? (*Genteel.*) I do worry so.

JOEY: There isn't going to be a next one. At least, not for some time.

BEN: Ho, reely? I think that's a good plan, h'abstinence makes the 'eart grow fonder. (*He sits on desk.*)

JOEY: I'm moving in with Reg.

BEN: (*After a pause*) I don't think he'll have you, dear, after your indiscretions and sauciness.

JOEY: Yes he will.

BEN: You'll go running after him, will you? How demeaning!

JOEY: Possibly. But it's better than having him run after me. I've been through that once, I couldn't face it again.

BEN: You love him then, your butcher's boy?

JOEY: Actually, he's not a butcher's boy, in point of fact. (*He picks up his briefcase and returns to his desk. Little pause.*) His father teaches maths at the university. His mother's a social worker. They live in an ugly Edwardian house . . .

BEN: (*After a pause, nods*) Of course. Quite nice and creepy. Creepy, creepy, creepy, creepy!

JOEY: I'm sorry.

BEN: Well, thank you anyway for the fiction. (*He sits on the hard chair by his desk. There is a pause.*) So you love him then?

JOEY: No. But I've got to get away from you, haven't I?

BEN: Really? Why?

JOEY: (*Sits at desk.*) For one thing, I'd like to get some work done. During your married year I did quite a bit. I'd like to finish it.

BEN: What?

JOEY: My edition of Herrick.

BEN: If the consequence of your sexual appetites is another edition of unwanted verse then you have an academic duty to

63

control yourself. Could I also mention, in a spirit of
unbecoming humility, that if I hadn't taken over your
studies when you were an averagely dim undergraduate,
you'd never have got a First. Your nature is to settle for
decent seconds, indecent seconds, in Reg's case.

JOEY: I know. But those were in the days when you still taught.
Now you spread futility, Ben. It creeps in, like your dirty
socks do, into my drawers. Or my clean ones, onto your feet.
Or your cigarette butts everywhere. Or your stubble and
shaving cream into our razor. Or your voice, booming out
nursery rhymes into every corner of this department, it
seems to me. Or your –

BEN: Shut up! That's rehearsed.

JOEY: Thousands of times.

*[BEN: (*After a pause*) He's going to get it published for you, isn't
he?

JOEY: (*Shrugs, after a pause*) Yes. He said he'd help.

BEN: (*Laughs*) And Appley Dappley has sharp little eyes. And
Appley Dappley's so found of pies.

JOEY: I can't help it. It's the only way I'll get ahead.

BEN: Into what? There's nothing left for you to get ahead in, it's
all in the past, and that thins out as the years go by. You'll
end up like Edna, sending out Dean's reports on any student
you haven't killed off, and extinguishing a poet or two in the
library. While it all rots away around you.

JOEY: Perhaps it won't rot away if – (*Pauses.*) I'd rather end up
like Edna than like you. Once you talked to me of literature
as the voice of civilization, what was it, the dead have living
voices –

---

*The passage in brackets was cut from the production the night before we opened.
I am re-instating it because it now seems to me a passage that, whether it should be
played in performance or not, conveys a great deal of useful information about
Butley's relationship with Joey and about his sexual nature. In the first
performance and all subsequent productions, this passage was replaced by the
following stage direction:

A long pause – during which BEN *goes to his desk chair and sits – the whisky bottle in
his hand.*

BEN: I hope not. I may have quoted . . . 'the communication/Of the dead is tongued with fire beyond the language of the living.' I can still quote it when the moment's right.

JOEY: And when will it be right again? It hasn't been with me since your marriage – since before it, really. It's been Beatrix Potter and passages and pastiches from Eliot . . .

BEN: I adjust my selection to the context. Why did you move back into the flat with me then?

JOEY: Habit, I suppose. I'm fairly feeble as both you and Reg point out to me. I don't like being alone, and I couldn't resist – I was actually quite pleased when your marriage broke down.

BEN: That's called friendship. (*Laughs.*)

JOEY: You should have stuck it out. With Anne.

BEN: Should I?

JOEY: But at least you slept with her. You sleep with women –

BEN: Not when I can help it. Mankind cannot stand too much reality. I prefer friendship.

JOEY: But it's the sort of friendship people used to have with me at school. Abuse, jokes, games . . .

BEN: It's only a language, as good as any other and better than some, for affection.

JOEY: But I've got these wrinkles around my eyes, and my neck will crêpe, just as you said. And you're fattening and thirty-five, just as you said, and we don't belong in a school or nursery any more. Reg is right. We're pitiful. We're pitiful together.

BEN: We're all pitiful, together or apart. The thing is to be pitiful with the right person, keep it from everybody else. And from yourselves whenever you can.

JOEY: Well then – well then – I can't keep it from myself any longer. I've been trying to keep you and Reg apart because I knew this would happen. But I've been longing for it, all the same. (*Pause.*)] I'm sorry it had to be today, what with Anne and Tom. I would have waited . . .

BEN: (*In senile professional tones*) Which shows you have no sense of classical form. We're preserving the unities. The use of messengers has been quite skilful. (*Pause.*) All right. All right. It doesn't really matter very much.

JOEY: What will you do?

BEN: (*After a pause*) Could you, do you think, staunch the flow of blood? (*He lifts his chin back.*)

JOEY: (*Comes over reluctantly, takes the piece of cotton wool* BEN *holds out to him.*) It's just a bubble. (*He hesitates, then bends forward with the cotton wool.*)

BEN: The trouble with – all these confessions, revelations, clean breaks, and epiphanies, shouldn't we call them these days? – is that – cluttered contact goes on. For instance, we still share this room. (*As* JOEY *steps away*) You're going to have to live with your past, day after day and as messily as ever. I'll see to that.

EDNA: (*Knocks, opens the door, smiles*) May I?

BEN: Of course. (*Laughs.*) Of course you may, Edna. It's your turn.

EDNA: Now you'll really be able to spread yourself. It's much more sensible. (*To* JOEY) I've moved out all my files. What can I do now?

(*A pause –* BEN *sinks into the chair in realization of the news.*)

JOEY: I can manage down here. (*He moves away, goes to the shelves, takes down his books.*)

EDNA: I'm glad I made one of you take advantage.

(JOEY *goes out with a load of books.*)

I've quietened down, Ben, you'll be glad to hear. But I'd like to say I'm sorry about my – my little outburst just now. I must learn not to be so sensitive. I suspect it's the only way, with this new generation.

BEN: They are rather frightening.

EDNA: Oh, I don't imagine you're frightened of them.

BEN: I haven't enough pride. I shall continue to throw myself on their mercy. (*He goes to Joey's shelves – takes down a pile of books and puts them on the desk.*)

EDNA: They weren't very merciful to Aristotle in the Senate House.

BEN: He had too many advantages. They couldn't be expected to tolerate that.

EDNA: (*Laughs*) Well . . .

BEN: (*Watches her*) I haven't congratulated you on your book.

EDNA: Wouldn't it have been awful if someone had got in ahead of me. Twenty years – I'm really rather ashamed.

BEN: Will you go on to someone else now?

EDNA: I don't know. (*She sits on the hard chair by Ben's desk.*) You know, last night I played a little game – I closed my eyes and turned over groups of pages at a time – and then I looked at a page. It was in the commentary on a letter from his sad wife. And I remembered immediately when I started working on it. It was in Ursula's cottage in Ockham, Surrey. I was still working on it when the summer term of the following year was over. I finished it during my first week back at Ursula's. I can even remember the weather – how's the book on Eliot, by the way?

BEN: It has a good twenty years to go.

EDNA: I'm sure that's not true. James is always saying that you get through things so quickly. I'm sure you'll be finished with Eliot in no time. Anyway, don't dally with him. Let me be a lesson to you –

BEN: (*Watching her*) Do you still go to Ursula's cottage?

EDNA: Oh, not in the same way. Ursula got married during chapter six. (*She laughs and goes to the door, stops.*) Oh hello. No, don't run away. (*She puts her head back in.*) Mr Gardner's here.

BEN: Oh! Right.

EDNA: Will you go in, Mr Gardner? (*She goes out.*)
(*GARDNER comes in. He is wearing a hat with feathers in it, a white Indian shirt, sandals, no socks.*)

BEN: (*Stares blankly ahead, then looks at him*) Well Mr Gardner – you're here for your Eliot.

GARDNER: Yes please.

BEN: Tell me, what *did* I say in the pub?

GARDNER: Well, I told you I couldn't stand Miss Shaft's seminars and you told me I was interesting enough to do Eliot, and that I ought to go and see James. You said he'd pass the buck back to you because whenever he had a problem he converted it straight into a buck and passed it. Actually, you called him Cottontail.

BEN: Did I? (*After a pause, he smiles.*) And here we both wonder fully are.

GARDNER: Yes (*Smiles.*) Thank God.

BEN: Well let's get going. (*He goes to the shelf, gets a copy of Eliot, brings it back.*) Can you start by reading me a passage, please. Don't worry if you can't understand it yet. (*He hands him the book, open.*) There. Do you mind?

GARDNER: No, I'd like that. (*He sits on the hard chair by Ben's desk.*)

JOEY: (*Comes in*) Oh sorry. (*He goes to his desk and begins to pack the contents of the drawers.*)

BEN: This is Mr Gardner, celebrated so far for his hat. Do you like it?

JOEY: Of its style.

BEN: Once – some years ago – I taught Mr Keyston. During our first tutorial we spent a few minutes discussing his clothes. Then he read me some Eliot. Today I'm actually wearing his socks. Those are the key points in a relationship that now goes mainly back.

JOEY: (*Opening drawers*) So you see, Mr Gardner, you'd better be careful. If you value your socks.

(GARDNER *looks at his feet: he is not wearing socks.* BEN *and* JOEY *look at* GARDNER's *feet, then* JOEY *goes on putting papers into his briefcase.*)

BEN: Please begin.

GARDNER: (*Reads*) 'In that open field.
　　　　　If you do not come too close, if you do not come too close,
　　　　　On a summer midnight, you can hear the music
　　　　　Of the weak pipe and the little drum
　　　　　And see them dancing around the bonfire
　　　　　The association of man and woman
　　　　　In daunsinge, signifying matrimonie –
　　　　　A dignified and commodious sacrament.
　　　　(JOEY *finished clearing, looks at* GARDNER.)
　　　　　Two and two, necessarye coniunction,

Holding eche other by the hand or the arm
Whiche betokeneth concorde. Round and round the fire.
(JOEY *looks towards* BEN, *they exchange glaces, then* BEN *looks
away,* JOEY *goes out, closing the door gently.*)
Leaping through the flames, or joined in circles,
Rustically solemn or in rustic laughter
Lifting heavy feet in clumsy shoes,
Earth feet, loam feet, lifted in country mirth
Mirth of those long since –'

BEN: So you're Gardner, are you?

GARDNER: (*Stops, looks at him in surprise. Smiles*) Yes.

BEN: Ninny Nanny Netticoat,
In a white petticoat,
With a red nose, –
The longer he stands,
The shorter he grows.

GARDNER: What?

BEN: I'm moving on, Mr Gardner. I'm breaking new ground.

GARDNER: Oh. (*He laughs.*)

BEN: Furthermore, I hate your hat.

GARDNER: I'm sorry.

BEN: Did you wear it when you bombed the Velium Aristotle?
And are you going to wear it for your raids on *Dappley* and
Parsley eh?

GARDNER: What?

BEN: It won't do you any good. Aristotle in his Velium stood
alone, vulnerable, unreadable and so unread. But *Dappley*
and *Parsley* are scattered in nursery consciousnesses
throughout the land. They can still be tongued with fire.

GARDNER: What are you talking about? – I wasn't anywhere near
the Senate House when that happened. I don't even know
what it was about, properly.

BEN: No, you're a personal relationships type of chappie, I can
sense that. Please go away. Go back to Miss Shaft.

GARDNER: What? But I can't – after all that trouble –

BEN: Trouble for you, fun for me. Go away, Gardner, and take
your plumage with you, I don't want to start again. It's all

been a ghastly mistake. I don't find you interesting, any more. You're not what I mean at all, not what I mean at all. I'm too old to play with the likes of you.

(GARDNER *puts the Eliot down, goes out.* BEN *puts the book back, sits at the desk, turns off the desk lamp and tries feebly three times to turn it on again. Curtain.*)

Wise Child

Wise Child was first performed on 10 October 1967 at Wyndham's Theatre, London. The cast was as follows:

MRS ARTMINSTER	Alec Guinness
MR BOOKER	Gordon Jackson
JERRY	Simon Ward
JANICE	Cleo Sylvestre

Director	John Dexter
Designer	Motley
Lighting	Richard Pilbrow

ACT ONE

*Inter-connecting rooms in a hotel. The one left of stage (facing) is
small, with a single bed, a large cupboard, a hard-backed chair, a
heavy lamp on the bedside table. The one right of stage is large, with a
double bed, a hand-basin, an armchair, a large cupboard.*

MRS ARTMINSTER *enters the large room, hurriedly. She is stout, tall,
dressed in a fur coat, has a small hat perched on top of her head, the
rim of which comes over her forehead, a veil hanging from it. She is in
her fifties. A small cluster of rinsed blue curls is visible, also heavy
make-up. She is burrowing into a large handbag, with a zip. She
takes out a quarter of a bottle of Scotch. Begins to uncork it when a
door bangs off-stage, and there are feet in the hall.* JERRY *comes into
the other room, and* MRS ARTMINSTER *thrusts the bottle into her coat
pocket.* JERRY *is slight, very pretty, with his blond hair cut short. He
looks about seventeen. He takes something out of his long raincoat
pocket, throws it on the bed, takes off his raincoat, throws it over the
chair, goes towards the connecting door when the door bangs again
off-stage. He freezes, then tiptoes to the connecting door. There is a
knock on his door and he opens the connecting door softly, enters with a
finger to his lips.* MRS ARTMINSTER *has been taking off her coat and
folding it so that the pocket is out of sight, over the armchair. She turns
with theatrical innocence as* JERRY *enters, begins to say something,
sees his signal and stops. He clicks the door shut. There is another
knock on his door, which then opens.* MR BOOKER *looks in.*

MR BOOKER *is about forty, plump, about the same build as* MRS
ARTMINSTER *and the same height. He wears spectacles, moves slowly
as if afraid of knocking into things. His spectacles are bi-focals. He
looks around the room, several times, withdraws his head. Then puts it
back in. Looks at the object* JERRY *has thrown on to the bed, and
advances towards it. He trips against the chair, nearly knocks it over,
turns around in a panic, and goes out.* JERRY, *who has been standing
by the connecting door, listening, then opens the door and slips in, just
as there is a knock on Mrs Artminster's door. He sees the object on the
bed (which is a wig) hurries over and stuffs it under the pillow.*

73

MRS ARTMINSTER: Come.

MR BOOKER: I'm just popping my head in to wonder how you are this evening, Mrs Artminster.

MRS ARTMINSTER: Still turning dizzy and faint now and then, I'm afraid to say, Mr Booker.

MR BOOKER: Oh, I'm sorry to hear that. (*Little pause, stares at her.*) But you've been out I see.

MRS ARTMINSTER: Yes, I did try a few steps down the street, until I was overcome.

MR BOOKER: Oh. Well, perhaps tomorrow you'll feel stronger and more like it. (*Little pause.*) Well. (*Withdraws head, puts it back in.*) I didn't see you go by my office, by the bye. (*Long pause. They stare at each other.*) I must be getting lax. I'm usually in the habit of keeping an eye out for passing guests, even when there aren't any. (*Little pause. Withdraws with a laugh, puts his head back in.*) Has Garfield come in yet, by the bye?

MRS ARTMINSTER: No, unless he's snatching a little doze. He may be very tired.

MR BOOKER: Been up to Little Munstering again, has he? I hope they're not giving him trouble. It's hard for a boy to control workmen, judging by my own experiences of the last month. (*Stares at* MRS ARTMINSTER. *She makes no reply.*) Well, perhaps I'll see him later on, if I pop up later, if I may?

MRS ARTMINSTER: Oh yes. That would be agreeable.

MR BOOKER: If I'm not intruding, that is?

MRS ARTMINSTER: No.

MR BOOKER: Well . . . (*Smiles, goes out.*)

(*Throughout all this* JERRY *has been standing by the door of his room, listening. When the door shuts he tiptoes into Mrs Artminster's room. She begins to speak. He raises a hand and she stops. There is a knock on his door, and* MR BOOKER *puts his head in again. Looks around, looks at the bed, goes over to it, stares at it puzzled. Puts his hand on the pillow, then goes out.* MRS ARTMINSTER *and* JERRY *stand facing each other, then when the door closes in the hall,* JERRY *crosses the room and sits down on the bed.*)

JERRY: So you went out then?

MRS ARTMINSTER: Yes, I did. Think I can spend the whole day in here, nodding and chattering to myself like one of your Dutch harlots?

JERRY: Where did you go?

MRS ARTMINSTER: Never you mind. (*Little pause.*) I went out, that's where. (*Crosses to the bed and sits down, back to* JERRY, *who is staring straight ahead of him. She turns and looks at him, shrugs, turns away.*) But it wasn't far because my dogs are barking, I can tell you. (*Takes off a shoe, sighs.*)

JERRY: (*Viciously*) Ooooh! Do you mind! They make my stomach jump!

MRS ARTMINSTER: What's the matter, dear, you can't stand your old mum natural you should have left her where you found her, shouldn't you? (*Takes off other shoe, massages foot, puts shoe back on.*) He's a bit (*tweaks her ears*) our Simon B. is, the way he's up after you every evening like a weasel for his rabbit.

JERRY: He makes me sick.

MRS ARTMINSTER: Yes, and who doesn't make you sick? Your old mum with her feet, Simon Booker with his smiles and helpfulness, the poor nigger Janice you sneer at too – you get above yourself, Jer, that's your problem. Not everyone finds you a sweet little tease. I don't for one, and Derek doesn't for another, and that's two that count.

JERRY: Derek, he doesn't count, not as far as I'm concerned.

MRS ARTMINSTER: Well, Simon Booker does. You keep dodging him and denying him and he'll be demanding the rent and throwing us out. (*Little pause, chuckles.*) He's a good man, and don't you forget it. There's not everyone would take us in just because I fainted in his lounge from shock and you begged him on your tiny knees. He's got the right to put us out on the pavement with a boot in each arse and don't you forget that either.

JERRY: I'm not worried about him.

MRS ARTMINSTER: Well I am Jer, it's me that's got to stay in here facing him while you dart in and out. He nearly said again about no guests officially until next week, I could see it from the way he was working his mouth, and he smells something's wrong, I could see it in his eyes.

JERRY: Eyes! He hasn't got any eyes! That's double glass in those spectacles of his, he can't see far enough to blink at it.

MRS ARTMINSTER: He can see you all right, oh, I've watched his features light up at your mere voice. He hasn't heard it raised like I have, in spite. The soft-hearted don't like being deceived Jerry. It kills the goodness in them.

JERRY: Yes, well you're right about him smelling something wrong, you make sure you stand three feet from him, or why don't you have a wash? The conveniences laid on. (*Indicates the wash-stand.*) You turn that knob and hot stuff comes out, called water.

MRS ARTMINSTER: Shut your mouth, I've had enough. (*Gets up and picks up her coat from the chair. The quarter bottle half slips out, she tries to thurst it back casually, her back to* JERRY. *He watches her.*)

JERRY: I can see you.

MRS ARTMINSTER: What? What can you see?

JERRY: You know what I can see.

MRS ARTMINSTER: None of your business, what you can see.

JERRY: Yes, it is my business what I can see. (*Gets up, goes over, stands in front of* MRS ARTMINSTER *with his hand out.*)

MRS ARTMINSTER: I don't care what you can see, you're not having it.

JERRY: Yes I am, Mum. (*In a sinister voice.*) Nine counties, Mum. (MRS ARTMINSTER *turns, stares at him, then slaps the bottle into his hand, crosses to the bed, sits down. Folds arms.* JERRY *stares at her, she unfolds arms, strikes her knee savagely, then refolds arms.*)

And where did it come from? (*Long pause.*) You stole it. (*Long pause.*) Where did you steal it from? (*Pause.*) Not from – not from Booker! You – you stupid old bitch.

MRS ARTMINSTER: He won't miss it. He wasn't in his office, he was peering down the street looking for we know who. (*Pause.*) He doesn't know it was there, it was in the back of his cupboard, I just plunged my hand in and that's what it wrapped itself around, so whose fault is that? (*Pause.*) There was bottles on bottles of it.

JERRY: He'll miss it all right.

MRS ARTMINSTER: No he won't. And what if he does? There's always the nigger to blame it on. Niggers are thieves aren't they? (*Pause.*) Anyway, he can't stand the sight of her.

JERRY: How do you know?

MRS ARTMINSTER: He likes you, doesn't he?
(*They stare at each other. Then* JERRY *throws the bottle on the bed and goes and sits down. He puts his head in his hands.*)
(MRS ARTMINSTER *looks at him tauntingly*) Derek would have understood.

JERRY: (*Viciously*) Derek isn't here, is he? (*Looks at her.*) You've still got gravy on your blouse from yesterday, what's the use my telling you to sponge it off?

MRS ARTMINSTER: Yes, the mention of Derek always brings the poison out in you. Just because Derek was a man you can't stand him.
(JERRY *leaps to his feet. They stand staring at each other,* MRS ARTMINSTER *tauntingly,* JERRY *in a rage.*)

JERRY: (*After a pause*) I didn't hear that, lucky for you. (*Looks at* MRS ARTMINSTER, *then goes into his room, takes a quarter of a bottle of Scotch from his jacket pocket, comes back.*) Here you are. (*Gives it to* MRS ARTMINSTER.) I was looking forward to giving it and now you've spoilt it.

MRS ARTMINSTER: Thank you, Jerry.

JERRY: (*In a martyred voice*) But you don't want it now, do you?

MRS ARTMINSTER: Don't want it? Oh, I want it all right. 'Course I do.

JERRY: But not like you would have if you hadn't stolen yourself one of your own.

MRS ARTMINSTER: (*After a pause*) I'll tell you what, Jer, you take this one and keep it for me (*gives own bottle*) and I'll start in on this one, and you can give me the other one when I need it.

JERRY: It's not the same.

MRS ARTMINSTER: No, it's better. It's two presents instead of one. (*Pause.*) Thank you, Jerry.

JERRY: (*After a pause*) That's all right.

(MRS ARTMINSTER *takes a swig.* JERRY *gets up and goes out to the wash-stand, comes back with a glass. Gives it to* MRS ARTMINSTER. *Smiles, then sits down beside her.*)

MRS ARTMINSTER: Jerry.

JERRY: What Mum? (*This has to be said half-ironically, half-tenderly.*)

MRS ARTMINSTER: Guess what?

JERRY: What?

MRS ARTMINSTER: I saw in Simon B.'s office.

JERRY: What?

MRS ARTMINSTER: I'm just telling you this, Jerry, I'm not saying anything. (*Long pause.*)

JERRY: Well, what?

MRS ARTMINSTER: There's a safe in there, Jerry.

(JERRY *doesn't answer.*)

Well?

JERRY: Well, what? (*Pause, turns and stares at her.*)

MRS ARTMINSTER: You all over. If I had my Derek along – a quick in, a swing of the jogger if Booker was fool enough to be hanging around, and out. That's the way Derek does things.

JERRY: Not any more he doesn't. Derek doesn't, does he? Not any more, Derek doesn't . So don't Derek me, you know it makes me sick to hear his name repeated without mercy. It's *me* that keeps you free. Me. Not Derek.

MRS ARTMINSTER: Free! You call this free! The only ideas that run in your head are to keep me in confinement, oh you enjoy yourself at my expense.

JERRY: Well, I'll tell you one thing, I wouldn't talk if I was taken. I'd lay all the blame on my own head, I wouldn't have you hunted across England. Would I? Would I? (*Glares at her.*)

MRS ARTMINSTER: (*After a pause*) No, Jerry, you wouldn't. I know that.

JERRY: And Derek – what is Derek? Big teeth and fat, that's what Derek is. Isn't he?

78

MRS ARTMINSTER: There's no denying he's big built.

JERRY: Fat, you mean. Don't you?

MRS ARTMINSTER: He likes his food, and where's the harm of that?

JERRY: It's no good his liking his food where he is, is it? Because there's only slops and hard bread, isn't there?

MRS ARTMINSTER: That's what you tell me, Jerry, yes.

JERRY: And you like your food too, don't you?

MRS ARTMINSTER: I'm only human, Jerry.

JERRY: So you're better off where you are, aren't you? (*Long pause.*) Aren't you?

MRS ARTMINSTER: I expect I am, Jerry, yes, as you say so.

JERRY: And Derek's no good to you, is he? He never was, was he? I'm the one you need, aren't I?

MRS ARTMINSTER: (*After a long pause*) Yes, you're the one I need, Jer. Ever since you brought yourself to me with your golden hair and cheeky smile I knew you for the one. (*Sarcastically.*)

JERRY: (*Getting up, walks around the room, slapping his hand against his thigh. Then he goes out, into his own room.* MRS ARTMINSTER *takes a long swig of whisky, braces herself. Stares at the door.* JERRY *comes back in.*) I got that feeling when I was out this afternoon.

MRS ARTMINSTER: Did you, Jerry, what feeling? (*Carefully.*)

JERRY: (*Pathetically*) You know.

MRS ARTMINSTER: Where your bones are china, and people are going to knock into you and you'll turn to powder.

JERRY: Glass, and it's not me they'll break, it's my bones.

MRS ARTMINSTER: Well Jer, as long as you're all right, what do your bones matter then?

JERRY: But my bones cut me up from the inside. *My own bones.* Every way I move I slice a bit more out of myself. That's the worst feeling. China doesn't cut you up like that.

MRS ARTMINSTER: What you need is a bit of fun, Jerry, to take you out of yourself. You've got no feeling of fun.

JERRY: (*Shaking his head, paying no attention*) Yes, and supposing it gets worse even? Because it doesn't matter what you know, it's what you are. I know my bones aren't made of glass, I know that.

MRS ARTMINSTER: That's right, they're not. They're made of bone, dear.

JERRY: But they'll cut me if I break up. I know that don't I? *That's* why I've got to move delicate , because of what I know *could* happen. It doesn't make any difference, it's all the same, what the doctors and magazines say. Have you noticed me when I'm moving delicate, Mum?

MRS ARTMINSTER: (*After a pause, looks away from him*) Yes, I have, Jer, and it's very ugly. You walk about me like spiders, I thought it was because you'd got corns.

JERRY: No, it's because of my glass bones, which I am, Mum, I am.

MRS ARTMINSTER: Corns are worse, dear, they're there and wishful thinking won't get rid of them. High heels bring *them* up.

JERRY: Yes, and then one day there's someone coming at me, because of the risks I take, and what do I do? I couldn't hit him, could I, I'd just be tearing myself open from inside, and what if I fell? What if I fell, Mum? (*Clutches* MRS ARTMINSTER.)

MRS ARTMINSTER: Derek doesn't have dreams like that, Jerry – yes, I know –

(*As* JERRY *stirs angrily*)

– but I've got to say his name, Derek doesn't have dreams like that. He sleeps at night, because he knows when he wakes up in the morning nobody's going to wonder at him. And if they do he shows an arm. It's people looking at you you can't stand, Jer, and you can't stand it because you can't look back at them from as good as they are thank you very much whoever you are. You keep a watch instead, and it's like my heart was tethered the way you keep it on me. (*Long pause.*) Was it my fault? Tell me the truth, was it my fault? No, one blow from Derek's jogger, he disabled himself that postman did, falling like a cripple in the wrong places. Is that justice? Is that what you expect? Derek was an expert, and don't you forget it, no Jer –

(*As* JERRY *walks impatiently about*)
– you listen to my piece until I've done. You nagging and
nine countiesing me, you think of Derek and what he was
and still is if I know Derek, and then you think of those glass
bones you talk about. Yes (*Long pause.*) Oh Jerry. Jerry.
Last month you was dreaming of being an eagle, why can't
you go back to that. (*Long pause.*) Yes, an eagle it was Jerry,
in Staines. Then Slough, Hitching, Baldock it changed itself
to glass bones. Reading, glass bones and cut up from the
inside. What next? (*Pause.*) That's why I say, find us a Little
Munstering and lie quiet. (*Long pause.*) Why don't you want
a girl friend, that's what I want to know? (*Long pause.*) You
tell me that, boy?

JERRY: Twits.

MRS ARTMINSTER: What?

JERRY: Twits. I said they're twits.

MRS ARTMINSTER: That's not the word. (*Pause.*) Oh, Jerry,
Jerry, Derek was everywhere with his muscle at your age, he
couldn't help himself. He built himself up with practice. He
was small and dainty when he was young, but he didn't
despise muscle. (*Pause.*) And he'd have their skirts up and
their panties down as soon as look at them.

JERRY: He was taken on top of one, wasn't he? The police
hammering at the door and smashing the windows to get
him, and he just lay there eyes glazed and grinning his pegs
out all over his fat face, if I know Derek.

MRS ARTMINSTER: *You* don't know Derek. (*Laughs.*) You don't
know Derek. (*Laughs again.*) Who do you know? You know
what they say, Jerry?

JERRY: What? What do they say?

MRS ARTMINSTER: It's a wise boy that knows its own, Jerry.
That's what.

JERRY: (*After a pause*) Well, I know my own mum all right, don't
I, on account of the police of nine counties would help me
find her if she was ever lost to me, wouldn't they?

MRS ARTMINSTER: There you are, that's what I mean. (*Gets up.*)
You have your dreams and I've got to listen to them even if

they're nightmares and not worth the bother. But me, me, what about me and my hopes for rest? I say Little Munstering and what do you help me towards that? Oh, it's one-way traffic with you, Jerry, all your way, and to hell with me, you treat me to threats and police to make me beg. That's your feeling.

JERRY: Little Munstering. There isn't any Little Munstering. You've done enough harm with your Little Munstering, with that Booker. *I've* got to answer the questions. *Me*. Because you can't shut up. Derek and Little Munstering. Little Munstering and Derek. You make me sick.

MRS ARTMINSTER: Yes, you're sick all right.
(*Long pause. They sit in silence, staring down at the floor.*)

JERRY: It's my nerves, I can't help it.

MRS ARTMINSTER: I know you can't, son.

JERRY: I always shout when my nerves are down. (*Long pause.*) It's the way they get at me. And you don't even ask me how I did.

MRS ARTMINSTER: Well, it's a funny trick you're up to, Jerry, and although I admire the brains of it, I don't understand it. And what I do understand, I don't like.

JERRY: 'Course you don't like it, I don't swing any of your joggers so the law can't touch me. And that's where the brains is. (*Long pause.*) But I still get nervous, don't I?

MRS ARTMINSTER: And that's what's funny about it. You don't like being looked at, and you earn your keep by showing yourself off. It's bound to get you down, son.

JERRY: Yes, well it's no good your telling me that, I know it, don't I? (*Long silence.*) Why don't you help me?

MRS ARTMINSTER: (*Cautiously*) Help you?

JERRY: Give me a test then. (*In a low voice.*)

MRS ARTMINSTER: (*After a pause*) No Jerry, you're too quick for me. I couldn't test you.

JERRY: Go on. Please.

MRS ARTMINSTER: To tell you the truth, Jerry, I'm not in the mood. I couldn't stand one of your tantrums.

JERRY: I won't. (*Long pause.*) I promise. Please.

MRS ARTMINSTER: No Jer, I'm not in the mood, I've told you.

JERRY: But you're in the mood for the sozzing you'll get into yourself, aren't you? You're in the mood to let me go off and do it tomorrow, it doesn't matter how my nerves are down, aren't you? You're in the mood for the pain and humiliation, because of the benefits, aren't you? You're in the mood to lie there and get fat, that's the only mood you're in, all the time. You're in the mood –

MRS ARTMINSTER: All right, Jerry. All right. There's one of your tantrums you promised we wouldn't have, but all right, anything for peace.

(JERRY *goes out of the room, takes the object out from under the pillow.*)

But it gives me the creeps, and that's my mood.

(JERRY *comes back into the room just as* MRS ARTMINSTER *stops talking.*)

JERRY: Well, you can't test me lying on a bed with a bottle at your lips, like a baby. Get up then.

(MRS ARTMINSTER *gets up and goes reluctantly to the chair, which is facing the other door.* JERRY *puts his head into the hall, obviously to see that the coast is clear. Looks back in.*)

Go on, you've got to stiffen up. You're power. Talk power.

(*Goes out as* MRS ARTMINSTER *readjusts herself in the chair, turning it so that the back is almost to the audience. During the following scene she talks with two voices, one pitched low and manly, with grotesque upper-class intonations, the other the voice she normally uses with* JERRY. *There is a knock on the door.*)

MRS ARTMINSTER: Come, come.

(JERRY *comes in shyly, wearing a blond wig which falls to his shoulders. As he advances there is silence.*)

Good God, what the hell is this?

JERRY: No, no. (*Takes the wig off and throws it to the floor.*) No. They don't say that.

MRS ARTMINSTER: Well, I'd be buggered, wouldn't I?

JERRY: Polite. They're always polite. (*Picks up his wig, goes out into the hall, shuts the door. There is a knock.*)

MRS ARTMINSTER: 'Min.

(JERRY *enters as before.*)

(*After a pause*) Name, old chap?

JERRY: Artminster, sir. Garfield Artminster.

MRS ARTMINSTER: 'Min Artminster, and have a pew, old chap.

(JERRY *comes in, sits down.*)

Now Artminster, handsome of you to come along, see us today. About a position in – in –?

JERRY: Technical side, sir.

MRS ARTMINSTER: 'Nical side, glad to have you aboard, 'trested to know, before we begin personal stuff, what experience in technical side you've had, Artminster wasn't it?

JERRY: Well sir, I put in my application form that I did two years at Hornsey Tech. sir, of the three-year course.

MRS ARTMINSTER: And didn't finish the course, Artminster old chap?

JERRY: Well, sir, I – (*Shakes his head.*)

MRS ARTMINSTER: Come, come, boy, speak up. No need to be 'fraid.

(JERRY *shakes his head again. There is a long pause.*)

Speak up, boy. (*Another pause.*) You don't just sit there blushing red, do you?

JERRY: Yes, I do.

MRS ARTMINSTER: Well, what am I supposed to do?

JERRY: Get embarrassed.

MRS ARTMINSTER: Oh, I am, yes I am. Well, old chap, so you're 'fraid you didn't finish the course. Now no need to be 'fraid of me old chap, you just tell me about why you got sacked.

JERRY: I wasn't sacked sir, they asked me to rest, for a little, sir.

MRS ARTMINSTER: Good, good, very good. Excellent. Now let me get your particulars down.

JERRY: I'm very willing, sir, like Mr Hempting says in his letter.

MRS ARTMINSTER: Hempting? Who's Hempting?

JERRY: He's a reference.

MRS ARTMINSTER: Who is he?

JERRY: Me.

MRS ARTMINSTER: Well, what do you say?

JERRY: He says I'm very intelligent and hard-working, and a bit of an individualist. (*Long pause.*) Then they ask me about my, you know – (*Pause.*) Go on then.

MRS ARTMINSTER: Now, I can see that you're an excellent chap, Artminster, and just what we want and all that, but there is a little problem here about your hair, which is too long for the kind of chap we have in mind for the position, I'm 'fraid, you'd have to get it cut, short back and sides sort of thing.

JERRY: No, sir.

MRS ARTMINSTER: Sorry, old chap.

JERRY: (*Mumbling*) A free country, sir.

MRS ARTMINSTER: Free country, cod's balls, old chap, what do you mean free country, you think you can walk into my office, your hair hanging down your shoulders, old chap, and tell me that it's a free country. Well, I'll tell you something, Artminster or whatever your name is, this is a free country, not because chaps like you want to get jobs with chaps like me with your hair hanging down to (*stops, and in own voice*) what you doing, then?

JERRY: I'm crying.

MRS ARTMINSTER: Cry – haven't you any respect for yourself?

JERRY: I can't help it. (*Pause.*) Get on with it.

MRS ARTMINSTER: (*After a pause*) Now look here, Artminster, old chap, no need for you take on, what I'm trying to say is, this is country where people can be people, no holds barred, but there's got to be decency , there's got to be order, I know it and you know it. And there are people on one side, like me, we keep things together and make things go, and we love our country, go down to our cottages in places like Little Munstering and we sit there and dream of decency and order, and that's all right, that's what it's all about, trees and an orchard of plums and a river with bridges over it, Jerry, and – and – Artminster, there's the other people who try to take it away from us, what we've put up and what we're holding together, want to get into my cottage in Little Munstering and loot it empty, or one night when I'm in the town flat with wife and kids, come through one of our

85

windows in the basement, where the bad catches are, come slipping up the stairs as easy as shadows, come like grease into the office, muscle the guard, smash the furniture, rob the desks, the safe, get away with what we've made, and start in again somewhere else. (*Pause.*) They're the other people, Artminster, and that's fair, we know them and they know us. They got their joggers, we got our police and it's all part of the same thing. But Artminster old chap, there's a third sort of people, just one or two of them, thank God, they're not with *them*, they're not with *us* they wear their hair to their shoulders and they snivel and con where the law can't touch them and the joggers are – what I mean, old chap, is you don't fit in anywhere, with your funny ways and your hair and that's why we can't give you the job, see, old chap? Now I don't mean to be hard, but what I'm trying to say is, where's the police if the police can't cure you? Where's the joggers – like the Peasbury Postman's attacker and his accomplice – if they can't take you in? I mean, who's to look after our wives and our kids from chaps like you, Artminster? You ruin everything. (*Long pause.*) That's why I can't give you the job.

(JERRY, *after a long pause, and wiping his eyes, gets up, goes to the door.*)

(*As* JERRY *stands at the door waiting*) Well, is there anything else, Artminster? (*In a very cocky voice.*)

JERRY: My expenses, sir. (*Long pause.*) I've got the chit, sir, you sent me. One rail fare to Reading from London, sir, first class, comes to two pound twelve, return; one lunch on train, sir, twelve shillings, one night in the Great Southern Hotel, two pound two shillings, sir, one lunch in Reading, sir. Seven shillings and sixpence. Five pound thirteen and sixpence, sir.

MRS ARTMINSTER: Five pound thirteen and six. You can't get five pound thirteen and six for a wearing a wig and snivelling. I mean, that seems a bit steep, Artminster.

JERRY: Well, sir, and then there's my mum, sir.

MRS ARTMINSTER: (*After a pause*) Your mother, Artminster?

JERRY: Yes, sir, she's sick, sir, and she has to come with me wherever I go, as she needs constant attendance owing to her habits, which she can't help, sir, being a polio victim from the neck down, and someone's got to feed her and bath her and – *other things*, sir, that's why I had to bring her with me. Up in the hotel. In a wheel-chair, sir. (*Long pause.*)

MRS ARTMINSTER: Jerry, you've got more ice-cold nastiness in you. I mean, why don't you put her in a home, Artminster, there are houses for old ladies in her sad condition.

JERRY: Yes, sir, I know sir, people are always trying to get her into a home but there are *things*, sir – (*Long pause.*) I love my Mum, sir, I couldn't see her taken away from me and clapped into a home. I love her, sir, and she needs me and relies on me, she's got faith in me. I couldn't be myself again if I let them catch her, sir, and put her away. Because she loves me back. (*Long pause.*) That's why I don't belong, that's why people are always after me, it's not because of the way I look, sir, it's because I've got this love in me for my mother that no matter what she'd done or who she was, I'd demean and humble myself to keep her free and happy, and they can see that and they don't like it, that love in me for Mum, they don't want to cut my hair off, they want to take the love out of me. So I don't care what you say about me, sir, there's no need for you to insult my mum because she can't help herself.

MRS ARTMINSTER: (*After a very long pause*) And they believe you?

JERRY: 'Course they do. Me being a bit off is one thing, it makes them cocky, but toting a wheel-chair mother about and setting her on and off the toilet turns their stomachs. They imagine me doing it, see, and they think of their own mums, and themselves lifting them on and off the toilet, and their hands feel different. They pay me the double expenses to get rid of me. (*Long pause.*) And they feel the feeling in me, about my mum, like I said, and they don't like it. I tell the truth, see. (*Long pause.*) See.

MRS ARTMINSTER: Yes, I admire it, Jerry, but I don't like it. That's the truth.

JERRY: That's because you don't know it, the way you do it, breaking in. Now let's do it straight.

(*There is a slight knock on Jerry's door.*)

Then you feel it.

MRS ARTMINSTER: No, Jer, honest I'm not up to it, I'll tell you what, we'll do it . . .

(*Voice fades as* JERRY *goes into the hall, and* MR BOOKER *comes into Jerry's room. Both doors close simultaneously. Then* MR BOOKER *crosses to the communicating door, raises his hand to knock, goes back, stares around the room, goes into the hall as* JERRY *enters Mrs Artminster's bedroom.*)

You must be Artminster, old chap.

JERRY: Yes, sir.

(*The door of Jerry's room opens again, and* MR BOOKER *steals in. He goes to the communicating door and puts his ear to it.*)

MRS ARTMINSTER: Good of you to come along, Artminster, hope you had a good trip, poor weather I'm 'fraid.

(MR BOOKER *stands up, hesitates, then knocks on the door.* MRS ARTMINSTER *and* JERRY *stare at each other, then* JERRY *goes to the hall door, and out.* MRS ARTMINSTER *gets up.*)

Enter.

(MR BOOKER *enters through communicating door.* JERRY *goes into his own room.*)

MR BOOKER: I'm not disturbing, I trust.

MRS ARTMINSTER: Oh no, I was just saying to Garfield that you'd be up shortly, as you'd promised.

MR BOOKER: Garfield?

MRS ARTMINSTER: Yes, he just went down the hall a minute to the toilet.

(JERRY, *who has been listening at the door, slips to the hall door, opens it and closes it, then walks to the communicating door. Puts his hand on the knob.*)

MR BOOKER: It's very odd, I thought I heard some voices, it must be me. (*Looks at* MRS ARTMINSTER.)

(JERRY *begins to open the door, realizes he is wearing the wig,*

takes it off, throws it out of sight, and enters.)
Oh, hello, Garfield, there you are.

JERRY: Hello, Mr Booker. May I come in a minute, Mother, unless you're busy?

MRS ARTMINSTER: Of course, dear, Mr Booker has just popped in for a chat, he knows how I like my bit of company and a gossip in the evening.

MR BOOKER: Well, how are things in Little Munstering?

MRS ARTMINSTER: Yes, how are things, dear?

JERRY: Oh, the place is coming along very nicely, thank you, they expect we can move in soon.

MR BOOKER: That's good news, good news indeed. Although not for me, of course, I shall be sorry to lose you.

MRS ARTMINSTER: You spoke to the gardener about the plum trees, Garfield?

JERRY: Yes, Mother. (*Little pause.*) He's planted them.

MRS ARTMINSTER: And how do the plums look.

JERRY: Lovely, Mother.

MR BOOKER: At this time of year?

JERRY: Well. (*Laughs.*) They're special plums. Early.

MRS ARTMINSTER: Why don't we make ourselves comfy, Mr Booker you sit down on the bed, and Garfield, stop your fidgeting dear, and take a pew.
(*They sit down,* MR BOOKER *on the end of the bed,* JERRY *on the side.*)
Now (*little pause*) what about the plumbing, Garfield, what do they say about that?

JERRY: Oh, they've fixed that.

MRS ARTMINSTER: Put the trimmings in, have they dear, like I instructed?

JERRY: Yes Mother.

MRS ARTMINSTER: That's a relief, seeing as they're so slow these days.

MR BOOKER: Oh they *are*, the way they stop for a smoke and a cup every five minutes. It's a wonder to me we're not all living on the streets, holding us up to ransom.

MRS ARTMINSTER: I know. I say the same to Garfield, it's the war that did it. Before the war service was service, work was work and money was money, they had to look to their jobs then, or unemployment and the dole was staring them in the face, instead of our being the beggars of Europe as we are now.

MR BOOKER: You can't tell me anything about plumbing and plumbers, there's a week left before we open and have you noticed the toilets? It doesn't matter what I say – and the overtime? I go down on my knees to them.

MRS ARTMINSTER: Overtime! Overtime from what, but having a good time at our expense, that's what I say.

MR BOOKER: *And* they use the guest toilets. There are perfectly good, clean toilets in the basement, I pointed them out and said that was one thing I was very strict on. But no, I catch them coming out of all the guest toilets without so much as a by your leave or a may I.

MRS ARTMINSTER: I know what you mean, Garfield, I hope you showed them the outside toilet by the bridge.

JERRY: Yes. Mother, I did.

MRS ARTMINSTER: And what did they say to that?

JERRY: They're using it, Mother.

MR BOOKER: Well, you must have a way with them, Garfield, I wish I could get that from our plumbers, they spend all their time winking at Janice. (*Little pause*.) By the bye, if I could just ask, where did you say Little Munstering was exactly actually? (*Pause*.) I was glancing at a map of the area just last night, to while away my insomnia, and I couldn't see a Little Munstering.

JERRY: It's outside Andover.

MR BOOKER: Oh, yes, very pretty countryside, lovely landscapes out there. That's where I was looking, by the bye, from Reading right through to Wiltshire. Is it to the south or North?

MRS ARTMINSTER: ⎱ North.
JERRY: ⎰ South.

JERRY: (*After a pause*) No, Mother, it's to the south, you're always bad on direction.

MR BOOKER: (*Shakes his head*) And I haven't even heard of it, that's the shameful truth. I like to know pleasant spots and nearby villages, for the guests' sake. They're not all travellers, you know, some of them have a real love of visiting the pretty places, how do you get out there, Garfield, by the bye?

JERRY: In a bus.

MR BOOKER: Oh dear, you don't have to tell *me* about our local bus service, the rudeness! Which number, by the bye?

JERRY: (*After a little pause*) 726.

MR BOOKER: Oh? To Hayler's Pond? It's out that way, is it? (JERRY *nods*.)
That's to the north. (*Little pause*.) Directly to the north. The 726. It's called the North Line Service. It even stops at Northlynne, North Hill and North Junction. The 726.

JERRY: Mother, I owe you an apology.

MRS ARTMINSTER: I always tell you, you should listen to your old mother, dear.

MR BOOKER: So Little Munstering's that way, is it?

JERRY: Yes.

MR BOOKER: On from the end of the route, I suppose. Up Hindley Lane –?

JERRY: I can't remember the name.

MR BOOKER: It'd have to be Hindley Lane. The rest is by-pass and the tracks to London, as I recall. Yes, and then you'd go along the field – Johnson's field and it'd be some way there, wouldn't it?

JERRY: Yes.

MR BOOKER: (*After a pause*) By the bye. (*Pause*.) I've been wondering if you remembered to telephone the Great Southern and explain about booking in here. They'll never believe it was a mistake – (*pause*) they'll think I stole you from them, especially as I don't even reopen for another week – (*pause*) although we're too humble to compete with the Great Southern. (*Laughs*.) Did you telephone?

MRS ARTMINSTER: It was the first thing I made him do as soon as I came to myself again.

MR BOOKER: I hope you don't think I'm fussing or nosy. I hate
people who are nosy. (*Little pause.*) By the bye –
(*There is a knock on the door.* JERRY *gets up and opens it.*
JANICE *enters. She is a tall, very pretty West Indian girl. She is
smiling.*)
And what's on today, at The Three Musketeers?

JANICE: Sausage. And there's liver, Mr Booker, sir.

MR BOOKER: Didn't you find out about the soups, Janice, you
know Mrs Artminster's been ill. She won't want liver, will
she?

JANICE: Oh no, sir.

MR BOOKER: Well then?

JANICE: Mrs Arminst, she always like the sausages, sir. Six
sausages, sir. Every night, sir. (*Smiles at*
MRS ARTMINSTER.)
(*There is silence.*)

MRS ARTMINSTER: And don't forget the Worcester, Janice,
tonight.

MR BOOKER: Well, it's good to see you've recovered your
appetite Mrs Artminster. Go then, Janice, Mrs Artminster's
hungry. (*Looks at* MRS ARTMINSTER.)

MRS ARTMINSTER: (*After a pause*) I like that girl.

MR BOOKER: Yes, she's a nice girl. (*Pause.*) Bit slow, though, in
some respects. (*Little pause. Then taps his forehead.*)

MRS ARTMINSTER: Oh, you won't find the intelligent ones over
here, oh no. They stay in the sun, where they belong.

MR BOOKER: Yes. They're very happy, a happy people. I'll say
that for Janice, she may be a bit – (*taps his forehead*) but she's
happy.

MRS ARTMINSTER: Yes, I like her.

MR BOOKER: Oh, I've nothing against her personally, she can't
help her habits after all, they're bred into her.

MRS ARTMINSTER: And you know what they say about them and
the way our white boys – (*in an excited voice*).

JERRY: Mother, I've –
(*Gets up, stands staring at her while* MRS ARTMINSTER *and* MR
BOOKER *stare at him.*)

MRS ARTMINSTER: What is it, Garfield, I must say you're very
    nervous tonight, the way you keep hopping about and
    gaping, it's rude dear.
    (JERRY *doesn't move.*)
    Come on then, you go and have a little nap – he's had a hard
    day, a mother can tell – come and give your old mother a kiss
    and lie down. (*This in a significant voice.*)

JERRY: Yes. mother. (*Comes across and gives her a kiss. Goes
    towards the connecting door.*)

MRS ARTMINSTER: Garfield was always the sensitive delicate one
    in our family, his brother Derek now, as tough as six
    wrestlers, and no holding him. But Garfield needs holding
    and looking after, he'd wither without it, he's got a loving
    nature, haven't you, Garfield?

JERRY: I don't know. (*Smiles with awkward shyness.*)

MRS ARTMINSTER: Oh, he has, I tell you. Come and give your
    old mother another kiss dear.
    (JERRY *stands awkwardly, then comes over. Gives* MRS
    ARTMINSTER *a kiss. Goes back to the door, opens it, goes
    through.*)

MR BOOKER: Well, you'll want to eat in peace. (*Having watched*
    JERRY *exit.*) So I'll leave you. Good night, Mrs Artminster.

MRS ARTMINSTER: Good night, Mr Booker, it was kind of you to
    cheer me up.
    (MR BOOKER *leaves the room.* MRS ARTMINSTER *fishes for her
    whisky bottle, begins to nuzzle it.*)
    (*Meanwhile* JERRY *is sitting on the edge of his bed, his hands
    clasped between his legs. There is a low knock on his hall door,
    and* MR BOOKER *enters.*)

MR BOOKER: I just wondered if you were all right, Garfield.

JERRY: (*Getting up*) Yes. Yes thanks.

MR BOOKER: Because I thought something upset you. (*Little
    pause.*) And if it did, I think I know what it was.

JERRY: No.

MR BOOKER: You're not upset?

JERRY: No.

MR BOOKER: Oh. Well – I didn't know you had a brother, Derek?

JERRY: Yes, but he's dead. Derek was a – he was a – he had a heart attack.

MR BOOKER: I'm sorry to hear that, Garfield. (*Long pause.*) (*Meanwhile* MRS ARTMINSTER *has come to the other side of the door, listened for a minute, nodded, and gone back to her chair.*) I had a close friend once. He wrote a book. (*Long pause.*) I'll tell you about him some day.

JERRY: Who?

MR BOOKER: The friend I was telling you about.

JERRY: Oh. Thank you very much Mr Booker.

MR BOOKER: Yes, he wrote the book when he was a priest. (*Pause.* MR BOOKER *is staring at* JERRY *intently.*) Do you ever go to boys' clubs, Garfield? I was just wondering, because my friend did a lot of work in the boys' club on Martin Street. I don't want to force you into anything, I hate people who do that, but I could show you around, if you like. (*Little pause.*) When you've settled into Little Munstering, I mean, and if we still – should happen to see each other. (*Laughs.*)

JERRY: Thank you very much, Mr Booker.

MR BOOKER: Garfield (*little pause*) is there any reason why you shouldn't call me Simon?

JERRY: Simon.

MR BOOKER: Called Peter. (*Little pause.*) The Fisher of Men. I'd rather you called me Simon. (*Little pause.*) After all, we've known each other for a week, haven't we, and that's a long time for a fisher of men. (*Little pause.*) I'm sorry, I'm a bit nervous myself tonight, I don't know why. (*Little pause.*) (MRS ARTMINSTER *has come back to the door to listen. She swigs sometimes from her bottle.*) By the bye, did you know our Gaumont was doing a festival of religious films shortly?

JERRY: No.

MR BOOKER: The truly great ones. I'd love to see them, but I hate going to the pictures by myself. (*Little pause.*) Do you like pictures?

JERRY: No, I – they hurt my eyes.

MR BOOKER: Oh? Have you got bad eyes too? We *are* in a poor way between us, what with our nerves and our eyes, aren't we? (*Little pause.*) Garfield, if there's any little problem you think I could help you with, you will come to me with it, won't you? No matter what it is. (*Glances towards the door.*) I know how difficult things can be.

JERRY: Thank you.

MR BOOKER: I mean it, Garfield. (*Stares at him.*) Would you like to borrow that book, then?

JERRY: What book?

MR BOOKER: The one my friend wrote. The priest. (*Little pause.*)

JERRY: Thank you very much.

MR BOOKER: I think you'd like it. (*Little pause.*) I think you'd understand it. (*Stares at* JERRY.) Well, good night, Garfield.

JERRY: Good night.

MR BOOKER: I'll get that book now, if you like.

JERRY: Well, I'm a bit – I don't think I could concentrate now.

MR BOOKER: I see. (*Little pause.*) Well, I won't lend it to you if you're not interested, you'd be liable to forget it, or put it away in your luggage, and it's a personal copy. Guests are very careless about our towels and soap without so much as a thank you. I'm sorry if I've been forcing myself on you, Garfield, I hate people who do that. I must have misunderstood. Good-night.

JERRY: No, it's not that, I'm just a bit – I'd like to read the book, honestly I would, Simon, but as it's so precious to you I'd be frightened of losing it.

MR BOOKER: I see. (*Looks at him.*) Well, perhaps tomorrow night then. (*Coldly.*)

JERRY: Yes, I'd like to borrow it tomorrow night, really I would, I'd be up to it then.

MR BOOKER: All right, Garfield. Good night then.

JERRY: Good-night, Simon.

MR BOOKER: Good-night. (*Goes to the door, opens it, stands looking into the hall.*) I'm sorry if I turn a bit funny sometimes, Garfield –

(JERRY *makes obscene gestures at him.*)

– it's that I'm out of the habit of talking, really talking to people since my friend – (*Turns.*)

(JERRY *manages to check a gesture.*)

I mean people I might care about – good night Garfield.
(*Exits.*)

(JERRY *makes one magnificently obscene gesture at the door, goes toward Mrs Artminster's door as she moves away from it to the bed.*)

MRS ARTMINSTER: Oh yes, he really delights in you, I could hear his voice, it was leaking under the door like oil. What'd he want then?

JERRY: He was going on about some priest, I don't know.

MRS ARTMINSTER: Oh yes, I bet his hands were up those skirts all right. But no, I mustn't sneer, I've got religious feelings too, and I don't like sneering at the chosen, I used to say to Derek he had the makings of a priest, he had strong thoughts about God, so our Simon Booker's entitled to his friend.

JERRY: What's the matter with you? Didn't you see the way he was asking us questions?

MRS ARTMINSTER: Because he's interested Jerry, that's why.
(*Little pause.*) It wouldn't hurt if you asked him a few questions, in politeness.

JERRY: What about?

MRS ARTMINSTER: *You* know what about.

JERRY: Now you keep your mind off that, I told you we're not doing anything like that.

MRS ARTMINSTER: Where's the harm in finding out, for the interest? Derek would have beaten it out of him in three minutes, but you've got your own way, Jerry, I'll give you that, you've got a way with homosexuals, you could wind him about your fingers and have the truth. A smile would get it for you.

JERRY: Shut up.

MRS ARTMINSTER: Yes, that's how you talk to me, isn't it? I'll tell you something Jerry, I'll tell you what you are. (*Long pause, swings legs off the bed.*)

(JANICE *comes in with a tray.* MRS ARTMINSTER *looks at her, looks at* JERRY, *smiles.*)

96

Oh hello, there you are dear, how kind.

(JANICE *smiles at* JERRY, *walks across the room with the tray, puts it on the table by the bed.* MRS ARTMINSTER *looks at* JERRY, *then at* JANICE.)

Why, what lovely ear-rings those are you've got on, Janice, I didn't notice those before, may I see them from closer to, dear? Sometimes a pretty object does more to rouse me than pills.

(JANICE *stands by the bed, smiling.*)

Oh yes, they look very fetching in those little lobes of yours, where did you purchase them? The only thing is I can't make out the design, could you bend a bit?

(JANICE *bends over the bed.* JERRY *glares,* MRS ARTMINSTER *looks at him, then takes one of the ear-rings between fingers.*)

JANICE: Mr Booker he gave them – ow! (*Straightening with a cry.*)

MRS ARTMINSTER: I'm sorry, dear. It seems to have caught itself in my fingers. Here it is, now let me punish myself by putting it back on. You start, Garfield dear, I know how peckish you get. Yes, Janice, bend a little lower, dear, it's nice to know there's no colour feeling in Mr Booker's hotel, black and white mix in, and how else are you going to raise yourselves, oops, now isn't that clumsy, my fingers have always been my weakest part for a lady, they're so chubby they make me blush, now I wonder where did it go?

(JERRY, *who has been watching, comes over to the bed.* JANICE *steps away,* JERRY *bends over the bed, there is a sort of tussle between them.*)

JERRY: Here it is, Mother.

MRS ARTMINSTER: Oh, thank you, dear. (*Little pause.*) *You* put it on for Janice, there's a good boy, to make up.

JERRY: I don't know how.

MRS ARTMINSTER: Janice will show you, won't you Janice?

(JANICE *giggles. Stands offering the side of her face to* JERRY. JERRY *stares at* MRS ARTMINSTER, *who stares back.*)

The girl's waiting, dear.

(JERRY *goes forward, stands a long way from* JANICE, *holds the ear-ring up.*)

97

Just pop it into the hole and screw, dear, you can work it out
for yourself.

(JERRY *holds the ear-ring out and seizes the lobe of* JANICE's
ear.)

JANICE: Ow! (*Giggles.*)

MRS ARTMINSTER: Closer, my dear, closer, you look as if you're
fishing without a pole. You've good eyes, don't worry about
pricking her. You move in on him, girl.

(JANICE *moves a little closer to* JERRY, *who shies away, then
braces himself and screws the ear-ring in.* JANICE *smiles at*
JERRY, *who moves back.*)

You've got him eating out of your hand, dear. Well, good
night, and we'll see you tomorrow.

(JANICE *goes towards the door, turns, smiles.*)

JANICE: Good night. (*Exits.*)

MRS ARTMINSTER: What's the matter, son, you look a trifle pale?

JERRY: You know what's the matter.

MRS ARTMINSTER: No, I don't, are you poorly again?

JERRY: You know how I hate their smell.

MRS ARTMINSTER: Do you dear, I'm very fond of it myself, it
makes my head swim, and Derek used to chase them till he
had them by the tail, pass my sausages, I'm ravening .

JERRY: (*Taking the sausages over*) Derek's dead.

MRS ARTMINSTER: What?

JERRY: I told Booker he's dead, I'll tell everyone, and he's dead
all right, you won't be seeing him again for twelve years.

MRS ARTMINSTER: Oh you evil boy, you'd like to see him dead,
wouldn't you? (*Eats a sausage.*) And you've never set eyes on
him.

JERRY: Oh yes I set eyes on him every time you talk about him, I
see him before me with every word, pegged-toothed, fat,
bullying all the small ones, oh I've set eyes on him all right.
Besides, I saw that photo in the papers.

MRS ARTMINSTER: His head was covered by a coat and he was
stooped over to get into the car. (*Eats another sausage.*) Aren't
you hungry?

JERRY: No.

MRS ARTMINSTER: Pass your plate, then.

JERRY: (*Viciously, watching* MRS ARTMINSTER *eat*) Can't you watch where the Worcester goes. Talk about ladylike.

MRS ARTMINSTER: If you don't like what you see, turn your eyes away, dainty-pants.
(*There is a silence.* JERRY *takes the plate away and puts it on the tray. Goes and sits down.* MRS ARTMINSTER *looks at him.*)
(*Taunting.*) Well, give your old mum a kiss then.
(JERRY *looks at her.*)
Well, you won't look at Booker, can't stomach the juices smell of Janice, who'll you kiss, Jerry? Not even your old mum? Go on Jerry, give your old mum a kiss (*pause*) like Derek used to do.

JERRY: (*Leaping to his feet*) He never.

MRS ARTMINSTER: Oh no? Oh no? *You* don't know what fondness is, for all your talk. (*Takes a swig of Scotch.*) Come on, Jerry, a kiddle, a cuddle, a knickery muddle, oh a cuddle, Jer, my youngest and prettiest won't give me a cuddle when I need one, oh he says he loves his mum, but no cuddles, no kisses.
(JERRY, *putting his hands to his face.*)
(*Watching him.*) Had enough, have you? (*Little pause, as* JERRY *doesn't move.*) Oh, come on, Jer (*pats the bed*) it's all right. What's the matter, son?
(JERRY *shakes his head.*)
What? Tell me.

JERRY: I don't know. I don't know. The way you go on at me.

MRS ARTMINSTER: Well, I don't mean harm, do I? (*Pause, then in a very gentle voice.*) You know I don't mean harm, don't you, Jer?
(JERRY *shakes his head.*)
(*Putting a hand on his shoulder*) Fond is fond, Jer, and that's what counts.

JERRY: (*Taking his hands away, looks at* MRS ARTMINSTER) Will you play then?

MRS ARTMINSTER: (*After a pause*) What?

JERRY: You know what.

MRS ARTMINSTER: What's the time?

JERRY: (*Looks at his watch*) It's early.

MRS ARTMINSTER: No it isn't Jerry, I can tell by my craving.
(*Seizes his wrist, looks at the watch.*)

JERRY: Just once. Three goes. That's all. Just three goes. (*Little pause.*) You said fond was fond, you did.

MRS ARTMINSTER: All right, but come on quick.
(*They hold out their fists, raise and lower them three times.*
JERRY *has stone and* MRS ARTMINSTER *has paper.*)

JERRY: You win.
(*Holds out his hand, palm up, and* MRS ARTMINSTER *hits him hard across it. Then they do it again, this time* JERRY *has scissors and* MRS ARTMINSTER *has stone.*)
You win.
(*Holds out his hand, palm up, in excitement.* MRS ARTMINSTER *stares at him a moment, then again hits him hard across it. Then they do it again, and this time* MRS ARTMINSTER *has scissors and* JERRY *has paper.*)
You win. (*Holds out his hand, palm up, head thrown back.*)

MRS ARTMINSTER: I'm not saying anything.

JERRY: What do you mean?

MRS ARTMINSTER: You know what I mean. (*Looks at him, then strikes him across the palm of his hand.*)
(JERRY *holds out his fists again,* MRS ARTMINSTER *shakes her head.*)

JERRY: One once, once, once, please, please.

MRS ARTMINSTER: (*Gets up, slaps hands together*) Fair's fair,
Fair's fair.
(JERRY *looks at* MRS ARTMINSTER *pleadingly, then gets up, goes into his room. Locks the door to the hall, opens a case. Takes a chamber-pot from under the bed. Meanwhile* MRS ARTMINSTER *is taking off shoes and stockings.* JERRY *returns, hands the box to* MRS ARTMINSTER, *puts the chamber-pot under the hot tap, goes to the hall door and locks it.* MRS ARTMINSTER *has taken a cigar out of the box, unwraps it.* JERRY *goes to the window, opens it wide. Collects the chamber-pot from the sink, hands* MRS ARTMINSTER *her whisky.*)

Aaah. Aaah. Where's a light then? (*Sniffing at the cigar.*)
There's one in my handbag, fetch it over.

(JERRY *goes over, gets the handbag, gives it to her.*)

JERRY: The trouble with you is you've got no control.

MRS ARTMINSTER: Control, don't talk to me about control.

(JERRY *crouches down and begins to swab at* MRS
ARTMINSTER'*s feet.*)

I could burst out, Jerry, burst out at any minute and expose
myself. (*Sighs contentedly, begins to hum.*) One day I'll do it,
and where'll you be then?

JERRY: Well, I'll know where you'll be, won't I?

(*Looks up significantly, but* MRS ARTMINSTER *is lying back,
smoking and sipping from the Scotch.* JERRY *goes back to
swabbing her feet.* MRS ARTMINSTER'*s hum rises into, 'On a
bicycle made for two.' Curtain.*)

ACT TWO

SCENE I

JERRY is standing before the mirror in the wardrobe, with a case open at his feet. He takes out the blond wig, tries it on, takes it off, puts on a tight black one with curls. Takes that off and puts on a long red one. Simultaneously MRS ARTMINSTER is sitting at a table, pouring tea from a pot into a cup and lacing it with whisky. Finishes the bottle, looks at it in dismay, puts it down. Then starts to put on lipstick and face powder from her handbag, occasionally taking sips from her cup. There is a knock on Jerry's door. He stuffs all the wigs back into the case as the doorknob is turned, goes towards the door, remembers his wig on his head, whips it off and is stuffing it into his pocket as there is the sound of the key in the lock. The door opens and MR BOOKER enters behind a large portrait in oils of a Jesuit of about forty-five – the colours of which are almost grotesquely vivid. The Jesuit is florid and bald.

MR BOOKER: Oh. (*Stops.*) Good morning Garfield, I didn't mean to disturb. I thought you must have gone out as you didn't answer to my knock. May I come in, if that's all right?

JERRY: Yes.

MR BOOKER: Thank you, because today's the day I hang the pictures. This is the one I've specially chosen for your – this room. What are your feelings about it?

JERRY: It looks very nice.

MR BOOKER: Just right for – here, don't you feel? I'm very proud of it myself for personal reasons. (*Props it against a chair and comes around, to stand beside JERRY.*) My pride is in the feeling that it catches the priestly qualities in particular. People don't use these words now, I know, but to my eyes he was a beautiful man on account of his Saintish face. He knew the meaning of compassion. It's there in the eyes. (*Points to them.*) It's that friend of mine I think I mentioned to you, done when he was a priest.

102

(*Picks the painting up, stumbles against the bed, comes back, picks up the chair and almost falls with both. Manages to hang the picture on a hook.* JERRY *watches coldly. The painting dominates the room.*)

Yes, the gift of myself he called it, which he said must be an ordained gift because of my optical weakness.

(MRS ARTMINSTER *has got off the bed and has been listening to this. Now leaves the room.*)

Now that he's gone, it's as if he'd taken the gift with him. (*Little pause.*) He said it would happen, he said I would have to wait, until it was risen up. (*Little pause.*) The gift I mean. (*Little pause.*) I telephoned last night, Garfield, by the bye.

JERRY: What? (*Looks at the picture.*)

MR BOOKER: To the Great Southern, Garfield. (*Stares at the picture.*)

JERRY: Oh? (*Little pause.*) Well, thank you very much, actually I've got to go now, because I've got an appointment at ten in Little Munstering.

MR BOOKER: That still leaves you time for a little talk, Garfield.

JERRY: Yes, well I like to be a bit ahead, you see.

MR BOOKER: I think you'd better spare me five minutes. (*Turns his head, to look at* JERRY, *then looks back at the picture.*) Because of my telephone call to the Great Southern. (*Pause.*)

JERRY: Well, what did you call about?

MR BOOKER: I think you know, Garfield.

JERRY: No, I don't.

MR BOOKER: I think you do. (*Turns head, looks at* JERRY, *turns back to the picture.*) It was about your reservations. There *were* no reservations, Garfield, in the name of Artminster. (*Little pause.*) Last night, when we were talking easily together, before you turned cold, I said to you that if you had any problems I would help you. In spite of your coldness I still want to help you, Garfield, because I think your coldness came from your problems. (*Turns his head.*) Why did you lie to me, Garfield?

(*While this has been going on,* MRS ARTMINSTER *has put down her mug and comes over to the door. She listens, bends down, looks through the keyhole, then quickly leaves the room, by the hall door.*)

JERRY: There must have been a mistake. Mother! (*As he hurries over to connecting door, opens it, stares around an empty room, enters followed by* MR BOOKER.)

JERRY: There must have been a mistake.

MR BOOKER: No mistake, Garfield. (*Turns his head.*) I should mention that being in the hotel world, I know how to speak to other hotel managers. No mistake, Garfield. (*Turns back to the picture.*) What is the problem that causes you to lie to me, Garfield?

JERRY: (*After a pause*) I – I have to do it, Simon, I have to.

MR BOOKER: Why? Why do you have to lie to me?

JERRY: Because of my mother. (*Goes and sits down on the bed.*) All my life, she's – (*Shakes his head.*) When I was little she was a clippie for the thirty-one bus route, Simon, and evenings she waitressed in Ned's Sandwich, all because of me. Derek didn't do anything, he was off with his friends, swilling down beer and getting into bad company, Simon, and doing things – I can't talk about them, they cause me pain, the things he did to me, I've never told her about them. So she had to bring me up herself, slaving to keep me in good clothes so that I could face the teachers at school, slaving to give me the best in the way of food, oh no, *I* never went short, not for anything, and *she* never said a word. Of course I didn't know when I was little what it meant to have a big boy like Derek who never cared for her although she cared for him, I didn't know what it was to be looked after like I was looked after.

MR BOOKER: Of course you didn't, Garfield.

(*Sits down on the bed beside* JERRY, *puts a hand on his shoulder.* JERRY *edges away slightly.*)

JERRY: Then when I was ten I got this thing in my bones, they were always breaking, like glass almost. And she – she asked Derek to help, and he wouldn't. So she borrowed money to have me sent to the most famous bone specialist in London. I spent two years in hospital, Simon, two years, and there wasn't a day she didn't come by with some toy or box of all-sorts or a bag of tiger's tails for me. Then out to slave at Ned's, and clippying, and cleaning at night, to pay back the money. (*Puts his face in his hands.*)

MR BOOKER: (*Putting his hand on* JERRY's *shoulder*) Don't blame yourself, child. Of course you can't.

JERRY: (*Taking his hands away*) And last year she got a turn, a bad turn, and when she came out of it, with me nursing her night and day, she was talking of – of – how there was this place we had, that had been left to her by Derek when he died of his heart attack, a cottage in Little Munstering, and we had to get to it. I can't tell her the truth, I can't, it's her dream of peace this cottage is, so I've had to pretend about it, and bring her here. What else could I do?

MR BOOKER: Nothing child, nothing. (*Little pause.*) And how did you come to find *me*?

JERRY: Well, there were Great Southern Hotel advertisements, Simon, all over the station, and I said Little Munstering was near here because it was all I could afford out of London, and she said, stay at the best, Garfield, we can afford it. So I pretended to look up the direction and saw the Southern, and I brought her here, that's when she – well, when she saw the lobby, because it wasn't what she thought it would be like at The Great Southern, and you said no guests until next week, that's why she fainted in the lobby. (*Little pause.*) I just chose it out of the book, Simon, because it was the same name.

MR BOOKER: Your moving finger stopped, Garfield.
(MRS ARTMINSTER *throws open the door of Jerry's room, arm raised in angry astonishment. Sees room is empty, drops arm, goes over to connecting door, takes fresh bottle of whisky out of pocket and begins to sip at it.*)

JERRY: What?

MR BOOKER: All your travelling and worrying have carried you here, here to the Southern, like Fate or – or – (*Looks at the picture.*) I'm glad you told me the truth, Garfield. Was it a pain to you to lie to me, child?

JERRY: Yes, Simon, it was.

MR BOOKER: She's a great burden to you, isn't she?

JERRY: Who?

MR BOOKER: Your poor mother.

JERRY: No, Simon.

MR BOOKER: I understand, Garfield, I understand what you feel. But let me say one thing to you, child, a most important thing. There are two kinds of human love, child, the love of gratitude and obligation, and the love that rises in us, free and spontaneous. The second love is the love that lifts the spirit up and out, against the tight bonds of life that seems to press us down and confine us in servitude. When this lifting comes we know the second love, the love that is freedom, the spouting forth of the heart, that buried fountain.

(MRS ARTMINSTER *comes over and listens by the door.*)

But we must never confuse the first love, of duty and obligation, which is imposed by dependants, child; with the second love, of spontaneous youthfulness in the spirit, which arises mysteriously; and which is a step towards the third love, which is the love of God in humility and therefore above the human. I myself was taught that by one who could stand straighter and pour himself more fully into those he loved, the word from the mouth that enters the mouth, the mouth that closes around the word and drinks the word in, the mouth and the word become one. In his case. (*Little pause.*) And by the by, Garfield, there are homes for the sick and ageing, there are doctors and comfort, on the medical health.

JERRY: (*After a pause*) But I – I couldn't – after all she's done for me – (*swallows, covers his face again*).

MR BOOKER: Lumps in the throat, Garfield, are compassion. Compassion merely. (*Little pause.*) By the by, child, how were you planning to pay my poor bill?

JERRY: I'm going to work it off. Every morning, when I say I've gone to Little Munstering, I go out and look for a job. That's where I'm going now, to find out about a chance of a position in an office. And I thought if I worked hard and saved, I

could get enough, one day, after I've paid you, Simon, for a
little cottage –

MR BOOKER: (*Standing up, raising* JERRY *up by the shoulders,
putting his hands on them, while* MRS ARTMINSTER, *who has
been watching through the keyhole, also rises, puts her hands on
the doorknob, thinks*) You will have a position, Garfield.

(MRS ARTMINSTER *opens the door.*)

There is a place for you. In Reading. I promise you that.

MRS ARTMINSTER: Oh you promise him, do you? What do you
promise him, and may I ask why you're resting yourself on
his shoulders?

MR BOOKER: (*Stepping away*) Oh, good morning, Mrs
Artminster. (*Laughs.*) Garfield and I were having a little talk.

MRS ARTMINSTER: About what, may I be permitted to be so bold
as to ask?

MR BOOKER: Oh, merely about a great friend of mine, who's
passed. (*Looks at the picture.*)

(MRS ARTMINSTER *steps forward and also looks at the picture.
There is a long silence. Then* MRS ARTMINSTER *steps away,
turns her back on* MR BOOKER.)

MRS ARTMINSTER: It's time you were running along, Garfield
dear, you've got a busy day in Little Munstering.

JERRY: Yes Mother. (*Makes for the door.*)

MRS ARTMINSTER: Garfield! (*Holds her head sideways, offering a
cheek.*)

(GARFIELD *comes back and kisses the cheek.*)

(MRS ARTMINSTER *straightens his tie, brushes at his lapels,
feels in his jacket pocket, takes out a comb. Gives it to him.*)

You know what Derek always says, about flat hair and
respect.

(JERRY *begins to comb it flat.*)

MR BOOKER: I must say, I thought the fashion these days was for
wild hair.

MRS ARTMINSTER: (*Turning, studies him*) You don't follow it
yourself do you?

MR BOOKER: I mean for the young lads.

MRS ARTMINSTER: That's as may be. (*Turns back to* JERRY.)

Garfield wears his hair flat as long as his old mother's around to see to it, no matter what advice other people may give. Now that looks very nice, dear, and off you go. (*Gives him a kiss on the cheek.*)

JERRY: Goodbye, Mother.

MR BOOKER: Goodbye, Garfield. Perhaps we'll have a chance to continue our chat later.

(JERRY *looks at* MRS ARTMINSTER, *who turns and looks at* MR BOOKER. *Goes out.*)

MRS ARTMINSTER: I see. (*Continues to stare at* MR BOOKER.)

MR BOOKER: Yes madame, what may I do for you?

MRS ARTMINSTER: Whose room are you in, dare I ask?

MR BOOKER: One of my hotel rooms, I think, madame.

MRS ARTMINSTER: Oh pardon me, I thought it was my son Garfield's room, as you'd let it out to him. I didn't know hotel owners were allowed into the rooms to caress the boy guests.

MR BOOKER: I beg your pardon?

MRS ARTMINSTER: Pardon is too weak a word. Mercy is what you should be begging for. What is it you're after with my Garfield? Fondling him.

MR BOOKER: Fond – fond – *I*, fondle!

MRS ARTMINSTER: Did you have your arms around him, or did my eyes deceive me? Where were you when he was getting into his clothes? Crouching at the keyhole?

MR BOOKER: (*After a pause*) I'll tell you what I was doing, madame, since you force it from me with accusations. I was getting the truth from him. The truth, madame.

MRS ARTMINSTER: The truth? What truth? And what right have you got to have it?

MR BOOKER: The truth, madame, in answer to some questions. About – it's you who compel it out of me – yourself, madame.

MRS ARTMINSTER: Who is this? Who is this before you?

MR BOOKER: (*Confused, after a pause*) You, I presume, madame.

MRS ARTMINSTER: You, you presume, madame. Well? Well? (*Pause.*) Where are your questions, madame?

MR BOOKER: (*After a pause*) I couldn't bring myself to torment you with them.

MRS ARTMINSTER: No? Would you prefer me to torment you with some of my own? Like about what I've just seen?

MR BOOKER: Very well, you leave me no alternative. I asked Garfield why he had told me an untruth about reservations at the Great Southern.

MRS ARTMINSTER: Untruth? What untruth?

MR BOOKER: (*Holding his hand*) And his answer, madame, was that because he loved you, you had to be deluded. Yes (*gesturing silence*) because, madame, of the shock of discovering that there wasn't any money, in spite of the bill you've been running up here, and that there isn't any cottage in Little Munstering, and that there isn't even a Little Munstering. And never has been and never will be.
(MRS ARTMINSTER *sways, with a hand to her head.*)
I'm sorry you've wrung this out of me, madame, and that it's caused you pain, but truth is truth, and even mercy can't temper it.

MRS ARTMINSTER: No money?

MR BOOKER: Not a penny.

MRS ARTMINSTER: My cottage!

MR BOOKER: Not a thatch. (*Pause.*) Nothing but a son who is wasting his life away for you.

MRS ARTMINSTER: You lie, you lie. (*Little pause.*) I can't believe it.

MR BOOKER: Can't, madame, or won't? Which is it?
(MRS ARTMINSTER *reels across the room.* MR BOOKER *grabs her by the shoulders and they tumble on to the bed.* MR BOOKER *clambers up, stares down, then runs out of the room.*
MRS ARTMINSTER *gets up, goes into the other room, takes a gulp of Scotch from the bottle in the bag. Goes back, falls across the bed, waits.* MR BOOKER *comes back with a bottle of Scotch, unscrews it, holds it to* MRS ARTMINSTER'S *lips. She gulps some whisky down. Moans. Straightens. Looks around the room. Looks at* MR BOOKER.)

MRS ARTMINSTER: What happened?

MR BOOKER: You had a turn.

MRS ARTMINSTER: Why? Did I receive a shock?

MR BOOKER: No.

MRS ARTMINSTER: Are you sure? I only get one of my fits from a bad shock, like when we came to the wrong hotel. (*Looks at* MR BOOKER.) You didn't shock me then?

MR BOOKER: No. (*Pause.*) We were chatting here, pleasantly, about Garfield.

MRS ARTMINSTER: (*Looking around wildly*) Garfield. Something's happened to him? Where is he?

MR BOOKER: He's all right, quite all right, madame.

MRS ARTMINSTER: But where is he?

MR BOOKER: (*After a little pause*) He went to Little Munstering.

MRS ARTMINSTER: Oh. Yes, well he's a good boy. (*Pause.*) What were you saying about him?

MR BOOKER: Merely that he was a most pleasant and modest lad, unusual in these times. And devoted to his mother. Also unusual.

MRS ARTMINSTER: And nothing more?

MR BOOKER: (*After a pause*) No.

MRS ARTMINSTER: (*Putting her hands to her head*) But voices sound in my head, words and insults. Lies to hurt. I hear lies in my head.

MR BOOKER: Oh no, madame, we even had a little laugh together. (*Little pause.*) Unless the lies come from deeper in, and are trying to force their way out.

MRS ARTMINSTER: And there's this evil picture of – of Garfield and some – some, can it be man? Cuddling up together? Can it be?

MR BOOKER: (*Handing her the bottle*) Here, madame, another drop to clear your brain.
(MRS ARTMINSTER *takes a swig.*)
How do you feel now?

MRS ARTMINSTER: Clouded. Troubled and clouded. Who is that creature? (*Points to the picture.*)

MR BOOKER: My – spiritual father, madame.

MRS ARTMINSTER: Spiritual – and yet you're here, aren't you?

(*Studies the picture.*) Why's he smirking in purple? (*Long pause.*) What did you say my Garfield went out for?
(MR BOOKER *walks to the picture, looks at it, turns to* MRS ARTMINSTER.)

MR BOOKER: I think you know, madame. The clouds and troubles in your mind are truth obscured. You know madame. (*Stares at her.*) Because of the possibility of his taking up a good position here, in my hotel, which we were discussing before your spell.

MRS ARTMINSTER: A position here? When he has an income and a cottage in Little Munstering? (*Long pause.*) And what were you offering? (*Contemptuously.*)

MR BOOKER: You were too delicate to ask. You only expressed your gratitude and your interest. (*Little pause.*) I was helping you to see the truth, which could be useful to you.

MRS ARTMINSTER: You're after something, Booker, and it's poison to me and my Garfield, whatever it is.

MR BOOKER: Madame, madame, at this very minute your son is standing before an interviewing board, cap in hand.

MRS ARTMINSTER: My Garfield is *proud*.

MR BOOKER: Yes madame, he's proud. And that's why he's selling himself to the highest bidder. He wants to keep your delusions alive.

MRS ARTMINSTER: Why are you doing this, Booker? I thought you were my friend, the way you came up to me every evening and helped to keep me cheerful. Now you go on and on, over and over, you tell me my Garfield's coming to work for you, why? Why do you want him? You've got that Janice haven't you? Why do you want my Garfield? What good can he do you?

MR BOOKER: (*After a pause*) Modesty is what I need at the desk. (*Sits down in chair.*) Breeding. Someone with the gift of quietness. *She*'s no Garfield.

MRS ARTMINSTER: Who?

MR BOOKER: Janice.

MRS ARTMINSTER: Who said she was?

MR BOOKER: I said she *wasn't*.

MRS ARTMINSTER: Why?

MR BOOKER: Well, she isn't, is she? I was comparing her to Garfield in quietness.

MRS ARTMINSTER: What's he got to do with it?

MR BOOKER: He's quiet.

MRS ARTMINSTER: Who said he wasn't?

MR BOOKER: I didn't.

MRS ARTMINSTER: Why? Why didn't you, Booker.

MR BOOKER: What I said was what I particularly admire about Garfield and what qualifies him for a post on my desk was that he wasn't like Janice, and what I said was that he was quiet. (*Pause.*) For his sake, madame, face the truth. That boy has gone out to get a position, and I can help him. Face it, madame, face it.

MRS ARTMINSTER: Oh yes, the sun rises and sets on my Garfield to hear you speak his name, but there's one thing I can't face because you won't tell me, and that's what you're after. But I can smell it.

MR BOOKER: (*Leaping to his feet*) Well, you've gone all the way down and shown yourself at last, haven't you, madame. (*Pause.*) But I couldn't expect you to understand. (*Pause.*) There's no one could understand, except someone who helped me once and took me under his wing.

MRS ARTMINSTER: And where is he now, this wing of yours?

MR BOOKER: He was persecuted. By people like you. (*Walks to the picture.*) Oh yes, they're against it in all the places, in all the Godless world. Even his own church turned against him. If a man has a loving heart they crucify him – as the Testament shows us. He – (*points to the picture*) that man, had to go to Canada.

MRS ARTMINSTER: Didn't take you along, eh?

MR BOOKER: We keep up a correspondence. And there are celebration cables – at Christmas and birthdays, on the blessed rising and transfiguration of Easter. He remembers, though the world forgets.

MRS ARTMINSTER: Well, you're not desperate, are you, or you'd go to him.

MR BOOKER: (*Turning*) The time came for me to suffer my own way, without going unto him.

MRS ARTMINSTER: Well, keep your suffering off of my Garfield. (*They look at each other.* MR BOOKER *turns to the picture, turns away from it.*)

MR BOOKER: There's no point in making an offer even, then?

MRS ARTMINSTER: An offer? For my son? Do you call him cattle, that you can buy or sell?

MR BOOKER: A fish, for the fisher of men. A lamb for the shepherd. Fish, fowl and soul, immortal soul, to work at my desk.

MRS ARTMINSTER: You offer me *money*?

MR BOOKER: I offer *you* money, as I offer *him* life.

MRS ARTMINSTER: Money?
(MR BOOKER *nods, goes to the picture.*)
You haven't enough money to buy my son from me.
(MR BOOKER *turns, stares at* MRS ARTMINSTER.)
Where? Where do you keep this money of yours, you keep boasting about? In some safe or other, I suppose, you'll be telling me next.
(MR BOOKER *nods.*)
(*After a long silence.*) Oh, you monster, How much do you think I'd sell him for?

MR BOOKER: I do not buy him. I buy you. I buy *from* you. I buy his liberty from you, it is you that I buy, and cast away. (*Pause.*) Never to return. (*Little pause.*) You may write, of course, on open postcards. (*Little pause.*) Two bottles of my Scotch are missing, by the bye.

MRS ARTMINSTER: Don't ask me, accuse the nigger. (*After a pause.*) Oh, I could say yes, just to have him set up in a position, to ease a mother's worry. (*Pause.*) Don't think I don't know what's the matter with me, with my dreams of Little Munstering and money to keep us on. Do you know what I want, Booker, just a view of bridges over a river from a little window, and orchards to tend as I get old. Do you think I haven't worked for it, Booker, worked and worked? (*Pause.*) I love my boy, and he loves me. We're bound together by it. And that's the trouble, because even if I listened to you, *he* wouldn't. He would fret after me. I'm not saying he wouldn't be better off, but he won't take up a position without me.

MR BOOKER: I'll talk to him. I'll make him understand. We know each other, Garfield and I. Two hundred pounds. If you help me.

MRS ARTMINSTER: How?

MR BOOKER: Tell him he needs to be free. Tell him you need his freedom for him. Tell him in a mother's love. And mention the satisfaction it would give you to know that he worked here, at my desk.

MRS ARTMINSTER: (*After a long pause*) I'll tell him. I'll tell him how much it means to me, this freedom. (*Pause.*) You know, Booker, once I had another boy. His name was Derek. Derek would have understood. He was muscle, Derek was, knew how to do a job and stay in himself. He didn't need me, to look after him. He didn't need to be looked after by me, Derek didn't. That was where our strength was – Derek and me. Now I'd like a look at him again, to remind me before it's too late. I'm old, Booker, old. I need my Derek now. (*Little pause.*)

MR BOOKER: Garfield will remember you.

MRS ARTMINSTER: What will he remember, Booker?

MR BOOKER: (*Going towards the door*) He will remember that you helped to set him free. I must go now. I have other rooms to visit, other pictures to hang.

MRS ARTMINSTER: And what about my two hundred?

MR BOOKER: When the choice is made. I'll be up this evening, as per.

MRS ARTMINSTER: You're a babe, Booker. I warn you that now, you're a babe in the wood, if you think it's going to be easy. I'll want that two hundred on the spot.

(*They stare at each other.* BOOKER *exits.* MRS ARTMINSTER *gets up, looks at the picture, goes into the next room, comes back for the whisky bottle, goes back into the next room. Then goes to the bed, lies down with the whisky bottle, begins to hum. Hums*

*louder – 'On a bicycle made for two' – Stops humming. Drinks.
Curtain.*)

SCENE 2

MRS ARTMINSTER *is lying on the bed, dozing. The bottle of Scotch a
quarter empty, is cradled in her arms. Jerry's room is in darkness. The
door of Jerry's room opens. His light goes on.* JERRY *enters.* MRS
ARTMINSTER *jerks awake, blinks, conceals the bottle under the
mattress.* JERRY *takes the blond wig out of his pocket and puts it in
one of the cases. Meanwhile* MRS ARTMINSTER *is arranging herself
on the bed.* JERRY *comes in. He sniffs, looks at* MRS ARTMINSTER
*suspiciously, sniffs again, then goes to the window and opens it.
Turns.* MRS ARTMINSTER, *who has been pretending to be asleep,
now wakes.*

MRS ARTMINSTER: Hello, Jerry. (*In a tender voice.*) Had a hard
day, son?

JERRY: I've had a terrible day, terrible. (*Sits down in the chair.*)
Load of twits think just because I sit there in my goldilocks I
don't have feelings. Laugh and clown and slobber their pity,
for the sake of five pound expenses. (*Little pause.*) There was
a little twit with Jew eyes and big lips and a fuzz of white
hair. I knew what he was up to, all right. They offer me a
position and I turn it down, then I don't get my expenses, do
I?

MRS ARTMINSTER: What did you say?

JERRY: I said yes sir, I wanted to be helped, and I kept looking at
his white fuzz, silky and noble, and I said of course I
couldn't cut my hair and the bit about a free country and
nothing in the advertisement. He said that was all right. *That*
stopped me.

MRS ARTMINSTER: You took the job?

JERRY: Had to, didn't I? But I kept my eye on his fuzz, all the
same. And he said twenty pound a week, starting Monday.

MRS ARTMINSTER: Twenty pound a week. That's high, Jerry,
very high, for someone without particulars.

JERRY: Oh yes, he was a bright Jew all right. I couldn't say no, could I?

MRS ARTMINSTER: (*After a pause*) So you've fixed yourself up then, Jerry, after all? I always said you were meat for the soft-hearted. All that cleverness and you got yourself caught. (*Shakes head.*) I knew it was coming.

JERRY: Wait a minute can't you, because he said, did I have any questions? He was waiting to see what I'd do, he knew I'd never turn up and he'd saved himself a five, and got himself some cheap laughs at my expense. And I said I was very grateful for the chance, and I'd be there nine sharp, a bit earlier because I'd want to get down to it straight away, a lot to learn and that, and he said no need, come at nine, and I said no, it was all right, I'd be there at eight because you needed to be set on the toilet and washed at seven, and fed your tea and porridge, and then I could leave you. That's when he began to get a bit worried, about whether I meant it, and there I'd be on the doorstep with my hair down my shoulders and eager, but he kept up his nodding and Jew grinning, and said anything else, and I said there was one thing, very personal, I didn't want to make him angry, and I sort of lay across the desk and whispered shyly into his face, still watching his fuzz, 'Pardon me, but yours is lovely, where did you get it? Was it made by hand?'
(*There is a long silence.* MRS ARTMINSTER *stares at* JERRY, *who is looking tense.*)

MRS ARTMINSTER: So what did he do?

JERRY: Shouted at me.

MRS ARTMINSTER: What did you do? (*Looks at him.*) You – ?

JERRY: Cried. (*Begins to slap his hands together, as if in agony.*) I cried. I couldn't help myself. I told you I can't help myself. It just came out. Any minute my bones was going to break into pieces and I'd be skin on his floor, with jagged ends showing through, I kept thinking of that, and what you'd say when you heard, and you crying over my box being lowered, these things kept going round and round, and then next thing I was out on the street, my expenses in hand and more,

and wiping my eyes, and I could feel them watching from the
windows, and people on the street staring, so I got down a
siding and out of my wig. Then I went to Dewbury and Son.
They took one look at me and signed the chit.

MRS ARTMINSTER: So how much did you take, in the whole day?

JERRY: Thirty pounds. But that's Reading done with. Word'll get
round. I'll write some letters tomorrow, there's hundreds of
firms in the north looking for boys with technical training.
They're warm in the north, I've heard that. Friendly and
hospitable.

MRS ARTMINSTER: And how much did it take off of you, this
thirty pounds? (*There is a silence.*) What I mean, Jerry, is
look at the state you're in, ragged and clenched up, you don't
know where you are? (*Little pause.*) Do you, son? You've got
a trick, and it's killing you off. What's the good of it, son,
what's the good of it?

JERRY: I don't know anything else, do I?

MRS ARTMINSTER: I could teach you.

JERRY: What could you teach me? Some of your joggering? So I'd
be like Derek, and end up where Derek is? No thank you.
No thank you.

MRS ARTMINSTER: You'd only have to do it the once. (*Little
pause.*) It'd be easy, no need for a real jogger. (*Little pause.*)
I'd do the joggering.

JERRY: Like you joggered the Peasbury Postman?

MRS ARTMINSTER: Derek did that, he forgot his own muscle, I
got more experience than Derek. I'd aim right. Jerry, Jerry,
all you'd have to do is keep a watch, give me the signals, we'd
be away. We'd find a place in the country, lie low, be
peaceful. He's got money in that safe.

JERRY: Who – ?

MRS ARTMINSTER: You know who.

JERRY: No. I've told you no. He'd have them after us in ten
minutes. He *knows* us.

MRS ARTMINSTER: No he doesn't.

JERRY: Well, he knows us like this, and they know you the other
way, you'd have nothing left. Everybody'd know us then.

MRS ARTMINSTER: We'd have a chance. We'd have a man's chance, more chance than Derek had.

JERRY: Shut up about him. I've told you, the police –

MRS ARTMINSTER: The police! Sometimes I'd rather be in a room with the police of nine counties than just you, Jerry, and that's the *truth*. I tell you I don't know myself, I'm lost, funny things happen to me when you're here. Woman's tricks I use now, and handbag cunning. Derek wasn't the only one famous for his muscles, and I'm not boasting. Where have *my* muscles gone, Jerry, and don't I have instincts? Don't I? You tell me, go on, tell me. There's that Booker downstairs sitting on a safe with a fortune in it, he told me as much, and what's my instinct about that? Mine. My instinct.

JERRY: (*Getting to his feet*) You're free, you're free and you're fed and you're looked after, that's your instinct happy, and you want to throw it away just for the pleasure of joggering Booker. Where'd your instinct be *inside*, *you* tell *me* that. (*There is a long silence. Then* JERRY *sits down, his hands clasped,* MRS ARTMINSTER *punches the bed, stops, looks at* JERRY.)

MRS ARTMINSTER: You could do it, Jerry. You could do it with a smile and your nerve. You could get into that safe, clean it out, and leave him babbling his nonsense while he watched you. He'd help you, he's that drunk with love. No need to jogger, no risks, nothing. You'd have something on him, if you did it right. (*Little pause.*) Just a drop of tenderness, you could keep your eyes shut.

JERRY: (*Clasping his hands over his ears*) I can't hear you.

MRS ARTMINSTER: For my sake, Jerry.

JERRY: I can't hear you.

MRS ARTMINSTER: All right, Jerry, but I've given you the chance. (*Quietly.*)

JERRY: I can't hear you.

(*There is a long silence. Then* MRS ARTMINSTER *gets up,* JERRY *watching with his hands still over his ears.* MRS ARTMINSTER *lifts up the mattress and takes out the Scotch.*

Takes a long drink. JERRY *takes his hands away.*)
Where'd you get it from?

MRS ARTMINSTER: I'm not talking to you, so don't ask questions.
(*Takes another drink.*)
(*There is a knock on the door.* JERRY *stares at the door, gestures at
the bottle,* MRS ARTMINSTER *puts the bottle on the table, in full
sight, stares malevolently at* JERRY.)
Enter.
(JANICE *enters, smiling. Stands just inside the door.*)

JANICE: Sausage and wooost from The Three Musketeers?

MRS ARTMINSTER: (*Looks at* JERRY) Come in, my dear, come in
for a moment.
(JANICE *advances into the room. She smiles at* JERRY, *who pays
no attention.*)
Garfield, what's your fancy tonight?

JERRY: I don't care.

MRS ARTMINSTER: Don't care was made to care, dear. (*To*
JANICE) You're looking very ravishing tonight, my sweet, and
you've got those lovely doo-dahs on again. They especially go
in black lobes, I envy you.

JERRY: (*Loudly*) I'll have the sausages. What do you want,
Mother?

MRS ARTMINSTER: I'd like a little woman's talk with Janice. Come
sit by me, dear. And have a sip of this. (*Shows her the bottle.*)

JANICE: Oh no, missus. Mr Booker, he say I've got to hurry your
supper, he wants to come up.

MRS ARTMINSTER: How kind everyone is being. Do you hear
that, Garfield, Mr Booker wants to come up? To see you, I'm
sure of it. Because he likes you, dear, doesn't he Janice?
(JANICE *laughs.*)
Does he like every stray boy who comes into this hotel, Janice?

JANICE: Mr Booker, he love boys' movements, he say. (*Laughs.*)

MRS ARTMINSTER: Do you hear that, Garfield? You're not the
only pebble on the beach, my dear. Tell me, Janice, what's
that steel cupboard with a knob on it that Mr Booker keeps in
his office?

JANICE: It's for valuable.

MRS ARTMINSTER: Is that where he wants to pop Garfield into, for safe keeping?

JANICE: Oh, he like Garfield. I hear him say to God, in his office.

MRS ARTMINSTER: Ah, it would be good for my Garfield to have a little taste of confinement. Perhaps he'd come to enjoy it, wouldn't you, Garfield, in Mr Booker's steel cupboard. Does the knob have a special number on it, Janice, for opening?

JANICE: Oh, big number. 3338967.

(*There is a silence.*)

MRS ARTMINSTER: What was that again, dear?

JERRY: I thought you had to go downstairs straightaway.

MRS ARTMINSTER: What was that number again, dear?

JANICE: Millions. 99999999. Very big number. (*Little pause.*) I don't know.

JERRY: You'd better get downstairs or there'll be trouble.

MRS ARTMINSTER: Pay him no mind, dear. I can see that we've got a lot to say to each other. It's not often I get a chance to speak with another lady, what with having to keep my eyes on him all the time. Come sit by me. Just for a minute. That's all I ask.

JERRY: Leave her alone.

MRS ARTMINSTER: I told you, dear, you're not being spoken to. (*To* JANICE) Oh he's very jealous, that one, a nasty, sulky boy. Come drink, my sweet – (*pours Scotch into the mug*) and tell me what you think of the taste.

JANICE: Mr Booker, he say don't touch alco.

MRS ARTMINSTER: This isn't alco, sweet, it's cereal boiled down and will do you good. Try it, come on, a little sip, try it.

(JANICE *laughs, comes over, sits down, takes the mug.*)

JERRY: Peasbury Postman. (*Little pause.*) Nine counties.

MRS ARTMINSTER: Fetch them here, then. There's some things I could tell them about a little freak of my acquaintance. Now my dear – (*To* JANICE) have a swallow and savour it. That's not drinking, what you're doing.

JERRY: I'll make trouble.

MRS ARTMINSTER: I thrive on it. So does a young lady like Janice.

JERRY: (*In a whisper*) Please. Please.

MRS ARTMINSTER: (*Puts her hands over her ears*) I can't hear you,
Garfield.
(*JERRY stands there, trembling, then goes into the next room. Sits
on the edge of the bed, bitterly.*)
Now what were you telling me about that Mr Booker? Go on,
another little sip.
(*JANICE takes one, giggles.*)
That Booker?

JANICE: He a good man. He read prayers. He speak to God.

MRS ARTMINSTER: Oh, does he? (*Pours more Scotch into* JANICE's
mug.) I know what he asks for, then. But what about his
cash, and how much does he keep?

JANICE: I don't know about that. (*Giggles again.*) He don't speak
to me, hardly. He's a good man, doesn't like my black girl
feelings, he say.

MRS ARTMINSTER: Well, we can see why he doesn't like the likes
of you, sweet, it's because you're too young and savage for
the likes of him, too full of the female sauces.
(*JERRY gets up, goes to the door. Crouches down and puts an eye
to the keyhole. Gets up, slams his hand against the door.*)

JANICE: Oooh. (*Giggles.*)

MRS ARTMINSTER: He's shy before the ladies, he and Booker are
two of a kind. He fancies you too much, white against black,
it gives him nightmares to think of it. (*Pause.*) And he's
probably thinking those bubbles of yours – another sip,
sweet – (*pours more into the mug*) – those bubbles aren't real.

JANICE: (*Holding out ear-rings*) Oh, they real. Mr Booker, he give
them to me because of the boy he teaching to pray.

MRS ARTMINSTER: Oh, teaching him to pray, was he? You saw
it?

JANICE: Yes.

MRS ARTMINSTER: Down on his knees, was he?

JANICE: Yes, Mr Booker, he down on his knees praying, and this
boy Henry he standing against him, arms out in Lord Jesus
Christ, he praying too, and moaning out to God, God, then
Henry, he very bad, he run off, and Mr Booker he say to me,

'Here are some ear-rings Janice,' and I don't to say he is a
religious man who like to pray with Henry, because the
people of this world, where is their heart and understanding.
Yes, they're real, these.

MRS ARTMINSTER: And those other bubbles, what about those?
Are they real?

JANICE: What bubbles? (*Takes a gulp of Scotch.*) Oooh. Where?

MRS ARTMINSTER: Those bubbles under your blouse, sweet.

JANICE: (*With a screech of laughter*) 'Course they are, yes indeed
they are.

MRS ARTMINSTER: I love you already, my dear, as if you were
white, but I don't believe you, no I can't. Because if they are
I might have to consider you for a photograph study in
Hearth and Lounge, wouldn't I? And then there'd be no
stopping you.

JANICE: What you saying?

MRS ARTMINSTER: *Hearth and Lounge*, dear, it's a popular ladies'
magazine, and a friend of mine is the owner. I promise to
send her pictures of local beauties I meet on my travels. I
don't like doing it, the girls get uppity, what with talk of film
contracts and easy stardom. But they don't accept false
bubbles, especially from darkies, they get police raids from
that. And those bubbles are false bubbles, admit it.

JANICE: These no false. These real as the Lord.

MRS ARTMINSTER: Oh no, my sweet, I'm afraid I can't believe
you, you're lying there, although it's no reflection on
yourself, only on the colour of your skin, which you can't
help.

JANICE: These real.

MRS ARTMINSTER: Now my dear, you'll anger me if you go on
like that, it's well known that black girls are born without
bubbles, it's your big flaw. If they was real you'd be on every
hoarding in the country. (*Pours Scotch into her mug.*)

JANICE: They real. They real. (*Pushes herself forward.*) Feel, go
on and feel.

(JERRY *comes over, his hand on the knob.*)

(MRS ARTMINSTER *stares at the breasts, gets off then goes over and pushes the catch on the door. Goes back to the bed.*)

MRS ARTMINSTER: No, because foam is firm and stuffing's soft,
and whether they're soft or firm they could still be false. No,
if they look right uncovered I may feel them as an extra
precaution. Then we'll talk about photographs, but not a
word of this to anyone else because I'll have all your darkie
cousins at my door.

(JERRY *tries the doorknob, pushes, slams the wood again, goes
and sits down on the bed. Puts his head in his hands.*)

JANICE: What you want me do? (*Giggles.*)

MRS ARTMINSTER: I was giving you permission, dear, to show
me your bubbles.

JANICE: Oh, you want see? (*Begins to unbutton her blouse.*)

MRS ARTMINSTER: No, no, do it slow and graceful, dear, a
button at a time and pausing often because it's more ladylike.
Remember this is a magazine for the upper-middle-class type
of person, and style is important. Now go to the far side of
the room and count ten before you even begin. Can you
count ten?

JANICE: One, two, three, fours –

MRS ARTMINSTER: (*Pushing her off the bed and giving her a pat on
the behind.* JANICE *totters from the Scotch*) That's it.
(JANICE *stands rigidly.*)
No, loose a little, girl, pluck idly at a button and smile about
you.

JANICE: One. Two. Three. Fours. (*Very loudly.*)

MRS ARTMINSTER: Ssh. Ladylike. Do it in your head, or have a
guess. Start again.
(JERRY *rises, walks around the room, then goes to the door, grabs
the knob, jerks viciously.*)
(MRS ARTMINSTER *pays no attention.* JANICE *begins to
unbutton her blouse.*)
No, on second thoughts, begin with the accessories. Ear-
bubbles off first. Just drop them on the floor, as if you had
tons of them stowed away. Which you will have if you reach
the fame I've in mind for you.
(JANICE *reels slightly from the Scotch, straightens, giggles.*)

JANICE: Don't know what you want.

MRS ARTMINSTER: (*Raising her voice.* JERRY *obviously hears and stands stock-still*) *I want you to strip*, that's what I want. Now do it, and do it quiet. (*Lowering her voice.*) You know what poses is? Poses?

JANICE: Poses?

MRS ARTMINSTER: Natural body postures. (*Puts a hand behind head, thrusts out bosom, turns her head.*)

(JANICE *imitates her.*)

Yes, that's good for a beginning, very good and talented. Now dear, ear-bubbles first. (*Settles back on the bed.*)

(JANICE *takes off her ear-rings, drops them.* JERRY *seizes the doorknob, shakes it. Lies against the door.* JANICE *stops for a moment,* MRS ARTMINSTER *makes a half-threatening, half-erotic gesture.* JANICE *lurches, giggles, begins to unbutton her blouse.* JERRY *walks around the room, striking his fist against objects. Stops suddenly, stares at the connecting door, runs towards it as if about to smash it down with his shoulder, stops at the last second. Turns around. Sits down on the bed, covers his face with his hands.*

Meanwhile JANICE *is peeling off her blouse and doing poses.* MRS ARTMINSTER *is lolling back.* JERRY *suddenly gets to his feet, as* JANICE *begins to undo buttons on her skirt. He runs towards the hall-door, opens it, rushes into the hall, from view, simultaneously there is a distant door banging,* JERRY *runs back into the room, glares about him, peels back the covers of the bed, leaps in, pulls covers up and turns face to the wall. Sound of footsteps. His bedroom door opens,* MR BOOKER *puts his head in, stares sightlessly around the room, withdraws. A second later his head reappears. He stares at the bed. Steps in very quietly, stands uncertainly.*

JANICE *is now stepping out of her skirt, stumbles mid-pose, recollects herself.*

MR BOOKER *goes to the middle of the room, stares intensely at the bed. Goes over to it. Puts a hand down on the covers, moves his hand up the covers, rests it on the pillow beside* JERRY's *head. He stares down at the head, suddenly snatches his hand away, goes across the room to the picture, looks at it, turns around, goes back on tiptoe to the bed. Stands at the head, hands folded in semi-prayer fashion across his chest. Puts his hand down again, strokes the covers.*

JANICE *has kicked off her shoes, clumsily, and is now rolling down her stockings, also clumsily.* MRS ARTMINSTER *is less relaxed on the bed.*)

MR BOOKER: (*In a long, yearning sigh*) Garfield. Oh Garfield. (*He sinks to his knees beside the bed and rests his face on the bed, beside* JERRY'S, *his hands folded into his lap.*) Oh Garfield. (JERRY *stirs under the covers, huddling tighter.*)

MRS ARTMINSTER: (*As* JANICE *moves back and forth, in movements that are gauchely erotic*) Oooooh. (JANICE *giggles and begins to unclip her bra.*)

MR BOOKER: Garfield.

(*Puts his hand on* JERRY'S *head, stares at him. A pause, then* JERRY *begins to stir under the blankets again, more urgently.* MR BOOKER *gets up quickly, tiptoes rapidly across the room and out of the door.* JERRY *immediately gets off the bed and runs to the connecting door, stops, stares at it.* JANICE *drops the bra,* MRS ARTMINSTER *is sitting bolt-upright, beckoning* JANICE *across the room with both arms.* JANICE *is walking towards her.* JERRY *turns, runs out of the room, into the hall, disappears, bursts into Mrs Artminster's room, runs in front of* JANICE. *Stops.*)

JERRY: Slut. Slut.

MRS ARTMINSTER: ⎫ Jerry!
JANICE: ⎬ What he say? (*Backing away.*)

JERRY: Black-skinned white-toothed monkey grinning, gibbering foul fur peeling off. Fur. (*This should be said in a low, almost muttering voice.*)

MRS ARTMINSTER: Jerry! (*Gets off the bed.*)

JERRY: Filth and fur holes and filth nigger slut nigger slut. (*Advancing on* JANICE, *who is backing away.*)

MRS ARTMINSTER: (*Grabbing hold of* JERRY *by the arm and trying to drag him away*) Shut up.

JERRY: You naughty. You naughty.

MRS ARTMINSTER: (*As* JANICE *runs past and out of the room, slaps his face. He reels back, then sinks on the bed, hands over his face. There is a long silence*) I told you. I warned you. You keep me choked up in what I want, I told you. What about my instincts, where are they? (*Little pause.*) You've only yourself to blame. There's things I need in spite of you. (*Pause.*) And to hell with the police. To hell with them. (*She stares at him, then sits down beside him. She picks up the Scotch bottle and has a drink.*)

(JERRY *sits with his face covered, then gets up, runs over to Janice's clothing, bundles it up and runs to the cupboard with it, stuffs it in. Turns, goes back into his own room. Walks around, straightens his bed, looks at it, turns again, goes back into Mrs Artminster's room.*)

JERRY: I knew what you'd be doing, guzzling at your bottle.

(MRS ARTMINSTER *looks at him.* JERRY *advances, stands before* MRS ARTMINSTER. *There is a long silence.*)

(*Pathetically*) Oh, I've had a bad shock, I came all over faint. They're so rude to me because of my hair, they laugh at me, and then I got that feeling about my glass bones and I had a nightmare or something. (*Sits down on the bed.*) There was darkness and smells and my heart stopped beating and inside I was splintering, and being cut and cut and I was bleeding, Mum, there was red running, I can't bear to talk about it. What can I do? (*Long pause.*) Mum.

(MRS ARTMINSTER *looks at him.*)

Mum?

(MRS ARTMINSTER *looks at the bottle.*)

Mum?

(*He rests back against* MRS ARTMINSTER, *who sits rigid, then puts the bottle down and puts an arm around him. Stares blankly ahead.* JERRY *cuddles himself into* MRS ARTMINSTER. *In a muffled, contented voice*) Mum.

(*Curtain.*)

ACT THREE

MRS ARTMINSTER *is lying on the bed, nuzzling from the bottle.*
JERRY *is standing before her, in his blond wig. He has a case beside
him. He takes a few steps across the room.*

JERRY: (*Turning his head sharply, three times*) See what I mean?
(*Swings head again.*) It doesn't swing. And if it doesn't
swing, it doesn't look natural.

MRS ARTMINSTER: What?

JERRY: You're not watching. (*Swings head again.*) I said it doesn't
look natural.

MRS ARTMINSTER: Oh, pardon me, I didn't know you wanted to
go in for looking natural.

JERRY: It's got to swing out when I turn my head, see. I can't sit
there looking straight ahead when they ask me questions, can
I? But if I turn my head and my hair stays pointing in the
same place, then they'll wonder. (*Swings his head again.*) It's
got too big inside. It's stretched.

MRS ARTMINSTER: Probably nervous sweat.

JERRY: I don't sweat, you know that. No, it's these cheap plastics
they line them with.

MRS ARTMINSTER: Oh, yes, well you think of cheap plastics
against my skin-line, and it doesn't stretch, it shrinks, on a
hot day it's like I was a baking potato.

JERRY: (*Tenderly*) Don't you worry, I'll get you comfy soon as
we're gone from here. The black one's nice though, isn't it,
Mum. (*Takes a black one out of the box.*) And still fits a treat.
(*Puts it on.*) But I don't know, I always see myself as blond or
red, to swing over my eyes. I feel naked in this.

MRS ARTMINSTER: Yes, well you look lovely and untakeable in
all of them, why don't you give it a rest, Jerry?

JERRY: What's the matter with you then? (*Takes off the wig, puts
it back in the box.*)

MRS ARTMINSTER: Nothing. (*Little pause.*) Perhaps I'm hungry,
that's what.

JERRY: Oh yes – (*shutting the box up busily*) well *I'll* slip out and get your sausages. (*Smiles.*) And Worcester. I'll pour half a bottle on.

MRS ARTMINSTER: You'll have to, won't you.

JERRY: I don't mind. (*Little pause.*) You know I like getting you things.

MRS ARTMINSTER: Nobody else is going to do it, is she? (*Stares at him.*) Not now.

JERRY: What do you mean? (*Goes out of the room into his own, with the box, puts it away, comes back in.*) It's no trouble, honest. (*Smiles at* MRS ARTMINSTER.)

MRS ARTMINSTER: You know what I mean. What I mean is, Miss Black-Bubbles isn't going to get my sausages for me, not now she isn't. That's what I mean.

JERRY: (*After a pause, slaps his leg*) You don't have to mention it.

MRS ARTMINSTER: Not mentioning it won't stop it from having happened. She'll remember it, won't she? And what's your Simon Booker going to say?

JERRY: What's it matter what *he* says.

MRS ARTMINSTER: It'll put him off you.

JERRY: What's that matter?

MRS ARTMINSTER: And I thought you was the one who didn't like trouble. We need Booker friendly, and you're the one that keeps him that way.

JERRY: We can leave here tomorrow, he can't stop us. (*Pats his pocket.*) I've got enough to get us to Leeds. We can go First if you want. (*Goes to the door.*) Like some chips?

MRS ARTMINSTER: I'm not hungry.

JERRY: You said you was.

MRS ARTMINSTER: Well, now I'm not. (*Little pause.*) You put me off my food, the way you talk about Simon Booker. There's something I like about that man, just because he's good and wants to help people doesn't mean you can go sneering at him.

JERRY: What are you saying, help people? What's the matter with you, you gone mad? I had him in there while I was – I was taking a doze, sniffing around at me and stroking at me and praying –

MRS ARTMINSTER: And what does that matter? He's got needs like everybody else and he's got other feelings on top of them. That man Simon Booker's had a hard life, but he's got it in him to be a good friend. What's more, he's climbing to the top in the hotel world, and don't you despise him for it. (*Finishes off the bottle.*)

JERRY: (*After a pause*) What you up to?

MRS ARTMINSTER: Nothing. I'm just telling you about a man, Simon Booker, who's got the makings.

JERRY: Well, he hasn't got the makings of me, I'll tell you that.

MRS ARTMINSTER: Yes, you've got it against nigger that she's juicy woman and against Booker that he's bent –

JERRY: Shut up. Shut up. Now what you up to?

MRS ARTMINSTER: Nothing.

JERRY: Oh yes you are. Now what is it?

MRS ARTMINSTER: Nothing, I tell you. It doesn't matter. I just don't like to hear evil nonsense about Simon Booker, who's got a religious nature and's willing to help. That's all. That's all I'm up to.

(*There is a long silence between them. Then* MRS ARTMINSTER, *avoiding* JERRY's *stare, gets up and goes to her bag, takes out the other bottle of Scotch and uncorks it.* JERRY *watches.*)

JERRY: Where did you get that?

MRS ARTMINSTER: This? (*Looks at the bottle.*) From a friend. (*Looks at him.*) Of a friend.

JERRY: What friend? Booker?

MRS ARTMINSTER: I can't tell you that. He swore me to secrecy.

JERRY: It was Booker, wasn't it? (*Little pause.*) You stole it.

MRS ARTMINSTER: I told you, I got it from a friend of a friend, and I can't say more. But he's got an interest in me, he was up here today making propositions.

JERRY: Propositions? To you? (*Laughs theatrically.*)

MRS ARTMINSTER: Yes, to me, and why not? Don't you think your old mum's got charms? There's more where you come from, Jerry, who prefer a mature lady and are willing to give her presents to prove it. (*Little pause.*) Perhaps Janice's got a brother she introduced me to, while you was out peddling your wigs. A sweet black boy, more like someone whose name you can't bear the sound of than he's like you, colour apart.

JERRY: (*Stares at her uncertainly*) You stole it.

MRS ARTMINSTER: Oh did I? What's the matter, can't you stand a little competition, son? It's you who made your mum this way, and if she catches other people's fancy, you've only yourself to blame, haven't you?

JERRY: You stole it. (*Whispered.*) You did, didn't you? You did.

MRS ARTMINSTER: What's the matter, son, got some more of the jelly-belly?

(JERRY *runs to the bed, flops on it, face down.* MRS ARTMINSTER *goes over to him.*)

'Course I only said perhaps – (*little pause*) and I didn't say it was my friend, did I? I just said a friend. Perhaps it was your friend. (*Little pause.*)

JERRY: Who? (*Beats his hands on the bed.*) Who? It was Booker, wasn't it? Wasn't it?

MRS ARTMINSTER: (*After a long pause, sighs*) 'Course it was Booker. (*Little pause.*) I stole it. (*Little pause.*) It doesn't matter.

JERRY: (*Sitting up*) I knew it all the time.

MRS ARTMINSTER: (*Sitting down, takes a drink, looks down at the floor*) Oh Jerry, Jerry. (*Long pause.*) Aren't I entitled to anything except what you make up for me? Where's my past, Jerry, gone along with my hope, that's where. (*Pause.*) We did twenty-seven jobs together, I taught him from when he was a green thug and nothing, till it took them a week to catch him, out in those fields where he ran about like a hunted animal. There's honour in that, I see it now. Four men held him down, and then they had to use handcuffs. He went silent.

JERRY: Oh did he? (*Little pause.*) They want you though, don't they? They haven't stopped looking, they're not going to stop, it said in the paper that postman was having his milk from a bottle like a baby. (*Little pause.*) They've been watching nuns in Andover. Where'd you be, without a son to

130

show you're a mother? (*Pause.*) So he must have talked, for
the remission.

MRS ARTMINSTER: You're a liar. You're a liar.

JERRY: No I'm not, Mum, and what's more you know it.

MRS ARTMINSTER: I hate you. (*Intensely and vindictively. Long
pause. They stare at each other.*) No, Jerry, I don't hate you, if
I hated you I wouldn't want to see you happy, and worry
about you, I'm sorry I said that.

(JERRY *shakes his head.*)

I'm sorry I said that, Jerry, I take that back, because it's not
true. (*Pause.*) You know that, don't you?

(JERRY *hangs his head.*)

What about a game of scissors and papers, Jer? (*Sits on the
bed, with fists out.*) Come on, Jer, I feel just like a game.
(*Pause.*) Jer?

(JERRY *looks up, puts his fists to his eyes.*)

J-e-r-r-r.

(*He comes over, sits down, puts out his fists sulkily, then lowers
them and shakes his head.*)

(*Very tenderly*) Yes, Jer, come on. Come on. (*Sharply.*) All
right, if you don't want to, that suits me.

(JERRY *raises his fists.*)

Now.

(*They raise and lower their fists three times,* JERRY *just a fraction
behind* MRS ARTMINSTER. MRS ARTMINSTER *does scissors,*
JERRY *does paper.*)

JERRY: Scissors cut paper.

(*He holds out his hand and shuts his eyes.* MRS ARTMINSTER
*looks at him, at his hand, then gets a piece of wood which is by
the window, and comes back. Sits down. Hits him hard across
his palm.* JERRY *receives the blow with head thrown back, in
martyrdom. They ready themselves and do it again. This time*
MRS ARTMINSTER *has stone and* JERRY *has scissors. She hits
his hand again. The game is repeated twice more, each time* MRS
ARTMINSTER *wins and hits his hand. On the fifth time:*)

MRS ARTMINSTER: I'm watching you.

JERRY: What?

MRS ARTMINSTER: I'm watching you.

JERRY: Well, I like that, who's winning then? You are.

MRS ARTMINSTER: Am I? Jerry, you're a cheat.

JERRY: Cheat! Look at my hand!

MRS ARTMINSTER: Yes, that's what I mean. We'll do it eyes closed, then we'll see.

(*They close their eyes, do it, although it's evident that* MRS ARTMINSTER *is watching.* JERRY *has stone and* MRS ARTMINSTER, *a fraction behind, has paper.*)

(*Hands him the wood*) Go on.

(JERRY *looks at the wood without taking it.*)

Go on. (*Menacingly*) I'm waiting, Jerry.

(JERRY *shakes his head.*)

Jerry.

JERRY: I can't.

MRS ARTMINSTER: Why not?

JERRY: Because I – because I hate violence, that's why.

MRS ARTMINSTER: (*After a pause*) Derek would.

(JERRY *stares at her, grabs the wood, turns his head away, swings down. It strikes* MRS ARTMINSTER *hard on the arm. She let's out a roar of fury, grabs the wood and flails him with it.* JERRY *crouches away, giggling and crying out.*)

JERRY: I'm sorry, I'm sorry, I didn't mean it, Mum, I didn't mean it. I'm sorry, Mum.

MRS ARTMINSTER: (*Striking more savagely*) I'm not your bloody mum. I'm not your bloody mum.

(*Stops, looks at the stick, then throws it across the room in disgust, stares at* JERRY *who is still curled up on the bed, giggling and whimpering, then shakes head.*)

It's no good, Jerry. It's no good. (*Little pause.*) It's wrong.

JERRY: (*Stopping*) What?

MRS ARTMINSTER: (*Standing up*) It's wrong, Jerry, you and me. We're wrong for each other. (*Long pause.*) I've got to take my chances and make my run, Jerry. I need a go for my freedom.

JERRY: You can't. You'll be taken.

MRS ARTMINSTER: I don't care any more. It's not worth it. Look at you. Jerry, look at you. And look at me. In these togs, at these games. I am fifty-three old, Jer, and I'm lost to myself. Lost. (*Little pause, then pleadingly*) All I need is a little cash, say two hundred, to help me get a start. (*Little pause.*) You help me, Jerry. (*Little pause.*) Please. (*Little pause.*) Please.

JERRY: (*Gets to his feet*) But – we're happy together, aren't we? We're happy. (*Little pause.*) I'll be better, honest I will. I won't do it again. I was only joking.

MRS ARTMINSTER: It's not the doing, Jer, it's the feeling behind it, and that's no joke. All the feelings, all of them. Glass bones, nigger smells, scissors and paper. (*Pause.*) It's just that I got to make my run, Jer, and finish like I started off. It's right. (*Little pause.*) Please.

(*There is a long silence.* JERRY *turns away, stands with his back to* MRS ARTMINSTER. *Shakes his head.* MRS ARTMINSTER *moves towards him, his hand out. There is a knock on the door.* MR BOOKER *puts his head in. Coughs. Then comes in, holding* JANICE *by the arm. She is wearing a man's dressing-gown.* MR BOOKER *looks at* JERRY.)

MR BOOKER: I'm very sorry to interrupt, with Janice, the truth is something unpleasant has blown up.

MRS ARTMINSTER: The truth is I told that girl never to darken our room again. What does she want now? (*Stares at* JANICE *scornfully.*)

MR BOOKER: The unpleasant fact is, I found her sobbing in one of the cupboards with nothing on virtually, I must say. She was sobbing and her breath was filthy with alcohol, which I don't and can't allow. Garfield, I'm sorry to make suggestions. She seemed to be saying something about being attacked by, the unpleasant truth is, Garfield, by you, although I confess it was difficult to make out.

MRS ARTMINSTER: Oh she did, did she? That's what she said, is it? (*Little pause.*) And you'd take the word of this – this – over my son Garfield you pretend to worry over? Well, I'll give you the unpleasant facts of the truth, if she can bear to stay in the room to hear it, and don't blame me if it's too strong for you, it's not my fault your present company is a nigger and a slut, even if she is decorated in your dressing-gown. Or do you want to tell it, Garfield, can you bring yourself to open your mouth on it my dear?

JERRY: (*Shakes his head*) No, Mother.

MRS ARTMINSTER: *She* came cavorting into my son Garfield's room when we were in here calmly waiting for our supper, and was going through my son's belongings with an open bottle of whisky he had purchased for me as a little gift. Oh yes, she was rolling with it, and singing one of her songs when Garfield found her at it, and accosted her with the truth about herself. And do you know what she did, oh yes, she began to strip herself down and offer herself at him until he was forced to come running in here to me, and I had to deal with her myself. *He* couldn't bear to look at her brazen nudity, he was that ashamed, could your dear?

(JERRY *shakes his head.*)

He was took sick with the sight of her.

MR BOOKER: I knew it. I knew it. I knew you were lying to me, how dare you, you animal. (*Shakes* JANICE.) Where are her clothes, by the bye?

MRS ARTMINSTER: Clothes? On her body, the last I saw them. I made her put them back, every stitch and tittle, before casting her out. What she's done with them since, I wouldn't know, and yes, animal is the word. It's the word Garfield used to me, and the word I used back at him. Animal. Garfield and I have been up here ever since, upset and sick, waiting for an apology from the animal. Haven't we, Garfield?

JERRY: Yes, Mother.

MR BOOKER: Well, what do you say? (*To* JANICE) What do you say?

(JANICE, *dazed and in tears, begins to cry audibly, shaking her head.*)

They're waiting for an apology. (*Shakes her again.*) You'd better say sorry, or there'll be no mercy for you. Even from where mercy's infinite and ever-abundant. (*Shakes her.*) Say you're sorry. Sorry, Say sorry.

(JANICE *begins to scream and jerk,* MRS ARTMINSTER *comes across and takes her by the other arm.*)

MRS ARTMINSTER: My son Garfield's waiting for the word.

(JANICE *thrashes about, and they control her by forcing her to her knees. She crouches with her head lowered, in front of* JERRY. *They have her arms forced up painfully.*)

MR BOOKER: Now Janice, say after me – 'Oh Lord, I do in my deepest sincerity repent for the blackness of my heart' – say it, 'Oh Lord I do –'

JANICE: Oh Lord, I do –

MR BOOKER: In my deepest sincerity repent –

JANICE: In my deepest sincerity repent –

MR BOOKER: For the blackness of my heart.

JANICE: For the blackness of my heart.

MR BOOKER: And furthermore, oh Lord –

JANICE: And furthermore, oh Lord –

MR BOOKER: For the foulness and depravity of my thoughts –

JANICE: For the foulness and depravity of my thoughts –

MR BOOKER: And my behaviour to your faithful servant –

JANICE: And my behaviour to your faithful servant –

MR BOOKER: Garfield Artminster.

JANICE: Garfield Artminster.

MR BOOKER: Amen.

JANICE: Amen.

(*They release her, she falls on the floor.*)

Amen Amen Amen Amen Amen –

MR BOOKER: (*Opening the door*) Now go to the basement room, where you will stay, until I see fit to redeem you. Go. Go I say.

(JANICE *crawls out of the room,* MR BOOKER *steps into the hall to watch her go.* JERRY *is now standing close by* MRS ARTMINSTER. MR BOOKER *comes back into the room.*)

(*To* JERRY) I never doubted for a moment, Garfield. I hope you believe that. I knew you to be innocent. I only hope you were satisfied with the confession and apology that were wrung out of her.

MRS ARTMINSTER: Yes, and it was no pleasure, I can tell you.

But you had it coming to you, Garfield, and I'm glad we got
it for you.

JERRY: (*Looks at* MRS ARTMINSTER, *comes to her, kisses her on the
cheek*) Thank you, mother.

MRS ARTMINSTER: (*Who has moved away*) 'Course it was Mr
Booker's apology mainly, Garfield. He thought it up.

JERRY: (*Turns to* MR BOOKER) Thank you.

MR BOOKER: (*Gently*) That's all right, Garfield. I was glad to do it
for you. You know that, I trust.

(MRS ARTMINSTER *goes towards Jerry's room.*)

JERRY: Where are you going, Mother?

MRS ARTMINSTER: I felt one of my turns starting up just now,
Garfield, and I thought I'd just lie myself down on your
bed –

(*As* JERRY *advances toward her*)

– no, no, dear. I'll be glad of the quiet. You two men carry
on without me. (*Looks at* MR BOOKER, *goes into Jerry's room.*)

(JERRY *stares at the door, turns.*)

MR BOOKER: Well. (*Takes a nervous step forward, stumbles against
the chair.*) Well, I'm glad that unfortunate nastiness has been
cleaned up. I hope you're not too upset.

JERRY: (*Looks at him, looks at the door of his room, sits down on the
bed*) No.

MR BOOKER: Good. That's good. (*Long pause, sits down in the
chair.*) May I?

JERRY: What?

MR BOOKER: (*Gets up, gestures towards the chair*) Sit down.

JERRY: Oh. Yes.

(MR BOOKER *sits down.*)

(MRS ARTMINSTER *is sitting by the door, listening. Suddenly
she gets up, comes into the room, walks across the room, collects
her bottle of Scotch, goes back to Jerry's room.* JERRY *and*
MR BOOKER *watch her.* JERRY *gets to his feet as she goes out,
then sits down again. There is a long silence.* MRS ARTMINSTER
sits by the door to listen, and sips from her Scotch.)

MR BOOKER: I was just wondering how you'd got on?

JERRY: What?

MR BOOKER: In your interview.

JERRY: Very well, thank you.

MR BOOKER: Oh, I see. (*Little pause.*) You've got a position
then?

JERRY: (*Gets to his feet, sits down*) No.

MR BOOKER: (*Eagerly*) Then you didn't accept?

JERRY: Yes.

MR BOOKER: You did accept?

JERRY: Yes.

MR BOOKER: I see. (*Long pause.*) You got on very well in your
interview in which you accepted a position, but you didn't
get the job?

JERRY: Yes.

MR BOOKER: I see.

(*Long pause, while* MR BOOKER *takes off his spectacles, wipes
them.* JERRY *sits staring at the floor, sometimes at his bedroom
door.*)

(*Putting his spectacles back on*) What actually happened then,
if I can take on myself the right to ask, Garfield?

JERRY: What?

MR BOOKER: With respect to the position you accepted but
weren't offered, as I understand it.

JERRY: They didn't want me.

MR BOOKER: (*After a pause*) I know how you must feel, to feel
rejected. That's the worst of all feelings. But Garfield,
Garfield, this rejection will be for the best, others have been
rejected before, as the Testament proves. (*Little pause.*)
Why didn't they want you, by the bye?

(JERRY *shakes his head. There is a pause.*)

You're upset, my child. I know it.

JERRY: (*Laughs*) Upset? I'm not upset. (*Raises his voice.*) I don't
care any more, I don't.

(MRS ARTMINSTER *nods, sips from the whisky bottle.*)

MR BOOKER: (*Intensely*) Yes, Garfield, you care. That's where
you're like me (*gets up*) and that's where you suffer. (*Walks
to the picture.*) It's called passion, after a sacred event of
love. Garfield, there are only a palmful of us, he used to

say, who can be naked before each other and face the
darkness. The dreadful darkness.

JERRY: Yes, yes, that's all right, isn't it? But what about the
smell, how can she face that. (*Raises his voice.*) You know
how, because she smells of it herself.

MR BOOKER: (*Little pause*) Yes, Garfield, you're right, of course,
I wouldn't have mentioned it for the world if you hadn't
brought the matter up. But we must be merciful and
remember that she can't help herself, although I've noticed it
personally every time I go in for a chat, and remember too
what cleanliness is next to.

JERRY: (*Looks at the door*) Peasbury. (*In a raised voice*) That's all I
have to say. Postman. At the top of my voice. (*Little pause.*)
Little Munstering (*spits*), that's what'd be left of Little
Munstering. And who'd be free then? Who?

MR BOOKER: (*Stepping towards him*) Yes, Garfield, you're right.
You *are* free. You're already free. She has a claim, of course,
and I won't forget it, don't you worry. (*Stops.*) Where's
Peasbury, by the bye?

JERRY: What?

MR BOOKER: Why did you say Peasbury?

(MRS ARTMINSTER *is sitting transfixed by the door.*)

JERRY: Because there was an attack at Peasbury, a bad attack,
that ended in a death almost.

MR BOOKER: (*Excitedly*) There'll be no danger of that in a home,
I promise you. Professional nurses, and a sum arranged and
put aside, for her tastes.

JERRY: It was death, as good as. You think of it, drooling food
out like a baby, helpless, dependent on a bottle. *That's* what
they say.

MR BOOKER: No, Garfield, *I* haven't said it, and I wouldn't say it
if you hadn't said it first. But the professional nurses will
wean her away from it, they've got new methods. (*Little
pause.*) You did say postman, by the bye.

JERRY: (*Who is facing the door, swings his back at* MR BOOKER)
Yes, I'll tell you about the postman. In Peasbury. Yes.

(MRS ARTMINSTER *scrambles to feet.*)

Why shouldn't I?

(MRS ARTMINSTER *enters the room.*)

I know what she's up to, and I don't care, see.

MRS ARTMINSTER: (*Entering the room, points finger at* JERRY)
Jerry! You utter, and Derek will get out special to see you.

JERRY: Derek out? (*Laughs.*) You know where Derek is? (*Looks at* MR BOOKER.) You know what you've got here?

MRS ARTMINSTER: Jerry!

(*There is a long silence.* MRS ARTMINSTER *and* JERRY *stare at each other,* MR BOOKER *stares at* JERRY.)

MR BOOKER: Garfield, please.

JERRY: Well, now I know you, don't I? I really know you.

MRS ARTMINSTER: Perhaps you do, and perhaps it's time you did.

(*There is another silence. Then* JERRY *turns and goes towards the door of his room.*)

MR BOOKER: (*To* JERRY's *back*) Garfield, listen to me, I beg you.

(JERRY *slams the door.*)

MRS ARTMINSTER: You've got to be tough, Booker, and deaf to his ravings. For his own good. He'll cling like a leech unless you use a box of salt.

MR BOOKER: But he's so upset, I don't understand.

MRS ARTMINSTER: 'Course he's upset, I warned you, didn't I?
But it's no good simpering at him like a lady. Now get at him.

MR BOOKER: But I – (*wrings his hands*) where *is* Derek, by the bye? I thought he was dead.

JERRY: (*Entering*) All right, you don't have to worry about me, any more. I'll leave you alone. I'm going.

MR BOOKER: Listen to me.

JERRY: (*To* MRS ARTMINSTER) I mean it. I'm off.

MRS ARTMINSTER: Are you, dear, then walk ginger on those bones.

JERRY: And you needn't worry, I'm not coming back.

MRS ARTMINSTER: (*Turning away from him*) 'Course not, or why say goodbye.

MR BOOKER: Garfield, let me speak to you for a moment, that's all I ask.

(JERRY *looks at* MRS ARTMINSTER *and turns away*.)

MR BOOKER: Please, Garfield.

MRS ARTMINSTER: Jerry, the manager of this hotel wants a word with you. I advise you to answer up, boy.

(JERRY *slams the door*.)

(*Whispering*) I told you. Force. Use force.

MR BOOKER: (*Strides to the door, knocks on it*) There's a little matter of fifteen pounds ten shillings outstanding before you can depart from these premises, Mr Artminster. One pound five per night, per cheapest rates. (*Waits*.)

(JERRY *is packing*.)

You are answerable for tonight, as you've stayed past checking out time two p.m.

(JERRY *pays no attention*.)

Fifteen pounds ten shillings, Mr Artminster. (*Pause*.) Garfield, I don't mean to be hard on you, I know what bad times you've gone through. I'm on your side, Garfield. I just want to talk to you about the possibility of a position on my desk.

MRS ARTMINSTER: Jerry, dear, this man is serious and to be trusted. I vouch for it.

(JERRY *stops packing a moment, and then goes on*.)

Walk in on him, you're the owner, aren't you?

MR BOOKER: You don't have to do anything you don't want to, Garfield (*opening the door as he talks*), just let me speak to you, and then say yes or no when you've heard out my heartfelt proposal.

JERRY: (*Turning, as* MR BOOKER *enters the room*) You get out. I know what you want, and you're not having it from me, see. I've been followed by the likes of you all over Victoria Station, except *they* weren't blind.

MR BOOKER: Garfield! (MR BOOKER *stumbles forward, falls on the bed*.) Oh, God, oh God.

JERRY: Don't God me any more your Gods, homo blindie.

MR BOOKER: (*After a long pause, during which* MRS ARTMINSTER *comes to the door, buries his face in his hands, shakes his head, then looks at the floor*) It's not fair. It's not fair. What have I had since he left me? I stand behind the desk with that slut of a nigger to talk to, and my weeks are garbage and Godless. Sad in the evenings, the afternoons dead to me, and the mornings I can hardly get out of bed from shame of my dreams. And then you came, Garfield, you came unto this hotel by accident that was Fate, and there were feelings again. I can't help my feelings, that are given to me. I've watched you, Garfield, as you've passed me towards the street, and I've come up here just for the gift of a chat with you. And you tell me that's evil and that I follow you all over Victoria Station in my blindness. And so I would, Garfield, I would follow you wherever you bid me, just so I can help and look after. That's my feeling, that's my feeling. (*Little pause.*) I want to be a good man, Garfield. Good. There's faith in me, to be brought out and put to service. (*Little pause.*) That's all I want, Garfield, and you talk to me as if you hate me for it. It's wrong.

JERRY: Wrong, oh yes. It's wrong. (*Looks at* MR BOOKER.) I've got my feelings and they're different from yours. What about her, and what she's just done to me? What about my feelings, do you think of them in your slobberings. My own mum.

MRS ARTMINSTER: (*Quietly*) I don't know the meaning of the word, where you're concerned, Jerry. I look at you and I see Stonehenge around my neck.

(JERRY *stands up and faces* MRS ARTMINSTER, *who comes over to him and puts his hands around her face.*)

Now I'll tell you something, boy. You're going to do what I say, because the time has come for me to make my run. And the time has come for you to show you've got real feelings for me, son, and let me go when I'm dying from lack of my freedom. Because whatever you think now, I've done my best for you, Jer, I have. Do you think I've come along with you from blackmail? Do you think you could contain me if there wasn't other feelings to hold me close? But now, Jerry, now I know, and you know too, and soon the whole nation will know and be after me for myself, and that's the way it should be, that's the way I want it. If you've ever trusted me before, you trust me in this. (*Steps away.*) You could do worse than Simon Booker. He'll look after you, he's promised me that.

MR BOOKER: (*As* MRS ARTMINSTER *and* JERRY *face each other*) I will, Garfield, I will. I've already forgotten your words to me. They'll never be mentioned between us.

JERRY: All right. (*To* MRS ARTMINSTER) All right. You know I couldn't speak out. You know that.

MR BOOKER: (*Standing between* MRS ARTMINSTER *and* JERRY) What do you say, Garfield? What do you say?

MRS ARTMINSTER: It's the best for all of us, Jerry.

MR BOOKER: A position at my desk (*reaches up his hands to put them on* JERRY'*s shoulders, withdraws them*) and your freedom to be as you like. (*Little pause.*) Garfield? (*Little pause.*) I'll do anything you say. (*Little pause.*) Full board and lodging, of course.

JERRY: (*Turning away, sits on the bed*) All right. (*In a dead voice*) All right.

MR BOOKER: You say yes? (*Steps forward, stands in front of* JERRY *with hands clasped.*) Oh Garfield.

JERRY: (*In a dead voice and shaking his head*) But you won't last without me.

MRS ARTMINSTER: But I'll be going in myself, Jerry, whatever the end. (*Draws a deep breath.*) Booker, do you know who you've been dealing with? No, you don't. You've been dealing with the Peasbury Postman's assailant's accomplice. Derek Stewbat's accomplice.
(*Little pause, while* MR BOOKER *sits gingerly down beside* JERRY *and stares at him, and then at the ground.*)
And now, Booker, I'm counting on you to let me have my two hundred, and give me the chance to get clear of here, as was agreed.

MR BOOKER: I'm a small establishment, Garfield, you know that. You've seen it for yourself. But if there's faith between us, Garfield, there could be miracles.

MRS ARTMINSTER: Jock Masters, Booker. Me. (*Laughs, points to his own chest.*)

MR BOOKER: (*Looking at him*) What?

MRS ARTMINSTER: Jock Masters.

MR BOOKER: Who's that?

MRS ARTMINSTER: The Peasbury Postman's assailant's accomplice.

(JERRY *stares at* MRS ARTMINSTER.)

MR BOOKER: Who?

MRS ARTMINSTER: Jock Masters.

MR BOOKER: Oh. (*Nods, turns back to* JERRY.) Yes, I don't deny that there are just the travellers, Garfield, and one or two from a better class who might stray in now we've got the decorating done –

(*While he is talking* MRS ARTMINSTER *has taken off her wig and comes to stand beside* JERRY, *looking down at* MR BOOKER. MR BOOKER *keeps his eyes fixed on* JERRY's *face.*)

– and there's things I've been thinking on Garfield, like travellers' specialities, which would be Janice for instance, sent up to the rooms.

MRS ARTMINSTER: Now about my two hundred you promised me, Booker.

MR BOOKER: But only with your permission and consent, Garfield. Nothing without that.

MRS ARTMINSTER: Look, if I'm to make my run, I want to get started. (*Puts her wig back on, angrily. It slips over one eye.*) Jerry, ask him for my two.

MR BOOKER: And I've often had a little dream, Garfield, vision-like, of a room set aside as a chapel.

MRS ARTMINSTER: Jerry?

JERRY: (*Looking up*) You said I wasn't yours. You said I was his now.

MRS ARTMINSTER: (*Sadly*) Jerry.

JERRY: You said you preferred Derek.

MRS ARTMINSTER: Oh Jer, how could you?

JERRY: And I was Stonehenge around your neck, you said, when you looked at me, and you wanted me off with Booker.

MR BOOKER: (*Looking at* MRS ARTMINSTER) Why did you say that about the Peasbury Postman's assailant, by the by?

MRS ARTMINSTER: So you wash your hands off of me, Jerry, do you?

JERRY: That's what you want, isn't it. Talk to him. (*Points to* BOOKER) He owns me, you said.

MR BOOKER: (*In a quiet voice, getting up, walking around* MRS ARTMINSTER, *studying the wig closely*) By the bye, didn't you say the name (*jerks off Mrs Artminster's wig*) of Jock Masters? (*Stands back.*)
(JERRY *leaps to his feet.*)

MRS ARTMINSTER: Thank you, Jerry. Thank you. I don't blame you for what you've done, no I don't. I just wish you hadn't done it so underhand, I just wish you'd let me have my run.

MR BOOKER: I think you said yourself that Jock Masters is the Peasbury Postman's assailant.

MRS ARTMINSTER: (*To* JERRY, *who is standing, frozen*) 'Course I knew I'd never make it, Jerry, just as you'll never make what you want. But I could have tried, couldn't I? (*Turns, makes for the door.*)

MR BOOKER: Oh no you don't. You're not going anywhere.

MRS ARTMINSTER: Keep your hands off me, homosexual, nobody mauls at Jock Masters.
(*He turns and grapples with* MR BOOKER, *who overcomes him easily, and forces him into a chair.*)

MR BOOKER: Telephone for the police, Garfield.

JERRY: I don't want the police.

MR BOOKER: Garfield, Garfield, this is a criminal I've got here. I couldn't let him get up and walk away, could I, in defiance of the law of the land?

JERRY: Why not?

MR BOOKER: Think of reputation, Garfield, and what would happen to the hotel if it leaks out that we harboured knowingly.

JERRY: I don't want the police. If you call the police, I'm leaving.

MR BOOKER: (*After a pause*) All right. But there must be no
return, and no communications. You must pursue your own
salvation and repentance, without reference to Garfield.

JERRY: (*As* MRS ARTMINSTER *gets up, takes his wig from*
MR BOOKER) You'll have to make your run in those togs.
You haven't got a suit.

MRS ARTMINSTER: I know that, Jerry, I'll take the risk. (*Goes
into the next room, collects zipper-bag.*)

MR BOOKER: It's all over now, Garfield, the end of that has come.
One day you'll look back on it and see what it was you had
here, with this person. And the guilt will have cleansed itself
out of you, and your restless spirit will be safe and settled.
How did you come to be mixed up with him in the first place,
by the bye?

(MRS ARTMINSTER, *who has come back into the room, walks
slowly and heavily as if worn out. She stands with her bag and
bottle, staring at* JERRY.)

MRS ARTMINSTER: It was in Ned's Sandwich, down by the
Stepney Graveyard, where I was hiding myself over a cup of
tea. Just after Derek was taken and there was descriptions in
the papers, and an identikit likeness. I'd walked past three
police that morning, but he knew me at once – (*shakes head*)
he knew me at once, this one did. He came to the table and
whispered to me that he could help or cry out, whichever I
preferred, it was like he was on the look-out. He took me
back to his room behind the Mile End tube and there were
the togs in a cupboard and a wig prepared, and a box of
lipstick and powders. I was garnished and out again before I
could think, and all the time he was talking to me, cool and
gentle. It was like he'd been waiting. (*Puts the bottle into the
bag, and zips it shut. Then walks across the room, with the same
dull tread, puts a hand to* JERRY's *face.*) And he's done his best
by me, I won't deny it. However far or little I run, Jerry,
there won't be a word about you in it when I'm taken. You'll
read about me in the papers, how I was hunted and trapped,
and there'll be questions and pain down at the station, when
the boys light into me, but I'll talk about every minute I was

free and there won't be a word about you in it. There's no
shame in being fond, Jerry, and I'll tell you now that I'm
fond of you. I always have been. I always will be.

JERRY: (*Sobs, straightens*) They're not checking the nuns at
Andover. I made it up. They haven't been looking hard for
weeks. (*Little pause.*) Derek didn't talk. (*Little pause.*) Just a
few more weeks and you'd be clear.

MRS ARTMINSTER: The time is come, son, as it was bound to
come. (*Turns away.*)

MR BOOKER: (*Taking him by the arm*) Yes Garfield, let the thief
walk in humility. There's a future to think of.

(MRS ARTMINSTER *walks slowly towards the door.* JERRY
makes an effort to run, MR BOOKER *hangs on to him and holds
him tight.*)

Let him go, Garfield. (*Gently*) It's what he wants.

JERRY: But she won't last without me, I know it.

MR BOOKER: He's in God's hands, Garfield.

JERRY: She hasn't got a chance.

MR BOOKER: (*To* MRS ARTMINSTER, *who is standing with hand on
knob*) Go. Go on. Go.

JERRY: (*Struggling across the room*) What'll happen to her?

MR BOOKER: (*Holds on to him*) God will protect him. Get out (*to*
MRS ARTMINSTER).

(MRS ARTMINSTER *opens the door and goes out. Shuts the door.*
JERRY *stares at the door for a second, listens to the sound of* MRS
ARTMINSTER's *feet, then swings around, dragging* MR BOOKER
*after him, clasps the heavy table lamp from beside the bed, and
swings it into* MR BOOKER's *face.*)

JERRY: It's your fault –
(*as* MR BOOKER *staggers back*)
– it's your fault (*hits him again, and when he falls, crying out,
kicks him in the face*), you spoilt it, homosexual. You spoilt it.
(MR BOOKER *lies on the floor, arms spread out.*
JERRY *stands staring down. Drops the lamp.*) Mum. Mum.
*There is a long silence, then the sound of feet coming down the
hall. The door opens and* MRS ARTMINSTER *stands there. Looks
at* JERRY, *looks at* MR BOOKER, *comes over. Bends down.*)

MRS ARTMINSTER: Now you've done it. He's dead, Jerry. You've done him.

JERRY: Well, Derek would have done that, wouldn't he? (*Looks at* MRS ARTMINSTER.) Yes, there's my muscles for you.

MRS ARTMINSTER: (*Takes a step back*) But you joggered him dead. This one's dead, Jerry. This Simon Booker's dead.

JERRY: You told me. You told me to jogger, didn't you. You told me to. Mum. Mum. (*Steps towards* MRS ARTMINSTER.) (MRS ARTMINSTER *sits down on the bed.*) What'll I do? What'll I do?

MRS ARTMINSTER: Do? (*Little pause.*) Why run, Jerry, run. Make for the crowded towns, or the open country. Cover yourself in twigs from ditches like Derek did, or sit on the bottom of London buses at rush hour like I did. Go where you're not known, or there's too many to care. Run, Jerry, run, that's what you do. Run while you got the time. (*Gets up, advances cautiously on* MR BOOKER, *begins to strip him at increasing speed.*)

JERRY: I don't know how.

MRS ARTMINSTER: You'll learn.

JERRY: Please (*as* MRS ARTMINSTER *goes on with the undressing*).

MRS ARTMINSTER: You've said your last pleases to me, Jerry, I can't hear them any more. Save yourself, boy.

JERRY: (*Sits down on the bed*) I won't.

MRS ARTMINSTER: (*Turns, looks at* JERRY) Then you'll be took. (*Turns back, begins to undress.*)

JERRY: I don't care.

MRS ARTMINSTER: (*As begins to swap clothes*) Don't care was made to care, Jerry. Can't you see I've had enough of it, locked away like one of your Dutch harlots in chains, my needs suppressed. Well, not any more. Look at me, Jerry, and what do you see. Jock Masters, that's what you see, boy. And that means I'll visit his safe on my way down, that's Jock Masters' way, and I'll find a way to open it, don't you worry. And I'll take half of what's there, and leave the other half for you, because that's Jock Masters' way too, and always has been.

(*While he is talking* JERRY *has been staring at him, then he gets up, goes into the next room with his case, goes to the wardrobe, takes out Janice's clothes and begins to exchange them, at speed, for his own.*)

Then you can go back to your wigs and whining, Jerry, I'll tell you again what I always told you, that game of expenses gives me the creeps, the thought of you sitting there, I don't know how you could do it. (*Stops.*) Scissors cutting paper, stones smashing scissors, eagles, glass bones – my own muscles going, tears spring up – there's no life in that, Jerry, and what you got against smells anyway? It wouldn't work, Jerry, I've got my own dreams, haven't I? What about Little Munstering then? (*Bends over and does up his shoes.*)

(JERRY *comes back into the room and stands waiting.*)

Yes, you see me now and know what I say. See who's back, Jer (*straightening*), Jock Masters, that's who's back. (*Turns. Stares at* JERRY.)

(*There is a long silence between them. Curtain.*)

Dutch Uncle

Dutch Uncle was first performed on 17 March 1969 at the Aldwych Theatre, London. The cast was as follows:

MR GODBOY	Warren Mitchell
MAY GODBOY	Megs Jenkins
ERIC HOYDEN	John Alderton
DORIS HOYDEN	Frances de la Tour
INSPECTOR HAWKINS	Patrick Magee

Director	Peter Hall
Designed and lit by	John Bury
Costumes	Sheila Russell

ACT ONE

SCENE I

The year is 1952. A living-room in a decaying house in Shepherd's Bush. The wall, right (the audience's right, that is), has a door leading into the hall. The wall, left, has a door leading into the bedroom. The back wall, left, has a door that leads into the kitchen. There is a door in the kitchen that also leads into the hall, but is not visible to the audience. Parts of the kitchen – the stove, sink, and parts of the hall – a door, opposite, that leads into the lavatory – are, however, visible to the audience when the appropriate doors are open. The furniture is as follows. Back stage, centre, a shabby sofa. An armchair to the right of it and slightly forward. Two hard-backed utility chairs, one left of sofa, one well away from the armchair and in front of it. On a small table, left, and close to the bedroom door is a gramophone and a pile of records. In the right corner of the room there is an enormous wardrobe, sticking out and carelessly placed. It is tall and deep, freshly varnished and covered with curlicues, etc. Next to it, against the wall and to the left, is a more conventional wardrobe, shallower and slimmer. Both wardrobes have drawers in their bases. On the other side of the enormous wardrobe and to its right, against the wall and close to the door that leads to the hall, is an alcove covered by two curtains that don't quite meet and don't quite reach the ground. The heels of shoes and a few inches of boxes are therefore visible, also sleeves of jackets, etc. The room is very messy. Bits of newspapers and women's magazines scattered about, a pair of woman's high-heeled shoes near the gramophone table, two empty packets of cigarettes on one of the utility chairs.

The curtain rises on the room, empty. There is a long silence, then a slight thumping noise from the large cupboard. The door opens and MR GODBOY *steps out. He is carrying a gas cylinder with a length of rubber tubing, very long, attached to its nozzle. He puts this into the alcove, hangs the rubber tubing so that it sticks out a fraction from between the curtain, goes to the door, looks casually around the room, then walks forward very quickly. With his left hand he slams the door shut, with his right hand he seizes the length of tubing, plunges it into a hole on the right side of the cupboard, then pulling the cylinder out, pretends to turn the nozzle with his right hand. Takes the tube out, puts it back as before, puts the cylinder back behind the alcove curtain, unlocks the cupboard door. Takes out of his coat pocket an enormous padlock, shut, with the key in it. Checks the padlock against the bolt, then holding the padlock, opens the cupboard door, steps inside, out of view, shuts the door behind him. Bangs on the cupboard door. The noises are muffled. Stops. There is a short silence then the door, right, opens and MAY GODBOY comes in. She is wearing a baggy dress and flattened shoes and an overcoat. She is carrying a basket with a greasy package on top. She puts the basket down, bends over it. While she is doing this the cupboard door opens a fraction. MAY stiffens, turns, stares at the cupboard, puts her hands on her hips in amazement. Then the door opens wide and MR GODBOY steps out, falters a fraction of an instant. The padlock, closed, is in his right hand. He closes the door fussily, keeping the padlock out of sight.*

GODBOY: Oh hello dear, I wasn't expecting you for another hour, you said.

MAY: What's that?

GODBOY: (*Slipping the padlock into his right jacket pocket, drops it to the floor, picks it up with a*) Whoops! (*Laughs.*) It's a cupboard dear.

MAY: (*Still staring at the cupboard*) What's it doing in here?

GODBOY: Oh no dear (*stuffing the padlock into his pocket*), it's not for us (*laughs*), it's for Eric and Doris. (*Little pause.*) As cupboard space was conditional on acceptance of terms for the upstairs apartment, legally furnishings have to be approved as adequate.

MAY: Who by?

GODBOY: Um, Eric and Doris that would be, dear.

MAY: And have they come complaining?

GODBOY: It's a matter of conscience also, dear.

MAY: Whose?

GODBOY: Mine, that would be, dear.

MAY: If it's for Eric and Doris, what's it doing down here?

GODBOY: It's merely for the time being, dear.

MAY: (*Looks at him, turns, picks up the basket, turns again*) And what was you doing inside it then?

GODBOY: Investigating it for capacity, dear, merely. (*Long pause.*) Would you like to have a look-see? (*Opens the cupboard door, makes a formal ushering gesture.*)

(MAY *walks closer to it, stares in suspiciously. As she does so* MR GODBOY's *right hand moves from the pipe hanging out of the alcove.*)

MAY: What for?

GODBOY: It's very capacious, dear.

MAY: Perhaps it is.

(*She steps away.* MR GODBOY *drops his hand.*)

But that doesn't mean I have to live in it. (*Walks across to the sofa, settles on it, takes off her coat, flings it on to the utility chair. It slides off, falls to the floor.*) What do you think I am, some class of hermit? (*Chuckles.*) Because no I'm not, no I'm not. (*She stares at him significantly.*)

GODBOY: (*Comes over, picks up her coat, folds it over the back of the chair*) Well dear, to tell you the truth, I've already been and placed some of your garments inside it. Your nightie and a frock you're fond of plus your comfy carpet slippers, dear, and other odds and ends.

MAY: Why?

GODBOY: Well, I thought we'd avail ourselves of the use of it, while we had it. Legally it's our cupboard until it's theirs. (*Looks at her.*) Anyway, if there's any article you can't find, it's likely to be in the cupboard waiting for you, you could peer in now for a check.

(MAY *swings her legs up on to the sofa.*)

But if I'm not here, give me a call so I can help you sort through . . .

MAY: Ooo, the headaches you give me, you make a fuss out of breathing.

(MR GODBOY *goes back to the cupboard, shuts the door, turns to the guppie case, scatters food from a packet into it.*)

GODBOY: I'm sorry, dear, it was just a little idea of mine.

(MAY *reaches down to the basket, picks the package up, opens it. It contains chips. She begins to pop them into her mouth.* MR GODBOY *turns, stares. She stares back at him, goes on eating.*) Tasty?

MAY: Is that what you been doing all afternoon, then?

GODBOY: (*Smiling*) Pardon, dear?

MAY: Messing about with cupboards?

GODBOY: Yes dear.

MAY: (*Knowing*) You sure?

GODBOY: There was a lot to be looked after dear. It had to be purchased first, then arrangements had to be made for its delivery, myself accompanying in the van, no laughing matter as you can imagine, then various matters arose in connection with the padlock I insisted on for security measures . . .

(*He hesitates, then boldly takes the padlock out of his pocket, flashes it at her, stuffs it away. While he is talking,* MAY *gets off the sofa and goes into the kitchen, leaving the door open.* MR GODBOY *hurries over to the sofa, picks up her coat, takes it to the cupboard, puts it in, shuts the door, as* MAY *comes back in, sprinkling vinegar over her chips.*)

(*Coming back to the centre of the room.*) And on top of that I had to supervise the placing of the cupboard, also no laughing –

MAY: Doris or Eric didn't drop down then?

GODBOY: No dear, as I was explaining, I was compelled to be out all afternoon.

MAY: Well, Eric was down looking for you while you was gadding about with cupboards; he wants to know when you're going to do some work on his Doris, if you're still up to doing work on anyone, that is . . . (*settling back on the sofa*) seeing as he says as he's asked you five times.

GODBOY: (*After a pause*) Yes dear, it's been a matter of waiting until the time is right, which it now is.

MAY: And there I was thinking you'd be glad to get your hands on her shy little toes; think of the liberties (*making prising*

gesture with a chip) while you was knocking off a corn.
(MR GODBOY *looks at her, then goes to the kitchen door, shuts it, comes back, sits down on one of the utility chairs, laughs, shakes his head.*)

GODBOY: I hope you don't joke like that around the neighbourhood, dear, on account of what you know it could do in the way of damage to my professional standing.

MAY: (*Sucks her fingers*) Oh and would it? (*Wags her head.*) What standing?

GODBOY: It might give people the unfortunate impression that everything wasn't right between us, dear.

MAY: It's unfortunate where the truth is, then. (*Pause.*) What about the standing that never stands because it's already had damage done to it according to your story and as I was the last to know?

GODBOY: (*After a long pause.*) Pardon, dear?

MAY: I've been thinking. How's your wound today? Throbbing, is it? Throbbing away?

GODBOY: It's merely been causing me a trifling pain, dear, thank you for asking. I managed to get down to the chemist for a prescription refill that'll assist me to doze off at night.

MAY: (*Sarcastic*) Well, that'll bring me some peace at last, won't it. (*Little pause.*) Your passion's been on the doze since the day we was married. (*Gets up, looks irritably around the room.*) And so's your foot-doctoring, so's your everything.

GODBOY: (*Watching her alertly*) As you know dear – are you looking for something?

MAY: Where's my coat?

GODBOY: I popped it in the cupboard. (*Gesturing towards it.*) I believe it would be fatal for me to practise full time owing to the effect on my pension and side-benefits, even my little family legacy would suffer.
(As MAY *goes towards the cupboard, he gets out of his chair.*)
And the fact that I'm perfectly willing to assist out on the wife of a tenant doesn't mean I have to go begging for it, merely, dear.
(*Sits down again as* MAY *walks past the cupboard to the alcove,*

pulls the curtain back, heaves the cylinder out of the way,
scrambles about on a shelf, knocking down bits and pieces of
clothes, then comes back wiping her hands on a large
handkerchief. MAY *blows her nose, settles back on the sofa as* MR
GODBOY *goes to the alcove, puts the cylinder right while*
pretending to be putting the clothes back.)

MAY: What's that?

GODBOY: Pardon, dear?

MAY: Those tubes and pipes?

GODBOY: Oh. (*Laughs.*) Merely a little device I was offered at the
chemist to try out a little experiment with merely, dear.
(*Straightening, he closes the curtain.*)

MAY: (*Looking at him*) All day I've been thinking about you. I've
got a surprise coming for you.

GODBOY: Pardon, dear? (*Brushing at his clothes*).

MAY: When we got started together you was brim-full of talk
about how you was going to swell up until you was too big to
handle on your own, as feet was feet and would always cause
pain and need doctoring, and all I seen you do in two years of
marriage is monkey about on that pension of yours and go on
about your wound and bother them down at the police
station. (*Points a finger at him as he comes back.*) Where else
was you this afternoon? (*Nods.*) Where was you? At the
police station, that's where you was, wasn't you?

GODBOY: (*Sits down.*) Indeed, dear, I did drop in for a chat this
morning.

MAY: (*Kicks off her shoes, sighs*) And what was you doing down
there this time?

GODBOY: Merely discussing, dear, as I said.

MAY: What?

GODBOY: (*After a pause*) Murder, merely, dear.

MAY: What murder?

GODBOY: James Ryan O'Higgs, the Dublin accountant and wife
and female tenant murderer, dear. The one who polished off
his wife and tenant in a week, and how he kept the police at
bay with clever lies, although they was – were suspicious
after the first. But still he kept on at it . . .

(*As* MAY *gets up, he watches her.*)

Chat merely, dear.

(*Getting to his feet as* MAY *goes to the cupboard.*)

What you might call shop.

(*Moving towards her as she opens the cupboard door: takes the padlock out of his pocket.* MAY *turns, looks at him. He has been walking furtively, now walks nonchalantly to stand beside her.*)

MAY: (*Looks at him with contempt*) No wonder you need medicine, the way you fill your brain up with stuff like that.

(*She moves closer to the cupboard as* MR GODBOY *slips behind her to the alcove.*)

Where did you say my slippers was?

(*He puts his hand against the cupboard door to shut it, takes the pipe in his right hand. He cannot of course see* MAY, *as the cupboard door blocks her from view.*)

GODBOY: That's right dear, in there dear.

(MAY *steps around from the cupboard, stands behind* MR GODBOY, *who is still poised, holding the pipe in his right, the door in his left hand.*)

He did it by gassing, May! (*in a shout*)

(*He slams the door as* MAY *puts a hand on his shoulder. He whirls around, laughs.*)

MAY: (*As* MR GODBOY *drops the pipe*) What's the matter with you, I don't care if he did it by eating them raw; let me through and why can't you leave my things alone.

(*As* MR GODBOY *steps away from the alcove, she bends down, knocking aside the cylinder, then comes out carrying a pair of slippers.*)

GODBOY: Those are mine, dear. Yours are in the cupboard.

MAY: They'll suit.

(*She puts them on. He watches her malevolently.*)

And talking of gas, you be careful; the number of times you left the oven taps on for no reason, it's a wonder you're still here. And now it's tubes and what.

GODBOY: (*Laughs*) Merely a device . . . (*Slips the padlock back in his pocket.*)

MAY: (*Turning her back on him*) Not that it matters. I've got a surprise for you.

GODBOY: Indeed? What sort of surprise?

MAY: You'll find out when it comes. (*She settles again on the sofa.*) And who was you having this chat with? Your Inspector Hawkins?

GODBOY: With Duty Officer Larkins, dear. (*Shuts the door, comes back.*) Although it's funny you should mention Inspector Hawkins, dear, as he did come in while I was talking to Duty Officer.

MAY: And has he remembered you yet?

GODBOY: His eyes were red-rimmed with fatigue and there was stubble on his chin; I garnered from Duty Officer's hints that he's been working twenty-four hours on the Merrit Street case – he wasn't in a condition to remember me.

MAY: But he's been at that station two months now, and you been down there every day of the week, how is it he don't remember you if you was so close to him in the war?

GODBOY: (*Stiffly*) I never said I expected him to remember me, May, I merely said in my capacity as Special Constable we'd come into contact before he was posted.

MAY: Ooooh! Well, to hear you tell it sometimes you was always at his side.

GODBOY: I admire him May, yes, and I've followed his career, yes, and I'm proud to have been in contact, yes, and that's all I've said May.

MAY: And yet he don't remember you even! Yes?

GODBOY: (*Looks at her coldly*) Inspector Hawkins will remember me all right, May, when the time comes.

MAY: (*Stares at him*) It's funny to me the way your voice changes at the mention of his name, why didn't you marry him instead.

(*Long pause.* MR GODBOY *is sitting stiffly.*)

And from what I hear you're not the only one's coming into contact with Hawkins. Who was he with?

GODBOY: (*Coldly*) Pardon?

MAY: Who was your Hawkins with?

GODBOY: He was in the company of a female constable.

MAY: That sounds like the Hawkins I've been hearing about.

GODBOY: (*Still coldly*) Doubtless she has a key part to play in the Merrit Street case, May, given the nature of the offence.

MAY: As long as she's female that's not all she'll have a key part to play in, constable or no constable, from what they say about Hawkins.

GODBOY: (*After a little pause*) There's always gossip about inspectors of a filthy nature.

MAY: Oh, he's of a filthy nature all right, ladies and Hawkins are never out of each other's sight, that's what I hear.

GODBOY: You're talking about Inspector Hawkins, May. There's not, nor never has been no stain on his record.

MAY: That's not where the stains would be. Manly Hawkins!

(MR GODBOY *sits staring straight ahead*.)

MAY: Isn't that what they call him?

GODBOY: That nickname was acquired because he's got the looks and manners of a born policeman. At first it was Irish Hawkins, but he soon put a stop to that, and then it was Mannerly Hawkins, from the respect he'd earned with his politeness, and then people got careless with it and it slipped into Manly, which only a few proven constables ever called him to his face and was – were allowed to get away with it in my hearing, if he thought highly of them to be on intimate returns. (*Little pause*.) As for the female constable, if she's working under Inspector Hawkins, and has been brought in special to do it, it's because she's developed a reputation in her own right. (*Little pause*.) I'm under oath to Duty Officer not to divulge what she's been requested to do in the Merrit Street case, I can only say she's in danger up to the hilt.

MAY: (*Laughs tauntingly*) If she's hanging about hoping the Merrit Street attacker will rip off her skirts to get in her up to the hilt, then that's Hawkins's idea of pleasure too, from what I hear, oh yes, what the Merrit Street attacker don't give her, Hawkins'll make up for.

(*Long pause*. MR GODBOY *sits staring straight ahead*.)

And I'll tell *you* something, I wouldn't mind being in her shoes. With *either* of them.

GODBOY: May I ask, May, may I ask where this gossip you've been
hearing's been taking place?

MAY: Never you mind where.

GODBOY: Because I don't believe you've had the pleasure of seeing
Inspector Hawkins in the flesh.

MAY: And he hasn't had the pleasure of seeing me the same way.
(*Laughs.*) It's a wonder to me they let you come snooping
around the station, you've got no business there, and as for
Manly Hawkins, he'd order you back to the corns and
bunions, which is where you belong, if he noticed you at all,
which he won't.

GODBOY: (*Laughs softly*) He'll notice me, May, when the time
comes.

MAY: Well, I won't be here to see it. (*Significantly picks up and
shakes the cigarette packs.*)
(MR GODBOY *looks at her, looks away.*)
And you remember I said that. (*Little pause, feeling irritably
under her.*) Where's my coat then?

GODBOY: Oh, I do believe I hung it in the new cupboard, dear.
(MAY *sighs, gets up, tramps across the room to the cupboard.*)

MAY: I have to do everything for myself in the place, why can't you
leave me alone?
(*As* MR GODBOY *follows her. She opens the cupboard, stands
thinking as* MR GODBOY *comes up behind her, then leaving the
door open, goes out of the hall door, right, leaving that open also.*
MR GODBOY *is fumbling for the padlock.*)

GODBOY: No dear (*laughs*), it's in the cupboard here.
(*Shakes his fist, then goes out into the hall after her. As he does so
the door, left, opens, and* MAY *comes tramping in holding some
cigarettes and matches, lights up as she settles back on the sofa.* MR
GODBOY *reappears through the kitchen door.*)

MAY: What you doing, following me about like a mongolese
idiot?

GODBOY: I thought you wanted your coat, which is in the cupboard
dear. (*Shuts the kitchen door, comes over to his chair, sits down.*)

MAY: What for? I'm not going anywhere – yet. It was me fags I
wanted. (*Taps ash on the floor.*)

(MR GODBOY *sits staring at her. After a minute gets up, picks up an ashtray from the gramophone table, puts it on the floor beside her, makes to sit down, then goes across, makes to shut the cupboard door, looks quickly at* MAY, *leaves it open and shuts the hall door. Comes back. Sits down. There is a silence.*)

My number one would have laughed, he hated the police.

GODBOY: I know he did, dear, but your first husband and myself was – were comparatively speaking two different kettles of fish.

MAY: Yes he was.

(*She draws on the cigarette, reaches down, stubs it out on the floor beside the ashtray without looking.* MR GODBOY *watches, then goes across, picks up the butt, puts it in the tray.* MAY *watches him.*)

He enjoyed himself, that one did. For one thing he liked goodbye parties.

GODBOY: (*Sitting down*) Pardon dear?

MAY: Nothing. I've got a shock in store for you, that's all. And the first of it is that Eric and Doris is coming down later.

GODBOY: (*After a pause*) Eric and Doris dear? (*In a controlled voice*) Indeed? Tonight dear?

MAY: That's right, but I'm not telling you why, because it's got pleasure in it, and you don't know what that is.

(MR GODBOY *after another pause, gets up, walks over to the cupboard door.*)

GODBOY: I was under the impression we was – were having a quiet night all by ourselves, dear. (*He shuts the cupboard door, comes back.*)

MAY: Was you? (*Points to the cupboard.*) Clear it out.

GODBOY: (*Sitting down*) Pardon, dear?

MAY: Clear it out. Kindly clean that cupboard out of my things, Number Two. (*Claps her hands.*) That you been kind enough to fill it up with. I'm going to be needing them later.

GODBOY: I don't understand dear.

MAY: You will soon enough.

(*There is a long pause.* MAY *claps her hands again.* MR GODBOY *gets to his feet, walks to the cupboard. Stops before it.*)

GODBOY: You want me to get your things out, dear, you actually
    mean?

MAY: That's right, and why should *I* do it (*lights another cigarette*),
    I'm not your slave.

GODBOY: (*Standing before the cupboard*) Dear?

MAY: What now?

GODBOY: Couldn't this trifling chore be left until later, dear?

MAY: No.

GODBOY: There's a question of fetching something in for Doris
    and Eric.

MAY: It's fetched, don't you worry.

    (*There's a pause.* MAY *claps her hands again.* MR GODBOY *steps
    inside the cupboard.*)

    I'm leaving you.

GODBOY: (*Puts his head out*) Pardon dear?

    (MAY *claps her hands.* MR GODBOY *goes back in.*)

    (*Shouting*) Are you still in love with me, dear?

MAY: (*Laughs*) What?

    (MR GODBOY *steps fluently out of the cupboard, shuts the door,
    hurries over to* MAY.)

GODBOY: I've been meaning to inquire for some time, May? (*Sits
    down beside her.*) It's particularly important for me to know
    the answer; I'd like to think there's been happiness for you
    this last two years.

MAY: That's what you like to think, is it?

GODBOY: (*Folds his hands into his lap*) You've got such an amusing
    wit, dear. (*Laughing.*) Oh dear.

MAY: I have, have I? (*Little pause.*) What you think you're doing
    then?

GODBOY: (*Smiling*) Pardon, dear?

MAY: Get back into that cupboard. I'm not going near it and don't
    you think I am.

GODBOY: (*Sits*) The truth is, dear . . .

    (MAY *claps her hands.* MR GODBOY *leaps to his feet, hurries over
    to the cupboard, steps inside. There is a pause.*)

MAY: (*Half singing*) Oh. I'm leaving you, leaving you, leaving
    you.

GODBOY: Pardon dear? (*Head appearing around the cupboard door.*)

MAY: I said, if you was the same kettle of fish as my Number One, you wouldn't have no wound, and if you had, it wouldn't stop you.

GODBOY: (*Steps out of the cupboard*) Specialists have done their best for me dear, and still I defeat them all.

MAY: If you was like Number One, you'd learn to handle me. (*Little pause.*) Once he give me a tanning, and I loved him the more for it.

GODBOY: (*After a long pause*) I have my own way of doing things, dear. Violence to a living creature is not in my nature.

MAY: What you up to, in and out of there like a rabbit from a top hat. Come on (*claps her hands*) Perkins, come on. (MR GODBOY *wheels around, goes back into the cupboard. Steps out again almost at once.*)

GODBOY: The truth of the matter is, dear, I'm not feeling exactly on top of myself.

MAY: Oh yes, it's about time for that, isn't it? And something else I've been thinking, if that wound's down there, why does it hurt you up there?

GODBOY: That's what defeats the specialists, dear. (*Clasping his head, comes over, sits down.*) All they know is, if they solve the one they solve the other.

MAY: (*Gets up, trudges over to the cupboard*) I knew I'd have to do it myself.

GODBOY: No, don't do it, dear, we can do it together after Eric and Doris have left. I'd enjoy that. Just the two of us.

MAY: By then it'll be just the one of us. (*Looks at him.*) I want everything to my hand. (*Nods.*) Besides, knowing Eric he'll forget to come, if there's something at the pictures he wants to see. (*She goes into the cupboard.* MR GODBOY *comes over, stands in indecision, looking yearningly in at her.*)

GODBOY: You say he's gone to the pictures. (*He half reaches for the padlock, takes his hand out, empty.* MAY *comes out with an armful of clothes, drops them on the floor.*)

MAY: That's where he'll be, if I know Eric, he'd be at the pictures

if Doris was dying and the world was changing to mud.
(*Goes in, comes out with more clothes, drops them down as* MR
GODBOY *comes closer*.)
You must be mad, filling this up with my things, then
turning on your wound to get off it. (*Goes in again.*) Oh yes,
and it's only the thought of seeing him . . .
(MR GODBOY, *sidling to the alcove, plunges his hand in behind
the curtain.*)

GODBOY: Yes, he forgot last time, didn't he, dear?
(*He slams the cupboard door shut, simultaneously there is a knock
on the hall door, right, and* MR GODBOY *opens the cupboard door
again. The shutting. The knocking. The opening. All should
come at almost exactly the same instant.* MR GODBOY *stands
holding the cupboard door open, having let go of the pipe. He is
smiling courteously.* MAY *comes out, looks at him, steps very
close, points a finger into his face.*)

MAY: Now what are you . . . ?
(*The knock comes again. She turns to the hall door, goes towards
it.* MR GODBOY *bends down, picks up armfuls of her clothes puts
them back into the cupboard, shuts the cupboard door, as* MAY
opens the hall door.)
I knew you wouldn't forget your May.
(*She stands aside, to let first* ERIC, *then* DORIS *pass. Smiles at*
ERIC. ERIC *is about twenty-five, thin-faced and pale. Black hair
slicked back.* DORIS *is about twenty, taller than* ERIC, *her lips
are bright red, her finger-nails scarlet. She is wearing a new-look
cotton dress, nylon stockings with seams, and stocky, high-heeled
shoes. She walks gingerly, with a slight suggestion of a limp. She
is holding a handbag pressed close to her stomach.*)

ERIC: Hello May. (*He is wearing a raincoat and scarf. He walks
across the room with one shoulder slightly hunched.*)

DORIS: Hello May.
(*She is watched closely by* MR GODBOY, *who is standing now to
one side, his hands over his crotch.*)

MAY: You're a relief for sore eyes, if you hadn't come I'd have
killed you.

GODBOY: (*Following* DORIS, *who has sat down on the sofa*) This is a pleasure, Doris (*in a low voice*).

(ERIC *sits down in one of the utility chairs, adopting a slouched, tough-looking posture.* MAY *comes to stand beside him, puts a hand on his shoulder.*)

MAY: See anything different in here?

ERIC: What? (*Stares around the room, shakes his head.*) No.

MAY: (*Bending her face close to his*) Gon on, something extra.

(ERIC *stares at* MR GODBOY, *who is standing between the armchair and the sofa.*)

ERIC: Him.

(*There is a pause.*)

I mean, last time he wasn't here, when we come down.

(*As* MAY *laughs.*)

DORIS: Yes, there's a –

MAY: Don't spoil it, Doris, let him guess. (*Sharply.*)

ERIC: (*Shakes his head*) What?

(MAY *puts her hands around his neck, pretending to throttle him. He hunches up, makes cinematic gagging sounds.*)

MAY: (*Jerks him upright*) Come on then.

ERIC: What?

(MAY *points* ERIC'S *face to the cupboard, pretends to throttle him further.*)

MAY: Ooo you! What's that then?

(*Little pause, as* DORIS *and* MR GODBOY *watch.*)

ERIC: Oh. (*Little pause.*) A shed.

(MAY *screams with laughter, wags* ERIC'S *head with her hands, as* MR GODBOY *sits down beside* DORIS. *Folds his hands into his lap, looks at her, looks at* MAY *and* ERIC.)

MAY: It's a cupboard we got for you, you midge, what do you think of it?

ERIC: (*After a pause*) It's big.

GODBOY: It was the most capacious obtainable.

(DORIS *nods.* ERIC *looks at the cupboard, puzzled.*)

MAY: Is that what you could do with?

ERIC: What for?

MAY: For locking Doris up in when she's naughty.

(*She laughs, sits down in the chair opposite* ERIC, *then pulls it close to him.* MR GODBOY *says something to* DORIS *in a low voice.*)

ERIC: What?

GODBOY: I was merely saying to Doris that I'd be able to deal with her tomorrow, if things go as planned.

ERIC: Oh.

(ERIC *looks at* DORIS, *who looks down into her lap.*)

MAY: (*To* ERIC) She's lucky, he hasn't touched a foot in six months, except his own, but he'll make an exception out of Doris, and if *you've* got anything coming up, I'll handle it. (*Slaps his knee, laughs.*)

ERIC: Oh, I'm all right, aren't I, Doris?

MAY: That's just the way of it, it's the poor ladies that suffer, it's a good job we don't get corns on our heels. (*To* DORIS.)

DORIS: On my heels?

MAY: On your heels. (*Nods solemnly, then bursts out laughing.*)

ERIC: (*Joins in*) You can't get corns on your heels.

GODBOY: (*To* DORIS) It's a fact that corns can cause as much distress to the whole system as ulcers, which is why I've made arrangements to attend to you properly, Doris.

DORIS: Well (*little pause, looks at* ERIC), I get a bit nervous at being tampered with, see?

ERIC: She's always been like that. Won't go near a doctor.

DORIS: Last time I went he – he – hurt me somewhere.

MAY: Where?

DORIS: Somewhere, that's all.

GODBOY: There's no cause for concern, Doris, I can assure you of that.

MAY: (*Leans over, slaps* ERIC's *knee*) You been doing any more your night-walks, then?

ERIC: What? (*To* MAY, *then to* MR GODBOY) Can you do for her, then?

GODBOY: Indeed. (*Nods at* DORIS.) I'll do for you, Doris.

DORIS: What will you do then?

GODBOY: There'll be a preliminary examination, Doris, to ascertain the extent of its growth, how deep in the imbedment goes, which will be followed by some probing.

DORIS: Probing? Oh.

MAY: (*Nodding her head at* ERIC) Here Eric, I heard you come in the other night, it was morning, almost.

ERIC: Oh. (*Nods. Then to* MR GODBOY) She won't like too much probing, she dead against being tampered with.

GODBOY: Probably a mere lotion will do the trick, or I could administer a little whiff, Doris.

MAY: (*Bends forward to tap* ERIC *on the knee*) What you do out there at night?

ERIC: (*Looks at her*) Nothing. (*To* DORIS) That sounds all right, Dorrie.

DORIS: That's all I'm having.

ERIC: Yes, that's her lot.

DORIS: A little whiff of what?

(MAY *wags her head irritably.*)

GODBOY: (*After a pause*) That will depend on what other symptoms it's been giving you, Doris, otherwise than its throbbing and its size.

MAY: That's enough, isn't it?

ERIC: What?

GODBOY: (*To* DORIS) Any other inconvenience above the pain?

DORIS: (*Shakes her head*) Whiff of what, what'll you –

MAY: (*Simultaneously with* DORIS *and to* MR GODBOY) Isn't that enough?

GODBOY: In which case the lotion applied on sterile pads, or a little whiff.

DORIS: Well, whiff of what?

MAY: (*To* DORIS) Why don't you show it to him now? Go on.
    (*There is a pause.* DORIS *looks down at her handbag, which she is clutching to her stomach.*)

MAY: Go on, give us a look.

ERIC: (*To* MAY) Here, she don't want to do that.

GODBOY: I appreciate that, Doris.

MAY: Oooo. (*Slaps* ERIC *on the knee.*) Aren't they the bashful two.

ERIC: She's like that. She don't like showing herself off.

MAY: It's only a corn we want to see. Go on, slip off your stockings, dear.

167

GODBOY: (*To* MAY) A chiropodist isn't permitted to take public liberties with his customer's feet, dear.

MAY: A chopidist isn't pitted to show his customer's feet, dear. (*Imitating contemptuously.*) Ooooh dear. Don't worry, chopidist, nobody wants to see people's feet at a party, it's music we want. Put a record on, Eric.

ERIC: What? Oh. Righto. (*Gets up, walks over to the gramophone, picks up a record, scans the cover closely and uncomprehendingly, puts it down, picks up another.*)

MAY: (*To* DORIS) You going to have a fling with the chopidist?

DORIS: (*Who is staring straight ahead*) I can't.

MAY: Course you can, what do you mean, can't?

DORIS: (*Voice quavering*) I can't dance with that foot.

MAY: Dance with the other one, then. (*Laughs.*) Or borrow one from the chopidist.

GODBOY: (*To* ERIC, *who has been watching him*) Eric, old boy, if you'll excuse my mentioning it, that one's not for dancing to.

ERIC: (*Who has been about to put the needle on*) What?

MAY: (*To* MR GODBOY) What do you know about what's for dancing to? Eric and me can dance to anything. (*Gets up, goes to the centre of the room, makes dancing movements.*) Put it on, Eric.

ERIC: Oh. Righto. (*Looks at* MR GODBOY, *looks at* MAY, *puts the record on.*) We'll just have a quick one, Dorrie.

(*The record begins. It is one of Churchill's war speeches.* ERIC *stands by the gramophone, bewildered.* DORIS *looks down at her handbag,* MAY *stands still.* MR GODBOY *gets up, walks right across, takes the record off, puts it back in its cover, goes back, sits down.*)

Who was that then?

GODBOY: (*After a pause*) That was Winnie, old boy.

(MAY *goes to the record pile.* ERIC *joins her, they begin to sort through the records.*)

(*To* DORIS) Five years ago there wasn't a man in this country wouldn't have laid down his life for Winnie, and glad to do it.

(MAY *whispers something to* ERIC, *laughs.*)

Of course the war wouldn't mean much to Eric, as he was

safe out of it, I'm glad to say for his sake.

ERIC: (*Turning*) What?

GODBOY: I was merely wondering, Eric, where were you precisely when the V-2s commenced dropping?

ERIC: Me?

GODBOY: In 1944 to be frank, old boy. Where were you precisely?

ERIC: (*Thinks, looks at* DORIS) I was in Wales, wasn't I, Dorrie, in that home?

GODBOY: Now refresh my memory, old boy, were there V-2s dropping in Wales?

ERIC: V – what? (*Little pause.*) Here, I never had nothing like that. (*Indignantly.*)

MAY: (*Puts a record on the gramophone*) What you going on at him for – you'd have ridden on a V-2 if they'd let you wear your special constable uniform. This one (*as the music starts*) was too nice and young to get messed up in that.

(*She holds out her arms, they start to dance,* ERIC *glancing apprehensively at* DORIS. MAY *leads* ERIC *further into a corner of the room, dancing amorously,* DORIS *and* MR GODBOY *watching.*)

GODBOY: Indeed Eric was to young for combat, and I don't hold it against him, Doris.

(DORIS *goes on watching the dancing, tense.*)

But there was – were some youths on the other side who weren't too young. Mere children of nine were issued with pitchforks and ordered to stand and resist. Those were the sort of people Winnie had to stamp out (*stamps his foot*) to make the country safe for the likes of Eric, who is a very pleasant boy, as I'm the first to admit. They didn't teach him to read in Wales then?

(*Little pause.* DORIS *shakes her head.*)

So frankly, between you and me, Doris, as May and Eric wouldn't understand as they naturally like to enjoy themselves, that's why I'm against having that record put on for joking at. Those were terrible days. (*Little pause.*) And that record brings back happy memories of them. How's your toe now?

(DORIS *shrugs*.)

I hadn't forgotten about it, Doris, there was something I had
to get out of the way first, which I'm dealing with now.

(*Looks at* MAY.)

(*The music stops.* MAY *does a grotesque curtsey.* ERIC *laughs,
looks towards* DORIS, *sees her face, stops laughing.* MAY *looks at*
DORIS *and* MR GODBOY, *keeps a hold on* ERIC's *arm.*)

MAY: What's he off on now, the double Dublin tenant and wife
gasser?

ERIC: What?

MAY: His head is filled with murder, that's all he thinks about,
isn't it, chopidist? That and Inspector Manly Mannerly Irish
Hawkins.

GODBOY: Indeed, dear, I keep in touch, merely.

MAY: (*To* ERIC) Come on, let's get our hands on something I've
got special in the kitchen.

(*Leads him towards the kitchen. He looks at* DORIS, *who glares
at him.*)

(DORIS *and* MR GODBOY *sit stiffly on the sofa, staring straight
ahead. There are noises from the kitchen, a crashing sound, a
scream of* MAY's *laughter. A pause. Then* MR GODBOY *gets up,
goes to the gramophone. As he does so,* ERIC *comes in, his coat
and scarf over his arm, looks at* DORIS, *who turns away from
him, plods across the room to the cupboard, opens it.*)

GODBOY: (*With his back to* ERIC *and* DORIS) My interest in
murder is connected to my interest in police work, Doris,
needless to say, which goes back a long way. My years as
Special Constable during the war naturally heightened my
interest. That's all there is to it, in spite of May's hints, I
hope you won't . . .

(MR GODBOY *turns, as* ERIC, *having shut the door of the
cupboard, walks back across the room to the kitchen door.
Watches him.* ERIC *looks at* DORIS, *whose face is still averted,
stands at the kitchen door.*)

ERIC: Well, I'll just . . .

(*He shrugs, nods, goes into the kitchen, leaves door open.* DORIS
sits staring ahead. MR GODBOY *looks towards the kitchen door,*

from which comes a scream of MAY's *laughter: goes towards it to shut it when it slams noisily from inside. He stops. Goes back to the sofa, sits down. There is a pause.*)

GODBOY: May has a funny sense of humour, she makes me chuckle out loud sometimes. (*Little pause.*) You can't understand the workings of murder until you understand the working of the police. The two things are connected. (*Little pause.*) Do you follow me there, Doris?

(*Throughout the following conversation there are noises from the kitchen, mainly of* MAY's *laughter, but gradually with* ERIC's *joining in.*)

DORIS: (*Shrugs*) I don't like the police.

GODBOY: (*Swings his head around, looks at her*) Indeed? I'm sorry to hear you say that, Doris, very sorry. Have you any grounds?

DORIS: (*Shrugs. After a long pause, looks down at her handbag*) They searched me once. In front of – people.

GODBOY: (*After a pause*) Well, Doris, justice has not only got to be done, it's got to be seen to be done. That's what makes our country great. (*Pause.*) I'm sure you'll admit they did a good job of it.

(*Long pause, as* DORIS *continues to stare down.*)

Pardon a little ignorance, unfortunately searching wasn't one of my duties, how far exactly did they authorize themselves to go?

DORIS: (*Whispering*) Everything. They took off me everything.

GODBOY: Indeed? (*Long pause.*) That would include, pardon my asking, to get the details straight in my head (*puts a hand to his head*), stockings, under-garments such as for instance camiknicks and bra, naturally? (*Little pause.*) Am I right in my guess?

DORIS: Me everything.

GODBOY: Yes, they've got to be thorough. (*Little pause.*) It was male officers took part in this.

DORIS: They was peeking. One of them was.

GODBOY: Superintending the legality, Doris, merely, that's all. Can you remember who it was precisely? Did you see his face?

DORIS: I don't know, I kept me eyes down.

GODBOY: (*After a pause*) Indeed. (*Little pause.*) As a matter of
    interest, Doris, and strictly privately, May's likely to go off
    on a little trip.
    (*Sudden scream of laughter from* MAY.)
DORIS: Oh? She never said.
GODBOY: No, I intend it to come as a complete and utter surprise
    to her. She won't know about it until she's on her way,
    virtually.
    (*Another scream of laughter.*)
    She's got it coming to her, she deserves a long rest.
DORIS: When's she going then?
    (*Little pause.*)
GODBOY: I've got it planned so that with luck she'll be gone by
    tomorrow.
    (*Waits through another scream.*)
    I think I can promise you that.
DORIS: That'll be nice.
GODBOY: (*Turns his head, looks at her*) I'm glad you've said that,
    Doris.
    (*The kitchen door opens, and* ERIC *puts his head around it. He is
    grinning.*)
ERIC: Who's for stout, then?
    (*Little pause.*)
GODBOY: No thank you, Eric.
    (ERIC *looks straight at* DORIS. *She stares ahead.*)
ERIC: Dorrie?
    (*She continues to stare ahead.*)
    Dorrie? (ERIC *looks at her a moment longer, withdraws, closes
    the door.*)
DORIS: Is she going a long way away?
GODBOY: Purley, probably. (*Little pause.*) I only mention it now
    merely so you won't wonder at her abrupt disappearance
    tomorrow.
    (*The door opens again.* ERIC, *grinning, puts his head in.*)
ERIC: Who's for a drop of something else, then?
    (MR GODBOY *looks at him,* DORIS *stares straight ahead.*)
    She's got a bottle of gin in there.

GODBOY: No thank you, Eric.

ERIC: Dorrie?

(She continues to stare ahead.)

What?

(Withdraws his head, shuts the door. There is a burst of laughter from MAY.)

GODBOY: *(After a pause)* How do you feel about that surprise news, Doris?

DORIS: *(After another scream)* It'll be quiet without her.

GODBOY: Indeed. *(Nods.)* That's one thing I'm expecting. *(Little pause.)* It would be best if I was to arrange our appointment now. *(Takes the padlock out of his pocket, puts it back hurriedly, takes out a diary.)* As you now realize I shall be free as of tomorrow on. I'll be ready to get down to it before it's too late. *(There is a silence.)* I'm referring to your toe, Doris. What do you say to tomorrow tea-time?

(MR GODBOY looks at DORIS, who shrugs nervously, looks down.)

Righto, tomorrow tea-time?

DORIS: What is, I mean, this whiff you was – whiff of something . . .

(The door opens. ERIC comes in. He is slightly drunk.)

ERIC: Comfy? *(Long pause.)* That May. *(Laughs.)*

DORIS: *(Looks at him vindictively)* May's going away tomorrow.

(MR GODBOY looks at her.)

ERIC: She hasn't said nothing.

GODBOY: Only you're to keep it quiet, old boy, it's a surprise to May, don't let anything drop.

(ERIC thinks. Laughs.)

Why do you laugh, old boy?

ERIC: Well, she keeps saying she's got a surprise laid up for you.

GODBOY: Indeed? What type of surprise precisely, Eric?

ERIC: She won't tell, she keeps tapping her nose and laughing over it, but I got a part in it.

GODBOY: Indeed, Eric, what's that?

ERIC: You got to wait. *(Holds up his hand.)* Eh, Dorrie?

(She stares ahead. There is a silence, then the sound of a lavatory

173

flushing off, right, and the door, right, opens. MAY *enters the room, one arm raised, she looks at* ERIC, *they lower their arms simultaneously and begin to sing.*)

MAY: (*As* MAY *advances on* MR GODBOY) Now is the hour.

ERIC: When I must say goodbye.

> (*They sing the song through,* MR GODBOY *and* DORIS *sitting staring straight ahead, until the last few lines, when* MR GODBOY *begins to sing. He sings the last line by himself as* MAY *throws herself laughing into* ERIC'S *arms and lights dim.*)

SCENE 2

Lights up. Half an hour later. DORIS *and* MR GODBOY *still sitting on the sofa, staring directly ahead. There is a sound of a door slamming, the kitchen-hall door, left.* MAY *comes in through the kitchen door, left. She is carrying a glass. She sits down on one of the utility chairs, left, drinks from her glass.* MR GODBOY *and* DORIS *watch her.*

DORIS: (*After a pause, voice quavering*) Where's Eric then?

MAY: (*Sipping from her glass*) Gone, dear.

> (*There is a little silence.*)

DORIS: Where?

MAY: Don't know. (*Little pause.*) Last I saw he was lurching down the hall. (*Looks at her sharply.*) Where's he go most nights, I hear him coming in all hours.

DORIS: (*After a pause*) For walks. (*Pause.*) He said he'd stop. He said he wouldn't any more.

GODBOY: Doubtless he'll come straight in up to the flat, Doris.

MAY: Doubtless. (*Little pause. Looks at* DORIS) What for? (*Little pause.*) Oh, drink puts Eric in a talking mood, we got the same problems, Eric and me. (*Shakes his head.*) But I'm getting over mine.

GODBOY: Pardon, dear.

MAY: She knows what I mean. (*Stares at* DORIS.)

> (DORIS, *after a pause, gets up, stands for a moment with her handbag, half opened, clasped to her stomach, then walks limping to the door, right.*)

(*Silkily*) Goodbye, dear.

(MR GODBOY *gets up, follows* DORIS, *holds the door open for her.*)

GODBOY: Good night, Doris.

DORIS: He said he wouldn't go out nights any more.

GODBOY: Don't you worry about him, Doris, he'll be back in no time. (*Little pause.*) And see you as arranged (*slapping his pocket*), tea-time.

(DORIS *goes out.* MR GODBOY *puts his head into the hall, watches for a second, then shuts the door, comes back.* MAY *drinks from her glass and watches him.*)

MAY: Coming tomorrow is she?

GODBOY: Pardon dear? Oh, yes, tomorrow seemed best.

MAY: Well, you'll have a free hand tomorrow.

(MR GODBOY *looks at her.*)

Not that a free hand with her's worth a eunuch's while.

GODBOY: Pardon dear?

(MAY *looks at him, shrugs, drinks.*)

(*After a pause.*) Well dear, that was a pleasant evening, I must say.

MAY: Must you? Why?

(MR GODBOY *stares at her.*)

Why must you say it?

GODBOY: I thought you must be enjoying yourself. (*Long pause.*) Who's for bed, dear?

MAY: Pardon, dear? (*Mimicking.*)

(MR GODBOY *laughs. There is a pause. He goes to the cupboard, swerves on to the guppies.* MAY *sits watching him. He turns, looks, nods, smiles.*)

GODBOY: Well, dear, (*stretches*) well (*yawns*) I need my bed, I must – (*stops himself*).

MAY: What for?

GODBOY: Why, for a good night's sleep, dear.

MAY: That what you think I need?

GODBOY: Par—

MAY: (*Simultaneously*) Pardon dear? A good night's sleep which is you curled up and clinging to the edge of your side like a winkle. A good night's sleep, which is me blinking into the darkness and thinking about what I had with Number One and how it won't never come no more. (*Little pause.*) Why do you wear two pair of pyjamas?

GODBOY: Merely, dear because I'm susceptible to cold, just as you prefer your hottie, why do you ask?

MAY: My hottie's got more bed-life in it than you have. (*Pause.*) You know what I'm trying to say to you?

GODBOY: No dear.

MAY: Can't you even guess?

GODBOY: (*After a little pause*) No dear.

MAY: More fool you, then. (*Slowly, significantly.*)

(*She gets up, goes to the kitchen, leaves the door open.* MR GODBOY *looks at the cupboard, then towards the kitchen door. Goes on tiptoe to the kitchen door, shuts it. Then hurries to the cupboard.*)

(*Flinging open the kitchen door*) Leave it open.

(MR GODBOY *stops, turns around.*)

Leave it open. I've had enough of you closing things up on me, now I'm after space.

(*She goes to the door, left, opens it, goes into the bedroom.* MR GODBOY *stares after her, then goes quietly to the cupboard, opens it. Goes to the alcove, checks the cylinder, then turns around, goes to the guppies.*)

GODBOY: Don't forget your night-things in the cupboard, dear. I've left the door open for you to make your selection from.

(MAY *appears at the bedroom door, holding a suitcase open. She stares at him. He stays bent away from her, gestures with his hands backwards.*)

I was merely reminding you of your nighties.

MAY: Yes, I'll be needing those. (*Significantly.*)

(*She walks across to the cupboard, steps in.* MR GODBOY *whirls round, suddenly remembers padlock, snatches it out, turns the key to open it, opens it, drops the key, picks the key up, makes a go at putting it back, then frantically puts it in his mouth, steals across, puts the padlock open and ready in the door-jamb hook, then key still in his mouth, whips to the alcove, grabs the tubing, reaches*)

for the door with his left hand, as MAY *steps out with the clothes.*
MR GODBOY *slams the door, whirls around.* MAY *turns as he*
holds the tubing behind him, walks up to him, puts her face close
to his.)
(*Shouts*) Stop slamming, I said.
(*She gives him a push with her arms.* MR GODBOY *steps back,*
swallows the key, as MAY *turns away.*)
Open it up again.
(MR GODBOY *stands watching, swallowing and coughing*
slightly as MAY *disappears into the bedroom, then gagging a*
little, opens the cupboard door, stands with the pipe held down,
waiting.)
(*Calling*) You wouldn't notice if the house was collapsing
around your eyes.

GODBOY: True, dear, very true.
(*He swallows experimentally.* MAY *reappears, begins to hum*
'Now is the hour . . .')

MAY: (*Stares at him*) What you doing then?

GODBOY: (*Holding the pipe behind him*) Thinking merely, dear.

MAY: About murder merely dear?
(GODBOY *laughs.*)
Or about how much you'd miss me merely dear?

GODBOY: (*Laughs again. Wags his head*) Oh May! (*Coughs again.*)
(MAY *comes towards him, stands in front of him.*)

MAY: Oooh *you.* (*Shakes her head.*) Ape!
(*Turns, plods back towards the door, left, stops, turns, goes back*
to the cupboard. MR GODBOY *watches tensely. She stands in*
front of it, half enters it. MR GODBOY *moves forward.* MAY
turns.)
No. (*Holds up a hand.*) No, not now you don't, no help from
you thank you. Go nurse your wound. (*Significantly*) You're
too *late.*
(MR GODBOY *stops, takes a pace back.* MAY *enters the*
cupboard. MR GODBOY *leaps forward. There is a knock on the*
door right. He stops, stares towards it.)
(*Now bending down, her buttocks sticking out of the cupboard*)
Answer it, then.

177

MR GODBOY *hesitates, then thrusts the pipe back into the alcove, goes towards the door, opens it a fraction.*)

GODBOY: Oh. (*Little pause.*) Hello.

(MAY *is now down on all fours, buttocks sticking out of the cupboard.*)

DORIS: (*But not distinct*) I can't find him.

(MR GODBOY *stares in agony at the cupboard, into which* MAY *has vanished. Holds the door open.* DORIS *walks gingerly a few steps into the room.*)

GODBOY: (*Stares at* DORIS) I should tell you in all fairness we was – were just preparing ourselves for beddy-byes. (*Laughs.*) Doris.

DORIS: (*Frightened*) Eric's not there!

GODBOY: Indeed!

(*He glances towards the cupboard.* MAY'*s buttocks reappear, slowly.* DORIS *watches.*)

Well, I can assure he's not with May or me, I'm afraid to say. (*Holds the door open wide.*) Have you glanced in your toilet?

DORIS: (*Shakes her head*) He's not there.

GODBOY: In which case I gladly give you permission to knock on our toilet.

DORIS: He's not there.

(MR GODBOY *watches* MAY *back out of the cupboard, an armful of clothes held to her waist. She looks at* DORIS, *shakes her head contemptuously, then goes across to the room left.*)

GODBOY: Indeed? Not in the toilets you say. You do surprise me, but it merely means he must be somewhere else.

(*He watches* MAY *come out of the room, go into the cupboard again.*)

DORIS: He said he wouldn't any more, he said, he does funny things when he's had too much.

(*She stares at* MAY'*s back accusingly.* MR GODBOY'*s head moves in anguish between* DORIS *and the cupboard.*)

GODBOY: Not to worry, Doris, my advice to you is to phone the hospitals from the corner call-box.

DORIS: Hospitals!

GODBOY: (*As* MAY *comes out again*) They have the authority to put you in touch with the latest accident cases and mortuary victims. So not to worry – May dear!

DORIS: No, he doesn't get hurt, he goes round and round, he says his head does.

GODBOY: Now Doris, that covers hospitals, mortuaries, toilets, which is all I can think of at the moment (*desperately as* MAY *comes back*), so pop upstairs and get a good night's rest. (*He steps in front of the cupboard with his arms out.*) May dear, did you hear that? Eric has mysteriously vanished!
(MAY *stops, looks at him, looks at* DORIS, *shakes her head contemptuously.*)

MAY: What a pair, oooh you lovely things, he's gone to clear his head, like I told you. (*Stares at* DORIS.) And if he *had* gone for a bit of something else, I wouldn't blame him.
MR GODBOY *resolutely stands before the cupboard as* MAY *tries to pass.*)

GODBOY: But we have reason to believe that the situation could develop into something more seriously tragic, dear. Doris is thinking in terms of fatal accidents.

MAY: (*After a moment, looking from one to the other*) I'll tell you something, the same what I've been telling him.
(*She nods to* MR GODBOY, *who as* MAY *goes to stand close to* DORIS, *is attempting to shut the cupboard door behind his back against a piece of hanging-out cloth.*)
Because this is the last chance I'll get as things down here have come to a head at last, and that's if you made your Eric welcome, he'd be up there, inside, and you know who I mean, who a man ought to be inside of. You don't give him what he needs, Doris Hoyden, and he'll do what I'm doing to him, who doesn't give me the same.
(*She nods at* MR GODBOY, *who has now turned around and is wrestling with the cupboard door face on.*)

GODBOY: Indeed dear, there's no doubt about that.

MAY: Or you'll end up like him, hanging about the police station and chasing after an Inspector Hawkins as if he'd do his work for him.

GODBOY: (*Shuts the cupboard at last, turns around, stands against the door grinning*) Exactly what I say to you, Doris, let the police handle it.

(*There is the squeal of tyres outside. Pause. They listen.*)

DORIS: Oh no, no, I'm not going near them.

MAY: Ooooh what a pair! (*Turns, goes to the door, stops, looks back, shakes her head, goes into the room, left.*)

GODBOY: Now Doris dear, as May says, not to worry, not to worry. Also as May says, there's the police outside near at hand, you could go and bother them, I merely mean (*goes to the hall door, right, opens it*) this tramping about isn't doing our corn any good, and the best thing for you all said and done is to aim for some shut-eye. (*He holds the door open, gestures usheringly out of the door, stops, cocks his head.*) And who's that coming in now if I'm not mistaken.

(*He steps out into the hall, DORIS behind him.*)

(*HAWKINS, as yet unseen, says something inaudible. MR GODBOY backs into the room, forcing DORIS back behind him.*)

That is my name, yes.

HAWKINS: (*Says something else.*)

(*MR GODBOY stands at the door as DORIS peers over his shoulder, stares in alarm, then hurries away, goes to sit down in a corner of the sofa, her face turned away.*)

GODBOY: Indeed, sir, indeed.

(*He stands aside to let HAWKINS in. His face wears an expression of bemused reverence. HAWKINS steps in, steps out again. His voice audible in a shout.*)

HAWKINS: All right boys, wait out in the car there and keep the engine humming, boys. (*He enters. He is wearing a smart suit, a carnation in his button-hole. And is carrying a trilby. He is tall, broad-shouldered, flush-faced, tough-looking, forty-five. He comes past MR GODBOY into the centre of the room, looks at DORIS, who is facing away, nods.*) Evening ma'am.

(*DORIS nods, mumbles, without looking at him. MR GODBOY stands staring at HAWKINS's back in a kind of rapture. Then holds out his hand, advances around him at the precise moment that HAWKINS revolves, so that again MR GODBOY's hand is held out to HAWKINS's back. Drops his hand, clears his throat as*

HAWKINS *turns again. They face each other.*)

GODBOY: Pardon me, sir, but it is Inspector Hawkins sir, isn't it? This is an honour, sir. (*Little pause.*) Indeed.

HAWKINS: Thank you, Mr Godboy, Duty Officer Larkin said I'd be known on the premises if I took the liberty of dropping in out of the night. (*Looks at* DORIS.)

GODBOY: (*Nodding*) We was colleagues during the war years, sir, in a manner of speaking, and recently since you've been back I've exchanged nods at you down at the station, sir, although doubtless you've been too much on the job to pay them much attention.

(*As he holds out his hand again tentatively,* HAWKINS *goes smoothly over to* DORIS, *at whom he has been smiling.*)

HAWKINS: And is it Mrs Godboy then?

(DORIS *shakes her head, looks away.*)

GODBOY: (*Coming over*) No, Mrs Godboy is busy in the bedroom, her work there is never done, as they say (*picks up quickly a few of the clothes* MAY *has dropped*), although I'm particularly anxious for her to meet you. (*Straightens.*) This young lady's from the upstairs premises, she's lost her husband for the moment. (*Laughs.*) May, dear! May! (*Goes over, knocks on the door.*) May! (*Opens the door, shoves the clothes in while calling out.*) There's someone here I'm anxious for you to meet.

(HAWKINS *has been standing close to* DORIS, *who sits tight, staring ahead.*)

HAWKINS: Lost your husband, have you, if he's missing too long, you call on us then.

GODBOY: May, dear, there's Inspector Hawkins himself in the parlour.

HAWKINS: (*Winks, nods at* DORIS) The husband we can't return, we replace. (*Laughs.*)

DORIS: (*In a whisper*) Thank you.

(MAY *appears at the door,* MR GODBOY *in front of her. She has a mountain of clothes in her arms.* MR GODBOY *steps around her, puts an arm around her waist, clears his throat to attract* HAWKINS's *attention.* MAY *stares at* HAWKINS *cynically.*)

HAWKINS: (*Turns*) I was just saying to the young lady, there's a pick of the boys at the station.

GODBOY: (*Laughs*) I've been hoping that you two was – would come face to face before too late, too long, I merely – the idea of it means a lot to me, this is my wife, Inspector Hawkins, May Godboy.

HAWKINS: (*Nods, smiles, revolves his trilby in his hands*) It's a great pleasure m'am.

(MAY *drops a few clothes from the top of the pile which* MR GODBOY *tries to catch, then bends down to pick up.*)

MAY: It's the dream of his life, to show you off at me.

GODBOY: (*Straightening, puts the clothes back on the pile*) Pardon dear? (*As a few more clothes drop from the bottom of the pile, laughs, bends down again.*)

MAY: And he only just pulled it off, a day later you'd have missed me.

HAWKINS: Now I call that flattering. (*Little pause.*) You're taking a trip, are you?

GODBOY: (*Now fishing between* MAY's *legs for an article of underclothing*) Pardon, sir? A trip (*laughs*), no, not that she knows of, eh, May dear, oops, pardon, dear.

MAY: I might be. (*Nods.*)

HAWKINS: (*Laughs*) Ah, the ladies need little trips as much as the ladies' husbands.

(*He turns, does a nod-wink at* DORIS, *who is still staring desperately ahead.*)

GODBOY: Pardon? (*Straightens, looks smiling from one to the other.*)

MAY: Have you come to arrest him, he spends all his time down at that station of yours he'd be better in the nog behind it.

GODBOY: (*Laughs, takes all the clothes out of* MAY's *arms*) Not even Inspector Hawkins can arrest me *before* I commit my offence, May dear. (*He goes into the bedroom.*)

HAWKINS: No, the truth, is m'am, that cruising around in the neighbourhood, with a spot of waiting ahead of me, I remembered Larkins mentioning Mr Godboy's name, and thinking to meet some of the people on top of it all (*turns, nods at* DORIS), I thought to myself, why not look in for a minute as the lights from your home were cheering up the darkness, like an invitation it seemed. (*Turns, nods to* DORIS *again.*) If I'm not intruding, that is.

MAY: Well, where's this female constable they're all talking about that's turned up so sudden, don't I get to see her?

HAWKINS: (*Little pause*) Is it Constable Hedderley you mean?
(*As* MR GODBOY *comes back out of the room, stands beside* MAY *again.*)
Well, to tell you a secret (*turns to look at* DORIS), Constable Hedderley's out on a very special duty just a minute or two away, so if you hear a strange commotion, as will be the ringing of police bells, the blowing of police whistles, the barking of police dogs, it'll be that Constable Hedderley's pulled it off and I'll be on my way in a hurry.

GODBOY: The Merrit Street case!

HAWKINS: (*After a pause, looks at* MR GODBOY) Well, and so it is. There's the mind of a natural policeman for you.
(MR GODBOY *swells proudly, looks at* MAY, *who turns her face from him.*)
I gave orders there was to be no gossip, so I'll be having a word or two that'll boil Larkins' ears in the morning (*laughs, nods at* DORIS), but there's no harm in mentioning it now, as you're under my personal eye (*nods to* DORIS *again*), the truth is that Constable Hedderley's under a street lamp and fiddling in the line of duty with suspenders and stockings and generally behaving temptingly, and all about Merrit Street the boys are scattered, waiting for the attacker to start his indecent assault on our provocative piece of bait, who's also carrying a handbag to tempt him further.

GODBOY: Masterly, Mannerly, Masterly.
(HAWKINS *looks at him.*)

MAY: Yes, that's nice, but what if he gets into this Hedderley before they get there, or can't stop him once he gets going. There's some men I knew, one in particular I was married to once (*looks at* MR GODBOY), couldn't have been bombed off a lady he'd get that —
(HAWKINS *laughs, winks-nods to* DORIS.)

GODBOY: Now my dear, all of Inspector Hawkins' finest combined can handle any man going.

HAWKINS: Don't you worry, m'am, Constable Hedderley will toss him off as soon as look at him.

MAY: Oh, will she! (*Lets out a screech of laughter.*)

(HAWKINS *laughs, nods towards* DORIS. MR GODBOY, *baffled, chuckles.*)

(*After a silence*) Yes, it's not only from him I heard about you, Manly.

(HAWKINS *looks at her. Chuckles.* MAY *chuckles.* HAWKINS *looks towards* DORIS, *who smiles awkwardly, goes on chuckling.*)

HAWKINS: Well no, no, I have to keep myself free to move in any direction. I can be to Hedderley's side in thirty seconds with the car waiting, so don't you disturb yourself on Hedderley's account, m'am.

GODBOY: That's what they mean by springing a trap, dear.

MAY: Yes, well I got to do some springing myself, out of my own trap.

(*She unwinds* MR GODBOY's *arm, which has replaced itself around her waist, goes back into the room, slams the door.* MR GODBOY *turns, stares after her, then opens the door, puts his head in as* HAWKINS *goes over, stands near to* DORIS , *smiles at her, nods.*)

GODBOY: What about a cup for Inspector Mannerly Hawkins, dear?

(MAY *says something inaudible but clearly abusive.* MR GODBOY *emerges, embarrassed, looks towards where* HAWKINS *was, then turns to where he is now, standing beside* DORIS.)

As I say, her work is never done. (*Little pause, then significantly*), although it soon will be, if I finish off a little plan of mine.

(*Pause.* HAWKINS *continues to smile at* DORIS, *who sits stiffly, smiling, staring ahead.*)

Would you care for a (*looks about him*) stout, sir?

HAWKINS: (*Shakes his head*) Oh, no, no, thank you very much, only if there's one available.

GODBOY: Indeed there is. (*He hurries to the kitchen.*)

HAWKINS: (*To* DORIS) I hope I haven't been frightening you, ma'am, with my talk of the Merrit Street rapist?

(DORIS *shakes her head.*)

We come into contact with such terrible things, we forget the peace of mind of the innocent. (*Little pause.*) Ah, but still the city's a place at night, a violent place, and there's not a corner in it you can't hear its horror come screaming for you, if you stand there listening still as a nun. (*Little pause.*) Do you know what I mean?

(DORIS *nods.*)

(*Looks at her.*) When I was a boy, and yourself a girl, we wouldn't have believed it then,

(DORIS *looks quickly up again, then down*)

would we? (*Little pause.*) And now I go about like all the nuns that ever were, waiting for the messages or listening to the screams, and it's only when I'm talking with someone like yourself, ma'am, that I remember there was a time of innocence for all of us. (*Little pause.*) And that's the truth.

(MR GODBOY *enters, carrying a bottle of stout, and a glass. As he pours the stout.*)

GODBOY: This is indeed good news about the Merrit Street case. It'll mean another feather in your cap, Man – Inspector, rape rates almost as high as murder in some quarters (HAWKINS *still looking at* DORIS)

although not (*significantly, handing* HAWKINS *the drink*) in my own personal opinion, frankly.

HAWKINS: (*Takes the glass, nods*) My best to you, Mr Godboy, ma'am.

(*Holding the glass in toast, quickly to* MR GODBOY, *then a fraction longer to* DORIS, *sips, stares about the room, sees the guppies.*)

GODBOY: (*Clears his throat*) In –

HAWKINS: (*Saunters over to the case*) Goldfish, now?

GODBOY: Um, no sir, in fact known as guppies, sir. Gups (*laughs*), we call them.

HAWKINS: And what nimble little fellows they are, darting this way and that (*bending over*), I like them, I like them for their speed.

(MR GODBOY *comes over to the guppie case, stands on the other side, bends over it.*)

GODBOY: Yes, they are quick, very quick. (*Puts a finger in reflectively.*) Inspector there's a question um I'd be interested to hear your personal view on.

(*As* HAWKINS *moves smoothly back to* DORIS, *sits down in one of the utility chairs next to her.*)

Do you think of your top murderer as a basically common or garden chap?

(HAWKINS *whimsically offers his glass to* DORIS, *who shakes her head, looks down into her lap.*)

I merely ask, because there's no doubt that some types of it are on the increase, although I've got no sympathies for the wounded veterans back from the front who lay about harmless old ladies for petty cash.

(*As again* HAWKINS *offers* DORIS *his glass, with insistent nods and smiles.*)

No, I've no time for them, that's a mixture of bad experiences and bad upbringing on the part of soft parents.

(*As* DORIS *is finally forced to take a sip.*)

No, I'm referring to a different specimen altogether, your cool-blooded killer who has the nerve and is prepared to go through with it to the final consequences, as in the case of O'Higgs, the wife and female-tenant gasser, for instance, merely.

(*He looks up, looks around, sees* HAWKINS *sipping from his stout, stares at him. There is a pause.*)

As you may remember, sir, I've had a little time on the force to my credit.

HAWKINS: Oh yes, a special constable wasn't it? (*Sips.*) Not quite a fully-paid up street-beater like myself.

GODBOY: Indeed. Unfortunately I was disqualified from submitting a full application owing to a mixture of age and a wound sustained in an accident. A rough-house that got beyond itself. (*Little pause.*) Children will be children, no blame was officially attached although malice was definitely involved. (*Comes over, sits down beside* HAWKINS *in the other utility chair.*) Pardon me. Of course, a lot of it was checking padlocks in the evening, Mannerly, giving tea to the bombed-outs which between you and me – and is no secret – made nuisances of themselves when in a state of shock and had to be restrained, and added to which there was molest-arrest – taking into custody. (*Shaking his head.*) I merely mean aliens who had no business in the country in the first place and had to be locked up in the interests of the security of the nation. (*Little pause, as* HAWKINS *sips again, looks towards* DORIS.) But mainly on the whole I was called on to assist in breaking the news in cases of fatal disasters. (*Little pause.*) I sometimes spent six hours a day in breaking tragic news, Inspector Manly, as you can imagine, I tried to do it politely but firmly. (MAY *comes out of the room, left, walks around to the cupboard, opens it, looks in.* MR GODBOY *watches, then as* MAY *looks in the second cupboard.*)

HAWKINS: So (*slowly*) you might say you did all our dirtiest work for us?

GODBOY: It was an honour (*watching* MAY) Hawkins, Manly, Inspector Hawkins. (*Laughs.*) Can I help dear?
(*As* MAY *comes back across the room, leaving the cupboard doors open, and entering the room, left.*)
Her work is never –
(*Interrupted by the slamming of the door.*)
Um (*Little pause*), indeed, it's because of my time on the force that I'm never likely to be one of those who'd forget our Pierpoint . . .

HAWKINS: Pierpoint?

GODBOY: Winnie, I merely mean, Inspector. (*Shakes his head, gets up, goes to the cupboard doors, shuts them.*) Pardon me, or runs about like lots of them do nowadays making a mockery out of due procedure in the country especially . . .
(*Comes back, stops, as the door, left, opens,* MAY *stands there for a second then slams the door.*)
Her work is never – (*laughs*) especially when it's an established

fact (*sits down*) that it's always properly and ceremoniously carried out with chaplains, doctors and officials in attendance.

(*Pause, looks at* HAWKINS, *who stares at him.*)

HAWKINS: (*After a pause*) Is it hanging you're talking about, then?

GODBOY: Indeed sir. (*Nods.*) It's my own personal considered opinion now you bring the subject into the open, frankly, that a man who is going to end up that way knows about it long before, from day-dreams and other symptoms, as in the case of (*little pause, looks at* HAWKINS *hard*) the gasser O'Higgs, for instance.

HAWKINS: (*After a long pause, drains off his glass, stares into it*) Mr Godboy – (*slight pause*) Mr Godboy, would you have something I could wash this down with, now?

GODBOY: Oh. Well, I'm sorry to say that was the last of the stout, there's nothing left in the kitchen except some gin and of course water.

HAWKINS: Now that would be very nice, that's very kind, a glass of gin and water would do the trick for me nicely, Mr Godboy.

GODBOY: (*Gets up, takes* HAWKINS' *glass*) An honour, Mannerly. (*Goes out into the kitchen.*)

HAWKINS: (*After a pause*) Tell me, ma'am, I think I've forgotten your name already, or never asked in my rudeness.

DORIS: (*In a low voice*) Doris Hoyden.

HAWKINS: Ah. (*Little pause.*) And I've never seen you before, Doris Hoyden?

(DORIS *shakes her head.*)

It's as if I'd had a peep of you sometime, there are little pictures going on in my mind, of a peep.

(DORIS *shakes her head.*)

It's the way you sit with your eyes down, lowered, that recalls – (*little pause*) well, it recalls all the girls of the village of my boyhood in Mayo, and none of the girls of the lonely policeman's life in the city of London. (*Leans a little closer.*) Are you one of those that likes to dance, now?

(DORIS *shakes her head.*)

Ah, but you'd be a natural dancer, I can see that, Doris, not one of those that leads a man, you'd know enough to give in to him in his movements.

(*He leans a little closer. The door right, opens, and* MAY *comes out. Looks at* HAWKINS *and* DORIS, *crosses in front of them.*)

(*Straightening away from* DORIS) Ma'am. (*Nods, smiles.*)

(MAY *stares at him, goes on out through the door, right.*)

Now there's a lady would dance a man back out through the doors of the Mother Church herself. Doris Hoyden.

(*He looks at her.* DORIS *stares down into her lap.*)

I've got a great feeling about you, let me ask you now—

(*Stops, as the door right, opens and* MAY *comes back in, carrying a lavatory roll. Simultaneously* MR GODBOY *comes out of the kitchen, carrying a glass of gin. He stares at* MAY *as she looks at* HAWKINS. MAY *continues across to the door, right.*)

GODBOY: Can I help, dear.

(MAY *slams the door.* MR GODBOY *nods, smiles hands the glass to* HAWKINS, *sits down. There is a pause as* HAWKINS *drinks.*)

I think you was mentioning the gasser O'Higgs. (*Little pause, stares at* HAWKINS.) In relation to which, it's my own personal opinion that a man like O'Higgs prepared himself for the rope in the knowledge that it was going to go off ceremoniously without a hitch. To snatch the noose away from him with talk of specialists is to take the first step back into the jungle as far as I'm concerned. It puts an end to his heritage. (*Stares at him.*) May I say again Mannerly, what an honour it is to have you in my home at last while I'm on the subject. (*Little pause.*) Did you ever mingle with someone similar to O'Higgs, before the event, so to speak, socially?

HAWKINS: O'Higgs? The only O'Higgs I ever knew had the purest tenor voice in the whole world, you could hear that voice through the screams of the City of London itself. (*To* DORIS) And what does your presently missing husband do, Doris, if I can ask?

DORIS: (*After a pause*) He's between.

HAWKINS: Between?

189

GODBOY: Between jobs, she means. Eric's being a bit unlucky at the moment, through no fault of his own, naturally, as he's totally unqualified.

HAWKINS: But still there's a great luck if he has you to come home to, Doris, for that's what a marriage means. Has he been missing from you long?
(DORIS *shakes her head*.)
A little bit of night-wandering he goes in for, does he?
(DORIS *shrugs*.)
When the mood comes over him to count the stars of the sky and the blessings of his home? (*Laughs*.)

GODBOY: Eric is one of those who have – has – who succumbs to a weakish head for alcohol, I'm sorry to say.

HAWKINS: (*To* DORIS) Well, he has a habit of turning up in the end, does he?
(DORIS *nods*.)
And that's a very pleasant habit for both of you, I think?
(DORIS *looks down. There is a long silence.* HAWKINS *stares at* DORIS, MR GODBOY *stares at* HAWKINS.)

GODBOY: Inspector, may I be so bold as to show you something? (*Gets up*.) It's merely this piece over here, a recent acquisition in a manner of speaking, for which I've got interesting plans.
(*As* HAWKINS *turns in his chair, goes to the cupboard*.)
Take a good look at it, sir, I'm particularly interested in your opinion.
(HAWKINS *leans over, pats* DORIS *on the knee*.)
(*Opens the cupboard door*.) I chose it myself. As you see, capacious. And around here, to the side, there's a hole, goodness only knows what for, Mannerly, originally.
(*Laughs, shakes his head, looks towards* HAWKINS, *who swings his head away from* DORIS.)

DORIS: (*Sidling down the couch*) Um, I've got to be um. (*In a low voice. Gets up*.)
(HAWKINS *also gets up*.)

GODBOY: It's worth pointing out there's enough room to get a fully grown adult in here even May Godboy, my wife, could be got in here, sir. (*Laughs.*)

(DORIS *limps hurriedly to the door.* HAWKINS, *following* DORIS *sidles ahead of her by the cupboard, so blocking off her exit.*)

HAWKINS: It's big enough to get into you say? Now isn't that amazing? (*To* DORIS.)

GODBOY: Indeed it is, sir. (*Gets into the cupboard.*) As I was saying, capacious enough for May Godboy herself, who could easily be accommodated.

HAWKINS: (*As* DORIS *goes around the back of him, opens the door, right*) May I just – for interest—

(*He closes the cupboard door, holds it closed with his left hand, catches* DORIS'S *hand with his right.*)

You're off upstairs then?

(DORIS *nods.*)

(*Stares at her.*) Well, perhaps we'll be seeing each other again, some people I see over and over again, and there's been a glimpse—

(*The door, left, opens and* MAY *comes out. Stops. Stares at* HAWKINS, *who releases* DORIS'S *hand.*)

Good night, ma'am (*to* DORIS), and my respects to your husband, I hope I'll be seeing him also.

(*As* DORIS *pulls away, stares at* MAY, *who shakes her head knowingly, goes out of the room.* HAWKINS *turns, looks at* MAY, *as knocking sounds come from within the cupboard.*)

(*There is a sudden blowing of whistles, yapping of dogs, shouts, from a few streets distance.*)

(To MAY) And there's Constable Hedderley calling.

MAY: Ooooh, everybody needs you so bad, don't they? Including my husband, where is he?

HAWKINS: Ah! (*Opens the cupboard door.*) I'm off to Merrit Street, Mr Godboy, I'll wish you good night and thank you. (*Leans in, shakes hands with* MR GODBOY.)

GODBOY: Merrit Street! You've done it then! Congratulations, Mannerly, congratulations, sir!

HAWKINS: Thank you, and good night.

(*Closes the cupboard door again, puts his hat on his head, goes out, right. His voice in the hall—*

All right, boys, all right, get moving boys, come on.
(*The front door bangs.* MAY *stands looking at the cupboard. It opens.* MR GODBOY *steps out.*)

GODBOY: Merely, um . . . merely . . . something I wanted
Mannerly to see.
(MAY *shakes her head at him, then points her finger at her head, revolves it slowly.*)
Well, the Merrit Street attacker has been taken at last, dear.
(*Looks at her.*) I wonder whose trail Mannerly will be on
next, perhaps some time he'll be up against someone who
knows the game inside out, and can give him a real battle of
wits.

MAY: He's already on her trail, isn't he? And he'd have her inside
out before your eyes and you wouldn't know what he was up
to.

GODBOY: Pardon, dear?

MAY: Do you know what I've been doing in there?

GODBOY: What dear?

MAY: I've been telling you something.

GODBOY: Indeed dear? What?

MAY: (*Looks at him, goes over to the sofa, sits on it. She is now
wearing shoes.*) What's the time?

GODBOY: (*Looks at his watch*) Ten thirty bed-time, dear.

MAY: Come sit by me.

GODBOY: (*Stares at her*) Well, I noticed there was still – were still
some things in the cupboard, dear, I thought we could do it
together.
(MAY *claps her hands, points to the floor beside her.* MR GODBOY
comes over, sits down on the edge of the sofa, gingerly, at MAY's
feet.)

MAY: You call that comfy?

GODBOY: (*Nods*) Thank you dear.

MAY: Well, I don't.
(*Gives him a push with her feet. He stumbles off the sofa.*)
Come on, let me have a last fling at your sad old head, as
that's the only part of you I'll remember as that's the only
part I'm allowed to touch. (*Points to the floor beside her.*)

(GODBOY *sits down on the floor, his head level with the sofa. She starts to knead his head gently.*)

GODBOY: You've got a long night ahead of you. Tomorrow, I merely mean, dear.

MAY: Oh shut up your niggidy-naggidy with your merely means. (*Little pause.*) Rest easy now and settle yourself back, because this is important. (*Slips her hand down his throat, then begins to undo his tie.*) It's your last chance.

GODBOY: Pardon, dear?

MAY: The trouble with you is you won't let go, that's what's defeating those specialists – if you've ever been to any. (*Pulls his tie off.*) I got a lot of life in me yet, that's what I been telling you, and if you'd just let me have a last-minute go at you everything could still come right. (*Puts a hand down his shirt, begins to rub his chest.*) There's a lesson to be learnt with taking a high hand, we all want it except for the freaks like Doris.

GODBOY: Doris, dear?

MAY: She won't give that boy what he needs. (*Shakes her head.*) But there's some men could make us follow after them like a wet puppy dog, and she'd better watch it, she's met her match, from what I see of Hawkins. What's this doing to you?

GODBOY: Making my chest nice and warm, thank you, dear. Can I take you to mean that Doris and Eric's marriage is definitely on a friendly type of basis?

MAY: She's not my idea of friendly, nor Eric's. And is *this* doing you good?

GODBOY: Yes, dear, thank you, although not too warm, it tends to tingle then – so Doris is against—

MAY: Tingle away, Number Two, tingle all over. Number One used to like this more than anything.

GODBOY: Indeed, dear?

MAY: Oh you and Number One is poles apart, one always up, two always down, and the horror of it is he's the one who's dead. (*Little pause.*) Does it make you green to hear me talk of Number One?

GODBOY: No dear, I enjoy hearing you reminisce.

(*There is a crash of the front door outside.* MR GODBOY *leaps to his feet, hurries over to the door, looks down the hall.*)

MAY: What is it?

GODBOY: It's Eric, dear. Eric.

(*Sound of feet in the hall, crashing.*)

Doris has been looking – what's happened to your trousers, Eric? (*Turns.*) He's gone.

MAY: What was the matter with him?

GODBOY: Nothing dear, except he looked out of breath and his trousers was – were torn.

MAY: (*Chuckles*) There's a boy after my own. If he's in the mood to do a bit of that on Doris, perhaps he'll save them both.

(*Claps her hands, points to the floor.*)

(MR GODBOY, *after a pause, comes back, sits down.*)

Don't it even make you green to see me having games with that Eric?

GODBOY: No dear, I particularly wanted you to have a pleasant evening, which was magnificently rounded off by the appearance of Inspector Hawkins himself.

MAY: Hawkins, O'Higgins, murder, wounds. I'd be better rubbing at a turtle. (*Removes her hand, lies still, stares at the ceiling.*) It's no go. No go. Last week it was my fiftieth birthday we was seeing out together and what did you do for it but spend the day creeping around them at the police station and the night sitting in your chair like a little white corpse. (*Long pause.*) I'm a warm woman, Perkins, everybody knows that, even your Manly Hawkins could see it in a wink, I'm a warm woman but the fire's going out. There's got to be hot coals to keep me banked, and you're turning me into embers, Perkins, embers. What'll happen to me if this goes on? What'll happen to me? (*There is a long silence.*) What do you say to me, then?

GODBOY: Dear. (*A pause. He sits staring ahead, his hands folded into his lap.*) If I haven't given satisfaction over the last two years, dear, it's because I've been waiting for me to see my path straight.

MAY: And do you see it straight to me, Perkins? (*Pause.*) Is that where the path's leading, into me?

GODBOY: No, dear. Now that Inspector Manly Hawkins has now called, after I'd given up all hope and was going to go ahead anyway, it can only lead to him, dear. (*Pause.*) I'm sorry.

MAY: (*Gets up. Stands looking down at him.*) What do you want with him? He don't want anything from you, it's someone else *he's* after. (*Nods at ceiling.*)

GODBOY: And yet he came, dear, on time exactly. (*Looks up at her.*) To me.

MAY: Well, I don't care no more. That was a chance I was giving you, Perkins, and I wanted you to take it. Remember that, it's all I ask now. (*Goes to the large cupboard, flings it open, looks inside.*)

(MR GODBOY *gets up, hurries over to the alcove, seizes the pipe, pulls it out, bends over, fishes for the cylinder, frantically pushes the pipe so that it falls into the guppie case, finds the cylinder, turns on the tap, drags the pipe out of the guppie case, turning around, as* MAY *steps out of the large cupboard, opens the door of the small cupboard, steps in.* MR GODBOY *slams the door of the large cupboard, pushes the pipe through the hole and simultaneously jerks out the padlock, puts it through, closes it, turns back to the gas cylinder. As he is doing this,* MAY *steps out of the small cupboard, with a hat on her head, glances at* MR GODBOY, *turns, stares at him, shakes her head, goes on into the room, left, reappears almost immediately with two suitcases, articles of clothing sticking out from under the lid, looks at* MR GODBOY, *who is now pressed flat, stomach first, against the cupboard door. Shakes her head again, walks through the kitchen door.* MR GODBOY *turns, his arms pressed back flat against the cupboard door.*)

GODBOY: (*Quietly*) Haw-kins. (*Staring blankly ahead.*)
(*Curtain.*)

ACT TWO

SCENE I

The following afternoon.
The curtain rises on the same set as in Act One, but the room is now
very neat. MR GODBOY can be heard and partially seen in the kitchen,
moving about. He comes fussily into the parlour with a new feather
duster, which he flicks here and there. He is wearing an apron.
Suddenly he stops, stands alert, then puts the duster down and goes to
the hall door, right. Stands listening, opens it a crack, peers out, opens
it wider.

GODBOY: (*Into the hall*) Doris.

> (*There is a little silence.*)

> I've just put the kettle on. (*Little pause – beckons with his*
> *hands.*)

> (DORIS *appears limping slightly more than in Act One. Her*
> *handbag is tightly clutched to her front. She stands at the door.*)

> I thought you'd forgotten, it looked as if you were passing
> me by. (*Laughs, ushers her in, makes to shut the door, is unable*
> *to do so. Opens it.*)

ERIC: (*Walks past him in a pair of bright new trousers.*) Hello.

GODBOY: (*Stares at him for a long moment.* ERIC *stares back at him,*
> *confused.*) Oh, you're coming in for a moment too, are you?

ERIC: (*Nods*) Yeah. (*Long pause.*) What? (*Short pause.*) Got old
> May off all right then, did you? (*Looks around.*) The place
> feels empty without her, eh Dorrie?

> (*Laughs nervously as* GODBOY *continues to stare at him.*)

> She certainly had a send-off from what we heard, eh Dorrie?

GODBOY: (*Walks briskly to the guppie case, sprinkles food on the*
> *surface, puts a finger in, waggles it*) Pardon, old boy?

> (ERIC *watches him, then comes to stand beside him as* DORIS *sits*
> *reluctantly on the sofa.*)

ERIC: You calling out goodbyes to May.

GODBOY: Oh, pardon me for waking you, yes, I did shout after her from the doorstep, I didn't mean to be heard. (*Puts the package back on the table.*) There, there, my little fellows, how's that for a feast?

ERIC: (*Looks at them closely*) Why they lying on top like that?

GODBOY: Because, old boy – (*stares a little closer*) they're dead.

ERIC: Oh, is that it.

(DORIS *lets out a little scream.*)

GODBOY: (*Picks one out, looks at it, drops it back in, wipes his fingers on his apron*) This is very upsetting, I don't mind admitting.

ERIC: How did it happen then?

GODBOY: Natural causes.

ERIC: Oh.

GODBOY: It can happen to anybody. Nevertheless it's a surprise. It's the last thing I thought would happen.

(*There is a long silence.*)

DORIS: (*Who has been sniffing*) Gas.

GODBOY: (*Swings towards her*) Pardon, old boy?

DORIS: I smell gas.

GODBOY: No there isn't, old girl.

(*There is a pause.* ERIC *sniffs. Another pause.*)

ERIC: What is it then?

GODBOY: Merely an unfamiliar odour, old girl. (*Walking across and taking off his apron.*) I've been boiling up some cabbage heads. Perhaps it's merely that. (*Folds apron carefully, puts it on the gramophone table.*)

ERIC: Can't help feeling sorry for them though. (*Puts his finger into the water.*)

GODBOY: Indeed, that's only human. (*Goes over to* DORIS.) Well, Doris, how are – ?

ERIC: It's funny thinking of them, they was here last night when we was clowning around enjoying ourselves, they was swimming around then, back and forward and up and down, and now today they're gone. Dead.

GODBOY: (*Listening, although facing* DORIS, *who is staring down into her lap*) Your husband Eric . . . (*with a smile*).

ERIC: Likely it was May's going did for them.

GODBOY: (*Turning*) You're talking nonsense, old boy, if you don't mind my speaking frankly to you as between friends, grief is unknown to fish.

ERIC: Is it? Oh?

(*As* GODBOY *turns back to* DORIS)

What grief?

GODBOY: Pardon, old boy?

ERIC: What grief? You said grief.

GODBOY: I merely mean, old boy, that those guppies would hardly go away from grief of May's passing, pass away from grief of May's going I merely mean (*long pause*), and if you work it out, if they knew enough to know May was going away they'd know enough to know she was certainly coming back as far as she knew.

ERIC: (*Laughs*) 'Course they didn't know she wasn't coming back.

GODBOY: (*Nods his head at him several times*) I'm glad we're agreed on that, Eric. (*Turns back to* DORIS. *Stops. Turns back to* ERIC.) They didn't know she was going, I also mean.

ERIC: Oh. (*Nods vaguely.*)

GODBOY: (*Turning back to* DORIS) How's it coming along today, Doris?

ERIC: What will you do with them?

GODBOY: The remains will have to be disposed of, naturally, old boy. (*Little pause.*) What kind of trouble has it been causing you today, Doris?

DORIS: It's all right today.

GODBOY: (*As* ERIC *comes across the room, and sits down in one of the utility chairs*) Really, Doris, my dear I was observing you closely as you limped across the room. We both know what needs doing to it. (*Turns to* ERIC.) Eh, Eric?

ERIC: (*Nods*) How will you dispose of the remains?

GODBOY: I will I will I will. (*Stops himself*). Pardon, old boy?

ERIC: Them gups.

GODBOY: They will have to be sluiced, old boy.

ERIC: Oh. Down the toilet you mean?

GODBOY: (*Nods*) Now Doris –

ERIC: (*Shaking his head*) Old May won't like that.

(GODBOY *stares at him.*)

No, she won't like having the remains sluiced, if I know
May.

GODBOY: I wasn't talking about May's remains, I merely mean
old boy, I was talking about the guppies' remains if you take
my meaning? (*Turning his head quickly.*) I like your dress,
Doris.

ERIC: What?

GODBOY: I was admiring Doris's dress.

ERIC: Oh? Where's my raincoat then?

GODBOY: Pardon?

ERIC: Well, wasn't it down here last night? (*Looks at* DORIS.)

GODBOY: (*Shakes his head. Stops shaking it as he remembers, then
shakes it more vigorously*) It was not. No.

ERIC: Well, listen, me and May was having a dance and I was
wearing it then, then me and May went into the kitchen for
the stout and gin and I was wearing it then, then May come
up to me and took it off me . . . (*looks around*) less she took it
with her.

GODBOY: I don't mean to cause trouble, old boy, but May
wouldn't be seen dead in that – in that – no, get that idea
right out of your mind. (*Little pause.*) It'll turn up where
you're least expecting it. (*Little pause.*) Righto, old boy?

ERIC: Oh. (*Nods.*) Righto.

GODBOY: Indeed you probably lost it when you went off in that
strange way.

ERIC: (*After a pause*) No, I wasn't wearing it then, no.

GODBOY: Where did you go anyway, we all sat here worrying
about you.

ERIC: Oh. (*Laughs hunches a shoulder.*) Out. I went out.

GODBOY: Yes, well Doris was in a state, it needed Inspector
Hawkins himself to calm her down.
(*There is a long pause.*)

ERIC: What was he doing here?

GODBOY: Merely visiting myself, old boy.

ERIC: Oh. (*Nods.*) You haven't seen my scarf then?
(GODBOY *stares at him coldly. There is a long silence.*)

(*Looks around him, stares at the cupboard, points at it.*) I know, I . . .

GODBOY: Now I don't mean to cause offence (*shouting*) but I'm getting tired of all these accusations of scarves and raincoats and sluicing May down the toilet, that is the guppies, where's your manners?

(*Long pause.* ERIC *stares at him in bewilderment,* DORIS *stares down into her lap.*)

Do I get my apology?

(ERIC *shakes his head perplexed. There is another pause.*)

DORIS: (*In a whisper*) Say pardon.

ERIC: Oh. Righto. Pardon.

GODBOY: (*Nods*) Least said, soonest mended, old boy.

(*He gets up, goes into the kitchen, leaving door open.* ERIC *looks at* DORIS, *who keeps her face bent. He looks away.*)

ERIC: (*Finally crossing his legs, begins to jog a foot up and down, whistles tunelessly.* DORIS *glares at him. He stops. Pause. Looks at her. She looks away.*) Honest, Dorrie, I was just walking.

DORIS: Walking?

ERIC: Just walking around, that's all.

DORIS: (*In a hiss*) And what about me, with that policeman, what was I meant to be doing while you was just walking around, with him walking around me. And them trousers you caught on barbed wire. What barbed wire?

ERIC: Well, I told you, there was this barbed wire –

(DORIS *turns her face away.*)

Anyway, you heard him, that policeman was just visiting.

(*Looks at* DORIS's *face.*) I love you, Dorrie.

(DORIS *pays no attention.*)

(ERIC *sits hunched. Begins to jog his foot again, looks around the room hopelessly, sees cupboard, gets up, goes over to it, stares at it closely, then tries handle. Pulls harder, then holds up the padlock.*)

Here, Dorrie!

(*She pays no attention. He peers between the door crack, gets down on one knee.* GODBOY *comes into the room carrying a tray. Puts tray down on the floor, picks up two cups, carries one to*

DORIS, *puts it beside her*.)

GODBOY: Sugar, my dear?

DORIS: Yes please.

GODBOY: What about Eric? Eric?

ERIC: Yes, please. (*Peering now with his face close to the crack*.)

GODBOY: (*Stirs Doris's cup for her*) There. Lots of sugar to sweeten your outlook on things. (*Chuckles, pats her shoulder*.) Not to worry, Doris. Not to worry. (*Nods, turns, walks across the room with Eric's cup, puts it down on the floor beside him, turns, walks eagerly back towards* DORIS.)

It's worrying does more harm than corns and ulcers put – (*Stops. Turns, looks at* ERIC.) Old boy?

ERIC: Yeah. (*Sniffing hard*.)

GODBOY: Haven't you got any respect, old boy? Haven't you got any? Any respect?

ERIC: What? (*Turns his head*.) What for?

GODBOY: For – for – for property, I merely mean.

ERIC: Oh.

(*Looks at* DORIS, *gets up. Stares at* GODBOY, *who is glaring at him*.)

DORIS: (*After a long pause*) Say pardon, Eric.

ERIC: Oh. Righto. Pardon.

(*Little pause, as* GODBOY *nods slowly*.)

GODBOY: Granted, Eric, as soon as asked. Now – (*gestures to one of the chairs*.)

ERIC: But I thought May said it was for us.

GODBOY: Indeed it is.

ERIC: Oh. (*Comes back to his chair. Sits down*.) But it's locked.

GODBOY: (*About to sit down, pauses*) Indeed it is.

ERIC: (*Looks at* DORIS) Well – ?

GODBOY: It'll have to remain locked until further notice, thank you for reminding me.

ERIC: Oh. (*Looks at* DORIS *again*.) But I remember see, that's where I put my scarf and raincoat, see.

GODBOY: (*Strikes his knee*) How many times do I have to tell you. (*Shouting*.) There's nothing in there except May's remains. (*Long pause. They all sit staring ahead*.)

By which I merely mean the bits and pieces of May (*falters*)
which she couldn't take with her and had to leave behind.
(*Little pause.*) If you take my meaning, old boy. (*Little pause.*)
Have you got those facts straight in your mind?

ERIC: Righto, yes, righto. Pardon.

GODBOY: (*After a pause*) Granted.

(*There is a long silence. They drink their tea.* DORIS *with her
head lowered,* GODBOY *genteelly,* ERIC *from the wrong side of
the cup.*)

(*To* DORIS) Excuse me speaking sharpish to your husband, I
don't mean you to take it personally. (*To* ERIC) It's just at the
rate he's going on funny things will be turning up all over my
parlour. (*Laughs.*)

(ERIC *laughs. There is another long silence.*)

ERIC: This cupboard then, that's got all this stuff of May's in it
and it's locked, are you still giving it to us then?

GODBOY: Indeed I am, yes, the sooner you get it up to your own
parlour the happier I'll be.

ERIC: Oh. (*Nods.*) Well (*looks at* DORIS) that's a bit funny, well, I
mean (*Laughs, looks at* DORIS), you're giving us this
cupboard and it's got May's stuff in it, and it's locked up so
we can't get into it anyway, and it'll take up all the room in
our room won't it? And I mean that's a bit funny. As we
can't get into it even.

(GODBOY *looks at him, goes over to the cupboard, bends down,
opens the drawers at the base, turns, folds his arms, looks at*
ERIC. ERIC *looks at* DORIS, *who looks away.*)

GODBOY: (*Quietly*) Any further complaints, Eric?

(ERIC *shrugs.* GODBOY *comes back, sits down, sips from his tea.*
ERIC *looks at him, looks at* DORIS, *looks at him again. Laughs
suddenly.* GODBOY *puts his cup into its saucer, stares at* ERIC.)

ERIC: No, I was just laughing because it's a bit funny getting a
cupboard you can't get into except in a bottom drawer and
it's as big as our room nearly and it's ponging away. That's
all.

(*Pause, while* GODBOY *looks at him,* DORIS *looks down into her
cup.*)

Well, you smell it, Dorrie. Go on, smell it.

GODBOY: (*Folds his arms*) Doris, be a good girl and smell it, will you Doris? As that's what your husband wants.

DORIS: (*Gets up, limps across the room, smells the cupboard, limps back*) It's not too bad. (*In a low voice, looks accusingly at* ERIC.)

GODBOY: Virtually odour free?

DORIS: I smelt far worse from that leak we had in the stove.

GODBOY: Thank you, Doris. (*To* ERIC) Well, old boy? (*Little pause.*) Eric?

ERIC: Um. (*Looks from* DORIS *to* GODBOY.) It's just that it smells funny to me. Gas in a cupboard. (*Little pause.*) It smells funny.

GODBOY: Oh does it old boy, and if it does I'll tell you why, it's because you're turning a bit nosy, frankly speaking. Righto. (*Little pause.*) Righto.

ERIC: (*After a pause*) Pardon.

GODBOY: Granted as asked. Now to change the subject to something pleasant, did you hear the news about Inspector Mannerly Hawkins' success in the Merrit Street case. He was here last night, wasn't he Doris, just prior to catching the man who's certainly helping him now down at the station, if I know Mannerly Hawkins. (*Laughs.*) Eh, Doris?

ERIC: Oh? (*Laughs.*) I heard something about that, yes. (*Looks around the room, begins to jog his leg.*)

GODBOY: Yes, if you hadn't run off like that, you could have met Mannerly too, Eric. Still, May and Doris met him, I'm glad about that. Eh, Doris? (*Smiles at her.*) He's got amazing instincts, Mannerly has. (*Turns to* ERIC.) What did you hear?

ERIC: Nothing, no. (*Shakes his head.*) Only when I was down at the um, 'bacanist's there was something I heard about this girl undoing her stockings or something and this chap went up to her, or something like that.

DORIS: When did you go down to the 'bacanist's?

GODBOY: (*Laughs*) That was no girl, Eric, that was Police Constable Hedderley.

ERIC: Who?

GODBOY: Hawkins' female accomplice, old boy.

ERIC: (*Angrily*) What was she doing there, then?

GODBOY: Pardon?

ERIC: Well, what was she taking her stockings off for then?

GODBOY: Bait, Eric, she was bait in the trap.

ERIC: Well, what'll happen to him, then?

GODBOY: Further promotion. Or another favourable mention from a judge.

ERIC: No, this bloke. The one you say they um . . .

GODBOY: With Mannerly Hawkins on the job, Eric?

ERIC: But suppose they get – got – I mean it's the wrong bloke?

GODBOY: I repeat, Eric – we're talking about Inspector Mannerly Hawkins.

ERIC: (*Thinks*) Well, but if he was a bloke coming home from going into the air to clear his brain for a moment, and happened to be in the area by mistake, see, and there was this girl pulling her stockings off and waving them at him, this – um, bloke he might come up to her, just from – well, and asked what she was doing larking about and if his brain was a bit fogged she could have got hold of him and pitched him to the ground bruising his shoulder something – see what I mean, it could be an accident, see. (*Long pause.*) No, I'm thinking, that's all. (*Little pause.*) No.

GODBOY: I say it again, Eric (*laughs*), we're talking about Inspector Mannerly Hawkins. Down there at the station he's dealing with a criminal second in value to a murderer himself. Mannerly doesn't make mistakes, Eric, as I ought to know.

ERIC: Oh. (*Little pause.*) That's all right then. (*Little pause.*) I mean if he's got someone he thinks did it, and he doesn't make mistakes, that's all right then. He can't grumble.

GODBOY: Who can't grumble?

ERIC: This chap they got.

GODBOY: Oh, he'll grumble all right, there's very few know how to help the police, Eric, very few like the gasser O'Higgs. After he'd been trapped with the corpse of his wife in an airing-closet, and the female tenant laid out on the kitchen table, stark, he knew his time was come. He sat down and wrote out a brilliant confession on the spot. Being in a lawyer's office he knew the language. There's very few men like O'Higgs, and an animal like the Merrit Street attacker wouldn't be one of them.

(DORIS *shudders*.)

What is it, Doris?

DORIS: I been having dreams about him, nightmares I mean.

ERIC: (*Looks at her, clears his throat*) Who?

DORIS: Him. People like him. The one was in Merrit Street.

(ERIC *gets up, takes his cup over to the record table, then wanders to the guppie case, stops in front of it, peers in, turns, wanders towards the cupboard, stops in front of it, raps on the door, stops himself, looks towards* GODBOY *furtively, then stands by the cupboard listening to the conversation between* DORIS *and* GODBOY.)

GODBOY: What sort of nightmares would those be, Doris?

DORIS: I mean, what could you do, if he got you? What could you do? And people, what would they think? There was one I was reading about in the States of America, he did things to girls with tape and shoe laces and stuffed their mouths with cotton-wool so the girls was helpless, and was powerless to struggle, and then he did other things to them. It wasn't their fault.

GODBOY: (*As* ERIC *abstractedly opens the bottom drawer of the cupboard, begins to unwind the length of pipe*) No Doris, if you were rendered incapable first, you'd be cleared of any blame.

DORIS: And when I was little there was this one he used to wait at bus-stops in his car, he was after us when we was little.

GODBOY: They're different, Doris. There's no excuse for that. I hope the authorities realize hanging's too good for them, what they need is medical treatment from specialists.

DORIS: But this Merrit Street one, he could've come through my bedroom window when I was all asleep and quiet, and done things to me, he could've bound me up and I couldn't have done nothing if he did it by force, while you (*to* ERIC) was walking the streets.

ERIC: (*Shakes his head*) Not to you, Dorrie, I wouldn't do that.

GODBOY: (*Looks towards him, leaps to his feet*) Now Eric what you prying into now, Eric?

ERIC: Well, it was in this drawer. (*Holds out the cylinder.*) It's got that gas smell to it.

GODBOY: (*Walking across to him*) Smell, smell, smell, all you talk about is smell. (*Takes the cylinder away from* ERIC, *thrusts it behind the alcove curtain.*) Now I'll tell you, old boy, I'm getting tired of telling you your manners in front of your own wife, you're interrupting a very pleasant conversation we're having. (*Turns, looks him in the face, very close.*) And there's another thing, old boy, what are your plans for the afternoon?

ERIC: What?

GODBOY: Because frankly, old boy, it's time Doris and me were getting down to it – her corn I merely mean, and it's medically a trifle funny to have a patient's husband loitering about in my cupboards. (*Long pause.*) What about going to the pictures?

(ERIC *looks at* DORIS.)

DORIS: (*Looking down into her handbag*) Could we do it tomorrow?

GODBOY: No Doris, I'm sorry to say I've got to get you over with, any moment now my time might not be my own.

DORIS: Well (*hesitates*), can't he stay then?

GODBOY: Again I have to say no, Doris, on general grounds. This is between you and me, my dear. (*Looks at her, then takes* ERIC *by the arm, leads him to the door, right.*) Now you go to the pictures, then you stroll about a bit, and then you look in on me, it'll be all over then as far as Doris is concerned, I merely mean we'll have had it off. (*Little pause.*) Righto?

ERIC: Oh. (*Shrugs.*) Well.

(*Looks at* DORIS, *walks past* GODBOY, *kisses* DORIS. *She turns her mouth away.*)

Well ta-ta, Dorrie.

DORIS: (*In a low voice*) Ta-ta.

(GODBOY *ushers him out of the room, stares after him, watched by* DORIS, *then shuts the door. Stands looking at* DORIS. *There is a pause. He comes and sits by her on the sofa, folds his hands into his lap, clears his throat.* DORIS *looks down at her handbag.*)

GODBOY: (*After a little pause*) How are you feeling now, Doris?

DORIS: Cold. I feel cold.

GODBOY: Cold, eh? That's a good sign.

DORIS: Is it?

GODBOY: It's when people get all heated up that inconveniences begin.

DORIS: Oh. (*Little pause.*) Can I have the fire on, then?

GODBOY: (*Leaps to his feet*) Indeed my – (*sits down again*). No, I'm sorry to say that might be a trifle risky under the circumstances. (*Long pause.*) Because of the little whiff I might be compelled to give you.

DORIS: (*After a long pause*) What for?

GODBOY: It's usual in these cases, Doris. (*Laughs.*) Never you mind your little head about that, dear.

(*There is a long silence.* GODBOY *turns his head and stares at* DORIS.)

I'm sorry about my treatment of Eric, he's a good lad. Above all, most likeable. (*Little pause.*) What was it precisely that attracted you about him?

DORIS: Well, it was that he looks like that Humphrey Bogart.

GODBOY: Oh, indeed my dear, you do surprise me there, my own impression of Humphrey Bogart on one viewing is of a trifle more educated man. But these things are a matter of personal taste.

DORIS: It's when he wears his raincoat.

GODBOY: His raincoat isn't in this room, Doris.

(*Long pause.*)

DORIS: Whiff of what?

GODBOY: Pardon?

DORIS: Whiff of something, you said.

GODBOY: Indeed. (*Nods.*) My own marriage to May was a blessing in its way. I didn't know what it was I wanted until I met her and found myself thinking about it. Fifty years a bachelor is a long time for a man, he dreams of what he is but he don't – doesn't do anything about it until fate compels

207

him. (*Looks at* DORIS.) I've followed Mannerly Hawkins'
career since the moment I saw him, down at the self-same
station he's returned to. There was something there that
bound us together, Doris. Did you know O'Higgs was taken
into custody by a man he'd worked with in his capacity as a
lawyer's clerk. He addressed some letters to him, personal
letters, from his final cell. They were eventually published in
a newspaper.
(*Long pause.*)

DORIS: (*Clears her throat*) Whiff of what, will it be?

GODBOY: (*Looks at her*) Whiff of the same thing I had to give to
May, Doris. (*Little pause.*) If it hadn't been for my wound,
things would have been different. I'd have been a different
man on the force. Mannerly Hawkins is a man. He's got the
authority.
(*Pause.*)

DORIS: It's funny. (*Laughs.*) It's not hurting me now.
(GODBOY *looks at her again, bends towards her, pats her on the
arm, gets up, arranges one of the utility chairs so that it's facing to
the left. He goes to the alcove, takes out a cardboard box.* DORIS
*watches. He comes back, clears his throat, stands holding the
back of the arranged chair. Bends over, pats the seat with his
hand.* DORIS *watches. Pats the seat again. Laughs.* DORIS *limps
over, sits down.* GODBOY *squares his shoulders, turns, stands
behind* DORIS.)

GODBOY: Kindly remove the shoe and stocking please. (*Stiffly,
then turns around and folds his arms over his chest.*)
(DORIS *slowly takes off her shoe, then her stocking.*)
Ready?

DORIS: (*In a low voice*) Yes.

GODBOY: (*Walks stiffly around the chair*) Would you mind just
stretching it out, Doris, so I can have a proper glimpse of it.
(DORIS *stretches her leg out.*)
(GODBOY *crouches down some distance from the foot, inspects it
carefully. After a little pause, whistles.*)
(DORIS *looks at him in alarm.*)
We just got to it in time. It's burgeoning fast. There'll be

danger if it's allowed to develop. (*Gets up, goes to the alcove, picks out a box from the back, then another one. Comes back, opens the top box, takes out small knives, pads, lotions, puts them on the floor.*) I've been a great admirer of yours, Doris. I expect you realize that.

DORIS: (*Watching him*) What?

GODBOY: We share similar ideas about things, Doris, very similar. (*Stares up at her.*) I appreciate what you was – were telling me about your dreams. (*Gets up, holding the second box.*) As I said to May, violence to a living creature isn't in my nature. That's why I was a bachelor for fifty years. (*Opens the box.*) Now I have to administer a whiff of something mild.

DORIS: Well (*in a shaky voice*), what is it?

GODBOY: It's to help you out.

DORIS: (*Shakes her head*) I don't want that.

GODBOY: Now Doris, I wouldn't want to have myself having to counter serious opposition. There could be dangerous responses made by your reflexes which could throw me off my stride. (*Laughs.*) It's a case of too many cooks can spoil the broth, merely.

(*He comes around to stand beside* DORIS. *She looks up at him. There is a long silence.*)

You won't give me any trouble, will you, Doris?

(DORIS *shakes her head.*)

(*Puts a hand on her shoulder.*) Thank you, Doris.

DORIS: What's that, then?

GODBOY: This. (*Holds the box up.*) This will make you laugh when you see it. (*Little pause.*) I'll have to ask you to slip it on in a minute of your own volition. It'll facilitate matters dreadfully for you.

DORIS: (*Makes a ghastly laughing sound*) But what is it?

GODBOY: It's an appliance you're familiar with. It'll even bring back childhood memories. I've done some alterations so that it comes in handy for what's got to be done. My own invention. (*Opens the box, shows her the contents, laughs.*)

(DORIS *stares down into it.*)

Righto?

(DORIS *shakes her head, starts to get up.*)

(*Pressing her down with his hand*) Righto.

(DORIS *subsides. Sits staring down into her lap. He comes round so that his back is to the audience, blocking her from view. There are slight struggling sounds. He keeps his back to the audience.*) There you are, it's the right size, it suits perfectly.

(DORIS *makes mumbling sounds.*)

(*Stands stiffly for a moment, puts his hands behind his back, twists them, his head up. Then bends.*) You look as right as rain.

(DORIS *mumbles.*)

(*Shouting*) You look as right as rain.

(*Little pause, further mumbling from* DORIS.)

As *rain*, I said.

(*Sounds of footsteps in the hall, right.*)

ERIC: (*Shouting*) I know, and I haven't got my raincoat.

GODBOY: (*Stands frozen by the chair. There is a pause, then tentatively*) Pardon?

ERIC: Dorrie!

GODBOY: What do you want?

ERIC: It looks like rain, and I need my raincoat, that's all.

GODBOY: It isn't here. I told you.

ERIC: Oh. (*Pause.*) How's it going then?

GODBOY: Doris is in excellent condition. (*Holding her shoulders as she struggles to rise.*)

ERIC: I'll be off to the pictures then.

GODBOY: Righto.

(*Sound of* ERIC *moving about outside the door, then a confusion of steps.* GODBOY *hurries over to the door, right, exposing* DORIS *for the first time. She is wearing a gasmask. He opens the door, right, stares down the hall then closes the door, turns the key in the lock. As he is doing this the door left opens, and* ERIC *puts his head in. Stares at* DORIS *as* GODBOY *steps away from the door, turns, sees him. There is a long pause.*)

ERIC: What are you doing in that, then? (*To* DORIS, *bursts out laughing.*)

(DORIS *makes mumbling sounds.*)

GODBOY: (*Hurries back, puts a hand on* DORIS's *arm*) You're interrupting a very important moment, Eric. This is no time for your jokes.

ERIC: (*Stops laughing. Looks grave. Lets out another snort. Stops*) I'm going to see *Flame and Arrow* with that Virgin Mayo and Burt Lancaster. (*Little pause.*) That all right?

(DORIS *stares at him.*)

Flame and Arrow. (*Bellows. Pantomimes drawing a bow.*)

(DORIS *nods.*)

(*To* GODBOY) It's outlaws in the woods. She don't like them, she likes cities. (*Little pause.*) It's where he catches her and keeps her chained by a chain around her neck. (*There is a little pause.*) It'll be good. (*Little pause.*) Righto. (*Little pause.*) Ta-ta then.

GODBOY: Ta-ta.

(ERIC *walks across the stage to the door, right, watched by* GODBOY, *tries the handle, finds it locked, steps away, comes back across the stage.*)

ERIC: Righto.

(GODBOY, *who has kept a hand on* DORIS's *shoulder, hurries after* ERIC *with a utility chair, puts it under the handle. Comes back, looks at* DORIS, *pats her on the shoulder. Goes to the alcove, takes out gas cylinder, length of pipe, starts to come back. There is a knock on the door, right. He turns angrily, puts the cylinder down, goes to the door, right. Puts his ear against it. Sound of footsteps.*)

GODBOY: (*Shouting*) I'm beginning to think your Eric is a trifle mad, Doris. If you'll pardon me for saying so. (*Unlocks door, opens it a fraction, peers out, opens it wider, then steps out of sight into the hall as the door, left, opens inwards, thus causing the chair to fall over.*)

(HAWKINS *enters, followed by* HEDDERLEY, *in a long police skirt, tunic, curls, etc.*)

HAWKINS: (*Stares down at* DORIS, *as* HEDDERLEY *takes up a position by the record table, hands behind back*) Well, and here's a pretty sight. (*Laughs.*)

(DORIS *stares up at him, then down into her lap as* GODBOY *comes back in through the door, left, stepping carefully over the chair. Stops. Stares at* HAWKINS.)

GODBOY: So you've come again! (*Reverently.*)

HAWKINS: I think we're interrupting something, Mr Godboy.

GODBOY: (*As* HAWKINS *turns back to* DORIS) No Mannerly, no. Please pardon the mess.

(*Goes to the door, left, picks up the chair,* HAWKINS *is now staring down at* DORIS's *leg. She draws it up awkwardly, sits with her hands clasped around her handbag.*)

We was – were just about to get commencing down to a nastyish business. (*Little pause.*) Doris's corn, I merely mean. (*Comes back, picks up the cylinder, carries it, with the tube trailing behind, to the alcove*) and a preliminary settling down I go in for as part of my technique. (*Comes back.*) Doris is a nervous girl (*bends over her*) so I slipped this on in a reminiscent vein about the old days. (*In a low voice, takes the gasmask off.*)

(DORIS *looks around, looks down at her handbag.*)

HAWKINS: Ah, and so it's you, Doris Hoyden. (*Crouches slightly to stare at her.*) But you're not still waiting for the wandering husband? (*Little pause.*) He wouldn't still be on the wander now?

GODBOY: He's just gone this second, Mannerly.

HAWKINS: (*Looks at* HEDDERLEY) Now isn't that a pity, then.

(HEDDERLEY *nods. There is a pause.* GODBOY *walks over to the alcove, the gasmask in his hands.*)

GODBOY: I'm merely, um, pardon me . . .

HAWKINS: Mr Godboy.

(MR GODBOY *stops, turns.*)

(*Comes towards him, revolving his hat in his hand. Stands thoughtfully for a moment, then puts his hand on* GODBOY's *left shoulder.* GODBOY *comes to attention, as if under arrest. Then* HAWKINS *moves to the cupboard, gives the padlock a flick.*)

Ah, and it's quite a lock you've locked your treasures up with. (*Turns, smiles at* GODBOY.)

(DORIS, *during this, picks up her shoe and stocking and begins to limp towards the kitchen door.*)

(*Quietly, still smiling at* GODBOY) Hedderley.

(HEDDERLEY *shifts around, stands beside* DORIS. DORIS *stops.*
HEDDERLEY *stares at the side of her face.* DORIS *is facing the
wall, right.*)

GODBOY: Yes, sir. (*Little pause.*) Unfortunately I can't put my
hand on the key at this precise moment, Mannerly, which
has got itself unfortunately lost somehow.

HAWKINS: (*Turns, looks down at the guppies*) And the charming
Mrs Godboy?

GODBOY: Unfortunately May Godboy is no longer with us just at
the moment, I'm sorry to say. She took that trip I was
hinting about last night.

HAWKINS: Did she now. (*Puts his finger into the water.*) Not as
sprightly as yesterday, I think.

GODBOY: (*After a pause*) A little run down, and in need of a rest,
now you ask, Mannerly.

HAWKINS: (*Still staring into the tank*) Not dead though?

GODBOY: No Mannerly . . . It's a kind of holiday.

HAWKINS: A holiday. (*Stirs his fingers around.*) How strange the
little creatures are, in their ways. How strange.

GODBOY: (*After a pause, laughs*) Very true, Mannerly, very true.

HAWKINS: Mr Godboy. (*Looks at him.*) What it is, Mr Godboy, is
that there's a little matter we're trying to get to the bottom
of.

GODBOY: Sir?

HAWKINS: (*Comes over, puts a hand on* GODBOY'*s shoulder again.*)
And I think you can help us, Mr Godboy.

GODBOY: (*Stares into his face*) Help you in your inquiries,
Mannerly. Yes, sir.

(*There is a long pause.*)

Do you want me to accompany you to the station, Mannerly?

HAWKINS: (*Shakes him gently by the shoulder*) Well, to tell you the
truth, we're on a little game of cat and mouse, and sometimes
it's better for the cat to sit beneath the mouse's lair. (*Tilts his
head, smiles.*) Isn't that the truth?

GODBOY: I've been expecting another visit, Mannerly, but I

didn't expect even you would be precisely – (*shakes his head in admiration*). May I say, whatever the outcome of your present inquiries, my congratulations are offered again on your Merrit Street attacker triumph. It will always be an honour, wherever I may end up, to recall that you sat in one of my chairs while it was happening. It'll be mentioned in my letters, Mannerly, from wherever I end up.

(HAWKINS *is looking towards* HEDDERLEY *and* DORIS *throughout this*.)

And of course similarly congratulations to Constable Hedderley, if that is Constable Hedderley that is.

HAWKINS: That is. Although Hedderley's a little modest about accepting congratulations this morning, aren't you now, Hedderley?

HEDDERLEY: Sir.

GODBOY: Even so, the Merrit Street attacker's a big feather to have had in her cap.

HAWKINS: (*Laughs, shakes his head, walks towards the centre of the room followed by* MR GODBOY, *still clutching the gasmask*.) Hedderley wouldn't know how to receive a feather like that, would you, Hedderley? Your whole nature's against it, isn't it, Hedderley?

HEDDERLEY: Sir.

GODBOY: (*After a pause, looking from* HAWKINS *to* HEDDERLEY *and* DORIS) That's in the best tradition, sir, of course. If I may say so personally, I think it's wonderful that the fair sex is being taken up, as long as they're not in it for the glamour merely of course.

HAWKINS: Hedderley?

HEDDERLEY: Sir.

HAWKINS: Did you hear what Mr Godboy said about the fair sex? Are you in it for the glamour?

HEDDERLEY: Sir. (*Shakes head*.)

GODBOY: (*After a long pause, during which* HAWKINS *looks towards* HEDDERLEY, *who continues to stare at the side of* DORIS'*s face*) Of course, even with the fair sex good officers are born and not made.

HAWKINS: Well, Hedderley, how would you answer Mr Godboy on that? Were you born, do you think, Hedderley, or were you made?

HEDDERLEY: Sir. (*Little pause.*) Made, sir.

HAWKINS: By whom were you made then, Hedderley?

HEDDERLEY: Sir. (*Little pause.*) By sir, sir.

HAWKINS: (*Turns, smiles at* MR GODBOY, *tilts his head, turns back to* HEDDERLEY)Now fill me in, Hedderley, on what you're doing at the moment?

HEDDERLEY: Sir. Nothing, sir.

HAWKINS: Well then, ask the young lady to turn around, it's rude to keep her on edge like that.

(HEDDERLEY *says something in a low voice to* DORIS, *who turns around slowly, clasping her handbag, her shoe and her stocking to her waist.*)

(*Goes up to her.*) Excuse our manners, Doris Hoyden, why don't you make yourself comfortable?

(*Gestures to the sofa.* DORIS *looks at him, limps over to the sofa, sits in its corner, tightly.*)

No, no, Doris, right in the middle, the middle of the sofa's the most comfortable.

(DORIS *shifts to the middle.* HEDDERLEY *looks at* HAWKINS, *who tilts head almost imperceptibly.* HEDDERLEY *sits down next to* DORIS, *on* DORIS's *left.* HAWKINS *turns one of the utility chairs around and straddles it, facing the other utility chair, which, after a hesitation,* MR GODBOY *turns around and also straddles.* HAWKINS *begins to revolve his hat in his hands.* HEDDERLEY *takes Doris's handbag from her, opens it, begins to go through it.* DORIS *sits staring down into her lap.* MR GODBOY *begins to revolve the gasmask in his hands. There is a silence.*)

GODBOY: So you're already on the trail of something else, Mannerly, after last night? (*Laughs.*)

HAWKINS: Ah (*shakes his head*) it's not all the city's wickedness happens at night, Mr Godboy, as you'd be knowing yourself, I think. (*Stares at him.*) There's a loneliness that comes with day-break that can turn a man's heart in his chest, isn't there? And fog the mind with the sorrow of us all.

GODBOY: Indeed, Mannerly? (*Staring back at him, revolving the gasmask in time to* HAWKINS' *revolutions.*)

HAWKINS: The evil's done by day-break, Mr Godboy. The morning has its own cries, and who can hear them if a policeman can't? How can a city live, if a city's lost its faith, and has its horrors locked in its households.

GODBOY: (*As* HEDDERLEY *opens Doris's compact, tastes its contents*) I can assure you, Mannerly, that key will turn up eventually.

HAWKINS: No, Mr Godboy, the key was thrown away by the fathers of the nation. (*Rubs his eyes.*) There's not the difference I used to think, when I was in the care of the real fathers, between the vocation of the priest and the vocation of the policeman. We're both of us lonely from discipline. (*Laughs.*) And who is there, in this city, can tell them apart, the sinners and the sufferers, if the policeman can't?

GODBOY: (*Confused*) There's no doubt that you can, Mannerly, your record shows it.

HAWKINS: (*Leans over, takes Doris's stocking from her lap, runs his hands along it, his hat on his knee*) But if loneliness can sour men into sinners, it's discipline can convert sinners into policemen. (*Begins to knot the stocking.*) Would there be something in the house can ease my throat from its preaching? (*Laughs.*)

(GODBOY *stares at him, puzzled.*)

A little drop of whatever it was you found for me last night, but only if you've got some.

GODBOY: Indeed, Mannerly, (*Little pause.*) Gin?

HAWKINS: What ever it was, water and something or other, I think.

(GODBOY *gets up, goes into the kitchen.*)

(*Turns to* HEDDERLEY *and* DORIS) Hedderley?

HEDDERLEY: Sir?

HAWKINS: Are you going through Mrs Hoyden's handbag, Hedderley? Is that what I'm seeing?

HEDDERLEY: Sir.

HAWKINS: And did you give Hedderley permission, Doris? (DORIS *shakes her head.*)

Well – and why don't you ask what Hedderley's up to then, as is your right?

(DORIS *looks down, shakes her head.*)

Ask anyway.

DORIS: (*In a whisper*) It's all right.

HAWKINS: (*Who has knotted the stocking several times, leans forward, letting it hang from his hand*) Ask Hedderley, Doris.

DORIS: (*In a whisper*) Why are you looking through my handbag?

(HEDDERLEY *hands it back to* DORIS.)

HAWKINS: (*To* DORIS) Demand an apology, Doris. (*Pause.*) Doris. (*Little pause.*) Doris.

DORIS: (*In a whisper*) Say pardon.

HEDDERLEY: (*After a pause*) Sorry, ma'am.

HAWKINS: (*Gets up, sits down on the right of* DORIS, *stares at her intently, as he unknots the stocking*) Doris, it's slipped my mind, what did you say your foot-loose husband's name was, Doris?

DORIS: (*In a whisper*) Eric.

HAWKINS: (*Glances at* HEDDERLEY, *who shakes her head imperceptibly*) That's right, and that's it. (*Little pause, puts hand on* DORIS's *knee.*) Between-Jobs Eric. (*Laughs, tilts his head.*) And tell me, Doris, aren't you perhaps suffering from loneliness with Between-Jobs always going away from you like that?

(DORIS *shakes her head.*)

So you're expecting him back, then, sometime between now and never?

DORIS: (*As* MR GODBOY *comes into the room, with a glass with water in it, and a bottle of gin*) He'll be back for tea, he said. (GODBOY *hands the glass to* HAWKINS, *who looks at* HEDDERLEY, *abstractedly takes the bottle from* MR GODBOY, *who is just about to pour, and pours himself a large gin.*)

HAWKINS: For tea?

GODBOY: Eric's a bit funny in his movements, but he's not one to forget his tummy, I'll say that for him.

HAWKINS: (*Swallows from his drink*) As long as you don't prefer him gone, Doris, and send word to him to stay away?

(*Squeezes her knee with his other hand, laughs, tilts his head at her.*)

(DORIS *shakes her head.*)

Ah, but then you'd be having a mother to turn to, if you felt lost beyond yourself?

(DORIS *shakes her head.*)

And no father either?

(DORIS *shakes her head.*)

(*Drinks some more, his hand still on* DORIS's *knee.*) Ah, and Hedderley's in the way of being an orphan too, aren't you, Hedderley?

HEDDERLEY: Sir.

HAWKINS: Which is why Hedderley took to the discipline of the policehood, isn't it Hedderley? (*Laughs.*)

HEDDERLEY: Sir.

HAWKINS: (*Tilts his head, laughs.*) Ah, there's been a glimpse, Doris. Somewhere. I know it.

(HAWKINS *hands the glass back to* MR GODBOY, *gets up,* HEDDERLEY *also gets up. Looks down at* DORIS, *puts his hand on her shoulder, then heads for the door, right, followed by* HEDDERLEY. MR GODBOY *runs ahead, unlocks the door, opens it for them.*)

(*Pauses by the guppie case, looks in, wags his finger about, looks at* MR GODBOY, *who is holding the door open.*) I might be back, Mr Godboy, I might be back.

GODBOY: (*Looks at him*) I know that, Mannerly. I'll be ready.

(HAWKINS *tips his head, then goes out, followed by* HEDDERLEY. MR GODBOY *goes out of the room, after them.* DORIS *looks towards the open door, right, then picks up the stocking, which Hawkins has left on the sofa, picks up her shoe and her handbag, tiptoes out into the kitchen left. There is a silence on stage, then* DORIS *reappears through the kitchen door, followed closely by* MR GODBOY. *He escorts her back to the chair, sits her in it.*)

There's the officer in a million for you, Doris. Inspector Hawkins. Mannerly Hawkins. Did you notice his courtesy in interrogation? The way he established that May Godboy was absent was a delightful piece of consummate skill. (*Looks down at her.*) But you're pale, my dear?

DORIS: What's he want then?

GODBOY: (*After a pause*) He knows, Doris, and I know, but I can't tell you. It's between Mannerly and me. He's working in the dark but he'll get there in the end. (*Little pause.*) With him, cat and mouse is an art.

DORIS: What's he want with Eric then?

GODBOY: (*Laughs*) Eric's got no place in this, he wouldn't bother himself with an Eric.

DORIS: Oh. (*Little pause.*) He had his hand on my knee, like last night again.

GODBOY: A red herring, Doris, that's known as. He had his hand on my shoulder, twice. (*Laughs.*) Twice. (*Turns, goes to the alcove, comes back with the cylinder, locks the door, right, picks up the gasmask, walks purposefully back to* DORIS.)

DORIS: No, I changed my mind.

GODBOY: (*Looks at her*) It's too late for that, Doris. It's now or never.

(*Bends over her, again a short struggle, straightens.* DORIS *is in the gasmask, sitting hunched.*)

He knows me for what I am, Doris, that's his secret, and soon he'll have the mouse, which is me, in his paws, and two's a better catch for him than one.

(GODBOY *picks up the end of the tube, thrusts it under the gasmask, turns the cylinder, wrestles with the knobs. As he is doing this,* DORIS *snatches the tube out. The gas comes out, holds it up.* MR GODBOY *turns.*)

Manley. Manley. (*In a long whisper.*)

(*Goes to* DORIS, *puts his hand on her shoulder, bends over her, sees the pipe* DORIS *is holding, grabs hold of it, takes a deep breath to exclaim, and still holding the pipe, reels away, grabs at the cylinder, turns off the tap, then crashing around the chair, sways to the sofa, watched by* DORIS, *who gets anxiously to her feet.*)

(*Lights. Curtain.*)

SCENE 2

A couple of hours later.

Lights on MR GODBOY, *sitting on the sofa, his head lolling. He appears to be asleep, his hands are pressed into his crotch. He leaps suddenly to his feet, sits down again, stares ahead, slumps forward, buries his face in his hands. There is a knock on the door. It opens tentatively.* ERIC *puts his head in, smiles at* MR GODBOY, *sniffs, makes a face.* MR GODBOY *stares slowly at him.*

ERIC: Hullo!

(*Comes in, carrying a small pail, smiles at* MR GODBOY *who is still staring at him. Goes over, puts the pail on the guppie table, turns, sniffs again, coughs, makes as if to say something, checks himself, smiles.*)

Um, didn't you say she'd be done now then?

(*There is a long silence,* MR GODBOY *looks at the cylinder on the floor, looks back at* ERIC. *Gets to his feet, walks over to* ERIC *slowly. Puts a hand in his shoulder.*)

(*Laughs nervously.*) Where is she then? Is she upstairs?

GODBOY: Eric, I regret to inform you that your wife has met with a fatal accident.

ERIC: (*Uncomprehending*) What?

GODBOY: She didn't suffer, sir, that must be the main consolation at a time like this. Her release was instantaneous.

ERIC: (*Worried, looks at him apprehensively*) Where's Dorrie?

GODBOY: (*His shoulders jump, goes back, sits down. Puts a hand to his head*) My wound is playing me up something terrible.

ERIC: (*Coming over to him*) Where's Dorrie?

GODBOY: An old wound. Pre-war. My dad did it to me, in a game with his belt.

ERIC: (*Shouting*) Where's my Dorrie?

GODBOY: (*Shouting back*) Don't you shout at me, old boy. A Special Constable's a Special Constable. (*Pause.*) Righto?

ERIC: (*Whimpering*) Where's my Dorrie?

GODBOY: I keep telling you. She met with a fatal attack, mistake, I merely –

(ERIC *begins to shake his head from side to side.*)

Would you mind restraining yourself, my personal giddiness
isn't helped by it.

(*As* ERIC *looks at him.*)

A great release must be your main consolation. Remember
your manners.

(*Staggers to the window, opens it, sticks his head out, comes back,
watched by* ERIC. *Goes to the guppie case, picks up the food
package, shakes it over them pauses, then puts his hands into the
water and bending down, splashes his face. Straightens. Turns.*)

ERIC: Where is she?

GODBOY: Whom!

ERIC: Dorrie!

GODBOY: (*Looks around, confused. Stares at* ERIC) I have reason to
believe that she must be laid out in the kitchen.

(ERIC *turns, makes as if to run to the kitchen.* MR GODBOY *seizes
his arm, they grapple,* ERIC *falls to the floor.* MR GODBOY *sits on
top of him.*)

This is bound to be a time of stress for you. I've had
experience of grief in happier days. Kindly stop bobbing up
and down, Eric, you're on my wound.

ERIC: Please, please, I've got to see her.

GODBOY: Why?

ERIC: I got to, she's my Dorrie!

GODBOY: There's nothing to see, merely her remains.

ERIC: Let me see her! (*Bucking frantically.*)

GODBOY: This is irregular. She's liable to be in a state of undress.

ERIC: (*Stops, stares up at* MR GODBOY) What have you done to her?

GODBOY: Don't you attempt to incriminate me, boy.

(*There is a long pause.*)

How was your pictures, old boy?

ERIC: It was all right, it was good.

GODBOY: Can that story be checked out. (*Cunningly.*)

ERIC: What?

GODBOY: I'm in the clear on this Eric, you're not good enough to
play cat and mouse with me. And I'll tell you why. I left May –

ERIC: May?

GODBOY: Doris I merely mean, alone in the cupboard –

ERIC: Cupboard?

GODBOY: Kitchen I merely mean, don't keep confusing me, Eric,
it's a cheap trick, left her alone in the kitchen when
compelled to fetch an emergency refill of my prescription.
When I came back, I found her already passed away on the
kitchen table and a moment later, although myself laid low
by my wound, heard you hammering at the door in a state.
(*Little pause, cunningly.*) You are in a state, aren't you? We
can agree on that?

ERIC: Let me go to her, please.

GODBOY: (*After a pause, gets up*) All right, Eric, I give you
permission. I'm inclined to believe your story, but I'm not
sure that a superior officer like Mannerly Hawkins would
take a favourable view.
(*Shouting the last part of this after* ERIC, *who has run into the
kitchen. Then goes to the sofa, sits down. Noises come from the
kitchen.* MR GODBOY *folds his hands into his lap, stares straight
ahead. After a moment* ERIC *comes out, stares at him.*)
I've been thinking, Eric, it would look strange to the police if
your wife was found dead in my kitchen. Kindly carry her
upstairs, to your own parlour, where she belongs.
(*As* ERIC *sits down, as if in shock.*)
While you're about it please remove that cupboard I went to
great annoyance to purchase for you. The ideal solution
would be for you to cram May –

ERIC: (*Listlessly*) Doris.

GODBOY: (*After a slight pause*) Doris, into the sea-trunk I noted
among your possessions. It would be best for your own sake
if you could get her in completely, try not to have anything
hanging over the edge, then hoist the sea-trunk on top of
May –

ERIC: Doris.

GODBOY: Nonsense, old boy, you can scarcely hoist Doris in the
cupboard on top of herself in the cupboard, can you?
(*Laughs.*) It's May that's in the cupboard.
(ERIC *looks at him.*)
It's May's cupboard, I merely mean, Eric, old boy. So you

222

hoist (*pause*) Doris in the sea-chest on top of (*thinks*) the cupboard and then there'll be real cat and mouse with Mannerly when he comes calling. Those are my plans for you, I've thought them all out.

(ERIC *continues to stare at him.*)

Now. (*Rubs his hands together.*) Did you get her garments?

(ERIC *shakes his head.*)

What did you make of (*thinks*) Doris's (*nods*) appearance?

(*Looks at* ERIC.) Did she look serene?

(ERIC *shakes his head.*)

(*Stares at him.*) Now, Eric, violence to a living creature –

ERIC: She isn't there.

(GODBOY *stares at him.*)

She isn't. No . . . (*Shakes his head.*)

GODBOY: Where is she then?

ERIC: I don't know.

GODBOY: (*Gets up, goes into the kitchen, comes out again, carrying the gasmask.*) Something's wrong here, old boy. You looked in the larder, did you? (*Half turning.*)

ERIC: She isn't there.

(*Pause, as* MR GODBOY *stands uncertainly.*)

Now you tell me, you tell me (*slowly, raises a finger menacingly*), you tell me where my Dorrie is. (*Gets up, goes over, puts his finger close to* MR GODBOY's *face.*)

GODBOY: (*Walks past him, to the door, right, opens it, puts his head out, freezes as steps*) Good evening, sir, this is an honour, although to tell you the truth I was just off for another of my refills. Prescription for my gammy . . .

(*Backs in, followed by* HEDDERLEY. *As he does so,* ERIC *backs out, in the kitchen, nearly closing the door.* GODBOY *enters, followed by* HEDDERLEY. *They stand facing each other. There is a long pause.* MR GODBOY's *shoulders jump. He chuckles.* HEDDERLEY *stares unblinkingly. Little pause.* HEDDERLEY *sniffs.*)

A minor accident with some gassed cabbage-heads. Boiled over I merely – Mannerly not with you then?

HEDDERLEY: Soon.

GODBOY: That's very kind of him.

HEDDERLEY: I'm looking for Eric Hoyden.

GODBOY: Indeed?

HEDDERLEY: He's not upstairs.

GODBOY: That's his story. Can it be checked out? (*In a low voice.*)

HEDDERLEY: I'm not empowered to force an entry. (*Little pause.*) Is there anything you can tell me about him?

GODBOY: He's a fine lad (*lowering voice slightly*), in spite of a mild history of violence.

HEDDERLEY: (*Takes out note-book, jots down. Then goes to one of the utility chairs, crosses legs, skirt slightly hiked, left stocking rumpled*) Yes?

GODBOY: It's not his fault he doesn't know his own strength. To look at he's a reed, so if other people don't know his strength, and he's not so quick frankly (*taps his forehead*) as other people, how can *he* know it.

HEDDERLEY: Yes? (*Writing.*)

GODBOY: Nothing is known against him in this house except his fondness for gas which he can't keep from talking about. (*Pause.*) In his quiet moments he's deceptively likeable.

HEDDERLEY: (*Writes*) Yes?

GODBOY: (*Coming closer*) His word's not to be trusted (*in a low voice, then stepping casually away*), he's got a wonderful sense of humour.

HEDDERLEY: (*Writing*) Yes?

GODBOY: (*As ERIC's face appears around the kitchen door, sees it*) I'll stand by Eric to the end. If you need a character witness, don't hesitate to call on me to speak out.
(ERIC *shuts the door.*)
He can't help his habits, they're second nature.

HEDDERLEY: Yes? (*Writing.*)

GODBOY: You're conducting this investigation very quietly and firmly, officer, and I'll be glad to report that to Mannerly.
(HEDDERLEY *stares at him, then puts the notebook away. Keeps staring at him.*)
The last I saw of Eric (*coming closer*), he was off after his

May. Doris. (*Little pause.*) What is the precise nature of the charges being laid against him?

HEDDERLEY: That depends on what he's done.

GODBOY: There's British Justice for you (*as* HEDDERLEY *recrosses legs*).

HEDDERLEY: Where's your wife? (*Quickly.*)

GODBOY: Still away, sir. (*Quickly.*)

HEDDERLEY: (*After a pause*) Why do you call me sir?

GODBOY: (*Laughs, shakes his head*) Pardon.

HEDDERLEY: When do you expect him back?

GODBOY: (*Quickly*) When she's rested.

HEDDERLEY: Who's rested? (*Quickly.*)

GODBOY: Doris . . . May. (*Quickly.*)

HEDDERLEY: (*Quietly*) I was asking you about Eric Hoyden. (*Gets up, takes a step towards him. Stocking slipping.*) Where is he?

GODBOY: Well, Eric's a law in himself. (*Shakes his head.*) I must say I don't know why I confused Doris and Eric like that, they're quite different kettles of fish (*laughs*) naturally.

HEDDERLEY: Your wife Doris?

GODBOY: Doris Godboy, my wife.

(*Nods, begins to rock back and forth, sees that Hedderley's stocking is slipping. Stares as* HEDDERLEY *flicks through the pages of the notebook, then stops.*)

No indeed. May. (*Slaps his forehead.*) May Godboy. Eric is Doris's wife.

(*The kitchen door opens softly and* ERIC *puts his head in.*)

HEDDERLEY: (*Steps very close to* MR GODBOY) Why are you staring at me?

(*As* MR GODBOY *begins to shake his head.*)

I need to adjust my clothing.

GODBOY: Pardon?

HEDDERLEY: (*As the door opens wider, throws her leg out, hoists up skirt.* MR GODBOY *stares, turns, hurriedly folds his arms*)

Kindly turn around, we're not permitted to interrogate from behind.

(GODBOY *turns slowly, stares straight ahead, a fixed smile on his face.*

HEDDERLEY *fiddles with suspender clip, then very sharply)*
Where is your wife?

GODBOY: Purley.

HEDDERLEY: We may need her to testify. Where can she be
reached?

GODBOY: Thatch Cottage, Mimosa Drive.

(ERIC *is staring transfixed at* HEDDERLEY's *leg. Takes a step
inside.*)
Failing that the YWCA. If she can't get into her Auntie's
house, she stays at the YW. They're very tolerant there.
(ERIC, *his mouth hanging open, shuffles another step forward,
begins to shake his head.*)
Failing that she may have gone to one of her other aunties.
She likes to go from auntie to auntie indiscriminate.
(HEDDERLEY *stands, as* ERIC *is about to shuffle forward again.*
ERIC *turns, goes quickly back out of the kitchen. There is a long
pause.* HEDDERLEY *and* MR GODBOY *stare at each other.*)
(*Clears his throat*) Does Mannerly use you often?

HEDDERLEY: Often.

GODBOY: (*After another pause*) How did you come to enter the
force, may I ask?

HEDDERLEY: Inspector Hawkins picked me out during a certain
period when I was frequenting coffee bars in the Notting Hill
area. He took me in hand, dealt with me like a Dutch Uncle,
and then when he'd finished showing me the ropes invited
me to apply for special duties.

GODBOY: He's got greatness in him.

HEDDERLEY: (*Stares at him, walks past to the door. Turns, smiles at
MR GODBOY*) What is your own attitude to violence?

GODBOY: I'm against some of it.

HEDDERLEY: Are you against discipline?

GODBOY: (*After a pause*) It's not in my nature to hurt a living
creature.
(*Little pause, as* HEDDERLEY *continues to smile at him.*)
Although my own sister used to apply it to me sometimes,
when I was little. (*Stares at* HEDDERLEY *as if transfixed.*) She
used to compel me to roll down my trousers and she spanked

226

me on my bare bottie. (*Laughs.*) She was only a few years older than me, but very strong. She wanted to join the force also. Unfortunately she fell victim to an unsavoury incident and had to leave for Dublin after the war. (*Long pause.*) She was like you in major respects.

HEDDERLEY: (*Nods*) Inspector Hawkins is for discipline. We'll be back later.

GODBOY: Thank you, sir.

(HEDDERLEY *looks at him, goes out, shuts the door. There is a long pause.* MR GODBOY *stands staring at the door, as if in a trance.* ERIC *comes in left, goes up to* MR GODBOY, *tugs at his sleeve.*)

What do *you* want?

ERIC: I want my Dorrie.

GODBOY: (*Blinking, shakes his head*) Do you, old boy, well I can't help you in that. All I know is that something funny's going on with regards to you as far as the police are involved. Things keep turning black for you.

ERIC: What?

GODBOY: They seem to be after you in connection with May. May Godboy.

ERIC: Well, I don't know about May, it's Dorrie –

GODBOY: (*Laughs smoothly*) Eric, Doris is old enough to look after herself, if indeed she's alive. It's May the police are calling in my help for. Cat and mouse is warming up, Eric.

ERIC: (*Shakes his head*) It's my Dorrie –

GODBOY: Now, Eric, if you've anything you wish to clear off your chest in respect to the gassing of May Godboy, tell me now.

ERIC: What gassing?

GODBOY: Where's her remains, Eric?

ERIC: What remains?

GODBOY: (*Points dramatically at the cupboard*) Remains of May Godboy.

ERIC: You said she was in Purley, I heard you.

GODBOY: Then as long as Mannerly and I can find her there (*walks away from* ERIC) there's nothing for you to worry

about, is there? (*Whips around.*) What did you do this
afternoon?

ERIC: I told you, I went to Virgin Mayo and Burt Lancaster.

GODBOY: Cinema alibis can be broken into shreds, Eric. Who's
your witnesses?

ERIC: I – I – (*points to the pail*) I got you those. Them gups!

GODBOY: Was Doris with you at the time?

ERIC: She was with you.

GODBOY: Oh, and was she here when you got back, Eric?

ERIC: No, that's what I'm –

GODBOY: Who's your witnesses, Eric?

ERIC: (*Thinks*) You are. (*Nods.*)

GODBOY: Indeed? All I know is that I was laid out on account of
my old wound and when I came to myself *you* was
hammering about with loose questions of May having died in
an accident. So who's your witnesses, Eric?

ERIC: Doris.

GODBOY: Hah. Hah hah. So it was *Doris* is dead.

ERIC: (*Shaking his head*) No, no, what I mean is May –

GODBOY: May!

ERIC: I haven't seen her.

GODBOY: (*Puts his face forward, hisses*) Witnesses, Eric, witnesses,
you need a witness, Eric, who's your witness, Eric, who?
Who? (*Following him across the room as he backs away.*)
(*The door right opens and* HAWKINS *steps into the room.*)
(*Whipping around.*) Good afternoon, Mannerly, I was hoping
you'd turn up, here's a real problem for you.
(ERIC *makes for the kitchen door, opens it, a figure in blue is
fleetingly visible. Closes the door, turns, faces the wall, left.*)

HAWKINS: (*Revolving his hat, walks towards* ERIC) Good
afternoon, sir, I don't think I've had the pleasure.
(ERIC *coughs.*)

GODBOY: Eric Hoyden, Inspector Hawkins is inquiring politely
after your name.

ERIC: Eric Hoyden.

HAWKINS: Well, I'll say this for you, you're a difficult man to put
a hand on, Eric Hoyden.

(*Puts his hand on* ERIC's *shoulder, turns him around slowly.*
ERIC *stands with his hands sunk into his pockets, head lowered.*)
And what do you know about all this, sir?

ERIC: What?

HAWKINS: And now what does *what* mean, sir, may I ask. (*Puts a
finger under* ERIC's *chin and lifts it up.*) What's *what* mean, sir?

ERIC: Nothing.

HAWKINS: Is it nothing, then, sir? You've no burglaries to tell me
about? (*Gives* ERIC's *jaw a little shake.*) No murders, sir?
(*Gives* ERIC's *jaw a little shake.*) No (*little pause*) indecent-
assaults-and-handbag-snatching to turn my ears with, sir?
(ERIC *attempts to shake his head.* HAWKINS *holds it steady.*)

ERIC: (*Pointing a finger at* MR GODBOY, *who is standing with his
hands behind his back*) He – he – he done something to my
Dorrie, he did.

HAWKINS: (*Still holding* ERIC's *jaw*) And have you done
something to *his* (*slight stress*) Dorrie, Mr Godboy?

GODBOY: I wouldn't touch her with a barge-pole, Mannerly.
(*Laughs.* HAWKINS *turns his head, looks at him.*)
I've got too much respect, sir.

ERIC: He did, he did, he told me himself she was dead.

HAWKINS: (*Removes his hand from* ERIC's *jaw, pats both his cheeks
simultaneously*) Well, sir, I can see you've nothing to fear
from the law, and certainly you wouldn't mind a little
inspection from one of my men. (*Little pause. Shouts.*)
Hedderley!
(*Whipping* ERIC *around to face the kitchen door as he does so.
The kitchen door opens simultaneously,* HEDDERLEY *comes in.*)
(HEDDERLEY *walks slowly toward* ERIC. HAWKINS *moves
away to stand next to* MR GODBOY. ERIC *stands transfixed.*
HEDDERLEY *stands facing* ERIC, *then puts arms about his
shoulders in a hug, sways about with him.*)

ERIC: Here! Here!
(HEDDERLEY *takes* ERIC's *hand and presses it against her right
leg, moves it up under the skirt.*)
Here! (*Bending over.*)
(HEDDERLEY *straightens, drops* ERIC's *hand, turns, nods once*

to HAWKINS. HAWKINS *beckons with his head.* HEDDERLEY
goes to him, they walk to the other end of the room, whispering.
ERIC *looks towards them, makes for the kitchen door, left.*)

HAWKINS: (*Without turning*) Would you be kind enough to hang
on a little, sir, thank you, sir.

(ERIC *stops.*)

(GODBOY *looks towards* HAWKINS *and* HEDDERLEY, *goes over,
takes* ERIC'S *arm.*)

HAWKINS: (*Turns*) Now that's a lovely pair of trousers.

(ERIC *looks down at his trousers, looks away.* HAWKINS
whispers to HEDDERLEY. GODBOY *fingers* ERIC'S *trousers.*)
(*Turning.*) Would you do Constable Hedderley the kindness
of permitting Constable Hedderley the use of your toilet?

GODBOY: Indeed, Mannerly, it's across the hall, Hedderley.

HAWKINS: (*Staring at* ERIC, *repeats*) Would you do Constable
Hedderley the kindness of permitting Constable Hedderley
the use of your toilet?

ERIC: (*After a silence*) What?

HAWKINS: Your toilet, sir. Constable Hedderley's in trouble.

ERIC: Oh. (*As* HEDDERLEY *comes towards him.*)

HAWKINS: Oh now, sir, you wouldn't be one of those citizens
who demands a search warrant from an officer desperate for a
toilet, sir, would you?

ERIC: Um . . . all right.

(HEDDERLEY *holds out a hand.*)

HAWKINS: Now where exactly did you say your toilet was, sir?

ERIC: Upstairs landing.

HAWKINS: Now there's great stress in the force on personal
hygiene, Constable Hedderley will be wanting to wash her
hands in your sink afterwards, could you let her have the
keys to get in with, sir?

ERIC: (*After a pause*) I lost them.

(GODBOY *puts his hand into Eric's trouser pocket, takes out the
keys, holds them triumphantly to* HEDDERLEY. HEDDERLEY
stares at them.)

HAWKINS: Mr Godboy, I think those are Mr Hoyden's keys, and
I advise you to return them to him immediately, Mr Godboy.

(GODBOY *looks towards* HAWKINS, *gives the keys to* ERIC.
HEDDERLEY *takes them from* ERIC.)
Manners, Hedderley!

HEDDERLEY: Thank you, sir. (*To* ERIC. *Goes out.*)
(*There is a silence.* HAWKINS *stands rotating his hat, smiling at*
ERIC. MR GODBOY *stands bewildered, looking from* HAWKINS
to ERIC. ERIC *stands hunched.*)

HAWKINS: (*To* ERIC) Now I think, sir, you were saying
something about *your* (*slight stress*) Dorrie, I think.

ERIC: He knows, he knows. (*Nods at* MR GODBOY.)
(*There is the sound of an upstairs lavatory flushing. They all stare
up at the ceiling. There are crashing sounds from above.*)

HAWKINS: Well, if anything's happened to that young lady,
there'd be some answering would have to be done, to the law
and to myself. (*Little pause.*) There was a young lady once,
permitting herself to be humbly searched down at the station
when she was innocent of everything but weakness of spirit,
and I caught a glimpse of her through a crack in the door
when she was standing with only her little hands for
covering, and then I was called off to a breaking and entering
and when I got back she was lost to me. Now I've been
looking for that young lady –
(*The door, right, opens.* HAWKINS *and* MR GODBOY *turn
towards it.* ERIC *stares quickly away as* HEDDERLEY *comes in
carrying arm-loads of handbags and a pair of trousers.* HAWKINS
and MR GODBOY *go on staring, as the door left, opens,* DORIS
puts her head in, ERIC *sees her, takes a step towards her.* DORIS
looks around the room, sees HAWKINS, *shuts the door.*)

ERIC: She's – she's –
(ERIC *turns, sees the handbags and trousers, stops. There is a
long silence on stage.* HEDDERLEY *drops the handbags, comes
towards* HAWKINS, *hands him the trousers.* ERIC *turns around
again.* HAWKINS *takes the trousers, shakes them out. They have
a large section missing at the fly.*)

HAWKINS: (*Strides across to* ERIC, *turns him around, takes his chin
in his hand*) So now we know what you do between jobs,
Between-Jobs Eric. You do the ladies of Merrit Street, sir.

(*There is a long silence.*)

GODBOY: You mean there were *two* Merrit Street attackers, Mannerly?

HAWKINS: Just one lucky one (*turns* ERIC's *face to the right, then to the left*) who must be thanking God (*turns* ERIC's *face up to the ceiling*) he's been taken at last. (*Releases him.*) We should have had you last night, Between-Jobs, all the misery of your guilt should have been over for you in the darkness of last night, if Constable Hedderley hadn't over-baited himself with heavy perfume and a skirt too tight it prevented him from running free. Isn't that so, Hedderley?

HEDDERLEY: Sir.

HAWKINS: Ah, while Constable Hedderley, coated in this perfume and hobbled at the legs, was throwing Between-Jobs around on the pavement, the dogs, unable to recognize Hedderley's natural body-odours, sprang straight at Constable Hedderley. Except, that is, for an elderly bitch with dirty habits who plunged straight for Between-Jobs, preferring the male smell of *him*, and tore this (*little pause, takes out of his pocket the cloth from Eric's trousers, complete with fly-buttons, and holds it against the torn trousers*) from the Merrit Street attacker. So (*to* ERIC) another day you had to suffer through, for your release.

GODBOY: And to think I left you alone in my kitchen with May!

ERIC: I wasn't going to – I wasn't going to – I'd made myself stop doing it. But she (*looks at* HEDDERLEY) he – she – was pulling her stockings up and smiling at me and winking and my head was buzzing from May's stout and gin, and I just meant to help out with something and the next minute she was whirling me about and holding me on the ground and his knee was in my back and her arm was around my throat and there was these dogs, these dogs . . . (*Covers his face with his arm.*)

(*Long silence.*)

HAWKINS: There, there, boy, it's all right. It's all over for you now. (*Little pause.*) Or will be when you tell us where our Dorrie is.

ERIC: She's in the kitchen.

GODBOY: Don't tell lies, Eric, it won't serve. You took her away somewhere this afternoon and gassed her or something like that, and we both know it.

HAWKINS: (*Takes a step towards* ERIC, *restrains himself*) Just tell us, son, and then we can have a good talk about the other matter down at the station.

ERIC: She was here, he done it, I don't know, she's – (*stops, looks at the faces*) I tell you.

(HAWKINS *looks at* HEDDERLEY, *turns, walks to the front of the stage.* HEDDERLEY *takes* ERIC's *arm, and leads him to the sofa, makes him sit down, bends over him.* MR GODBOY *stands somewhere between* HAWKINS *and* HEDDERLEY, *his hands behind his back.*)

HAWKINS: (*Turns his head to* MR GODBOY) When I was a little boy, Mr Godboy, over there in County Mayo –

(GODBOY *nods attentively.*)

I had a dream of devotion, a lonely life given up to salvation. I dreamt that as a boy, I did.

(HEDDERLEY *bends over* ERIC, *does something to him,* ERIC *cries out.* MR GODBOY *turns his head, looks towards the sofa.*)

And come Sundays there was a special pond I'd walk to, deep and calm it was, and there in the long afternoon I'd sit and think of what was open to me to be done –

(HEDDERLEY *makes* ERIC *cry out again.* GODBOY *again looks towards the sofa, takes a step back to it.*)

And of the little I have to give. And my dog whiskers up to some doggy mischief at my feet or behind me in the bushes. (*Shakes his head, smiling.*)

(HEDDERLEY *makes* ERIC *cry out again.* GODBOY *takes another step back.*)

And somehow in those days the sun was always shining, yes it was, or that's the way I see it now, from the black heart of the big city. When I look back to it from no more Sundays in Mayo. (GODBOY, *who has been standing, looking down at* ERIC, *his hands behind his back, watches* HEDDERLEY *bend over* ERIC *again.*)

And yet somewhere in the back of my mind is the picture,
I'll keep it there through disciplining and pain, of what it is
I've lost.

(GODBOY *leans over and does something experimental to* ERIC.
Then HEDDERLEY *does it. Then* ERIC. *In a see-saw rhythm.*)

ERIC: (*Screaming out*) I tell you she was there, larking about in the
kitchen.

GODBOY: I won't have you telling lies about my kitchen,
Between-Jobs.

HAWKINS: (*Smiling*) Through disciplining and pain I hug it to
me, that Sunday afternoon when I dreamed of devotion, by
an eternal pond, in an eternal sunshine, and I –

(DORIS *puts her head around the kitchen door, stares at the scene
on the couch, takes a few frantic steps in, stops.* HEDDERLEY
and GODBOY *go on working on* ERIC.)

(*Turns, sees* DORIS.) – am boy eternal.

(*Goes over to* DORIS, *takes her gently by the arm, leads her to the
centre of the stage.*)

GODBOY: Where is she, Between-Jobs, where is she, where?

HEDDERLEY: Where? Where?

(*They bend simultaneously over him.*)

HAWKINS: (*Puts a finger under* DORIS's *chin, tilts her face up*) And I
am boy eternal, Doris. I thought you'd been taken from us
(*very gently*), where have you been, Doris?

(ERIC *lets out a long shout.* HAWKINS *looks towards them as*
GODBOY *turns his face around. He is laughing, sees* DORIS, *nods
to her, turns back to* ERIC. *Begins to do something, suddenly
stops.* HEDDERLEY *stops.*)

Hedderley. (*Nods to the kitchen door.*)

(HEDDERLEY *helps* ERIC *from the sofa, takes him into the
kitchen.*)

Mr Godboy. (*Nods again to the kitchen door.*)

(GODBOY *hesitates, looks at* DORIS, *follows* HEDDERLEY.)

And Hedderley, there's to be only gentleness now,
Hedderley.

HEDDERLEY: Sir.

HAWKINS: Mr Godboy?

GODBOY: Sir.

(*They go into the kitchen, shut the door.* HAWKINS *stands looking at* DORIS, *who clutches her handbag to her stomach, stares at the ground. There is a long pause. Then* HAWKINS *puts his hand through* DORIS's *arm, leads her to one of the utility chairs, sits her on it. Doris's handbag drops from her lap, its contents scatter over the floor. She makes a move to pick it up.* HAWKINS *restrains her, pats her knee, crouches at her feet, begins to put her things back into the handbag.*)

HAWKINS: Are you frightened?

(DORIS *sits hunched.*)

Of course you are. I think it's part of your nature, isn't it? (*Pause.*) Isn't it?

(DORIS *nods. Shuts her handbag firmly, puts it back in her lap, stays on his knees.*) And why has Eric been out in Merrit Street, grabbing at the ladies and their handbags then? (*Croningly.*) Is it because you wouldn't let him near you, is it because he didn't know how to come near you, is it because you're frightened, Doris?

DORIS: (*After a pause*) He didn't mean it. Not Eric.

HAWKINS: (*Strokes her foot*) Is he any good to you, Doris? (*Little pause.*) And is he, now? (*Takes her shoe off.*)

DORIS: (*After a pause*) Don't know.

HAWKINS: And what good are you, Doris, all by yourself while Eric's away from us all? Will you get yourself taken away again by another Eric, poor Eric. Will you?

(DORIS *shrugs into a hunch.*)

What do you want, then, Doris?

DORIS: Don't know.

HAWKINS: And who knows what you're wanting, Doris? (*Stands up slowly, stands over her, looks down.*) Who?

DORIS: (*After a long pause, lifts her face to his. Pause*) You? (*Whispered.*)

HAWKINS: And who'll make you a good girl, Doris?

DORIS: You.

HAWKINS: And who did I get a glimpse at, once, down at the station, and nude?

235

DORIS: (*Staring up*) Me. (*Whispered.*)

HAWKINS: (*Bends down, kisses* DORIS *on the mouth. Raises her up by the arms, kisses her again, passionately*) So what do you want, then, Doris?

(DORIS *staring into his face, whispers something inaudible.*)

(*Releases her slowly, looks at her.*) Hah! (*Slaps her playfully on the rump.*) Hah! Hedderley!

(*The kitchen door opens.* GODBOY *enters, stands aside with his hands behind his back as* ERIC *enters,* HEDDERLEY *holding his arm up behind him.*)

ERIC: Dorrie, Dorrie, you all right, Dorrie?

(DORIS *looks down, her handbag clasped to her stomach again.* HAWKINS *nods to* HEDDERLEY. ERIC *is released, stands upright.*)

HAWKINS: Are you all right, Doris?

(DORIS *looks at him, nods.*)

ERIC: I couldn't help it, Dorrie, I couldn't, it's 'cause I love you, Dorrie.

HAWKINS: Well, Doris, I think he's expecting an answer, have you got an answer for him?

(DORIS *looks at* HAWKINS, *shakes her head.*)

There's no answer for you, son. (*Goes to* ERIC.) You were going to come to me in the end, you see, and you'll be glad of it, in the end, you see. (*Little pause.*) Think of it, while you were slipping through my net I was sitting here, beneath your home, waiting for you without either of us knowing it. Something called me here, it was your own cry that called me here, son, and that's why I came. There's always a reason for accidents. The reason was that you were waiting for me, what else could it have been? Think of that.

GODBOY: (*Coughs, he has been standing restlessly during* HAWKINS'S *speech*) There could be other reasons, Mannerly, you could have come because someone –

ERIC: (*Swings up an arm, points his finger at* GODBOY, *stares at him*) It was you, you. (*There is a long silence, then cries out as if in revelation.*) He done for May!

(*Another silence. They look at* GODBOY, *who puts his hands*

236

behind his back, swells his chest.)

GODBOY: That's who it's been between, Mannerly, all along. Cat and (*takes a step forward*) mouse.

ERIC: (*Nodding*) He done for May!

GODBOY: Where do you think she's concealed then?
(*Smiling at* HAWKINS, *who is looking at* ERIC.)
All along?

ERIC: (*Draws a deep breath, bursts out*) In the cupboard! In the cupboard, what's full of gas!

GODBOY: Mannerly? (*Smiling at him.*)

ERIC: That's it, the cupboard!

GODBOY: Quiet, rapist, people like you is two a penny nowadays.

HAWKINS: (*Goes to* DORIS, *takes a hair-pin out of her hair, then as* ERIC *takes a step forward, without turning around*) Hedderley.
(HEDDERLEY *takes* ERIC'S *arm again.* HAWKINS *goes over to the cupboard, bends down, fiddles the hair-pin into the lock.* GODBOY *turns, smiles at* ERIC *disdainfully, walks across to* HAWKINS, *stands beside him.*)

GODBOY: I want to say, Manly, you've cracked open something big here, that'll be a feather in your cap in all the newspapers. I've waited for you to show up here, waited and waited, and you did, Mannerly, just on time. Our turn together was doomed. Cat and mouse Mannerly, as you said yourself, the big mouse is in your paws at last.
(*As the lock clicks and* HAWKINS *stands upright.*)
Permit me, Mannerly, it's all I ask now the moment is come (*takes the door*), here is what you've been waiting for, here is what was calling out to you.
(GODBOY *stands, stares* HAWKINS *in the face, then flings the door open.* HAWKINS *stares inside, then comes back to* DORIS, *nods to* HEDDERLEY. HEDDERLEY *pushes* ERIC *across the room past* GODBOY *who is staring blankly into the cupboard.* HAWKINS *follows, one hand resting carelessly on* DORIS'S *rump. She is limping, clutching her handbag tight.* ERIC *suddenly breaks free of* HEDDERLEY, *and plunges into the cupboard, comes out again, holds up his raincoat, shows it to* DORIS.)

ERIC: I said it was in there, didn't I, Dorrie?

(*Struggles defiantly into it.* HEDDERLEY *takes his arm, they go out.*)

HAWKINS: (*To* GODBOY) There's a lot of confessing to be made. And don't worry yourself about Doris, what she needs is only a Dutch Uncle talking to. (*Looks at* DORIS.) I'll be showing you the ropes myself, Doris. (*Puts his hat on.*) Goodbye, Mr Godboy, goodbye.

(*Replaces his hand on* DORIS's *rump. They go out.*

GODBOY *stands alone, staring after them. Then goes and sits down on the sofa. Sits staring ahead. A long wait. Then he gets up, goes forlornly over to the guppie case, is about to shake some food in, checks himself, picks up the pail, goes off stage, right. There is a pause.*

MAY *appears through the kitchen door, carrying her bags. Drops them on the floor, takes off her coat, drops it on the sofa, looks about her, goes back into the kitchen. Sounds of a lavatory flushing.* GODBOY *comes in, puts the guppie case on the table, pours the guppies from the pail into it, scatters the food. Stands for a moment, back to the audience, then turns, looks at the cupboard, goes to it, stares in, steps in completely.* MAY *comes out of the kitchen door, smoking a cigarette, looks about her, then walks across the room towards the door, right, passing the cupboard. As she does so she slams the cupboard door shut, goes on out of the room, tapping ash. Curtain.*)

Spoiled

for Beryl

Spoiled was first performed at the Haymarket Theatre, London, on 24 February 1971. The cast was as follows:

HOWARTH	Jeremy Kemp
DONALD	Simon Ward
JOANNA	Anna Massey
LES	Peter Denyer
MRS CLENHAM	Pamela Pitchford

Director	Stephen Hollis
Designer	Anthony Holland
Lighting	Joe Davis

ACT ONE

SCENE I

The stage is divided. Three-quarters of the stage space, on the right,
shows the living-room and one quarter, on the left, shows a small spare
room, referred to in the directions that follow as the bedroom. A wall
with a door upstage, opening into the bedroom, divides the two rooms.
The living-room is large, comfortable, middle-class intellectual and
casual. A table with books and a lamp stands in the window and
against the wall downstage of the window a smaller table also with
books and a lamp. Against the wall upstage of the window is an old
upright piano and piano stool. The main door to the rest of the house is
facing us upstage right. Through this door can be seen the hall, with
the foot of stairs upstage. The kitchen can be seen through a hatch,
which is on the left of the main door in the living-room. Running along
the back wall of the living-room, under the hatch, is a shelf-unit with a
lamp, a tray of drinks and a hi-fi unit on it. The speakers for the hi-fi
are on a shelf above. Books fill other shelves on the back wall and
shelves above the piano.
The bedroom area, left, has baby paper on the walls and is cluttered
with a desk against the back wall, with a lamp and two single chairs,
a carry-cot against the dividing wall downstage and parts of a larger
cot upstage of the door. A folding bed, made up and hidden with a
cloth cover is folded and stands against the wall, left.
The action starts in the living-room.
HOWARTH *and* DONALD *are seated at the table,* HOWARTH *in the*
elbow chair right, DONALD *left.* DONALD *has a bicycle satchel on the*
floor beside him, HOWARTH *has textbooks on the table in front of him*
and a briefcase on the floor. As the curtain rises DONALD *stoops to pick*
up three textbooks which he has knocked on to the floor. HOWARTH *is*
eating a biscuit.
HOWARTH: In the event of almost any catastrophe 'je suis desolé'
will do nicely.

DONALD: Um, je suis desolé.

HOWARTH: Yeah. A phrase like that's worth five marks in the oral. It might be worth contriving a small accident, like stumbling over the examiner's toes, to get it in. Don't hurt him, mind.

(DONALD *laughs*.)

OK. Expliquez-moi, monsieur Donald Clenham, pourquoi vous êtes en train d'apprendre le français?

DONALD: (*Nervously*) Um, um, parce-que je veux apprendre le français.

HOWARTH: (*Waits, smiles*) Elaborate. Don't be afraid of boring him.

DONALD: Um, um, parce-que je veux voyager en France et parce que il est, um, c'est une langue très intéressant.

HOWARTH: Now Donald, think. (*Pause.*) Une langue intéressant?

DONALD: Oh, um. (*Laughs.*) Um, un langue intéressant. Um . . .

HOWARTH: (*Looks at him, eyebrows raised*) Well, at least now you're consistent. But wrong.

DONALD: (*After a ghastly pause*) Une langue intéressante . . . (*Tentatively.*)

HOWARTH: Mmm, huh. OK. (*Smiles.*) Can you relax? You're terribly tense today. Why?

DONALD: No, I'm all right. Well . . .

HOWARTH: Is it because the exam's on Monday?

DONALD: (*Shakes his head*) Well . . . I suppose I keep thinking about it, sir.

HOWARTH: Don't make it worse than it is. Look, today's Saturday. You've got all day tomorrow. Don't suffer before you have to. What are you going to do for the rest of the weekend?

DONALD: (*Shrugs*) Nothing really. Go for a bicycle ride with a friend and . . . well, do some work.

HOWARTH: Fine. But don't do too much, eh? Get your mother to throw you out of the house, to the cinema or something, eh? (DONALD *nods*.)

No, really. I'm all for your translating a few passages, but for God's sake don't work yourself into a state. In fact, I'll give you a ration of passages to take home, and you stick to those. (*Rises, goes up to hatch, brings out a biscuit tin, helps himself to a biscuit.*) Mm? (*Looks at him, smiles.*) By the way, there's something I've been meaning to ask you. What have you been using for a dictionary?

DONALD: Just a um, little one.

HOWARTH: Got it with you?

(DONALD *nods. Then, clearly embarrassed, he bends over, picks up his satchel, fumbles in it and picks an exercise-book out of the satchel. A folded picture from a magazine drops from the exercise-book onto the floor.*)

DONALD: The thing is, my mum got it for me. (*Picks a very small dictionary out of the satchel, holds it up.*) She just went into the shop and asked for one and this is the one they, um . . .

HOWARTH: Keep it for a weekend in Paris. (*Hands him the little one and picks up an enormous Cassells dictionary from the table.*) But you borrow this one for this weekend, eh? (*Hands him the big one.* DONALD *notices the photograph on the floor and hurriedly puts his foot over it.* HOWARTH *sees this.*) It's an extremely lucky dictionary. Even if you don't use it, it'll communicate a certain impressive confidence. I've lent it to hundreds of boys at school just before exams, and always with satisfactory results. Let it calm you down.

DONALD: Thank you, sir. I'll bring it back afterwards, straightaway.

HOWARTH: OK. Are you up to a dictation?

(DONALD *grabs the photo from the floor and puts it in his satchel.* HOWARTH *notices this.* DONALD *nods, draws an exercise-book to him.*)

Let's see. (*Flickering through the pages of a textbook.*) What with you twice a week and five classes at school twice a week, I can never remember. (DONALD *puts the dictionary in his satchel and looks through his exercise-book.*) 'Ce matin-là Jean avait parlé beaucoup de blés et de ce qu'il appelait la "culture intensive" . . .'?

DONALD: Yes, we've done that one, sir.

HOWARTH: 'Un homme voyageait dans un pays de

montagnes . . .' (HOWARTH *looks at* DONALD, DONALD *nods*.)

Yeah, I remember that, um, 'Il y a, à Vérone, des jardins'.

(DONALD *shakes his head*.)

All right. (*Gets up, saunters to the window, puts his hand in his pocket*.) Ready?

(DONALD *nods, pushes his satchel clumsily aside*.)

'Il y a, à Vérone, des jardins à l'italienne où l'on monte par une série d'escaliers et de terrasses. J'y passai l'après-midi dans un terrible perplexité. D'en haut, je découvrais . . .'

(DONALD, *as* HOWARTH *reads, is still clumsily attempting to get ready . . . He knocks the satchel off the table, kneels, shoves papers and books back inside*.)

DONALD: (*Gets up, is desperately scrabbling*) Sorry, sir.

(HOWARTH *stands watching, as* DONALD *sits down, and gets a pencil out of his pencil-case*.)

Um, sorry sir.

HOWARTH: All right? 'Il y a, à Vérone.'

(HOWARTH *continues to read the dictation piece*. DONALD *breaks the point of his pencil, scrabbles in the pencil-case for a sharpener and starts to sharpen his pencil over the satchel.* HOWARTH *notices this and breaks off*.)

This isn't a good idea. Not now, anyway. Shall we give it a rest?

DONALD: (*Sits looking down at the table, mutters inaudibly*) Sorry, sir.

HOWARTH: Mmmmm. (*Looks at him thoughtfully*.) Donald, if the worst comes to the very worst, and you don't *feel* like it on Monday morning, you can always take it the next time around, can't you?

(DONALD *nods*.)

So why does it matter so much? You know, I'm generally telling boys at this stage that they've got to care more. In your case perhaps you should really try caring less.

DONALD: (*Nods again*) Except, well. (*Looks at him*.) It's my mum, sir. She's expecting me to get it, and – because it's the third time and that. (*Laughs*.)

HOWARTH: She'll be angry with you?

DONALD: No, no, she won't – no, but she, well . . . worries.

HOWARTH: Parents do tend to. Especially mothers.

DONALD: Yes, sir.

HOWARTH: (*Pause, looks at him, as if thinking*) Look, do you think she'd spare you for the weekend?

DONALD: Sir?

HOWARTH: Then we could take things at their own pace, eh? We could get through a bit of work, and calm each other down. I'd hate to think that all we've done over the last six weeks is going to slip away in a nervous weekend. (*Pause.*) Eh?

DONALD: Well . . . (*Stops, stares at him blankly.*)

HOWARTH: Do you think she'd mind?

(DONALD *shakes his head.*)

Or would *you* rather not?

DONALD: (*Looks down, mutters shyly*) Don't want to put you out, sir.

HOWARTH: I wouldn't have asked you if I thought you'd be putting us out. We'd both be delighted to have you. So the question for you to answer, frankly and fearlessly, is whether you want to. Do you?

DONALD: (*Nods, looking down*) Thank you very much indeed, sir.

HOWARTH: Good. Very good. Now we *can* relax . . . although, first you'd better phone your mother.

DONALD: Sir. (*Gets up.*)

HOWARTH: It's just in the hall there.

DONALD: Sir. (*Nods, walks across the room.*)

(HOWARTH *stands for a moment, stroking his chin, then makes a sudden face, as if grasping that he's done something he hadn't really intended. He spots Donald's satchel, looks down at it, starts to bend to pick it up.*)

(*Reappears at the door.*) Um, the only thing, um, we're not on the telephone.

HOWARTH: Oh. Well, you'll have to let her know, of course. Is there anyone else you could phone? You could ask *them* to ask *her* to phone us or . . . (*Shrugs.*) It's very complicated, isn't it?

DONALD: Well, there's some people next door – sometimes they let us use their phone.

HOWARTH: There you are then.

DONALD: Sir. (*Goes out.*)

(HOWARTH *shakes his head, bends down and takes out the folded paper, opens it, looks at it, makes a little whistle of amused surprise . . . is about to put it back into the satchel, when the door opens and* DONALD *reappears. He shoves the folded paper into his back pocket.*)

I just remembered, um. (*Laughs awkwardly.*) They're away this weekend. They've gone to visit her auntie . . . she lives in Bexhill.

HOWARTH: Oh dear. Well, perhaps we'd better think again. I can't keep you here without letting your mother know, and it's scarcely worth your cycling all the way home and back again.

DONALD: I don't mind, sir. I mean, it wouldn't take me long.

HOWARTH: Your mother might not be in.

DONALD: Oh yes, sir. She doesn't go out until later. She's doing the matinée . . . that's at two thirty.

HOWARTH: (*Reluctantly*) Well, in that case . . .

(*The sound of the door slamming.*)

JOANNA: (*Off*) Hello!

(JOANNA *opens the door. She is carrying a bundle of clothing . . . scarlet, curtain-like, and a plastic carrier bag.*)

HOWARTH: Though it seems rather a business . . .

JOANNA: (*Entering between them, looks at* DONALD) Hello, Donald – it is Donald, isn't it?

HOWARTH: (*As* DONALD *smiles, nods awkwardly*) Yes. Donald Clenham.

JOANNA: (*Shaking hands with* DONALD) Well, hello, Donald.

DONALD: Um, hello, um . . .

JOANNA: I've got your gear. (*Drops the stuff on the couch.*) I've just got to nip up to the butcher for the joint. I won't be long.

HOWARTH: OK.

(JOANNA *smiles, goes to the kitchen door and through.*)

Well, what do you think? (*To* DONALD) If it *is* going to be difficult. Mmmm?

JOANNA: (*Reappearing from the kitchen*) Have you finished, or are you going on a bit?

HOWARTH: Actually, we were just deciding that very question. Why?

JOANNA: Well, I just thought if you *were* going on, why doesn't Donald stay and have a bite . . . only scrambled eggs on Saturday, I'm afraid. (*To* DONALD.)

DONALD: Mmm, well . . . mmm . . . (*Laughs, looks at* HOWARTH.)

HOWARTH: As a matter of fact, darling. (*Laughs.*) The question we were attempting to decide was whether or not Donald should stay for the weekend.

JOANNA: (*Looks at him, a fractional pause*) Oh, lovely. (*To* DONALD) Do.

HOWARTH: That is, if we're all right for sheets and things.

JOANNA: We are. (*Smiling over-politely, directly at* HOWARTH.)

HOWARTH: Actually, there are *other* problems. We can't think how to get hold of Donald's mother.

JOANNA: Donald's mother? (*After a pause.*) She'd be very welcome too, of course.

HOWARTH: (*Laughs again*) No no . . . to let her know where Donald is.

JOANNA: (*Laughs*) Oh, I see. (*Suddenly naturally.*) Oh, manage it somehow please, Donald. We'd love you to.

HOWARTH: (*In relief*) Yes, come on now, Donald, let's think.

JOANNA: (*Looks at* HOWARTH) Well, I'll see you later. (*Looks at* DONALD.) Both of you, I hope.

(*Severe look at* HOWARTH *as she goes out, shutting the door.*)

HOWARTH: (*Smiles*) There you are, you see. My old lady isn't a problem, I'm sure yours won't be.

DONALD: No. Well, I'll go around on my bike then.

HOWARTH: Good. That *is* settled then, isn't it? At last. (*Pause.*) Do you want to go now, or shall we have another go at that dictation?

DONALD: (*Pause*) I don't mind. I mean, well, the dictation . . . if that's all right.

(HOWARTH *goes to the box and picks it up.* DONALD *sits down at the table.*)

HOWARTH: 'Ce matin-là Jean avait parlé beaucoup de blès et de ce qu'il appelait la "culture" . . .' No, that wasn't the one. Ah, 'Il y a, à Vérone, des jardins à l'italienne . . .' (*Stops.*) Have you ever thought that the major stresses in life come from the most minor embarrassments? Mmm– I mean, that we spend an enormous amount of energy and feeling on the most trival worries . . . the ones that we forget about almost immediately. Mmmm?

(DONALD *smiles, bewildered.*)

A random thought, and not worth interrupting a dictation for . . . Now – 'Il y a, à Vérone des jardins à l'italienne où l'on monte par une série d'escaliers et de terrasses. J'y passai l'après-midi dans une terrible perplexité. D'en haut, je . . .'

(DONALD, *during this, has secretly looked anxiously at his watch. He holds up his hand for attention, like a child in class, looking towards* HOWARTH *in a panic.* HOWARTH *stops and looks at him.*)

DONALD: She leaves for the cinema at two, for the matinée.

HOWARTH: Yeah?

DONALD: Well, if I go later, I may be too late.

HOWARTH: Oh. Well then, you'd better go now, hadn't you? (*Snaps the book shut, smiles.*) Get it over with once and for all, anyway. This could go on all afternoon.

(*There is a ring at the bell.*)

Is that all settled, then? (*Smiling, goes out of the room.*)

(DONALD *puts on his jacket and looks hurriedly through his satchel.*)

HOWARTH: (*Off, at the front door*) Yes?

LES: (*Off*) Sorry to interrupt. My name's Les. I'm looking for Donald Clenham.

HOWARTH: (*Off*) Oh, come in, come in.

(*The door opens.* HOWARTH *comes back in, accompanied by* LES.)

HOWARTH: For you, Donald. Les. (*Looking at* LES.)

(DONALD *puts down the satchel.*)

LES: Hello, Don. I'm sorry to interrupt. You said half-past and I thought perhaps I'd missed you . . . that you'd already gone. There was another turning you could have meant. I thought I'd been waiting at the wrong one.

DONALD: I'm sorry. I – I . . . (*Looks at* HOWARTH, *then at* LES *again*) . . . forgot.

LES: That's all right. (*Pause*.) Do you want me to wait on a bit, then? Or what?

DONALD: Well, I can't come, you see.

LES: Oh. (*Little pause*.) That's all right.

HOWARTH: (*Who has been looking at* LES) I'm sorry, the fault is entirely ours. We persuaded Donald to stay for a bit, and in the confusion of arrangements *everything* got forgotten.

LES: That's all right. It doesn't matter. We were only going for a ride. (*Pause*.) It doesn't matter.

HOWARTH: (*To* LES) I know you, don't I?

LES: I was at St Martin's for a while, sir.

HOWARTH: Yes, I thought you were. About three years ago. (LES *nods*.)
Grant. Leslie Grant.

LES: (*Nods*) I never had you for French, I was in Mr Wales's class. I was only there for two years . . . and Mr Holliday's.

HOWARTH: You left early, didn't you?

LES: Sir. (*Slightly embarrassed*.)

HOWARTH: (*Pause*) What are you doing now?

LES: Same as Don . . . I'm in Crabtree's.

HOWARTH: Oh. Which part?

LES: (*Laughs, embarrassed again*) Well, in cutlery . . . at the moment. Mainly I'm on sales in cutlery, sometimes in toys.

HOWARTH: And do you like that?

LES: Well, not too much. (*Looks towards* DONALD.) Eh, Don?
(DONALD *laughs awkwardly. Pause.*)

HOWARTH: I'm sorry. Still, you'll probably be able to move on . . . or out.

LES: We hope so. (*To* DONALD *again*.) Eh, Don?
(DONALD *again laughs awkwardly*.)

HOWARTH: Well, I'm sorry I've mucked up your Saturday ride.

LES: No, it doesn't matter. We can go tomorrow, can't we, Don?
(*A slight pause.*)

DONALD: Well, I'll be here tomorrow, Les, actually.

LES: (*Pause, still quite easy*) Oh. (*Pause.*) Oh well, that's that,
then. It doesn't matter.

HOWARTH: But look here, if you're going to be in this area – I
mean, if you feel like coming out – do drop in for a cup of
coffee or tea.

LES: Oh no, I wouldn't want to interrupt . . .

HOWARTH: (*Pause*) You wouldn't be. We're bound to need a
break. The idea is to get a bit of French into Donald in as
relaxed a way as possible.

LES: Oh, well, that's very kind of you. Thanks very much. I don't
know if I will be in the area . . .

HOWARTH: No, but if you are.

LES: Well, thank you, sir.

HOWARTH: How extraordinary, you two knowing each other.
You never told me you knew an old St Martin's boy, Donald.

DONALD: Well, Les said . . .

LES: I said I was sure you wouldn't remember me.

HOWARTH: You see, I do. I was sorry you . . . had to leave.

LES: Yes. (*Little pause.*) So was I. I might have learnt some
French. (*Laughs*)

HOWARTH: (*Laughs*) Well, um, Donald, if you're going to see
your mother . . . we've been trying to think of ways of letting
Donald's mother know that he's staying with us.

LES: Oh, I'll tell her. I might as well go back anyway.
(HOWARTH *looks at* DONALD.)

DONALD: Oh, well, thanks, Les. Thanks.

LES: No trouble. It's only just around the corner from us. (*To*
HOWARTH) If she's not there, I'll put a note through the
letter-box, OK?

HOWARTH: Perhaps you'd better give her our phone number . . .
6371.

LES: 6371. I always remember numbers. (*Smiles at* DONALD.)
Good luck for Monday if I don't see you, Don.

DONALD: Thanks.

LES: Goodbye, then.

HOWARTH: Goodbye.

(LES *goes out.*)

Perhaps under the circumstances, you should see Les down the path, eh?

(DONALD *nods, and hurries out.* HOWARTH *stands for a moment, then moves up to the hatch, reaches through for the biscuit tin and takes a biscuit. There is the sound of the front door. He crams the biscuit into his mouth, gulps it down hurriedly.* JOANNA *comes in with the shopping bag, stands looking at him ironically.*)

(*Swallows furtively.*) I know. Don't say it.

JOANNA: But has he mysteriously doubled? I passed two of him cycling down the path.

HOWARTH: (*Laughs*) No, just a friend he'd arranged to meet.

JOANNA: Ah, gone to get more friends for the weekend perhaps? Will they come back as four? (*Goes out into the kitchen.*)

HOWARTH: Darling, I'm terribly sorry. But I did apologize.

JOANNA: (*Returning*) Did you? How?

HOWARTH: I kept glancing at you abjectly.

JOANNA: Well, what came over you?

HOWARTH: I don't know.

JOANNA: Richard, I ask compassionately.

HOWARTH: (*Pause, shakes his head, takes her hand and speaks directly to her, kindly*) Well, I do know. He's got his O level on Monday – he's failed twice already – and he's in a state about it. He lives alone with a repressively anxious and Catholic mother, who'll almost certainly demoralise him thoroughly before the weekend's out. So, I thought . . . (*Shrugs.*) It might just make the difference. (*Pause, kisses her hand.*) Do you mind?

JOANNA: Yes. (*Hand on his shoulder.*) But I'd be a bitch if I made a fuss, wouldn't I? When the cause is so good. (*Kisses him.*)

HOWARTH: Well, how are you, then?

JOANNA: Roughly as you see me. I've had a very stimulating morning. I asked Matthews why there was a layer of beef around the fat, like a blanket to keep it warm, and at the

supermarket I caused – and then took part in – a scene about
the size and colour of the eggs. I wanted large brown ones
and they had tiny white ones, that look as if the chickens
have stamped them out with machines. In other words, I
succeeded in making myself into a harridan, and in the fridge
I've got beefy fat, and a dozen shiny, white little eggs.

HOWARTH: Poor darling.

JOANNA: Yes. How did you get landed with him in the first place?

HOWARTH: Who? Donald? He's the one that Catholic priest
wrote to the school about – O'Toole, Father O'Toole. His
dad died when he was three, his mother's had to work to
keep them both. He didn't do too well at school, is now
doing something or other at that shop you hate – Crabtree's –
and wants to better himself, I suppose. After his French he's
going to try for maths and a few other subjects – with Father
O'Toole's letters to help, no doubt . . . if he gets his French.

JOANNA: And will he?

HOWARTH: It depends, I should say, almost entirely on his nerve,
and whether he knows enough. No, probably not. His nerve
is bad and he doesn't know enough.

JOANNA: But you're going to have a go?

HOWARTH: Yes.

JOANNA: All right. But you shall make it up to me. What with
vanishing for rehearsals while I sew up your costumes,
introducing nervous boys into the house, and no doubt a
briefcase full of marking . . .

HOWARTH: I shall – make it up to you.

JOANNA: But there's something else. (*Sternly.*) You've been at the
biscuits.

HOWARTH: What?

JOANNA: What? (*Imitating him.*) The crumbs are clustered around
your lips. (*Pokes him in the stomach.*) You're . . . (*poke*) . . .
not . . . (*poke*) . . . to . . . (*poke.*) It's bad for you to be fat.
(*Slaps him.*) And it's self-indulgence, and on top of
which . . .
(*The doors opens,* DONALD *comes in, stops and looks at them
awkwardly.*)

254

(*As* HOWARTH *steps away*) Oh, hello. How did you get in?

DONALD: (*Pause*) The door was on the latch.

JOANNA: Of course it was. (*Laughs.*) Well, you've fixed it all up, which is lovely.

HOWARTH: We really must do that dictation. Come on, Donald, we'll go next door until lunch.

JOANNA: It's very cluttered in there.

HOWARTH: It's all right. Besides, we'll be out of your way.

JOANNA: (*As* HOWARTH *and* DONALD *go out*) But you don't have to be.

(HOWARTH *appears not to have heard. Blackout.*)

SCENE 2

That evening.

In the small room, DONALD *kneels searching in his satchel, takes out a copy of* Mayfair *and shakes it, puts it back, goes quietly to dividing door and opens it very carefully. He sees there is no one about, so enters and looks on table, sits left of table and starts silently to rehearse the moment when he dropped the photograph, putting his foot out in the way he did before. Still puzzled, he kneels left of the table to look under it. As he does so* JOANNA *enters.*

DONALD *starts, rises.*

JOANNA: (*Closing door*) Did I frighten you?

DONALD: Um, pardon, I didn't know. I was looking for Mr Howarth . . . I mean, whether he was back yet.

(JOANNA, *behind the sofa, takes one of the cushions from the left end to the right end, preparatory to sitting there.*)

JOANNA: No, he's still rehearsing – at least I presume he is. These school plays are meant to be for the students, but every year he always seems to grab a small, but plum, part for himself. This time he's one of those bishops in Henry Fifth, which means a lovely costume for him and hours of needlework for me. Were you looking for him under the table?

DONALD: (*Laughs falsely*) No, there was a bit of paper, um, it must have fallen out of my satchel.

JOANNA: (*Looks around the floor*) In here?

DONALD: No, it's probably in there. It wasn't anything
important. (*Little pause, then goes back into room.*)

JOANNA: Where are you going?

DONALD: Well, I'd better get back . . .

JOANNA: Oh, do sit down. You can't spend the whole time here
working, and besides, we've scarcely exchanged a word all
day.

DONALD: Well, I haven't finished that translation passage he set
me.

JOANNA: (*Smiles*) Sit down, please. (*With quiet authority.*)
(DONALD *looks at her, comes across, sits down.*)
(*Picks up the edge of the material, and the needle, begins to sew –
suddenly laughs.*) Very satisfactory. I'm trying out a
completely new technique – quite authority – and it works
. . . at least, it does with you. You can go now if you insist.

DONALD: No, that's all right.

JOANNA: Are you very on edge? Before an examination is hell,
isn't it?

DONALD: No, I don't feel too bad this time. Not really.

JOANNA: Good for you. (*Smiles, pauses.*) You work at that big
shop – Crabtree's.

DONALD: Yes.

JOANNA: It's very grand. I only go there on days when I feel
impregnable. Which I'm certainly not at the moment. What
do you do exactly?

DONALD: Well, I help out in accounts.

JOANNA: Oh, *do* you? You must have a very good head for
figures, then?

DONALD: No, I just, you know, take the letters around and – that.

JOANNA: I see. Anyway, you're not one of the supercilious
salesmen – the ones who put people like me in their places?

DONALD: Um, no. No. (*Laughs.*)
(*There is a silence.*)

JOANNA: I did have one very nice experience in Crabtree's. When
I was working on the *Argus* – which, come to think of it, was
up to three months ago – being pregnant makes me feel that

256

anything before that was about six years away. (*Laughs,*
DONALD *smiles dimly*.) Well, it was my first year as a
reporter, a real reporter, and I remember I went in to buy
something very ordinary – spoons, I think – and they only
had these Swedish things at about nine and six each, and the
boy said why didn't I try Woolworth's. So, I made one of my
scenes, and it ended up with my seeing the manager, who
was very snooty . . .
(DONALD *laughs*)
. . . and said much the same thing – I really could have
murdered him. Well, the next week I got my first real
assignment, which was to interview the manager of
Crabtree's about a special fair or sale they were having. It
was delicious, strutting impassively into his office.
(DONALD *laughs again, evidently realizing it's expected*.)
Unfortunately, I was far too green and nervous to take
advantage. *Now* I would have murdered him this side of
libel. (*There is a long, appalling silence*.) I don't know what on
earth he's up to. He was meant to be back . . . (*looks at her
watch*) . . . half an hour ago. I expect he's got involved –
some lame duck – (*Embarrassed*.) I mean, some wretch who
can't get his lines right – um, tell me. (*Hurriedly*.) What's he
like as a teacher? I always hear from him what his pupils are
like, but never from them what he's like.
DONALD: (*Looks at her, looks down*) Well, he's very good. (*In a
mumble*.)
JOANNA: I don't mean he's ever gossiped about you – except in
the most flattering way. (*Laughs*.) God, how awful. It must
sound as if I'm fishing, but I can't help taking advantage.
You know, you're the first of his pupils I've ever had a
chance to grill. (*Waits*.)
DONALD: Well, he's got a very good accent.
JOANNA: (*Laughs*) Yes, that must be quite a help.
DONALD: (*Pause*) And, um, well, it's when he explains
something, then I understand it. When my teachers at school
used to explain things, I didn't always understand . . . not
really.

JOANNA: Ah, I see. He makes you want to learn, is that it?

DONALD: Well, if I go on getting it wrong, then it's like I'm sort of – well, you know, letting him – Mr Howarth – down.

JOANNA: There you are, you see. I've been married to a teacher for three years. My teachers . . . I either hated them and ragged them unmercifully, or I had the most ghastly crushes on them. (*Laughs.*)

(DONALD, *puzzled, laughs.*)

Which is why I'm probably so uneducated.

DONALD: (*Nervous laugh*) Yes . . .

JOANNA: Oh dear, (*Yawns.*) I feel sleepy all the time these days. It's because I eat so much. I hope you haven't been letting him pilfer cakes and biscuits from the kitchen. He's on a diet this term – next term he's doing the football, so I can let him relax a little.

(DONALD *nods.*)

Does he? Steal from there? (*Gestures towards the kitchen.*)

DONALD: Steal? No, no. Well, I don't know.

JOANNA: Mm. He's very sly. I find chocolate and biscuit crumbs in his pocket. (*Pause.*) Well, I could find worse, I suppose.

(DONALD *gives a little giggle* – JOANNA *looks at him – she yawns again.*) Oh dear, I'm sorry. I suppose I might as well go to bed, if I'm going to. (*Stretches.*)

(DONALD *gets up.*)

No, why don't you stay here. It's much more comfortable.

DONALD: Well, I've got my stuff in there, um . . .

JOANNA: Oh. Well, in that case, *I'll* stay on the sofa. (*Swings her legs up.*) There!

DONALD: (*Uncertainly*) Well. (*Sits down.*) Um . . .

JOANNA: You *can* go, if you want. I shan't take offence.

DONALD: No, it's all right.

JOANNA: Well. (*Smiles.*) It's very nice of you. (*Pause.*) You will excuse me if I just close my eyes . . . and you pop off the second you want to. (*Closes her eyes, keeps them closed.*)

(DONALD, *after a moment, looks at her, kneels and looks under the table again.*

The sound of a door closing downstairs.

DONALD *retreats back into his bedroom with the satchel. He sits at his desk and writes out a translation during the following scene.* JOANNA *sits up.*

HOWARTH *comes in, with his briefcase.*)

JOANNA: Well? (*Looks at her watch.*)

HOWARTH: I'm sorry. There was a bad case of stage fright. I had to do some soothing down. How are you, then?

JOANNA: Intolerant.

HOWARTH: Oh. Not of me, I hope.

JOANNA: Only by association.

HOWARTH: Oh. Where is he?

JOANNA: Oh – smoking pot in the kitchen, or out in the fields raping a peasant . . . Or, yes, possibly next door in one of his more serious moods having a go at his French, do you think?

HOWARTH: Well, I'd better go in.

JOANNA: No, you don't. (*Takes him by the wrist.*) He's only just gone – you can spare me five minutes. *He* did.

HOWARTH: Oh? What did you talk about?

JOANNA: (*Pulls him down beside her, puts her arms around him*) Well, he wanted to know about our sex life. (*Taking his arm.*) Very prying, and slightly coarse in his approach. Lost his temper and called me a swollen tart – said he was looking forward to the day when you and me and our kind were swept aside. Frankly, some of his ideas struck me as a little wild, but he'll probably settle down in a few years' time and have babies like the sad rest of us.

HOWARTH: You don't like him, then?

JOANNA: How would I know? He's been here all day, in a trance of shyness at lunch and supper, and concealed from view for the rest of the time. But I do just wonder why, of all the pupils you've ever taught, this is the only one I get a chance to look at.

HOWARTH: He's a special case. None of the boys at school need this sort of attention – for obvious reasons.

JOANNA: Really, I'm not against him, you know. It just seems odd, in this day and age. It's not as if I was being *de haut en bas* to him. He was being *de bas en haut*, or whatever it is, to me.

HOWARTH: He wasn't. It doesn't exist.

JOANNA: Don't school-teach me, thank you.

HOWARTH: Sorry.

JOANNA: You are prickly, aren't you? All through lunch you behaved as if I were going to assault him – warning glances at me, protective smiles for him.

HOWARTH: Well, it was an ordeal for him.

JOANNA: Thank you. (*Laughs.*) Oddly enough, he makes *me* feel quite shy – which is why I chattered at him. Does he have any girlfriends?

HOWARTH: I don't know. He's just as inaccessible to me, darling. (*Mitigatingly.*)

JOANNA: Well, you're not inaccessible to him. He managed a few words about you.

HOWARTH: Oh? (*Little pause.*) What?

JOANNA: He said he liked to please you. That's why you're a good teacher. (*Pause.*) No, that's what it came to. What he really meant, of course, was that you've got a sexy personality. (*Little pause.*) And you're very self-indulgent.

HOWARTH: Self-indulgent? It's . . . (*looks at his watch.*) . . . ten thirty on a Saturday evening. I've been cramming Donald all day, and ever since supper I've been rehearsing a school play – and shortly I shall have to mark exercises for Monday – after, that is, a spell with Donald again.

JOANNA: You're not!

HOWARTH: I've got to.

JOANNA: Can't you do them tomorrow?

HOWARTH: Yes, but I shall have to do a few of them tonight as well. Donald's not the only one taking his O levels next week.

JOANNA: Well, bloody hell, it sounds like self-indulgence to me. It's only because it's a respectable activity that you get away with it. You know, I could, if I were feeling nasty, remind you that last weekend, which you spent almost entirely at rehearsals, you only managed to calm me by promising me this weekend – all to myself.

HOWARTH: (*Stacking exercise books in a pile on the table*) I know. I
  have apologized.
  (*There is a silence.*)
JOANNA: Doesn't he have any friends at all?
HOWARTH: Friends? Who? Donald? (*Looks through O-level
  dictation book.*) I don't know. He's got one – the one that came
  this morning. I suppose he's got friends, like any other
  ordinary young man.
JOANNA: Not so ordinary. He's too pretty to be ordinary. Even if
  he's totally innocent about his looks now – of course, when he
  finds out, he'll probably turn into a monster.
HOWARTH: Then I shall have to watch him with you, won't I?
JOANNA: Oh, don't worry. I'd never have fancied him.
HOWARTH: Poor Donald. Why not? (*Starts to correct an exercise-
  book.*)
JOANNA: Perhaps because he'd never have fancied me. He seems to
  get on best with the older man. (*Giggles.*) Anyway, this is a bit
  strong – I'm meant to be the one in the interesting condition
  and we spend all our time talking about how . . . (DONALD
  opens the door, coughs awkwardly) . . . uninteresting your
  house guest is.
DONALD: Um, I'm – I've finished that, sir.
HOWARTH: Poor Donald – I didn't mean to keep you, uh . . . (*Gets
  up.*) Anyway, I'll join you now.
JOANNA: Donald can join *you* – in here. It's much more
  comfortable, and I'm going to bed. And, by the way Donald,
  I've made him confess – he eats cakes and biscuits with you,
  doesn't he?
  (DONALD, *as* HOWARTH *smiles irritably, stares at her, then at
  him.*)
  You might as well come clean too.
DONALD: Oh no, he doesn't eat anything.
JOANNA: You've never even seen him eat *one* biscuit?
DONALD: No. No, I haven't.
JOANNA: (*Looks at him, slightly startled*) You know, I don't believe
  you, though thousands would. (*Laughs.*)
  (DONALD *laughs and looks at* HOWARTH, *who raises a stiff smile.*)

JOANNA: Anyway, you're to be my ally tomorrow. You're to leave
fatter than when you came, and he's to be . . . (*punching*
HOWARTH's *stomach*) . . . thinner when you leave.

HOWARTH: It sounds like a very good way to reduce me. (*Sharply
to* JOANNA) You'd better go and get your books then,
Donald.
(DONALD *goes out, leaving his door open.* HOWARTH *turns
away, walks to the table, and sits.*)

JOANNA: (*Sotto voce*) You're not prickling again. I was only trying
to cover up.

HOWARTH: It's all right.

JOANNA: Do you think he heard?

HOWARTH: I hope not.

JOANNA: You're not very reassuring.

HOWARTH: Well, I can't *be* sure, can I?
(*The door opens again.* DONALD *comes in, carrying his satchel.
He comes to the table.* JOANNA *sits on the sofa and starts to sew.*)

JOANNA: By the way, Donald, did you find your bit of paper?

DONALD: Um, no.

JOANNA: I'll keep my eye open for it.

DONALD: No, it doesn't matter, it's nothing. Just a stupid –
picture. *I* don't want it. (*Violently.*)

JOANNA: I see.
(HOWARTH *smiles slightly. He holds out his hand for Donald's
exercise-book.* DONALD *takes it out of his satchel and sits.*)

HOWARTH: (*Looks at the exercise-book*) Well, we wouldn't say,
would we, that the sun was about to go to bed, even if the
French do. What do we say?

DONALD: Mmm – it . . . (*thinks*) . . . sinks.

HOWARTH: Or sets, or goes down. Mmm-huh, well, all right, but
you don't really, do you? 'Mount' a hill – I mean, one
mounts a horse in English and that's about all these days.
What do you do to a hill?
(JOANNA *looks for her scissors in her work basket.*)

DONALD: Oh, climb it.

HOWARTH: Yeah. You see, you're still being a little lazy, really.
(JOANNA *looks in a tin on the piano. It rattles.*)

When you know what a word is – I mean, its literal translation – then think from that to the word we'd use. Do you see? . . . So. Mmm-huh, a little *wave*, a little grey *wave* on the horizon?

DONALD: Cloud, I mean. (*Laughs.*)

(JOANNA *goes into the bedroom, opens and shuts a drawer in the desk.*)

HOWARTH: 'Course you do, it's common sense. He's standing on top of a hill and he's looking across the plains, so even if the first word that comes to mind is a wave, then think about it. What is a wave, by the way?

DONALD: Um, um, um . . .

(JOANNA *returns. Opens a drawer in the shelf-unit. Looks in a tin which rattles.*)

HOWARTH: We had it just the other day.

DONALD: Um, orage. Orage.

HOWARTH: L'orage is the storm. (*Correcting his pronunciation.*) Well, it was in that piece – and it sounds – (*breaks off as* JOANNA *rattles the tins again*) – sounds roughly like, um . . . (*Turns, looks at* JOANNA, *who has opened the tin, is looking inside it.*) No?

DONALD: It's um, um, um – (*Puts his hands to his face.*)

(HOWARTH *watches him.*)

Vague. (*English pronunciation.*) Vague. (*French.*)

HOWARTH: (*Laughs*) Good boy!

(JOANNA *shuts the drawer, turns and goes out of the room.*) Now. (*Folds his hands, smiles at* DONALD.) Est-ce que vous voulez parler avec moi un peu, monsieur?

DONALD: Oui, monsieur. (*Tensely.*)

HOWARTH: (*More relaxed*) Take it easy. Whoever does it with you, just imagine it's me, and we're amusing ourselves for a few minutes, mmm? This really *is* marks for jam. OK? Où habitez-vous?

DONALD: J'habite en Angleterre.

HOWARTH: D'accord. Vous vous appellez Donald Clenham et vous êtes de quelle nationalité?

DONALD: Anglais.

HOWARTH: Êtes vous sûr?

DONALD: (*Hesitates*) Oui, monsieur.

HOWARTH: Bon. Mais vos parents sont de quelle nationalité?

DONALD: Ma mère est anglais – (*remembers the gender*) -se, mais, mon père était . . . (*pause, desperate guess*) Eer-eesh.

HOWARTH: Irlandais.

DONALD: Irlandais.

HOWARTH: C'est ça que j'ai pensé. En ce cas, vous avez une imagination bizarre, non?

DONALD: Um – um –

HOWARTH: Bizarre, curious, extraordinary, extravagant. (*French.*) Bizarre! (DONALD *laughs.*) Mais, c'est vrai. Tous les Irlandais sont très imaginatifs, non? Et vous avez, vous-même, les yeux, les cheveux et la charme d'un irlandais, non? Est-ce que tu pense que tu as la charme d'un irlandais?

DONALD: (*Laughs*) Je l'espère.

HOWARTH: Et qu'est-ce que vous aimez faire, pour vous amuser?

DONALD: J'aime bien à chanter.

HOWARTH: Et vous chantez bien?

DONALD: No, sir . . . Non, monsieur.

HOWARTH: Bien sur, vous chantez bien. Tous les irlandais chantent bien parce qu'ils sont très sentimentaux.

(JOANNA *enters.* HOWARTH *turns to her.*)

Hello, I thought you were going to bed.

JOANNA: When I've finished your costume. (*Sits on the sofa.*)

HOWARTH: Why don't you leave it till the morning?

JOANNA: I'd rather find some other way of amusing myself in the morning, thank you.

HOWARTH: Well, I'm sorry it's such a job.

JOANNA: Well, it wouldn't be if you'd try it on.

HOWARTH: Well, I can't right now, can I?

JOANNA: Well, it would only take a moment.

HOWARTH: (*Turning to her irritably*) We're in the middle of some French.

JOANNA: Yes, I realize that, but as I've spent three hours sewing it together, I thought you might spare me thirty seconds trying it on. (*Pause, angrily.*) After which I'll take myself off to bed.

HOWARTH: (*Sharply*) OK.

JOANNA: Oh, don't bother.

(*She throws the robe onto the sofa and goes out.*)

HOWARTH: (*As she goes, making peace*) I don't mind . . . (*Pause, turns to* DONALD.) Oh dear, I seem to have disgraced myself. (*The door bell rings.*)

Oh, God! (*Goes off to answer the door.*)

MRS CLENHAM :(*Off*) Good evening, I'm Mrs Clenham, Donald's mother.

HOWARTH: (*Off*) Oh, come in.

MRS CLENHAM: (*Off*) I'm sorry to bother you like this.

(DONALD, *recognizing his mother's voice, rises.*)

HOWARTH: (*Enters, holding the door*) Donald, your mother.

MRS CLENHAM: (*Stepping in*) Pardon me for coming like this. I tried to contact you on the telephone but Les must have given me the wrong number. I brought some things over for – my son.

HOWARTH: Well, we're very glad to see you. I'll just tell my wife. (*Goes out, closes door, calls off-stage.*) Darling!

MRS CLENHAM: Hello, Donnie.

DONALD: Hello, mum.

MRS CLENHAM: (*In a low voice*) Are you all right?

DONALD: Yes, I'm fine.

MRS CLENHAM: It was a bit of a shock, getting Les's message.

DONALD: I'm sorry, mum, I couldn't think how else to let you know. They . . . you know – it was a bit difficult.

MRS CLENHAM: Then Les giving me the wrong number . . . I dialled and dialled down at the shop, and I kept getting this man . . . he was very rude in the end. I was getting very worried.

DONALD: I'm sorry. (*Slightly irritable.*)

MRS CLENHAM: That's all right, Donnie. It doesn't matter. Anyway, you're all right then? It's very kind of them to ask you.

DONALD: Well, he's giving me a hand with revision – dictations and that. Right through. We were just in the middle of an oral.

MRS CLENHAM: Well, I'll be going straight back. (*Puts the brown paper carrier bag she has been carrying on a chair.*) Here, I've brought your pyjamas and tooth-brush and your razor. (*Getting a cake-box out of the bag*) And here's a cake. It's one of those orange gateaux.

DONALD: (*Looks down at the cake*) Oh.

MRS CLENHAM: You give it to them, Donnie, as you know them. (HOWARTH *and* JOANNA *re-enter*. DONALD *puts the cake in the carrier bag, puts the bag on a chair.*)

HOWARTH: Mrs Clenham, this is my wife. (*Shuts the door.*)

JOANNA: How do you do? (*They shake hands.*) Oh, do sit down. Would you like some tea or coffee or a drink?

MRS CLENHAM: (*After a quick glance at* DONALD) No, thank you. There's a bus back in a minute, it's the last one.

JOANNA: Oh, what a shame you've got to rush off.

MRS CLENHAM: I'm sorry I came up so late, but it was difficult because Les gave me the wrong number. And then I didn't get his note until I was off in the evening from my work.

JOANNA: Oh, I see . . . what do you do?

MRS CLENHAM: Well, I'm at the Rex. At the cinema. (DONALD *giggles nervously.*) (*After a glance at* DONALD.) I'm the usherette there.

JOANNA: Oh, I've always thought that must be lovely, seeing films as part of your work.

MRS CLENHAM: Oh yes, well most of them I see ten times in a week.

JOANNA: Yes, that must be a bit boring. (*Pause.*) Are you sure you haven't time to sit down?

MRS CLENHAM: No, thank you. I've got to get the bus. It's the last one. I just wanted to give my son some things.

JOANNA: I do hope you don't mind our stealing him for the weekend.

MRS CLENHAM: No, it's very kind of you to help him. (*Turns to* HOWARTH.) Thank you very much.

HOWARTH: Not at all. It's a pleasure.

MRS CLENHAM: (*Turning to* DONALD) Well, goodbye Donnie.

DONALD: Goodbye, mum.

MRS CLENHAM: And I'll be thinking of you on Monday.

DONALD: Thanks.

MRS CLENHAM: (*Crossing to* DONALD) Goodbye Donnie. (*Kisses him.*) And don't forget tomorrow's Sunday.

DONALD: No mum.

JOANNA: Why don't you walk your mother to the bus stop?

MRS CLENHAM: Well, it's very cold. You'll need your coat, Donnie.

DONALD: Yes, mum. (*Goes into the bedroom and collects his jacket.*)

MRS CLENHAM: (*Crossing towards* HOWARTH) Do you think he has a chance, then?

HOWARTH: Yes, yes, I certainly do.

MRS CLENHAM: But not certain to pass, then?

HOWARTH: Well, these things are slightly in the lap of the gods, unfortunately, Mrs Clenham. But we're doing our best. (DONALD *returns, waits nervously.*)

MRS CLENHAM: If anybody deserves to pass the exam and better his chances, Donnie does. He's not one for pushing himself forward, more's the pity. Of course I'm glad of that but he's . . .

DONALD: (*A nervous laugh*) Yes, mum.

MRS CLENHAM: Well, thank you very much.

JOANNA: Not at all.

MRS CLENHAM: Thank you.

JOANNA: Good-night.

MRS CLENHAM: Good-night. (*Goes out.*)

DONALD: (*To* HOWARTH, *out of nervousness*) Good-night. (DONALD *follows* MRS CLENHAM *out.*)

HOWARTH: Well, there goes the lady who's responsible for the state of Donald's nerves. (*Laughs and watches* JOANNA *who is touching the costume.*) Shall I try that on as we seem to have a moment?

JOANNA: No thank you.

HOWARTH: Oh, come on, Jo.

(DONALD *enters, stays by the door, closes it.*)

JOANNA: (*To* DONALD) That was very quick.

DONALD: Um, she made me come back. She said it was too cold.

JOANNA: Oh, very wise. You can't afford to get anything now. Well, I'll leave you in peace.

(JOANNA *goes off and closes the door.* DONALD *comes to the table and sits.* HOWARTH *sits on the arm of the sofa.*)

HOWARTH: I think we've done enough for one evening.

DONALD: Yes sir. (*Pause. Puts the book in his satchel.*) I'm sorry about that, sir.

HOWARTH: What? (*Looks at* DONALD.) About what?

DONALD: My mother. (*Pause.*) Her coming out here like that.

HOWARTH: But you've got nothing to apologize for. She just wanted to make sure you were all right.

DONALD: Yes sir. It's because she worries, sir.

HOWARTH: Yes, you've already told me that.

DONALD: Sir.

HOWARTH: Having parents is terribly difficult, one of the most difficult things in life – up to a certain age, anyway. Very few boys, in my quite extensive experience, aren't mortified by their mothers or their father or both, but they wouldn't feel mortified if there weren't a muddle of other feelings as well – protectiveness and, well, love and sheer irritation, which generally comes from vanity. We want those we love to be admired, and we feel for ourselves as well as for them when we suspect they aren't. (*Pause.*) From what I can make out, I think your mother is an admirable woman. (*Little pause.*) It must have been very hard for her.

DONALD: (*Nods, and in an emotional whisper*) I know that, sir.

HOWARTH: Yes, I'm sure you do.

(DONALD *nods again, emotionally.*)

Mmmm. (*Little pause.*) By the way, tell me about our mutual friend, Les.

(DONALD *looks at him.*)

Are you two very friendly?

DONALD: Well . . . yes, well, as he's at Crabtree's and he lives near us and that –

HOWARTH: I got the *impression* you were quite close.

DONALD: Yes, well, I see him more than anyone else. He comes around in the evenings and we have lunch and that. (*Shrugs, smiles.*)

HOWARTH: Uh huh. You must like him then?

DONALD: Yes. (*Now slightly worried, and defensive.*) Well, he's all right. (*Little pause.*) We're going to go to France together next holidays.

HOWARTH: Really? What does your mother think about that?

DONALD: Well – (*Laughs.*) I haven't told her yet. She doesn't like Les too much. I think she quite likes him, but his parents are divorced – he lives with his mum – and as we're Catholics . . .

HOWARTH: Ah, yes. I remember the business about the divorce. It was *one* of the reasons he left us – his mother took him away. His father was bad about maintenance, and Les had to go out to work. There are two little brothers, aren't there?

DONALD: Sisters.

HOWARTH: Yes, of course – it would be sisters. (*Smiles. Pours himself a whisky.*) What's he like now?

DONALD: Well, he's very nice. I mean, he's always, you know – helping me, doing things for me. Lots of times, things I don't even think about – or well, even need – you know, he does them.

HOWARTH: But you don't always enjoy it as much as you feel you ought to?

(DONALD *looks at him, as if not understanding.*)

DONALD: Sorry?

HOWARTH: I just mean that people – friends – sometimes get on our nerves, like parents. They do more than we want them to do.

DONALD: Well, once or twice – Once, I couldn't go into Crabtree's because mum hurt her back, and I had to take her to the doctor's, and Les, he thought I was just swinging it because he didn't know about mum, and he went around telling people I was ill, that he'd seen me the night before and I had a temperature with the flu. So, when I phoned up and said it was my mum that was ill, *they* thought I was swinging it too. But he was only trying to help, that's all.

HOWARTH: Were you angry?

DONALD: Well, he got a bit upset.

HOWARTH: So you apologized? (*Smiling.*)

DONALD: He was a bit upset. It didn't matter. I mean, I shouldn't have lost my temper.

HOWARTH: Why not? (*Pause.*) If he did something bloody silly and interfering . . .

DONALD: I don't know. He takes it very hard.

HOWARTH: Les never told you about St Martin's?

DONALD: No, well, just that he was there.

HOWARTH: One of the reasons Les left St Martin's was because of the difficulty between his parents. But there was another reason. (DONALD *turns and looks at* HOWARTH.) He was getting – well, a little too fond of one of the other boys. He kept writing him letters – love letters, in fact – and generally behaving – desperately. The other boy took the letters to the Headmaster – at least, his parents did. They'd found them in his satchel, and the Head was – he's a kind man, but not the world's most proficient psychologist – and he was a little clumsy about the whole thing. Unfortunately – or from some points of view, perhaps, fortunately – Les's mother said she wanted to withdraw him while all this was going on, and the Head, who, as I've said is a kind enough creature, and normally under the circumstances would have done something to keep the boy on, let him go. So . . . (*Looks at* DONALD.)

DONALD: (*After a long pause, in horror*) D'you mean he's a homo?

HOWARTH: It's not the word I'd use – ever, no. But boys, particularly at that age, can be sexually very confused. They're as much homosexual from necessity as they're heterosexual in their – (*gestures*) – dreams. Mmm. The point, as far as their future happiness is concerned, is whether they grow out of it. The world, thank God, is learning not to judge homosexuals as if they were criminals. *But*, homosexual boys – men – (*shrugs*) – do have a tendency to make emotional claims, to develop habits of dependence that

can lead – if the other person is normal – to difficulties. Do
you see?
(DONALD *nods*.)
Relationships in even the most ordinary of circumstances can
be difficult enough, God knows – (*laughs*) – *and* depend
upon habits. Joanna and I have the dieting thing, for
example. It doesn't mean very much – at least, as far as
actual eating goes – but it's become a familiar part of our
lives, a habit that's a kind of reassurance, really. All right,
but other habits – and in less ordinary circumstances –
habits, say, where Les makes a nuisance of himself – like that
little business at Crabtree's, because he's possessive, well,
cares too intensely, let's say, and then gets too upset when
you're quite rightly irritated, so that *you* apologize – that
sounds a little too like a marriage to me. You might be drawn
in further than you want. I'm only telling you all this because
at school it's a part of my job, perhaps the most important
part, to pass on what little information my experience has
given me – and because you said you and Les were going to
Paris together – perhaps I shouldn't have told you this – I
thought I ought to warn you about possible complications. I
certainly don't want you to do anything more than think
about it all.

DONALD: (*Pause*) I didn't know about that, – about Les, sir –
except my having to apologize to him all the time. I mean,
that used to get on my nerves, but I didn't know about that.

HOWARTH: (*Pats* DONALD's *arm, relaxed*) Oh, don't worry. I
know you like girls. (*Smiling*.)

DONALD: Sir?

HOWARTH: Well, you do like girls, don't you? I know you like
looking at them.
(DONALD *laughs, looks at him; is overcome with
embarrassment*.)
I'm trying to be exquisitely tactful – (*takes out of his pocket the
folded picture*) – and return your property to you without a
fuss. It fell out of your satchel in all your comings and goings
this morning.

DONALD: No, it's not mine, sir.

HOWARTH: Oh, Donald. Come on, take it. I know it's yours.

(DONALD *goes to take it.*)

Just a minute, there's something you can explain to me –
(*takes the picture back, opens it out*) – the boots. What's the
appeal of the boots? (*Points to them.*) The rest of it gets to me,
in my own thin-blooded way. Proud breasts, pertly up-tilted
– (*tracing lines with his finger*) – saucy little nipples, suave
hips, an exciting sheen on her flanks and a vee of shadows,
which is what she wears instead of pubic hair. I always
wonder whether it's rubbed out on the negative or shaved off
before they take the photo. But the boots – what's the appeal
of the boots?

(DONALD *stares down, transfixed . . . makes a giggling noise.*)
Mmmm? (*Smiles slowly, then laughs.*)

(DONALD *also laughs.*)

It's not fair. I know exactly what the appeal of the boots is.
Here. (*Hands the photo back to* DONALD.) The real thing, of
course, is trickier. It tends not to go about nude in boots,
with all the embarrassing bits removed – unless you
specifically ask it to – and it's very much in love with you.
The real thing tends to be hairily human, with all that that
implies.

(*The door opens.* JOANNA *comes in in dressing-gown and
slippers.*)

Et voilà, c'est tout pour ce soir, Monsieur Clenham.

JOANNA: And high time. If Donald's going to keep fit for Monday
morning, he'd better get his sleep.

(DONALD *gets up, carries his satchel into the bedroom, leaving
the door open.*)

HOWARTH: Good-night!

JOANNA: Good-night!

(DONALD *puts his satchel down on the desk in the bedroom and
returns to the main room.*)

DONALD: Oh, my things. (*Collects his mother's carrier bag from the
chair.*)

JOANNA: You do know where the bathroom is?

(DONALD *goes to take the cake-box out, half lifts it from the bag,
then, too embarrassed to give it to* JOANNA, *puts it back and
hurries out of the main door.*)
I'm a bitch. I've been brooding in my bath and you are a
terribly good teacher, aren't you?

HOWARTH: Quite good.

JOANNA: (*Hand on his shoulder*) And it's because you're all the
things I blame you for – a liar, self-indulgent, lovable, sexy
and exhibitionist.

HOWARTH: Am I lovable?

JOANNA: (*Caresses his head*) Well, quite lovable. But you're very
lovable with him. I admit it. He's not very bright, is he?

HOWARTH: No, not very.

JOANNA: And you make him brighter than he is, which must be
one of the gifts of a teacher.

(HOWARTH *points ruefully to the pile of exercise-books and
reaches for one.*)
Oh you're not, are you?

HOWARTH: Darling, I've got to.

(*Pause.* HOWARTH *starts correcting the exercises.*)

JOANNA: Do you think I'm more like a flower or a cow? I've been
reading novels about pregnant ladies, and when they're
written by men, we're languid and dream-like, curiously
beautiful, in touch with the mystery and other balls about
creation. Our faces open as flowers, etc., etc., but when
they're written by other ladies, especially the ones with
degrees, we're always cow-like, sow-like, lumpish and
clumsy. Which do you think I'm like?

HOWARTH: Mmmm?

JOANNA: Cow, sow or flower?

HOWARTH: Flower.

JOANNA: A flower with a urine test on Monday. You know, that
Doctor Lafflin treats my bottom half like his wife's handbag,
and my top half like an idiot son – but he does accept my
little glass jar with a twinkle. The only time he's at all
personal, is when he twinkles at me, and as I'm either
holding or have just handed him a glass of my pee, I can

scarcely twinkle back at him, can I, without seeming insane
or obscene. Which do you think I am? Insane or obscene?

HOWARTH: You're not insane.

(DONALD *comes back in, wearing pyjamas and slippers and
carrying the bag and a pile of his clothes with the cake-box on
top. He smiles at* HOWARTH *and* JOANNA *and goes in to the
bedroom, puts his clothes on a chair.*)

JOANNA: What has he got in that cake-box?

(DONALD *turns on his bedroom light.* JOANNA *goes to the
bedroom door and knocks.*)

DONALD: (*Puts the cake-box on top of the folded bed*) Yes?

JOANNA: Donald? Are you all right in there? Got everything?

DONALD: Um, yes, thank you. It's very nice.

JOANNA: Good.

DONALD: (*Coming into the main room*) The only thing is – um – is
there a bed?

(JOANNA *and* HOWARTH *laugh and* JOANNA *goes in to the
bedroom, followed by* DONALD. HOWARTH *follows to the door.*)

JOANNA: I'm so sorry, it's all made up. It only takes a second.

(JOANNA *hands the carry-cot to* DONALD *who puts it against the
wall.*)

I'm sorry about all the baby stuff, I was afraid you'd take all
the nappies and rubber knickers as a joke in bad taste.

(*Hands the cake-box to* DONALD, *takes the cover off the folded
bed and wheels it into the centre of the bedroom.*) It opens this
way –

(DONALD *puts the cake-box on the chest of drawers, unfolds the
bed, which is ready made up.* JOANNA *puts away the bed-cover
and brings out a rug.*)

HOWARTH: (*Stepping forward to help*) Can you manage?

DONALD: Yes thank you, sir.

JOANNA: Donald, you're to stop calling him 'Sir'. You're a guest,
and besides, it ages me.

HOWARTH: Yes, we're Richard and Joanna from now on.

JOANNA: Now, is that all right then? There's an extra blanket if
you want it.

(HOWARTH *goes out of the room and sits at the table again,*

JOANNA *follows.* DONALD *straightens the rug on the bed then comes into main room.*)

DONALD: Um – the only thing – is there a church?

HOWARTH: Yes, there is. St Mark's – it's next door to the post office, a one-minute walk.

DONALD: Oh yes, I saw it.

JOANNA: What time have you to be there?

DONALD: Well, seven o'clock.

JOANNA: Seven!

DONALD: Well, I could go to the eleven o'clock mass, I suppose.

JOANNA: Is that all right? Lovely. We'll remember.

DONALD: Um, well, good-night, sir. Good-night, Mrs . . .

JOANNA: You've forgotten already!

DONALD: (*With difficulty*) 'Night then, Richard. Good-night . . .

JOANNA: Joanna.

DONALD: Good-night, Joanna.

JOANNA: Good-night, Donald.

(DONALD *goes into the bedroom and closes the door. He turns out the light and gets into bed.*)

And what about you? I've suddenly realized I'm very neurotic, and only a cuddle will cure me.

HOWARTH: (*Having turned back to his exercises*) Say half an hour?

JOANNA: That's no use to me. I'll be asleep in three minutes, as you well know. Give me one now, on account.

(HOWARTH *turns and draws her to him. He cuddles her.*)

Mmm, well, all right, if you promise to cuddle me if I'm asleep. I need some basic soothing.

HOWARTH: I promise.

JOANNA: Mmm. (*Suspiciously, goes towards the door.*) 'Night, Richard. (*Imitating* DONALD.)

(HOWARTH *looks after her, then goes back to his exercise-book, then gets up. He goes to the hatch, brings out the biscuit tin, takes about four biscuits out. He sits down, takes a biscuit and continues to mark the exercise-book.*

The lights dim to suggest the passing of about half an hour, then the one light by Howarth's table up, and HOWARTH *still marking.*

DONALD, *from his bedroom, has begun a low, keening sound. He is sitting up hunched together and rocking backwards and forwards in his sleep.* HOWARTH, *at first not noticing, goes on working. The keening noises get louder.* HOWARTH *looks up, looks at Donald's bedroom door, as the stage fills with the noise.* HOWARTH *gets to his feet, goes to the bedroom door.*)

HOWARTH: (*Knocks*) Donald, Donald. Are you all right?
(*The noise stops, then starts again.*)
(*Opening the door and turning on the light – tenderly*) What's the matter? Are you all right?
(HOWARTH *goes into the bedroom, bends over the bed, gently pushes* DONALD *back on to the pillow.* DONALD *stops moaning and sinks back, still asleep.* HOWARTH *straightens the blanket.*)
All right then, there you are. There. Now go to sleep. (*Comes back to the door, is about to shut it.*)

DONALD: (*In a strange voice, intimately insolent*) 'Night Richard.
(HOWARTH *stands with his hand on the knob, then turns out the light and closes the door gently. Curtain.*)

ACT TWO

SCENE I

The Howarth living-room. The following morning.
In the bedroom the bed has been made neatly and a chair from the desk has been placed by the door.
The action starts in the living-room. DONALD *is sitting at the table, pen in hand, exercise-book before him.* HOWARTH *is standing by the window, the dictation textbook in his hand.*

HOWARTH: And you say you can't remember it?

DONALD: Um, I don't think so.

HOWARTH: Sure?

DONALD: Yes.

HOWARTH: Mm. I must have done it at school. Right – I'll read it through again – by the way – (*smiling*) – did you sleep well?

DONALD: (*Looks at him, slight pause, almost apprehensive*) Yes, thank you, um, Richard.

HOWARTH: You gave me quite a turn.
(DONALD *looks at him, smiling awkwardly.*)
(*Smiling*) Don't you remember?
(DONALD *shakes his head.*)
You were – I don't know what you were doing. Keening.

DONALD: I –I'm sorry.

HOWARTH: Don't be silly. There's nothing to be sorry about – but did you know you do it?

DONALD: Well, sometimes I – I make this noise, mum says.

HOWARTH: Actually it's very effective – quite eerie. (*Pause, as* DONALD *looks down, mortified.*) Have you ever seen anyone about it? A doctor?

DONALD: I think mum mentioned it once to, um, Father O'Toole.

HOWARTH: And what did he say?

DONALD: That I'd grow out of it.

277

HOWARTH: (*Little pause*) Then just when I thought I got you
    quieted – (*smiling*) – you said, with a really quite unnerving
    lucidity, ''Night, Richard.' You don't remember that,
    either?
    (DONALD *shakes his head.*)
    (*Laughs.*) It actually chilled my blood. (*Laughs.*) You
    sounded so – accomplished. Well, I'll read it through again.
    Ready?
    (DONALD *nods. As* HOWARTH *reads, he runs his pen along the
    top of the lines.*)
    'Ce matin-là Jean avait parlé beaucoup de blès et de ce qu'il
    appelait la ''culture intensive'', mais il ne possédait aucune
    notion sérieuse d'agriculture. (*Looks up sharply.*)
    D'agriculture. (*Repeating it, with a slightly knowing
    exaggeration.*) Félicie, haussait parfois les épaules. Philibert
    – (*looks at* DONALD) – jetait de temps en temps vers elle un
    regard de sympathie, et une fois il avait chucoté: – ''Ne
    vous fachez . . .''
    (JOANNA *comes in, goes to the sofa for her handbag. She smiles
    at* HOWARTH. *He smiles back at her. She looks in her
    handbag.*)
    '''Ne vous fachez pas. Votre frère dit des bêtises, mais cela
    fait passer le temps.'' Mais Félicie l'arrêta . . .'
    (JOANNA *makes an apologetic gesture, goes over to the shelf and
    picks up a bunch of keys.*)
    'Mais Félicie . . .' (*Stops.*)
JOANNA: Sorry, darling. I'm going to try and get a cup of coffee
    from the Haywards. I'll be back at lunchtime. The joint's
    on.
HOWARTH: OK. See you then.
    (JOANNA *smiles at* DONALD, *who smiles back, withdraws.*)
    'Mais Félicie l'arrêta court. Chut! Faîtes-moi donc le plaisir
    de vous occuper de ce qui vous regarde! (*Sound of door
    closing.* HOWARTH *glances out of the window.*) Elle s'était
    mise en colère. Elle était bonne mais vive, et toujours prête
    à s'emporter . . . (*Waves out of the window.*) . . . à
    s'emporter, surtout quand il s'agissait de sa famille.' OK?

(DONALD *nods.*)

(HOWARTH *saunters towards him.*) You didn't make any
corrections, did you?

DONALD: No.

HOWARTH: (*Leans over him, runs his finger rapidly along the lines*)
You were quite right not to. Well, that's very good, isn't it?
Except for this. One little mistake. But otherwise very
good. (*Pause.*) Well done.

DONALD: Well – it seemed easy – I don't know why.

HOWARTH: Don't you? (*Pleasantly, with a hint of underlying
menace.*) Really? Probably just a matter of confidence, eh?
(DONALD *nods.*)
(*Pointing at the exercise-book.*) Of course, your little mistake
was a stupid one. '*Une* fois' – not only did I say it quite
distinctly, but you *know* perfectly well that 'fois' is
feminine.

DONALD: Well, um, that's meant to be an 'e' there. (*Points.*) It's
just splodged.

HOWARTH: So it is. Well, that makes it perfect. Something to be
proud of. Could you stand doing another? A very short one.

DONALD: (*Nods*) The only thing is – (*in a mumble*) – I'm
supposed to be in church.

HOWARTH: (*As if not having heard, overlapping* DONALD'*s speech*)
No, I think you'll find all these too easy. Have a go at this.
Just a few lines – no splodges, mind. (*Smiles.*)
(DONALD *sits listening.* HOWARTH *recites from memory.*)

'Ange plein de gaieté, connaissez-vous l'angoisse,
La honte, les remords, les sanglots, les ennuis
Et les vagues terreurs de ces affreuses nuits
Qui compriment le coeur comme un papier qu'on froisse?
Ange plein de gaieté, connaissez-vous l'angoisse?

'Ange plein de beauté, connaissez-vous les rides,
Et la peur de vieillir, et ce hideux tourment
De lire la secrète horreur du dévouement
Dans des yeux ou longtemps burent nos yeux avides?
Ange plein de beauté, connaissez-vous les rides?'

OK? (*Looks at* DONALD, *who has clearly not understood a word.*)

DONALD: Well . . . (*Shrugs.*)

HOWARTH: Have a go, anyway.

(HOWARTH *speaks at dictation speed, pausing between every two or three words*.)

> 'Ange plein de gaieté, connaissez-vous l'angoisse,
> La honte, les remords, les sanglots, les ennuis
> Et les vagues terreurs de ces affreuses nuits
> Qui compriment le coeur comme un papier qu'on froisse?

(DONALD *writes, clearly completely confused, shaking his head.*)

Am I going too fast?

DONALD: No.

HOWARTH: Good. 'Ange plein de gaieté, connaissez-vous l'angoisse?' How's it going?

DONALD: Well, not really – (*Laughs nervously.*)

HOWARTH: Well, perhaps I'd better stop there. Eh? Look through it then.

(DONALD *does so.*)

> 'Ange plein de gaieté, connaissez-vous l'angoisse,
> La honte, les remords, les sanglots, les ennuis . . .

(*Crosses the room, looking down at* DONALD's *attempt to do the dictation.*)

> 'Et les vagues terreurs de ces affreuses nuits
> Qui compriment le coeur . . .

(DONALD *abandons the attempt, sits staring blankly down at his book.*)

> . . . comme un papier qu'on froisse?
> Ange plein de gaieté, connaissez-vous l'angoisse?'

(*Pause.* DONALD *looks at* HOWARTH.)

Well?

DONALD: I, um, got a bit lost.

HOWARTH: Could you understand it?

DONALD: Well, some of it.

HOWARTH: Then translate what you've got, and see if you can work backwards, filling in the blanks, so to speak. Not

exactly examination practice, but a test of your – um . . .
(*Gestures.*)

DONALD: Well, that'd take a bit of time.

HOWARTH: (*Looks at him*) We've *got* time.

(HOWARTH *picks up a newspaper from the sofa and stands by*
DONALD, *reading.* DONALD *stares at his exercise-book, rocking
backwards and forwards slightly as he did in his sleep.*
HOWARTH *turns back to look out of the window.* DONALD
*bends over his exercise-book helplessly, picks up his pen,
frowns, scratches down some words, shaking his head,
shrugging, then looks towards* HOWARTH. HOWARTH *pays no
attention.* DONALD *writes down a few more words. There is a
long pause,* DONALD *staring towards* HOWARTH.)
Well?

DONALD: Well, I got some of the words . . . (*In a mumble.*)

HOWARTH: Mmm – huh. (*Picks up Donald's exercise-book.*)
'Ange' – hip. My pronunciation must be a joke. 'Hanche' –
hip. 'Ange' – (*drawing the word out*) – angel. (*Laughs again.*)
Your first sentence appears to read, then, 'Hip plan of the
limp' – 'limp?' – oh, I see. (*Laughs.*) 'Gaieté' – gait – limp –
ingenious, 'do you know,' 'connaissez-vous,' *well* done, –
'l'angoisse' 'the English' – Didn't you even grasp, from its
rhythms and rhymes, that it was a poem?
(DONALD *shakes his head.* HOWARTH *takes down a copy of*
Les Fleurs du Mal, *opens it at the poem 'Réversibilité' and
puts it down contemptuously in front of* DONALD.)
Look at it.
(DONALD *does.*)
(*Pointing out each word.*) Literally – 'Angel, full of gaiety,
do you know the anguish, the shame, the remorse, the sobs,
the tedium and the vague' – what did you put for 'vagues'?

DONALD: (*In a mumble*) Um, 'waves'. (*Starts to weep.*)

HOWARTH: Of course. 'The tedium and the *vague* terrors of
those frightful nights which compress the heart like a paper
that one crumples. Angel, full of gaiety, do you know the
anguish?' Mmmm? There's only one word there, actually,
that you don't know – 'froisser' – to restrain or crumple –

eh? There are no grammatical difficulties?

(DONALD *shakes his head.*)

And the fact that it's a painfully beautiful *poem* shouldn't have worried *you*, should it? As you didn't *register* it was a poem?

(DONALD *shakes his head.* DONALD *stares at him, puts his hands to his eyes. There is a silence.*)

Well – do you think I'm being unfair?

(DONALD *shakes his head.*)

(*With his back to him, still looking out of the window*) Do you think I'm being cruel?

(DONALD *shakes his head.*)

Well, I am. And do you know why? (*Turns around.*)

(DONALD *shakes his head.*)

(*Crossing to* DONALD.) Oh yes you do. (*Leans across, picks up Donald's exercise-book, flicks back through it, hands it to* DONALD) What's this?

DONALD: (*After a pause*) That dictation, sir.

HOWARTH: I do five of these a week, so it's scarcely surprising that I can't remember which I've done with whom. But *you* remembered, didn't you? From the first sentence. (*Little pause.*) Didn't you?

(DONALD *sits hunched, looking down.*)

Didn't you? Mmm?

DONALD: Sir.

HOWARTH: Because you wanted me to give you good marks? (*Contemptuously.*)

(DONALD *shakes his head.*)

Because you wanted to impress me?

DONALD: (*After a pause, in a mumble*) Sir.

HOWARTH: But it's cheating. And that's a very serious matter. (*Gently.*) I don't mean cheating *me*, about which I care not one damn, but cheating yourself, about which I do care. Don't you see?

DONALD: Sir.

HOWARTH: You don't have to impress *me* with anything. At least, not in this way – that's something one keeps for one's girlfriend, or whatever.

(DONALD *weeps, uncontrollably.*)

Even so, I was unfair, wasn't I?

(DONALD *shakes his head.*)

I think I was insulted, and the very last thing you wanted to do was insult me. In fact, you wanted me to praise you – and what, after all, could be more flattering that that? Mmmm? (*Very gently.*) Donald?

(DONALD *goes on looking down, crying.*)

Donald (*Pause.*) Donald.

(DONALD *looks up slowly.*)

I'm sorry. (*Smiling.*)

DONALD: (*His voice shaking*) Sorry, sir.

HOWARTH: No, you're not to be. Not now. And the 'sir' you already know about.

(DONALD *looks up, attempts to smile at* HOWARTH's *smile.*)

Donald, you do worry me, you know.

(DONALD *begins to say* 'sir', *checks himself.*)

You're very attractive – my wife says you are – and you're not at all stupid, although I think you think you are, and you laugh – when you laugh, which is not nearly often enough – terribly nicely. But you give off an impression of – what? – well, as if you're permanently frightened. (*Pause.*) You are, aren't you?

DONALD: (*In a whisper*) Yes.

HOWARTH: Of me?

DONALD: (*Looks down*) Yes.

HOWARTH: But not badly frightened of me? At least, not frightened in a bad way?

(DONALD *shakes his head.*)

Well, that sounds about right. (*Laughs.*) But your trouble is – may I tell you what the trouble is?

(DONALD *nods. Looks at* HOWARTH.)

Your trouble is not that you're frightened but that you don't realize that, on the whole, other people are frightened too, you see. They are. Always. Why, I'm even a little frightened of you.

(DONALD *looks at him, laughs slightly.*)

But I am. I expect you judge me, don't you, in the way that
we half-consciously judge *everyone* we know. Perhaps you
find me pompous, silly, boring, fat? A trifle fat? Anyway,
putting on weight?

(DONALD *sniffs and laughs simultaneously.*)

But I am. Joanna tells me, and I feel it, other people – my
students – must notice it. Well, that doesn't matter – there
are other things I could be judged for – humiliated because of
– just like you. That's the point, you see. But where I have a
slight edge over you is that I know that other people are as
frightened as I am. Of being found out. We all are. It's the
great human secret. Do you believe me?

(DONALD *is staring at him as if hypnotized.*)

But perhaps we go some way towards overcoming it by
talking of it. Perhaps you and I needn't be more than a
necessary little bit frightened of each other again? (*Smiling.*)
Eh? (*Little pause.*) How do you feel?

(DONALD *looks at him, looks down, there is a long pause, begins
to cry again very slightly.*)

You're not unhappy, are you?

(DONALD *shakes his head.* HOWARTH *puts his hand on*
DONALD's *shoulder.*)

You're not crying though, are you?

(DONALD *shakes his head, puts his arm to his eyes.* HOWARTH
goes over to DONALD, *puts his arm around his shoulder.*)

Donald, don't.

(DONALD *sits, his arm still over his eyes.*)

(HOWARTH *removes his arm gently.*) Got a handkerchief?

DONALD: (*Fumbles in his pocket, takes out a handkerchief, blows his
nose, wipes his eyes, draws a breath, then in a brave, trembling
voice*) I'm sorry.

HOWARTH: You're not to say sorry to me – ever again. People
who say sorry all the time are simply doing dirt on
themselves, mmm?

(JOANNA *opens the door, comes in, stops.* HOWARTH *steps away
from* DONALD. DONALD *blows his nose.*)

JOANNA: I'm sorry. (*Little pause.*) Only it's gone eleven. (*She is carrying a basket of shrubs.*)

HOWARTH: Gone eleven?

JOANNA: Donald's church.

HOWARTH: My God (*Looks at* DONALD.) I completely forgot.

DONALD: Um, it doesn't matter, it was my fault.

JOANNA: (*Advancing into the room*) Well, hadn't he better get along. He won't be too late. (*Goes on out of the door, leaving it open.*)

(DONALD *looks at* HOWARTH.)

HOWARTH: All right? (*In a low voice.*)

(DONALD *nods and fetches his coat from the bedroom.*)

OK. See you then (*Smiles.*)

(DONALD *goes out.* HOWARTH *stands for a moment, looking towards the door, then goes over to it.* JOANNA *comes, in, carrying two vases.*)

(*Taking one from her.*) Here, let me.

(*He takes the larger of the two vases from her and places it on the table.* JOANNA *closes the door and puts the smaller vase on a stool.*)

How are you, then?

JOANNA: (*Busy*) Preg-nant.

HOWARTH: Poor darling. How were Peter and Sally?

JOANNA: Out.

HOWARTH: Out?

JOANNA: Yes. Not in. (*Takes the vase* HOWARTH *has placed on the table over to one by the window.*)

HOWARTH: Well, it looks as if we have the house to ourselves for a change. (*Goes over to the table, starts arranging the books.*) What shall we do?

(JOANNA *goes over to the sofa.*)

JOANNA: Peel. Peel the potatoes. Top and tail. The sprouts. In a minute. (*She picks up the other vase of flowers and takes them into the lounge.*)

HOWARTH: Poor darling. Can I help?

JOANNA: What was that all about?

HOWARTH: What all about?

JOANNA: In here. Between you two. He was crying, wasn't he?

285

HOWARTH: Yes. I was a little tactless. I pushed him a bit harder than I meant to.

JOANNA: I see. (*Little pause.*) Does it happen often?

HOWARTH: Happen often?

JOANNA: With your other boys. At school.

HOWARTH: With my other boys?

JOANNA: (*Sharper*) You're developing an extraordinary trick of repeating all my questions. Did you know?

HOWARTH: Well, you're asking some extraordinary questions. Did you know?

(*There is a pause.* JOANNA *looking at the Sunday paper,* HOWARTH *looking at her.*)

Well, what do you mean, happen often? If you mean, do I usually reduce my boys to tears, the answer is no, I most certainly do not. If you mean, is there occasional tension between us, the answer is yes, when the other party is someone like Donald. (*Little pause.* JOANNA *puts down the paper and listens.*) There *have* been tears in my time. As in the time of any schoolmaster, I should think. The boys are vulnerable and the masters impatient. The resulting concussion is – sometimes – unpleasant. It's one of the hazards of the profession. It generally means I lose a perfectly clean handkerchief, as I did with Donald. (*Little pause.*) As a matter of fact, I merely caught him doing something silly – a kind of useless cheating – and nagged at him because of it more than I should have, and his – his nerve broke. Not his strongest point at the best of times, as his 'mum' warned us. It was my fault. And I said so. (*Little pause.*) I feel upset enough about it, you needn't worry. And I particularly dislike showing myself a brutal bungler in front of you. OK?

JOANNA: (*Looks at him – there is a pause*) Come here.

HOWARTH: What?

JOANNA: Come on. Please. OK?

(HOWARTH *goes over,* JOANNA *takes his hand, raises it to her lips, kisses it.*)

HOWARTH: (*Sits on the sofa with his arm round her*) Have you noticed it's when people apologize to each other that the tears come?

JOANNA: (*Gives him a kiss*) I'm sorry.

HOWARTH: (*Gently, after a moment*) But where are the tears?

JOANNA: Oh, I can manage them if you want?

HOWARTH: No thanks. (*Indicates Donald's door.*) Enough is as good as a feast.

JOANNA: Feast? With all those biscuits inside you? (*Prods his stomach.*)

HOWARTH: I – (*Laughs.*) We had a sort of elevenses.

JOANNA: Give us a kiss, pig.

(HOWARTH *does so, then straightens up.*)

But why should he cheat?

HOWARTH: What? (*Shrugs.*) Why do boys ever cheat? Because it's easier than not.

JOANNA: But it's not an examination or anything. Why should he cheat with you?

HOWARTH: Well, I don't know, I suppose because he wanted to get a good mark, I suppose. Or for his self-esteem, which, God knows, needs boosting.

JOANNA: You mean, to win your approval?

HOWARTH: Not mine necessarily – at least, not personally. Probably just because his nerve is weak – and it's not tested when you do well.

JOANNA: Perhaps his nerve is weak because his feelings are strong. He wanted *you* to respect him – after all, if he cries when *you* find him out –

HOWARTH: Well, I expect I'm the only teacher ever to take the mildest interest. (*Sits at the table.*) The question is, what would he have done if Father O'Toole had caught him cheating? (*Starts to mark exercise-books.*)

JOANNA: (*Looks at him*) When I was out, I suddenly got frightened. (HOWARTH *turns to her.*) I didn't go to the Haywards at all.

HOWARTH: (*Looking at her anxiously*) Oh, why not?

JOANNA: It was stupid, but I suddenly remembered the last time I went – (*swings her legs off, looks at* HOWARTH) and Sally

talked all the time of her forceps delivery – did you know
Tom was a forceps – they caught his head with the forceps
and tugged it out. Although you wouldn't think so to look at
him now – his head's enormous. This last week all I can
think about is what could go wrong.

HOWARTH: But you're supremely healthy – everyone keeps
saying so.

JOANNA: Yes, but is he? Or she? Or – I don't know. I don't know
if I'm up to what every woman's meant to fulfil herself in.
The Americans just put you under about a week before, and
you wake up with a baby or two, all sluiced down and
probably gift-wrapped. (*Stands up.*) God, I'm boring. You've
no idea how nervy I feel, from how boring I sound. (*Bends
down with a sigh, turns on the radio. It is Bach. She smiles at*
HOWARTH, *goes out.*)

HOWARTH: (*Listens to the music, then goes to the door, shouting*)
Darling – you're not at all boring.

JOANNA: (*Returning*) Sprouts or peas?
(HOWARTH *goes over to her, kisses her on the cheek, cuddles
her.*)
Peas or sprouts?

HOWARTH: (*They kiss, he laughs*) Both, possibly?

JOANNA: All right, but you do the potatoes then. The elephant
and the pig. (*As she does a few steps of a lumbering dance.*)
(*There is a ring at the door-bell, only just audible.* JOANNA *looks
at her watch.*)
Back already? I always heard that was the Catholic system –
little but often. (*Goes out.*)
(HOWARTH *returns to the table. Sound of voices, then footsteps.*)
(*Enters with* LES.) Darling – a friend of Donald's – Les.

LES. Sir.

HOWARTH: Oh – (*getting up*) – hello. (*Little pause.*) I'm afraid
Donald's out – he's gone to church.

LES: Oh, I thought he'd go to the early morning mass – he
usually –

JOANNA: We've been corrupting him, I'm afraid. We always sleep
late on Sundays.

(*There is a pause.*
Glances at HOWARTH, *puzzled, then back to* LES.) Anyway, do sit down.

LES: Oh, well, thank you. (*Sits down.*)

HOWARTH: (*Still standing*) Um, well, you cycled, did you?

LES: Yes. (*Little pause.*) I wasn't sure what time you meant me to come exactly, you said coffee or tea and I thought that's either eleven or in the afternoon. (*Laughs.*)

HOWARTH: (*To* JOANNA) Um, I suggested to Les that if he should be cycling this way today, he look Donald up. They were going for a ride together yesterday.

JOANNA: But if you cycled, you must be exhausted.

LES: No, I'm used to it, we go out every week almost.
(*There is a pause.*)

HOWARTH: That's two of your rides I seem to have messed up.

LES: Oh, it doesn't matter. We can go next week. Well – (*Makes as if to rise.*)

JOANNA: Darling, what about a drink? Or would you prefer tea or coffee, Les?

LES: No, well, that's all right, thank you very much.

JOANNA: Well, *I'd* like a drink.
(HOWARTH *goes to the door, shuts it, goes over to the shelf, pours a sherry, brings it back, gives it to* JOANNA.)
You work in Crabtree's too, do you?

LES: Yes, in the cutlery.

JOANNA: Oh, really? I tried to get some spoons there once, but they were so expensive.

LES: Yes, I know. I always tell people to try somewhere else.

JOANNA: (*Laughs*) Like Woolworth's?

LES: Yes. (*They both laugh.*)

JOANNA: (*Taking her drink*) Darling, I'm sure Les could be persuaded. Have a *small* sherry – you know it makes sense.

LES: Oh, well – thanks very much.
(HOWARTH, *after a fractional hesitation, pours* LES *a very small sherry.*)

JOANNA: Have you known Donald long?

LES: Well, since just after I left school.

JOANNA: You weren't at school together, then?

HOWARTH: No, actually Les was at St Martin's for a short time.

JOANNA: Really?

HOWARTH: (*Handing* LES *his drink*) Although we scarcely knew each other.

LES: Yes, I was only there two years, I had to leave early.

JOANNA: Oh? (*Interrogatively.*)

HOWARTH: Which is how he came to miss me.

LES: That was one of my regrets. (*With sudden intensity.*)

JOANNA: How very flattering. (*To* HOWARTH.)

HOWARTH: Yes. (*Laughs.*) The best way to keep one's reputation is not to have it put to the test.

LES: Everybody at school said you were marvellous and – well, Don says the same.

JOANNA: I must have more of this – hang on a minute. (*Goes out.*)

HOWARTH: (*After a pause*) Well, I'm sorry Donald isn't here, after all your exertions.

LES: He'll be gone a long time then, will he?

HOWARTH: I don't know how long these things last – but I'm afraid I'll have to do a bit of French with him –

LES: Oh, I see.

HOWARTH: He's getting such a lot done – I'm terrified of breaking the spell. (*Little pause.*) I'm sorry.

LES: (*Finishes his drink*) No, it doesn't. (*Shakes his head, gets up.*) Well, perhaps I might as well get back anyway.

HOWARTH: Well, at least you've got the weather, mmm?
(LES *looks at him uncertainly.*)
Still, I'm glad you could drop in.

JOANNA: (*Comes back in*) Oh, you're not going?

LES: Well, I've got to get on.

JOANNA: Oh, what a shame.

HOWARTH: Les wants to get as much of the sun as he can.

JOANNA: Well, it's been *very* nice . . . (*Holds out her hand.*)

LES: Oh, well, thank you. (*They shake hands.*)
(*As they do, there is the sound of the door closing, footsteps.*)

JOANNA: Ah!
(DONALD *comes in, stops when he sees* LES.)

LES: Hello, Don.

JOANNA: You got back just in time. That was lucky.

DONALD: Well, there wasn't an eleven o'clock mass.

JOANNA: Oh dear, I am sorry. Let's all sit down again, at least, and have another drink.

LES: Oh, well, thanks, but if you're going to be working? (*Looks at* HOWARTH.)

JOANNA: Surely you're not going to do anything before lunch?

HOWARTH: Um, no, no, not now – (*Looks at his watch.*) – I shouldn't think. Do have a drink.

JOANNA: Do sit down. (LES *sits down again,* HOWARTH *pours sherry for* DONALD.) Les was just telling us that he never got to do French with Richard at St Martin's.

LES: Of course we don't need French at Crabtree's – (*Contemptuously*) – but we're going to France next holiday – and now Don'll have to do all the talking, eh, Don?

JOANNA: To France? How exciting!

(HOWARTH *gives* DONALD *his sherry.*)

LES: Yes, we thought we'd take our bikes, you know, just put them on the boat and then sort of cycle off – we thought we might even get to Paris, eh, Don?

(DONALD *nods.*)

JOANNA: It sounds marvellous. You know, I think Donald's having you on, darling. He's really getting up his French so he and Les can have a naughty holiday together. (*Goes into the kitchen.*)

(*There is a silence, then the sound of saucepans from the kitchen.* DONALD *sits.* LES *lifts his glass, sees it is empty and sets it down again.*)

LES: (*To* DONALD) I thought I'd ride up to Farlington.

DONALD: Oh. (*Nods.*)

LES: But I won't if you want to go up there next week.

DONALD: No, that's all right.

LES: Anyway, I can go and see what it's like, and we can go up again. Just take a quick look this time, you know, find out where the café is. (*Laughs.*)

(DONALD *nods.*)

(*Pause.*) Well, um, I suppose I'd better be getting on. (*Gets up.*)

HOWARTH: Yes – that's quite a trip, Farlington. (*Gets up.*)

DONALD: Yes. (*Also gets up.*)

JOANNA: (*Raises the hatch and speaks through it*) Darling, ask Les if he'll stay to lunch.

(*There is a pause.*)

HOWARTH: Les was just saying he was going to cycle up to Farlington.

JOANNA: Well, he'll be having lunch on the way, won't he? So why not have it here.

HOWARTH: (*Pause*) Yes, do.

LES: Well, I don't want to cause trouble.

HOWARTH: No trouble.

JOANNA: Well? Is he, or isn't he?

HOWARTH: Yes, he'd love to.

JOANNA: Good. (*Shuts hatch.*) Potatoes, darling!

(HOWARTH *goes out.*)

LES: How's it going, then?

DONALD: All right (*goes into his room, hangs up his coat on a chair.*)

LES: (*Looks at him, clearly worried and follows him to the doorway of the bedroom*) Is this your room then?

(DONALD *comes out, sits down at the table and starts to get on with his work.*)

I met your mum on the street – she was just coming back from church.

DONALD: Oh?

LES: (*Laughs*) She said to find out how they liked the cake.

DONALD: Oh. Yes, well, they liked it.

(*Pause.*)

LES: (*Sitting opposite* DONALD) Well, it's all right then, is it?

DONALD: What?

LES: Well, you know – everything.

(DONALD *shrugs, looks at* LES.)

(*Looks at him, looks down.*) Didn't you want me to stay to lunch then?

(DONALD *shrugs.*)

I see. I'm sorry, Don. I mean, she asked me, didn't she. I
didn't want to be rude to your friends. I didn't know *you*
didn't want me.

DONALD: (*After a pause, looking at* LES) Well, you know now,
don't you. (*In a mutter.*)

(LES *turns, goes out of the main door. The front door slams.*
JOANNA *enters.*)

JOANNA: Has Les gone?

DONALD: (*Gets up*) Um, Les had to go after all, he just
remembered he had to do some shopping for his mum, and
the shop'll be closed.

JOANNA: Oh!

DONALD: He said to say sorry.

(*Blackout.*)

SCENE 2

*The Howarth living-room. Evening. The hatch is open, and through it
come sounds of* HOWARTH *and* DONALD *washing up, and their
voices, quite distinct.* JOANNA *is at the piano, picking quietly the
melody of 'Danny Boy'.*

HOWARTH: Maintenant, tu le prends *ou* vous le –?

DONALD: Prenez . . .

HOWARTH: Pour le secher. Et moi, je vais laver cette assiette –
donnez-le-moi, mon enfant, s'il vous plaît. Merci – oooops!
(*Sound of a plate crashing to the floor.* JOANNA *stops playing the
piano, looks towards the door.*)
Well, what do you say now?

DONALD: Um, je suis desolé.

(HOWARTH *laughs.* JOANNA *cocks her head to one side,
ironically.*)

HOWARTH: (*Raising his voice*) Darling!

JOANNA: (*Slightly parodying*) Yes, darling?

HOWARTH: (*Looking in through hatch*) I'm afraid there's been a
little – (*in French*) – accident, darling.

JOANNA: Oh, that's all right, darling. Not to worry.

293

HOWARTH: It was only one of the plain white ones.

JOANNA: Oh, that's *good*.

HOWARTH: Sorry, darling.

(JOANNA *begins to play again*.)

Non, non, laisse-la. Et le café, c'est prêt?

DONALD: Oui, c'est prêt.

HOWARTH: Bon – ça, c'est pour madame.

(DONALD *wearing an apron, appears at the door, carrying a mug of coffee. He wipes the base of the mug on his apron and puts the coffee on the piano*.)

JOANNA: Do you know the words?

DONALD: Well, um, not properly.

JOANNA: I bet you do.

DONALD: Well . . . (*Nods*.)

JOANNA: And sing them beautifully?

(DONALD *laughs, shakes his head*.)

(*Smiles, and as* DONALD *turns to go*) Come here.

(DONALD *comes back apprehensively*.)

(*Strikes a chord*.) Go on. Please.

DONALD: Well. (*Shakes his head, laughs*.) I can't.

JOANNA: Please! (*Plays again. Starts to sing the first few words*.)

Oh, Danny Boy . . .

(DONALD *joins in and they sing together*.)

JOANNA: ⎫
DONALD: ⎭ . . . the pipes, the pipes are calling . . .

(JOANNA *stops singing and* DONALD *goes on alone*.)

DONALD: From glen to glen, and down the mountain side.

The summer's gone and all the roses falling.

(HOWARTH, *from the kitchen, puts a coffee mug on the hatch-shelf, moves quietly in to the doorway*.)

'Tis you, 'tis you must go and I must bide.

But come ye back when summer's in the meadow

Or when the valley's . . .

(HOWARTH *appears from the kitchen, wearing an apron and carrying a mug. He stays in the doorway, staring at* DONALD.)

. . . hushed and white with snow,

And I'll be here, in sunshine or in shadow,

Oh Danny boy, oh Danny boy I love you so.

JOANNA: (*Ending the song*) I knew you'd have a beautiful voice.

HOWARTH: All the Irish do. It's because they're so sentimental.

(HOWARTH *shuts the door.* DONALD *takes off the apron and leaves it on a chair.* HOWARTH *turns to the hatch, brings down the coffee mug there to* DONALD *at the table, puts his own coffee mug on the table.* JOANNA *gets up, picks up her coffee cup and goes over to the sofa. She sits down and looks towards* DONALD. DONALD *sits at the table, gets his books and makes as if to begin some work.*)

JOANNA: I'm sure you shouldn't, Donald. You've been at it all afternoon.

(DONALD *looks at* HOWARTH.)

HOWARTH: (*Looking up*) Perhaps you should give it a rest, but you can have a little dictation for a night cap, if you want.

JOANNA: So come and talk.

(DONALD, *reluctantly, takes his coffee and sits by* JOANNA.) May we?

HOWARTH: (*Takes off his apron, sits at the table and begins marking books*) What? Mmm, go ahead.

JOANNA: He never minds when he's marking. Tell me more about your Paris adventure.

DONALD: Well, I'm, um, I don't think I'm going to Paris.

(*Glances towards* HOWARTH.)

JOANNA: Oh? (*Puzzled.*) Les seemed to think it was all arranged.

DONALD: Yes, well, I don't think I'll go. (*Clears his throat.*)

JOANNA: I'm sure you would have enjoyed it. I did at your age – and every age since. Won't Les be very disappointed?

DONALD: (*Shrugs*) Well, he can go on his own.

JOANNA: Will he? (HOWARTH *looks at them.*)

DONALD: (*Shrugs again, laughs awkwardly*) I don't know, but I'm not going.

JOANNA: I see. Wouldn't you enjoy Paris with Les, then?

DONALD: (*Shakes his head*) No.

JOANNA: Why not?

HOWARTH: Poor old Donald. He's getting quite a grilling.

(JOANNA *looks towards him, shocked, then turns back to*

DONALD. HOWARTH *looks back at his books.*)

JOANNA: I'm sorry. (*Silkily*) Am I grilling you?

DONALD: No. No, it's all right. (*Laughs.*)

JOANNA: I may ask you a question or two – by way of conversation?

(HOWARTH *lifts his head and looks towards them.* JOANNA *looks at* HOWARTH. DONALD *glances towards him.*)

(*Very silkily*) Well, may I, sir?

HOWARTH: (*Laughs*) Darling . . .

JOANNA: Good. (*Turning back to* DONALD) You were saying you wouldn't enjoy Paris with Les.

DONALD: I just don't want to be with him – making his scenes and that.

JOANNA: Scenes? I thought you were friends.

DONALD: Not any more. He gets on my nerves.

JOANNA: I see. Poor Les, no wonder he didn't stay for lunch. (*Sips coffee.*)

HOWARTH: He didn't stay for lunch because he'd forgotten the shopping.

JOANNA: (*Looks at* HOWARTH, *pause, looks back at* DONALD) What does he do that gets on your nerves? (*Little pause. Looks at* HOWARTH.) May I ask? (*This meant genuinely.*)

DONALD: (*Glances at* HOWARTH) Well, he's odd. (JOANNA *looks back at* DONALD.) There's something wrong with him. He's always depending on me and nagging at me.

JOANNA: Well, I agree that does sound unpleasant – like a wife. (*Laughs. Looks at* HOWARTH.)

DONALD: Yes. (*Nervous laugh.*)

(JOANNA *looks back at* DONALD. *There is a pause as if the conversation is finished.* HOWARTH *goes back to his exercise-book.*)

JOANNA: Why do you think he's like that – with you?

(DONALD *looks across at* HOWARTH *for help.* JOANNA *follows his gaze across to* HOWARTH. HOWARTH *looks down at his books.*)

DONALD: Well, because, um, his feelings are confused. (*Little pause.*) He's a homo – (*checks himself*) – sexual.

296

JOANNA: (*After a pause*) Really? (*Pause.*) Has he told you he is? (DONALD *glances towards* HOWARTH *again.* JOANNA *follows his glance.* HOWARTH *looks towards them, and pretends to go on correcting.*)

DONALD: No, but I can see it now. I really knew it before. I mean, from the way he was always depending on me and making me apologize for things that were his fault. I always knew there was something with him.

JOANNA: But what *exactly* put you on to him – it must have been very recent. *He* certainly doesn't realize yet that you know.

DONALD: (*Looks towards* HOWARTH. *There is a long, embarrassing pause.* HOWARTH *looks at* DONALD.) Well, um, Richard – (JOANNA *turns to face* HOWARTH) – when he saw him and knew who he was from school, he warned me about him.

HOWARTH: I don't think I quite did that, Donald.

JOANNA: What *did* you say? (*Pleasantly*) Or is it something private that I oughtn't to know?

HOWARTH: Merely something to the effect that people are what they are, and that we haven't the right to judge them. Donald was slightly worried about Les's tendency to cling. He was finding him a bit oppressive.

JOANNA: Clearly not the person to go to Paris with. (*To* DONALD.)

DONALD: No, that's what Richard said too.
(JOANNA *looks at* HOWARTH.)

HOWARTH: Well, again, not quite that, Donald. All I meant – or at least meant to mean – was that if you're going to be forced into someone's company a great deal, then you've got to be sure of the company. I wasn't prescribing, I wouldn't dream of doing so. (*Goes on with his marking.*)

JOANNA: (*Watches him*) But this thing at school – that you knew about. *Is* it private?

HOWARTH: No – well, yes, of course it is. (*Pause.*) It was just the usual schoolboy business. He got a crush on another boy, and there was a little – (*shrugs*) – trouble, but it's not for publication – I'm sure Donald knows that.

JOANNA: (*Ironically*) Well, I'll try and guard my tongue too. But

I suppose boys grow out of that. I actually wrote anonymous love letters to one of my teachers.

HOWARTH: The point is – (*sharply*) – that Donald – Les, I mean – hasn't grown out of it – at least from what Donald tells me. Anyway – (*laughs*) – it's a bit hard. He just dropped in to be, um, friendly, and we seem to be giving him a bit of a going-over between us. I mean what I said about not judging.

JOANNA: We are mean, aren't we? (*Looks at* HOWARTH, *clearly furious, gets up and goes out of the room into the kitchen and shuts the hatch from the other side.*)

(*There is a silence.* HOWARTH *goes on marking.* DONALD *looks towards him, then looks down.*)

HOWARTH: (*Marking, not looking up*) One of the facts of marriage, Donald, is that ladies, when in an advanced state of pregnancy, tend to be a trifle, um, dramatic, poor dears. Still – (*looks at* DONALD) – you will be careful never to repeat to anyone – and particularly Les – what I told you about him.

DONALD: Oh, no. (*Shakes his head.*) No.

HOWARTH: Anyway, perhaps you'd better get an early night, eh? – in view of tomorrow. (*Turns, smiles at him.*)

DONALD: (*Rising*) I thought we were going to do that last dictation, you said. I'll be all right for that.

HOWARTH: (*Hesitates, then regretfully*) I think we've left it a bit late really.

DONALD: Oh. (*Disappointed.*)

HOWARTH: Good-night.

DONALD: (*Takes the dictionary and satchel, makes for his bedroom door – stops, turns, looks at* HOWARTH) If – if I get through my O level, would you help me then? With my A levels?

HOWARTH: I don't know, Donald.

(DONALD *looks at him for a moment, then turns, goes into the bedroom. He turns on the light there, puts down the satchel, takes off his tie, hesitates, picks up the dictionary and returns to the living-room.*)

DONALD: I just remembered – I mean, I might forget it in the morning. (*Puts it down on the table.*)

HOWARTH: Oh yes, I can't let you have all the luck, can I?
Someone else may need it sometime. (*Smiles.*) I've got a lot
going on at school at the moment, and next term – when
I've finished with that blasted Bishop – I've got to organize
the French play, and then I've got the football, the colts,
and of course there'll be the baby. (*Smiles.*) But I'm sure
we'll manage *something* – for your A levels.

DONALD: Thank you, Richard.

HOWARTH: Because, you know, you're going to pass tomorrow –
and I want you to go on. I intend to take all the credit.

(DONALD *smiles.*)

Now you go to bed.

(DONALD *turns, goes back to the room.* HOWARTH *goes back to
his marking. There is a pause. The door opens.* JOANNA *comes
in, picks up the cups, etc., then goes out again.* HOWARTH
watches her. She comes in again.)

JOANNA: Donald gone to bed?

HOWARTH: Yes. What about you?

JOANNA: Has he gone to the bathroom yet?

HOWARTH: Um, I don't know. I don't think so.

(JOANNA *sits down.*)

You going?

JOANNA: In a minute. (*Coldly.*)

(HOWARTH *looks at her, then turns back to his marking.*
DONALD *comes out of the room, in trousers and shirt with
sponge bag. He looks towards* JOANNA *and* HOWARTH, *then
hurries out.*)

Now then, what the hell were you up to?

HOWARTH: What do you mean?

JOANNA: Were you trying to put me in my place?

HOWARTH: (*Laughs contemptuously*) Of course not.

JOANNA: Then I assume your odd turns of phrase – grilling,
going over, etc. – were an attempt to cover up your own
indiscretions.

HOWARTH: What indiscretions?

JOANNA: Your revelations about Les – but then you were
covering a lot of territory – moral and psychological – do

you do that with all your boys?

HOWARTH: You're being very offensive. (*Little pause, they stare at each other.*) The occasion doesn't usually arise. He asked me my advice about Les and I gave it to him. Yes, come to think of it, I'd do that with any boy – I consider it part of my job. He simply got hold of the wrong end of the stick, that's all.

JOANNA: Well, that's certainly a bad omen for his examination – if he makes such a hash of understanding you in English. (HOWARTH *shrugs.*)
Well?

HOWARTH: Well? (*Little pause, he throws his pen down on the table.*) What do you want me to do – tell him he's a bloody little fool for getting it wrong? I've already been extremely tactless with him once today, the last thing I want to do is mess him up again, especially with the examination in the morning. With the chance he's got.

JOANNA: Richard. (*Pause.*) Richard, look at me, please. (*Politely.*)

HOWARTH: What?

JOANNA: That's better. You've been dodging your eyes all round me for weeks – except once or twice when you've glared at me. (*Looks away.*) Perhaps I'm not very pleasant to look at.

HOWARTH: What?

JOANNA: Do you think I don't know? Nine months of just getting fatter and squatter, and going on at you about foetal stages and membranes splitting and shows of water and bottles of urine, not to mention vomiting at the beginning and lying all over the place now. Do you think *I* don't feel it – with *my* tendency to cling?

HOWARTH: Don't be silly.

JOANNA: And off and on I think, who *would* want to lie beside this swollen sow, *not* flower, and then I think, well, hell, it's just as much your doing, so you can damn well lie beside me and like it. (*She smiles sadly.*) But you don't like it, you haven't liked it for months, and there's nothing I can do about that. Nothing at all. I can't stop you from being disgusted by me, not by law or love.

HOWARTH: Disgusted?

JOANNA: Don't do that. Not now. If you need time to think, just ask for an intermission. I won't scream.

(HOWARTH *gets up, goes over to her, bends down, kisses her on the cheek and sits beside her.*)

Thank you. But think about it. When did you last kiss me properly? When I was three months gone?

(*The door opens,* DONALD *comes in.*)

DONALD: (*Turning, smiling*) 'Night, Joanna.

JOANNA: 'Night Donald.

DONALD: 'Night, Richard.

HOWARTH: Donald.

(DONALD *goes on into his room, puts down his sponge bag and clothes, turns out the light and gets into bed. There is a pause.* HOWARTH *attempts to kiss her properly.*)

JOANNA: Don't be ridiculous. (*Gently.*) Do you know what I've found out this weekend? I don't like good teachers.

HOWARTH: Don't you?

JOANNA: They really are self-indulgent. All this business with Donald – moralizing, philosophizing, gossiping, weeping, advising – it's just self-indulgence. You don't know anything about anything at all, not really.

HOWARTH: (*Smiling*) Not really.

JOANNA: Least of all yourself.

HOWARTH: Least of all myself.

JOANNA: And you're not, actually, charming me one little bit. (*Gets up.*)

HOWARTH: (*Gets up*) Darling . . .

JOANNA: This isn't a good time to find you out.

(HOWARTH *steps back, as if he's been hit.* JOANNA *turns, goes to the door.*)

HOWARTH: You can't leave it just like that –

JOANNA: You're busy.

HOWARTH: That can wait, darling! I – (*Gestures to the exercise-books.*)

JOANNA: No, it can't wait. You be as long as you like, Richard. Because I'm bloody tired and want to be asleep. (*Opens the*

301

door, goes out, closes the door.)
(HOWARTH *stands for a moment, makes a gesture of frustration and anger, then goes to the door, stands there, hesitating, then opens the door and goes into the hall as if to call* JOANNA. *Pause. He goes into the kitchen and comes back munching on a biscuit, looks at Donald's door, then sits down, carrying the biscuit tin and begins marking. There is a slight dimming of light in the lounge to suggest the passing of time.*)

DONALD: (*As the lights start to fade, cries out in his sleep*) Please . . . please . . . please . . .
(*The lights fade out and fade up again. In the living-room the centre table-lamp on the shelves is on, with just a pool of light round the table where* HOWARTH *is still working. In the bedroom, the lights are on and* DONALD *is discovered, moaning and rocking himself to and fro on the chair, still asleep.*
HOWARTH *hears the sounds, rises and goes to the bedroom door, knocks. No answer.*)

HOWARTH: Donald, Donald – (*He goes in, leaves the door open.*) Donald! Donald!
(*He gently puts his hand on* DONALD'S *shoulder.* DONALD *wakes with a start, looks up at* HOWARTH.)
It's all right, Donald. It's all right.

DONALD: I'm sorry, Richard, I'm sorry.
(DONALD *suddenly clasps* HOWARTH *round the waist, burying his face against him.* HOWARTH *gently raises* DONALD *up from the chair.* DONALD *puts his arms round* HOWARTH.)

HOWARTH: There's nothing for you to be frightened of. Not here.
(DONALD *starts to cry.*)
Donald, don't. Don't. (*Puts his arms round him.*) There there, my Donald, there, my dear old Donald. There, I'm on your side. I care about you, you know I care about you. I'll see that nothing can harm you.
(*Still embracing* DONALD, *but now with more feeling, he closes the door, then takes* DONALD'S *head in both his hands and turns his face to his.*)
(*The lights fade out.*)
(*As the lights are fading.*) Donald, Donald . . .

(*After a pause a beam of light comes up in the living-room, focused on the back of the sofa.* JOANNA, *in dressing-gown, is seated there, her head bowed. She raises her head to face the bedroom door and a beam of light comes up in the bedroom, focused on the chair beside the door.* HOWARTH *is sitting there, head raised.* DONALD *is in bed, but the bed and the rest of the bedroom is in darkness.* HOWARTH *looks at* DONALD, *gets up slowly and leaves the bedroom for the living-room, closing the door. The light fades in the bedroom and increases in the living-room.* HOWARTH *steps into the living-room and is going towards the door when he sees* JOANNA. *They stay staring at each other for a long time, then* JOANNA *rises and slowly goes to the door and opens it.* HOWARTH *slowly goes past her and out of the room.* JOANNA *follows and closes the door.*

After a pause the morning light slowly builds, strong sunlight seen through the curtains which are still shut, and we are into Scene Three.)

SCENE 3

The Howarth living-room. Morning.

DONALD *wakes, sits up in bed, hunched over for a minute. He hears a noise from the kitchen and gets quickly out of bed and starts desperately and hurriedly to dress, takes off his pyjama jacket and puts on his shirt, does not stop to put on his tie.*

JOANNA *enters, looks toward the bedroom door, crosses to the window and opens the curtains by their pulley cord. Morning light floods the room. She crosses to the table, pushes the school books downstage on the table to make way for the tray, slowly goes out again to the kitchen. After a pause she returns with a tray having on it tea, bread and butter and knives and forks, places it on the upstage side of the table. All this while* DONALD *has been hurriedly dressing and cramming his possessions into the carrier bag.* JOANNA *leaves the table and has reached the door when* DONALD, *dressed and carrying his bag and satchel starts to open the door. He sees* JOANNA *and leaps back into the bedroom, begins to close the door.*

JOANNA: (*Still in her dressing-gown, sees the door closing*) Donald!

DONALD: (*Opens the door slowly, carrying the carrier bag and satchel*) Um, 'morning, Joanna.

JOANNA: Good morning, Donald. Your breakfast's ready. Would you sit down?

(DONALD *sits at the table.* JOANNA *goes out into the kitchen.* DONALD *puts his things on the floor beside him.* JOANNA *returns with a plate of scrambled egg.*)

Here you are. (*Sets the plate down in front of him on the tray and starts to pour him out a cup of tea.*) What time have you got to get to work?

DONALD: I'm going to the examination hall. It's in the town hall. Um, at nine o'clock.

JOANNA: Well, you'd better hurry then, it's already half-past eight. Sugar? (*Passes him the basin from the other side of the tray.*)

(DONALD *nods, helps himself to sugar.* JOANNA *sits by the table, watching him.* DONALD *drinks tea, his hand trembling and slowly starts to eat the egg, acutely conscious of her presence.* JOANNA *rises slowly, takes the biscuit tin from the table up to the hatch, puts it through and closes the hatch. She continues watching* DONALD. DONALD *takes another sip of tea and one more forkful of egg to his lips. He can't eat, looks at* JOANNA, *puts the fork down.*)

All right? Nothing else I can give you?

DONALD: No, thank you. No. That was very nice. Um – (*Gets up and picks up his things.*)

JOANNA: (*Goes over to the door*) Richard! Donald's just leaving. (*Goes out to the kitchen.*)

(DONALD *stares nervously towards the door, his arms full with bag and satchel.*)

HOWARTH: (*Enters*) Good-morning, Donald. Condemned man ate a hearty, um – (*Gestures towards the table – there is an appalling silence.*) My god, your dictionary. (*Goes to the table, picks it up, hands it to* DONALD.)

DONALD: Um, no, it's yours. (*Tries to hand it back.*)

HOWARTH: I know, but – look. I want you to have it, it's a very lucky dictionary, I –

DONALD: I – I – can't. (*Shakes his head, tries to give it back.*)

HOWARTH: Why not?

DONALD: Well, it's not – I mean it's too er . . .

HOWARTH: Nonsense, bloody nonsense, it's not too anything, except wrong of you not to let me give it to you. I – I need you to have it, Donald. Please.

DONALD: (*Takes the dictionary emotionally*) Thank you, Richard. (*Looks down at it.*) You won't be helping me with my A levels, then?

HOWARTH: (*Gently*) No, Donald.

(DONALD *nods, suddenly makes a low, sobbing noise.*)

DONALD: I don't know what I'm going to do. (*He starts to cry.*)

HOWARTH: (*Shuts the door quickly and goes back towards* DONALD, *not close to him*) Donald – what, look, what happened, it was one of those, well, the kind of thing, it could happen to anybody, it caught us, um, me, the thing is to forget what happened, in the end it won't matter, but try to remember me as a teacher. And a friend. I am your friend, Donald.

DONALD: Yes, Richard.

HOWARTH: It won't matter, nothing will matter except that we, we liked each other, from our different, um, rafts. (*Long pause, puts his hand on* DONALD's *shoulder, glances towards the door.*) And when you've got your O levels and all the A levels you want, because you will, Donald, and when you're doing, doing – (*moving away*) what you want to do, think of that, eh?

DONALD: Sir.

HOWARTH: And Donald – if – well, you won't tell anyone about it, will you, ever? Not Les – no one?

DONALD: (*Looks down, whispers*) No, sir.
I'm sorry, sir. I'm very sorry.

(*Pause.* JOANNA *comes in.*)

JOANNA: (*Entering to between them*) It's getting on.

HOWARTH: Yes, you'd better go.

(JOANNA *sees the dictionary* DONALD *is holding.*)

JOANNA: (*Tentatively*) Isn't that ours? (*Looks at* HOWARTH.)

DONALD: (*Holding out the book as if to offer it back*) Well – Richard said –

JOANNA: Oh, I see.

(*She goes to* DONALD *and gently pushes the book back into his hands.*)

Good luck in your examination, Donald.

DONALD: Thank you, Joanna.

HOWARTH: (*Still at other side of sofa*) Yes, Donald, good luck.

DONALD: Thank you, sir.

(JOANNA *goes out.* DONALD *follows without looking back. Pause.* HOWARTH *slowly crosses to a chair by the table, pulls it away from the table and sits. Pause.* JOANNA *returns, closes the door. She is carrying the cake-box. She crosses down to* HOWARTH, *to his left and holds the box out to him.*)

JOANNA: To say thank you with.

(*Curtain.*)

The Caramel Crisis

The Caramel Crisis was first transmitted by BBC films on 25 April 1966. The cast included:

CARAMEL	George Cole
CLOON	Richard Pearson
LAME	John Le Mesurier
MCWITHERS	Bryan Pringle
SIR ROY	Kynaston Reeves
MRS CLOON	Barbara Miller
MRS LAME	Rosamund Greenwood
MRS MCWITHERS	Edna Petrie
MRS PORTLY	Winifred Dennis

Director	Naomi Capon
Producer	Paul Allan
Music	Norman Kay

INT.MCWITHERS'S OFFICE. DAY

The board, MCWITHERS, LAME, CLOON, *are watching someone leave the room.* MCWITHERS *stares aggressively.* CLOON *modestly, with a suggestion of appreciation.* LAME *smiles in a superior fashion. The departing person is not seen. Sound of his footsteps receding. Noise of door opening and closing.* MCWITHERS *leaning back, drawing on his cigarette, and then confidently.*

MCWITHERS: Well, what do you think? What do you think? Cloon?

CLOON: Er, yes, he, well, certainly wants the job. Excellent medical qualifications, experience, and other things. Seemed, er . . .
　　(LAME *smiles in a superior way.*)
　　. . . seemed interested and anxious to, anxious to –

LAME: Anxious to please. Yes, I wondered if you'd noticed that. I agree with you there, Cloon. One hundred per.
　　(*Little pause, while* MCWITHERS *frowns and* LAME *continues with his superior smile. Between* LAME *and* MCWITHERS, *there should be a suggestion of rivalry –* MCWITHERS' *bluster against* LAME's *intellectual poise. In fact,* LAME *leads,* MCWITHERS *pretending that the ideas are his own.*)

MCWITHERS: Come on then, Lame. (*Laughs.*) Let's have *your* version.

LAME: There it is. Anxious to please. (*He waits, pretends to be surprised by the confusion around him.*) This, I mean. Everything just a little too right, a little too bright, a little too good, and a little too true about our friend, Reenis.

CLOON: Peenels.

LAME: (*Stammering slightly*) Pen, er, Renels, pen, er whatever it is. (*He tries to sound contemptuous, but somehow recoils from the confusion of the name. Then, recovers himself*) He *wants* too much. Wants the job, I mean. What does McWithers think?

MCWITHERS: I've said it before, I'll say it again. It's not smartness we're after. Not cockiness. Not flash, flash, flash.

We want a good doctor, yes, and above all a reliable man. You can always tell a reliable man by his look. (*Pause.*) We'll know the one we want. Know him as soon as we clap eyes on him. Because he's reliable. (*Laughs.*) Eh, Cloon? (*But looks sideways at* LAME.)

CLOON: (*Nods*) Only, er, actually we've seen, er, five. There's only the one left.

LAME: (*Paying no attention*) We won't pick him, will we? That's the way it goes on a good selection. Meeting, communication, recognition. He'll pick us.

CLOON: Yes. But . . .

MCWITHERS: Oh yes (*he settles comfortably and confidently back*), we'll know, all right. There's always one. Always one.

LAME: (*Meditatively*) A connection. A correspondence.

MCWITHERS: Look out for the reliable man.

CLOON: Yes. Only . . .

LAME: Osmosis. Osmotic. We'll perceive him osmotically. (*Laughs.*) Is there such a word?

CLOON: (*Vaguely*) Yes, well, the next one . . . (*he picks up the application form and stares at the photograph on it*) is the last one, actually.
(*They look down at the photograph. A buzzer sounds. They look up as the* SECRETARY *opens the door.*)

SECRETARY: Doctor Caramel.
(CARAMEL *crosses the room. He is seen as a hazy outline. He sits down.*)

LAME: . . . degree, Doctor Caramel. Distinguished, may I say? (*Looks down at the papers*) – and then, mmm yes, internships, mmm yes, three years – with, mmm yes, mmm, two years, mmm – huh.

MCWITHERS: Had experience in large factories, I see. That's important. *We're* a large factory. One of the largest. We're very large indeed. And we've got a good medical staff, good reputation, good equipment, good supplies. You'd be in charge of all that. All of it. At the centre of it.

LAME: Your duties will be complex, of course. At first glance simple, in reality complex. This, for example. Three

thousand men here, three thousand bodies, which comes to
God knows how many limbs, fingers, ears, locks of hair
(*laughs*) you'd be responsible for. (*Laughs.*) The work they
do is highly unskilled (*laughs again*) and therefore highly
dangerous. One hundred per dangerous. This, I mean. Last
month in the western block alone two chaps lost their
fingers – one each, actually (*laughs again*) in the Sicrex cogs,
one chap got his hair caught in the mill loading nexus, one
chap had his (*sudden confusion*) had his, oh, thumb (*with
relief*) sliced right off, and . . . (*as* LAME *goes on camera fixes
on* CARAMEL's *face, imperturbably nodding*)
. . . fainted dead away from what Doctor Leak calls
monotonous tension, and this, mark you, and this is the
western block alone. Apart from the western . . .
(*After a long close-up of* CARAMEL's *face during* LAME's
*monologue, camera settles by his face, to suggest a rounded part
of it, and concentrates on the board, who go on eagerly talking
at him.* LAME *didactically, with gestures and nervous laughs.*
MCWITHERS *aggressively, with ponderously emphatic
movements, and* CLOON *getting in a worried sentence here and
there. But this is all mime.*)

CARAMEL: (*Voice over*) Westerns're certainly not what they used
to be, oh no, all confused now with talking and stuff like
that, and no action, violence, stuff you can thrill to, but if
I'm lucky there might be a good thriller on with Glenn
Ford as a policeman chopping them down with the side of
his hand and no conversation except blows and shots and
deadly stuff, a blood-bath. (*Pause.*) Will there be a bath at
the hotel?

CLOON:
LAME: } Oh bound to be, a big one, yes, really big.
CARAMEL: } (*Voice over*) We're a large factory. One of the
MCWITHERS: } largest. Very large indeed.

LAME: Have you had any experience of sycnex cogs?
CARAMEL: (*Voice over*) Like my mother's . . .

311

CARAMEL: (*Voice over*) Only *she* won't be there screeching at
me all the time to come out, and turning off
the gas, screech, screech, screech.

LAME: (*Voice over*) That's all right then, we have rather a
lot of trouble with them.

MCWITHERS: Have you got any questions, Cloon?

CLOON: I must say, your testimonials seem very sound.

CARAMEL: (*Voice over*) I can't help it that I like baths,

CARAMEL: (*Voice over*) And she has no right to keep me out of
them.

We do have rather a lot of accidents . . . depending,
need we say it? On the weather. Odd how
accidents rise as the temperature drops. I call it

LAME: the Healman paradox.

CARAMEL: (*Regally*) Yes. Yes. It does make a difference.
Naturally it does.
(*Nervously, under the impression he is being thought foolish*)

LAME: But I don't have to tell *you* that. Of course not. This, I
mean . . . This report proves what I've just been saying.
(*Fades away, face becoming indistinct.*)

CARAMEL: (*Testily*) Chatter, chatter, chatter. Why are they
chattering so much? I hope they won't come chattering after
me all the time, once I'm comfortably settled, the fat one is
nice though, I like him, he looks as if he'd leave people
alone.

MCWITHERS: (*Comes sharply into focus*) . . . a good flat, with lots
of room for a family. Of course, you haven't got a family.
(*Laughs.*) But if you did have a family, there would be room
for it.

CLOON: (*Anxiously*) As long as it was a very little family, really.

CARAMEL: Does it have a bath?

MCWITHERS: A bath?

LAME: Exactly. A bath. This is very much to the point. Does it
have a bath? Yes, Doctor Caramel, (*glancing slyly at*
MCWITHERS). I think you'll find *all* the hygiene facilities in
Healman and Co. are adequate. Do I read you right?

CARAMEL: (*Again majestically*) I'm glad to hear it.

312

(*He proceeds in his dream voice.*)

(*Voice over.*) Nice, nice, nice, one I can sink into with just my head sticking above the water, but why are they keeping me so long, I won't have time to go to the cinema if they chatter, chatter, chatter unless I go *after* dinner and have my bath when I come back, and perhaps I can say I have an important engagement.

MCWITHERS: (*Overlapping* CARAMEL's *speech, coming into focus*) We'd like you to take up the appointment : . . soon Doctor Caramel, if we offer you the position. Leak wants to wrap it up by the fifteenth.

CARAMEL: Oh, yes.

LAME: Good. Excellent. One hundred per.

CLOON: Yes.

MCWITHERS: (*Jovially*) Well, perhaps you have some questions, Doctor Caramel? Huh?

CARAMEL: No thank you. (*Rises slowly.*) Everything seems quite acceptable.

CLOON: (*Staring up at him*) Acceptable?

CARAMEL: Yes, thank you.

LAME: (*Significantly, to* CARAMEL) Acceptable. Exactly.

CARAMEL: Yes, thank you.

MCWITHERS: That's right.

CARAMEL: Goodbye.

THE BOARD: Goodbye.

(CARAMEL *goes to the door and steps out.*)

CARAMEL: (*Voice is heard from outside*) I might just make it to the nearest cinema if I get a taxi, taxis are warm, deep and warm, so are cinemas, and baths, baths are . . .

(*Door clicks shut. We see the eager faces of* LAME *and* MCWITHERS, *the worried face of* CLOON.)

LAME: (*Exuberantly*) Got him. Got him. Got him.

MCWITHERS: He's the reliable man. No doubt about that, eh. Lame?

LAME: He knows it too. And that's why we want him. Yes, McWithers, *that*'s why we want him. Eh, Cloon?

CLOON: Yes, er, but only don't you think there was something a

313

little – I mean, that was a funny question about the bath, and he looked, well, half-asleep, almost.

MCWITHERS: He's not flash, if that's what you mean. No. If it's the flashy man you're after, then Caramel's not the man for you. He's just a solid, reliable man, a stayer. (*Glares humorously at* CLOON.) Myself, I've said it before, I've no use for the flashy man. Nor has Sir Roy. Sir Roy wants men who will last.

CLOON: (*Fingering his tie*) Yes.

LAME: (*Tapping his nose in thought*) You see, he'll be out there now, waiting to be told that he's the man we want. Waiting, confidently waiting, to be told. How do I know? Osmosis. (*Laughs.*) Shall we see what he says to our offer, then? (*Rises jauntily, followed by* MCWITHERS, *with* CLOON *in the rear.* LAME *opens the door, he and* MCWITHERS *stare.* CLOON *can't see, as his view is being blocked, but he stares at their backs.*)

CLOON: Isn't he, er, there then?

MCWITHERS: Of course he isn't. (*Wheeling angrily around*) Why should he hang about. (*Triumphantly, to* LAME) It was in the bag.

LAME: (*Rather desperately*) He knew. He knew. And *that* precisely, is why he's gone.

INT. CARAMEL'S FLAT. DAY

The hall and bathroom of the medical flat. Lots of soaps, bath-salts, etc., in the bathroom. A telephone in the hall, on a little table.
CARAMEL, *enveloped in an enormous towel, pads into the bathroom. He is carrying a book – a sensational paperback (on the cover a girl bound to a chair, gagged, in limited underwear, and a man holding a gun). He is humming, a little, and happy. He climbs into the bath, and settles back in the water, after arranging the book on a contraption to support it. Suddenly there is a knocking on the front door. In the conversation that follows the camera is on* CARAMEL.)
LAME: (*Out of shot*) Hello, hello.

CARAMEL: (*Not interrupting his reading*) Hello.

LAME: (*Out of shot*) Well, um, (*at a loss*) are you comfortable in there? Having a bath? (*Laughs.*)

CARAMEL: Oh, thank you.

LAME: (*Out of shot, after a pause*) Well, er – I've just been to see the methodical medico, Leak. He's looking forward to handing over to you and collecting his pension. (*Laughs.*) Seven injuries this week. Seven.

(CARAMEL *subsides into the water until his ears are covered, then bobs out.*)

CARAMEL: Yes, yes. Look, have you got a television set?

LAME: (*Out of shot*) What? (*Pause.*) A television set? (*Little pause.*) No, no, we never watch television, my wife and I.

CARAMEL: I said *I* haven't got a television set.

LAME: (*Out of shot, confused*) I see. Haven't got a television set? A goggle box? (*Laughs.*)

CARAMEL: (*Pounding the water with his hand, in exasperation*) Yes, I haven't got one. Shouldn't there be one for the flat? I should think they'd put one in. (*He ponders, then craftily*) For relaxation.

LAME: (*Out of shot*) I see.

CARAMEL: (*Displaying something like impatience*) I said, what about a television set?

LAME: (*Out of shot*) Yes, I see. (*Pause.*) Are you going to be long in the, er, bath?

CARAMEL: (*Now displaying indignation*) I've only just got in. (*Pause.*)

LAME: (*Out of shot*) I see. Well.

CARAMEL: Goodbye.

LAME: Yes, well . . .

(CARAMEL *sits listening to* LAME's *footsteps retreating.*)

CARAMEL: They'd better get me a set. It's preposterous that I haven't got one.

(*He settles back with his book. Chuckles at something on the page.*)

INT. CORRIDOR. DAY

One of the corridors of Holman. During this scene the three of them walking up and down. LAME *and* MCWITHERS *close together.*
CLOON *a little excluded, sometimes being squeezed against the wall.*

LAME: A trifle odd, perhaps to come out with it just like that. A trifle odd, and oddly trifling. (*Laughs.*) But one mustn't worry.

MCWITHERS: (*Heartily*) He knows what he wants, that's all. I like that in a man. You know where you stand with a man if he knows what he wants, and says that he knows . . . (*Sentence gutters out.*) What he . . .

LAME: Precisely. I'm with you one hundred per. But we do have this weensy problem of the set.

MCWITHERS: If we stand straight with him, he'll stand straight with us. That's always good.

CLOON: Should I, er, speak to Sir Roy's secretary about the set?

MCWITHERS: So he was, really, actually *in* the bath, you say? At, er, three, was it three you said, in the afternoon?

LAME: This I *have* said, already, four times to be precise.

MCWITHERS: Yes, well he probably had his reasons. (*Pause.*) Being a doctor and that.

CLOON: I could mention it, er, to Sir Roy's secretary? I'm sure he could think of something.

MCWITHERS: (*With false joviality*) No, no, no, no, no. No, no. No, man, no. We've got a battery portable at home. Never use it anyway. No need to bother Sir Roy with this. No, no, sounds strange if you don't know the chap.

CLOON: (*Humbly*) Well, er, I suppose we don't, really. None of us do, do we?

MCWITHERS: (*Angrily*) Of course we know him. Of course we do. (*Laughs.*) We appointed him.
(*Camera settles for an instant on* CLOON's *face, which is very thoughtful. Fades.*)

THE CARAMEL CRISIS

INT. CORRIDOR OUTSIDE CARAMEL'S FLAT. DAY

A close-up of the flat door, from behind which are coming mysterious slapping sounds.
Slap, slap, slap, slap (pause), slap, slap, slap, slap (pause), slap, slap, slap, slap (pause), with one variation – slap, slap (pause), slap, slap (pause), slap, slap, slap, slap, etc.
Then MCWITHERS *appears in the corridor. He is whistling unconvincingly. He knocks on the door. No response. He knocks again. Still no response. Stoops, puts his eye to keyhole, then rises and turns away. Suddenly slapping noises begin again. After a while slapping noises become faint.*
MCWITHERS: Caramel! Caramel! Are you there? It's me,
McWithers. McWithers here, Caramel.

INT. CARAMEL'S FLAT. DAY

Quick cut to naked feet, padding down the flat hall then up to CARAMEL, *carrying a portable television set, which he arranges on the hall table – telephone having been put on the floor – so that it can be seen from the bath.*

INT. CORRIDOR OUTSIDE CARAMEL'S FLAT. DAY

Cut back to MCWITHERS, *looking both angry and bewildered.*
MCWITHERS: (*Hoarsely*) Caramel?
  (*Pause. Then he creeps back and listens – the sound of gun-fire punctuating a Western ballad is quite distinct.*)

INT. CARAMEL'S BATHROOM. DAY

CARAMEL *dabs at his chest with an enormous sponge and stares, wide-eyed, at the television. He is engrossed in it, so that when the telephone rings, its shrillness is discordant. A slight pause, while*

317

CARAMEL *adjusts his responses – a frown of irritation, followed by a sudden smile of recollection – to suggest that he was expecting a call. He leans over the side of the bath, picks up a television controller and almost cuts out the sound, leaving a low murmer in the background. The telephone is still ringing, but he keeps his eyes on the screen as he leans over and picks up the receiver. He then has the receiver in one hand, the control in the other.*

CARAMEL: (*In a dignified voice*) Dr J. D. Caramel speaking. Thank you for phoning so promptly. About these supplies. (*There is a clicking noise.*) Hello, are you there?

SWITCHBOARD OPERATOR: (*Voice over, telephone*) Hello, Mr Caramel?

CARAMEL: (*A trifle testily*) Now I wanted to change the order, this is very urgent because I'm extremely busy, from *one* box to two boxes. One of . . . (*Another clicking sound, more telephone noises.*) Hello, hello. (*Testily beating his hand against the side of the bath, but still gazing at the television.*)

SWITCHBOARD OPERATOR: (*Voice over, telephone*) Mr Caramel? This is exchange. Mr Caramel. We have a call for you from Whitstable. Are you willing to accept the charges?

CARAMEL: (*Jerking upright*) Whitstable. No, no. (*In a panic, then gathering himself together and attempting to resume his dignified voice.*) J. Campbell speaking.

SWITCHBOARD OPERATOR: (*Voice over, telephone*) (*Puzzled*) Mr Caramel?

CARAMEL: Campbell. Campbell. This is Henry Campbell.

MRS CARAMEL: (*Voice over, telephone*) Hog, hog, hog –

CARAMEL: Caramel is not known at this number. Goodbye. (*He scrambles receiver onto telephone. He is now sitting bolt upright, gazing ahead, his mouth hanging open. The television control is still in his other hand. The room suddenly fills with:*)

MRS CARAMEL: (*Voice over, telephone, furious*) A hog, I say. Only a hog spends all his time in the bath. Only a hog steals his dead brother's papers. His own dead brother, who slaved and slaved to qualify. Only a hog lives off his widowed mother's pension, and wears his dead brother's clothes, and wears his shoes, only a hog, yes, a hog, hog, hog, would . . .

(CARAMEL *recoils and as he does so, presses the button of the controller so that the last 'hogs' are cut off by the sound of gun-fire.* CARAMEL *blinks, focuses on the screen, and gradually the smile of comfort and pleasure returns to his face. He drops the controller and settles back in his bath.*)

INT. MCWITHERS'S OFFICE. DAY

LAME *is sitting on the desk, legs crossed and slightly hunched.* CLOON *is standing sideways to the desk, with a sheet of paper in his hand.* MCWITHERS *is sitting. The office consists of the desk, telephone, and perhaps a photograph of McWithers's wife – a wedding photograph.*

LAME: How – precisely – much was it?

CLOON: Sixty pounds, eleven shillings and ninepence halfpenny.

LAME: Well, yes, (*struggling for insouciance*) that's a tidy little sum, in a sloppy sort of way. (*Laughs.*) Yes. Sixty pounds, eleven shillings and ninepence halfpenny. Most of that – (*appears confident and casual, clearly is neither*) – on medical supplies, doubtless? Bandages, syringes, forceps, this kind of thing?

CLOON: (*Impassively reading*) Two boxes of frozen eclairs, six hundred cigarettes, tipped, six hundred cigarettes, untipped, a carton of crisps, and a box of salt. Five bottles of whiskey. An electric blanket. An electric razor. A tin of olives. A box of Turkish delight. Two bars of milk chocolate and a carton of fruit gums. No, er, medical supplies here. (*Pause.*) No cash either. (*Pause.*) Ordered by telephone. (*Long pause.*) Perhaps we ought just to mention it to Sir Roy's secretary. Or I could write to Sir Roy himself enclosing the canteen bill. If I wrote a polite note, explaining that I thought he'd be interested in the bill, (*pause*) he wouldn't mind. Er, too much. Er, he might even be pleased.

MCWITHERS: No, no, no. No, man, no. He won't be pleased. (*Gazes at* CLOON, *then at* LAME.) Remember that Sir Roy's very sick. A very sick old – er – man.

CLOON: Yes.

LAME: Extremely sick.

MCWITHERS: Look, look, he doesn't start until tomorrow. Officially he doesn't. *Of course* (*stands up and slaps the table triumphantly*), look, he wants to pay for the canteen stuff out of his salary. Look, this is all right. All he's done is – (*pause, blankly, then as if inspired*) – he needs a vacation. Needs to rest up, relax, take baths and – and – and watch television. He's going to start on a big responsibility tomorrow. (*Pauses again.*) I *admire* him for relaxing. I think he's all right. It *shows* he's all right. It shows we were right to pick him. He's a solid man, an independent man. We want independent men. We need them. We don't want yes-men in Healman, do we?

(*Glares at* CLOON.)

CLOON: No.

LAME: (*With assumed brightness*) I'm with you one *thousand* per. (*He exits.*)

MCWITHERS: Sir Roy doesn't want yes-men in Healman, does he?

CLOON: No.

MCWITHERS: No. He *does not*.

(*He leaves the room. Camera settles on* CLOON's *thoughtful face.*)

CLOON: No. No, he doesn't.

INT. LAME'S SITTING-ROOM. NIGHT

A stiff, fashionable, ridiculously uncomfortable armchair in which LAME *is sitting. He is reading the* New Statesman, *but partially looking over the top.* MRS LAME *is seen only partially. She is basket-weaving.*

LAME: He starts work tomorrow.

MRS LAME: Will it be all right, do you think?

LAME: No.

MRS LAME: Never mind, my little cream pickles.

(LAME *stares at her yearningly.*)

You've something on the tip of your nose.
(LAME *touches his nose.*)

LAME: It's a pimple. (*Then, self-pityingly*) A worry pimple.
(*Yearns more insistently.*)

MRS LAME: Well, we'll listen to the Third tonight. There's always something extra special on a Tuesday.
(LAME *goes back to his* New Statesman. *Speaks wheedlingly from behind it.*)

LAME: I don't want to listen to the Third, my darling. I don't *want* to hear any music.

MRS LAME: What would you like, my little pineapple? (*Her voice is detached.*)

LAME: (*After a pause*) I want to be comforted. (*Lowers the* New Statesman *and stares at her desperately.*)

MRS LAME: The Third will comfort you. You know it will.
(*Pause.* LAME *strokes the tip of his nose.*)

INT. MCWITHERS'S BEDROOM. NIGHT

Large bed. MCWITHERS'S *face is illuminated by a pool of light from a bedside lamp. He is smoking a cigar.* MRS MCWITHERS *in the darkness, beside him, her hair in rollers. She is making low, sobbing noises.*

MCWITHERS: He'd better be there tomorrow. (*Small pause.*) I wish you'd stop that. It's what every husband wants. All men want that.
(MRS MCWITHERS *moans. Automatically and abstractedly.*)
Shut up, shut up, shut up.
(*Little pause.* MRS MCWITHERS *moans.*)
I know he'll come. He'll show up all right. He'll do his stuff.
(*Little pause.* MRS MCWITHERS *moans.*)
If you don't stop that I'll pinch you.
(*Little pause.* MRS MCWITHERS *gasps.*)
That Lame thinks he's smart, does he? I've got my eye on him. I *trust* Caramel. (*Stubs out cigar, then rolls over, towards*

the shadow of his wife, and shouts) You do want me really, don't
you? I know you do.

(*Increased sobs.*)

Answer me, you'd better answer me or I'll give you you know
what.

(*Little pause.* MRS MCWITHERS *gasps.*)

INT. CLOON'S KITCHEN. NIGHT

A kitchen stool, on which CLOON, *with his toes turned in, is sitting. The
hand passing him the coffee is all that is seen of* MRS CLOON, *but it
should be a very plump hand. While this conversation takes place, her
presence is registered by sinister kitchen noises – saucepans being
scraped, perhaps, or crust being grated – anyway, something that
contrasts grotesquely with the sound of her voice, which is sweet but also
menacing.*

MRS CLOON: All I can say, Dirk, (*scrape, scrape*) is that I do hope
you know what you're doing.

(CLOON *is fiddling with the spoon, examining it first, then rapping
it nervously against the saucer.*)

CLOON: Yes, I hope so, my dear.

MRS CLOON: Be careful with the spoondle, Dirk.

(*Scrape.*)

CLOON: Spoondle?

MRS CLOON: The spoon. It's called a spoondle. The top-let unscrews
for use as an olive skewer. (*Scrape, scrape.*) And if you're
wrong, Dirk, they won't want you any more. If you're wrong,
and McWithers finds out you've written to Sir Roy, Dirk.

CLOON: I know, my dear.

(CLOON *is fiddling about with the spoon quietly.*)

MRS CLOON: And I, for one, won't blame them. (*Scrape.*) You
know that, don't you, Dirk?

(*Particularly dreadful scrape, which causes* CLOON *to twitch
nervously.*)

CLOON: Yes, my dear.

(*He stirs coffee with spoondle.*)

THE CARAMEL CRISIS

INT. SIR ROY'S STUDY. NIGHT

A wheelchair, with SIR ROY HOLMAN *in it. Small tables around him, with lit candles on them. A table in front of him, on which is Cloon's letter. There is a stick across* SIR ROY'S *knee. He is being fed gruel by a hand holding up a spoon.* MRS PORTLY'S *hand should be covered with bracelets, rings, etc. and should jangle when she plies the spoon.*

MRS PORTLY: (*Cockney, sweet, flirtatious voice*) You could do it yourself, you know you could. It's just you and your tricks. You're as spry as a monkey in a barrel of peanuts.

SIR ROY: (*In a wheezy voice, rapping the letter on the table with the end of the stick*) I'm going to the factory tomorrow, to have a word with Cloon.

MRS PORTLY: There you are, you see. If you're nimble enough to get up to the factory, you're nimble enough to feed your own mouth.

SIR ROY: (*Makes a hideous sound that is probably a laugh*) I'll break them, break them to pieces, if they've made a mistake. (*Gruel leaks out of his mouth, dribbles down his chin, and is trapped by the spoon – with a jangle of bracelets.*)

MRS PORTLY: Oh, you. You'd break everything, if you had your way. (*Pause.*)

INT. MCWITHERS' OFFICE. DAY

MCWITHERS *is sitting at his desk with the telephone. During this conversation* LAME *is constantly touching the tip of his nose.* CLOON *is standing behind* MCWITHERS.

MCWITHERS: *All* the sheds? You've tried all the sheds?

CLOON: Yes.

MCWITHERS: And he's not in any of them?

CLOON: No.

LAME: (*Meaninglessly*) Mysterious. A man of mystery. (*He attempts his usual, nervous laugh, dabs at his nose instead.*)

MCWITHERS: But God man, it's half-past eleven. Half-past

323

eleven. (*Pauses, then, his voice brightening.*) Perhaps he's had an accident? Do you think he's had an accident?

CLOON: No.

LAME: Indestructible man of mystery. (*Laughs again, in the same ghastly way.*) Super-duper-one-hundred-per man of mystery. (*Pause.*)

MCWITHERS: Well, it's all right. I'm sure it's all right.

LAME: (*Pulling himself together*) Someone must have heard something from him this morning? Something?

CLOON: (*After a little pause, then with a suggestion of relish*) Yes. (*Little pause.*) He phoned down to the shop. (*Pause.*)

MCWITHERS: (*Carefully, but expecting the worst*) What did he want?

CLOON: He wanted another carton of potato crisps.

MCWITHERS: Potato crisps? Well. Well. Potato crisps, eh? Potato crisps, eh? (*Stops pacing and with thundering decisiveness.*) That's one thing we can stop.

(*He looks to* CLOON, *who now has a funny little smile on his face. At* LAME, *who is more hunched – one shoulder higher than the other – than before, and trying to whistle.*)

We can stop that. That's all right. We can put a stop to that sort of thing.

(*He picks up the receiver, shakes it, then shouts into it.*) Switchboard?

SWITCHBOARD OPERATOR: (*Voice over, telephone*) Yes sir.

MCWITHERS: Listen to this. It's McWithers here. Now pay attention to me.

SWITCHBOARD OPERATOR: (*Voice over, telephone*) Yes, sir.

MCWITHERS: Now don't accept any calls from the medical flat. Do you understand me? *Under no circumstances* are you to accept *any* calls from the medical flat. We're putting a stop to it.

(*Replacing receiver*) We've put a stop to that, all right.

LAME: (*Jerking upright*) *If* he put through a call this morning, *and* nobody's seen him since – *then* he's probably still here.

CLOON: (*Showing repressed excitement*) Yes.

LAME: And he won't answer the phone.

324

CLOON: (*Almost shrilly*) No.

MCWITHERS: (*Staring at* CLOON) Pull yourself together, man. Everything's all right. Everything's quite all right.

LAME: So what we can do is – go up and get him. Bring him down. Fire him. Tell everyone he was – was taken ill. Get hold of that other man, Penners, –

CLOON: Rennis.

LAME: (*Stroking his nose*) Reenis, yes, yes, get hold of him. Quickly. This we can do. Without worrying Sir Roy in any way.

MCWITHERS: That's right. That's right. Sir Roy's a very sick man. He mustn't know a thing. Mustn't bother him with this trivial business. Let's go to it.

(*He goes towards the door,* LAME *follows,* CLOON *doesn't.* MCWITHERS *calls to* CLOON)

Come on, man. Come on.

CLOON: Yes, Yes. I've just got to, er, make a little call.

INT. CARAMEL'S FLAT. DAY

CARAMEL, *humming, is in the bathroom. The bath is full and steamy, but* CARAMEL, *fully dressed, is spreading objects out on a table beside it. A thriller. A bottle of salts. A glass of whisky. Three packets of crisps. An apple. He could be shown passing from the hall into the bathroom, and out again, several times, and with the various objects in his hand. Suddenly there is a banging. He stands still, alert. During the first part of this only he is shown.* MCWITHERS *and* LAME *are only voices.*

MCWITHERS: (*Out of shot*) Caramel! (*Imperious*) Caramel!

LAME: (*Out of shot*) It's us. (*Facetiously*) Time to come out now, Caramel.

MCWITHERS: (*Out of shot*) Open up, man.

(CARAMEL *stands in the hall, the apple in his hand, looking irritated. He takes a bite of the apple and listens.*)

(*Out of shot*) Caramel.

CARAMEL: (*Frowns, scratches cheek with apple, then quietly*) Yes.

MCWITHERS: (*Out of shot*) We want to see you, Caramel.

LAME: (*Out of shot*) Caramel.

(CARAMEL *takes a bite of apple, looks wistfully towards the bathroom.*)

MCWITHERS: Are you there!

CARAMEL: Yes. Yes. What do you want?

MCWITHERS: (*Out of shot, shouting*) *Want*, man? It's nearly twelve o'clock. You were meant to be on duty at eight thirty. (*A little pause, and then in a conciliatory voice.*) Did you forget? I expect you thought you weren't on until later. We'd better hurry down there, Caramel. There's at least one case on monotonous tension waiting for you.

(*Long pause, while* CARAMEL *does nothing.*)

Caramel?

CARAMEL: Yes?

MCWITHERS: (*Out of shot*) Are you coming?

CARAMEL: I'm not very well. I'm feeling a little feeble. I've been off my food.

MCWITHERS: (*Out of shot*) What's the matter with you, man?

CARAMEL: Measles. I've got measles.

LAME: (*Out of shot*) Measles?

INT. CORRIDOR OUTSIDE CARAMEL'S FLAT. DAY

MCWITHERS *and* LAME *in low conference.*

MCWITHERS: Caramel. Caramel. We'd better take a look at you.

CARAMEL: (*Out of shot*) Why?

LAME: You may need help. There may be something we can do.

INT. CARAMEL'S FLAT. DAY

CARAMEL *is sitting on the edge of the bath. He pulls the coffee table forward.*

CARAMEL: (*Ponders a second, then*) Well, I'm short on entertainment if I'm going to be cooped up here with measles

for a long time. Could you get me some books and
magazines. I'm very fond of thrillers.

MCWITHERS: (*Out of shot, beating on door*) Open up. Open the
door, do you hear?

CARAMEL: You'd better go away, because I've got to lie down
now.

LAME: (*Out of shot*) No. You must open the door.

CARAMEL: You'll get mumps, if you come in. You don't want
mumps do you?

LAME: (*Out of shot*) I thought you said you had measles?

CARAMEL: Yes.

INT. CORRIDOR OUTSIDE CARAMEL'S FLAT. DAY

MCWITHERS *is pressed close to the door,* LAME *is standing beside
him.*

MCWITHERS: (*In pleasant, supplicating voice*) Listen, Caramel. I
appointed you. Lame and me. We liked you at once. We
chose you because you're the right man for the job. I said you
were a solid man. Do you hear that, Caramel, a solid man? I
said you were just the kind of man Sir Roy likes, Caramel. I
said you were a *stayer.*

CARAMEL: (*Out of shot*) Oh, don't worry. I'm not going.
(LAME *lets out a hysterical laugh.*)

MCWITHERS: If Sir Roy finds out, there'll be trouble. (*He taps on
door.*) Terrible trouble. He's a very sick old man. He gets
upset. (*Taps again.*) But it'll be all right. If you come down
now and look after the monotonous tension case, it'll be all
right.

CARAMEL: (*Out of shot*) Who's Sir Roy? I haven't met any Sir
Roy, have I?

LAME: (*Turning as there is the sound of a door opening at the end of
the corridor*) Here's Cloon. Where's he been, anyway?
(*He has turned right round and is staring aghast.* MCWITHERS
turns, too, and is also aghast. CLOON *is pushing* SIR ROY *in his
wheelchair.* SIR ROY *has his rug over his knees, and his stick*

across his rug. His head is hanging down. CLOON's *face is
solicitously close to his.* SIR ROY *lifts his head up, and coughs.
His face is full of senile venom.*)

SIR ROY: Get me to the door.

(MCWITHERS *and* LAME *surge around him, but he waves his
stick at them.*)

No, no. I want Cloon. Cloon to push me.

(CLOON *pushes him to the door, as* LAME *and* MCWITHERS *fall
back, behind the chair.* CLOON *stands beside the chair, close to
the door.*)

MCWITHERS: Yes, sir. Everything's fine, sir. We've sorted things
out. You're a very sick old man, sir.

(LAME's *hysterical laugh is heard.*)

No, I mean Doctor Caramel is a very sick old man. He's been
struck down by a – by a – sickness, sir, but he's a good man,
sir. Reliable. The man we want.

SIR ROY: (*Making feeble gesture with stick*) Tell him to open up,
Cloon. Tell him I want to see his face. (*Pause.*)

CLOON: (*Rapping on the door*) You'd better open the door,
Caramel. Sir Roy has come. I advise you to open the door at
once. Sir Roy intends to speak to you, and he wants to see
your face.

(*He steps aside importantly, leaving* SIR ROY *alone facing the
door.*)

CARAMEL: (*Out of shot*) What does he want to see my face for?

SIR ROY: (*Gestures with his stick, and begins to cry out hoarsely, but
his voice gathers a manic strength as he goes on, ending in
something close to a scream*) Smash it down. Smash it down,
Caramel. (*Brandishes the stick feebly.*) Smash it down. Smash
you down. Smash you down, Caramel. Smash.

(*This screamed, as with appalling strength and in a crazed
frenzy, he suddenly launches himself out of the chair, the stick
held above his head to deliver a blow at the door. He brings the
stick down at the precise second the door opens. He falls into the
hall.*)

THE CARAMEL CRISIS

INT. CARAMEL'S FLAT. DAY

MCWITHERS: Quick man, quick. You're the doctor. Look at him. Is he all right? Quick man.

(*As* CARAMEL *comes slowly forward:*)

He might have broken something.

(CARAMEL, *eating crisps, comes between* CLOON *and* LAME *and stares with curiosity at the broken figure for a time. Then:*)

CARAMEL: I expect he's broken everything. He's very old, from the look of him. He shouldn't be hurling himself about like that, at his age.

(*Noises and cries from the floor, as if in agonized reply.*)

LAME: (*Hysterical, to* CARAMEL) What can we do? Oh, God, what can we do?

CARAMEL: Oh well, I should get him to a hospital if I were you. (*Slight pause, then in a dreamy voice.*) Hospitals are very comfortable.

(*He turns away from them.*)

MCWITHERS: Yes, yes. We'll rush him to a hospital and save him. It'll be all right if we save him. He'll be grateful.

CLOON: (*Staring down, dully*) Yes. Save him.

LAME: The telephone. Phone for an ambulance.

CLOON: (*Starting into life*) Yes, the telephone.

(*Goes to pick it up, but is shouldered aside by* MCWITHERS, *who shouts:*)

MCWITHERS: I'll do it. *I'll* do it. *I'll* save him. (*Grabs the phone, glares at* CLOON, *who shrinks back.*) Hello, switchboard. Hello. Listen to this. This is me, do you understand?

SWITCHBOARD OPERATOR: (*Voice over, telephone, brightly and mechanically*) I am sorry sir. We cannot accept any calls from the medical flat at this time.

MCWITHERS: (*Kneeling*) Hello. No, no. It's all right. It's perfectly all right. This is urgent.

SWITCHBOARD: (*Voice over, telephone*) I am sorry, sir. We are cutting you off now. (*Click.*)

MCWITHERS: (*Pounding the telephone bar*) Hello. Hello. Hello. Hello.

(*Long pause.* CLOON *places his hand on* MCWITHERS' *shoulder.*)

MCWITHERS: (*Drops the telephone, turns around.*)
It's no good now. It's all right.

LAME: I'll do it from downstairs. From downstairs.

MCWITHERS: (*Stands up, then dully as if in a trance*) Yes, but it's no good, you see. It's all right. Everything is . . . (*Voice trails off.*)

CLOON: Yes.

(*During this,* CARAMEL *has disappeared. He now reappears with a small bag in his hand, and his pockets stuffed with bags of crisps. He slips past them and out of the door.*)

INT. CORRIDOR OUTSIDE FLAT. DAY

CARAMEL *goes down corridor, past the wheelchair. His dreamy voice floats back.*

CARAMEL: (*Voice over*) Ridiculous nonsense never leaving people in peace. Coming crashing up to *my* flat, shouting and dying everywhere, chatter, chatter, chatter, trouble, trouble, trouble, and trouble with *her* too, if I have to go back there, (*pause*) but anyway if I take a taxi I could get to a cinema for the first performance, and if it's a Western it'll be worth it, an old-fashioned simple Western with . . .
(*Voice fades away as he rounds a corner.*)

INT. CLOON'S KITCHEN. NIGHT

MRS CLOON *is icing a cake. She is out of shot except for her hands.*
CLOON, *on his stool, sits staring blankly down at an olive on the spike of the spoondle.*

MRS CLOON: (*Out of shot*) Yes, well Dirk, I warned you. You're finished there now, you know. McWithers and Lame will see to that. They'll force you out, now the old man's gone. *They'll* have all the power now. You know that, don't you, Dirk?

CLOON: (*Still gazing at the olive on the spoondle*) I know, my dear.

MRS CLOON: (*Out of shot*) Well, Dirk, what are you going to do?

Can you tell me that? What are you going to do? Nobody will
as much as look at you now, Dirk. What will you do?
(CLOON *plucks the olive off the top, looks down at the pointed
end of the spoondle as the scraping noise rises and rises, to an
almost unbearable pitch. For a second his face goes mad, his eyes
fix on where his wife would be, he holds the spoondle up so that it
becomes a menacing weapon, then the noise subsides, his face
returns to normal, and he pops the olive into his mouth.*)
CLOON: I don't know my dear. (*Pause.*)

INT. LAME'S SITTING-ROOM. NIGHT

LAME *sits in his ridiculous chair, a bowl of soup in a deep, black,
ridiculous bowl, a large almost flat spoon, on his lap. His knees are
pressed together.* MRS LAME *is unseen, but she makes little slurping
noises as she talks – soup-drinking noises.*

MRS LAME: (*Out of shot*) Why are you looking so sad, (*slurp*) my
little cactus? I thought it all turned out well. You're very
sad . . .

LAME: Am I?

MRS LAME: (*Out of shot, slurp*) . . . and I don't know why.

LAME: (*Staring intensely towards her*) It's been difficult. A shock.

MRS LAME: (*Out of shot*) They're doing Stravinsky, 'Rites of
Spring'. (*Slurp*) 'Rites of Spring' will relax you.

LAME: (*Almost in tears*) I don't *want* Stravinsky. I want *you*. I want
you to relax me.

MRS LAME: (*Out of shot*) The Stravinsky will do you good. He's
your favourite modern. (*Slurp. Her voice becomes coldly
affectionate*)And afterwards I'll pop your pimple. It's ready
for popping. (*Slurp.*)
(LAME *strokes his nose and stares at her.*)

INT. MCWITHERS' BEDROOM. NIGHT

MCWITHERS' *head in the pool of light from the lamp, as before. His*

331

face is mad with triumph. Beside him there is the dark bundle of MRS
MCWITHERS.

MCWITHERS: It's all right. I knew it would be. (*Chuckles*) I knew
it would be. They'll have a big burial, and then we're in. I'm
in. Oh, (*chuckles*) there'll be some changes. (*Chuckles*)
Cloon. (*Voice becomes sinister.*) Cloon. (*Little pause.*) Lie still.
Why do you always roll away from me. You've got a duty to
me. (*Little pause.*) I'll see about Cloon. I'll settle with him all
right. I'll settle with Lame too, later on. (*Chuckles.*)
(MRS MCWITHERS *has begun to whimper.*)
Shut up. I haven't done anything yet.
(*He laughs. Rolls over, props himself up on his elbow, shows a
hand, as if to grab her, but there is a click, and the lamp goes off.*
MRS MCWITHERS *whimpers. Darkness.*)

Sleeping Dog

The Sleeping Dog was first transmitted on BBC TV on 11 October 1967. The cast included:

SIR HUBERT	Marius Goring
LADY CAROLINE	Rachel Kempson
GREATORIX	Denys Graham
CLAUD	Johnny Sekka
YOUNG MAN	Nicholas Critchley
SIR GEOFFREY	Peter Graves
BARMAID	Wendy Ascott
Screenplay	Simon Gray
Producer	Graeme McDonald
Director	Warris Hussein

EXT. COLONIAL BUNGALOW IN AFRICA. NIGHT

Long shot. The bungalow is brilliantly lit, curtainless.
Sound of a woman's voice singing to a piano 'Somewhere over the Rainbow', which goes straight into group-singing of 'For He's a Jolly Good Fellow'.
Then a plump man, not properly seen for the darkness, comes out on to the porch. The music stops.

SIR HUBERT: Whitey, Whitey. Here, boy. Come on, boy. Come along.

> (*Other shapes join him.*)

VOICE ONE: (*Slightly tipsy*) What's the matter?

VOICE TWO: Whitey's gone.

SIR HUBERT: Come along, come along. Chocolates, Whitey. Whitey, chocolates.

OTHER VOICES: Whitey, chocolates, here boy, here sir.

> (*The piano starts again, woman's voice singing 'Somewhere over the Rainbow', leaving the plump man on the porch. Then he too turns, goes in.*)
> (*Mix. Exterior Bungalow. Same shot of the house, now completely silent. The plump man on the porch.*)

SIR HUBERT: Whitey, Whitey, here Whitey.

> (*There is a silence, then sudden rustlings, bird cries. Close-up of* SIR HUBERT'*s face, lips open. Then shot of the garden, which appears to be full of strange but human shapes, figures in feathers, tribal kit, but none of these seen properly. Back to* SIR HUBERT, *staring intently.*)
> (*Tentatively*) Whitey, Whitey?
> (*Silence, then rustlings, wing flappings, parrot voices.*)

PARROTS: Whi-ey. Whi-ey. He-ah, Whi-ey, hah, hah, hah.

> (SIR HUBERT *stares around, licks his lips, then bellows:*)

SIR HUBERT: Whitey.

> (*More flapping sounds from parrots, to shot of running movements in the garden.*)

PARROTS: Whi-eee hee hee.

335

(*There is a sudden silence. Long shot of the house, the figure on the porch joined by a lady in a long, white dress.*)

LADY CAROLINE: Did you hear him?

SIR HUBERT: No. No. Er, just the birds. Whitey, Whitey, sir. Come along.

(*This is met by complete silence. Then long shot to the sound of muted chucklings and flappings.*)

(*Fade.*)

EXT. COTTAGE. DAY

A large cottage in the country, set in a lawn, with a drive cutting through. It is mid-afternoon. There is a car in the drive, facing the french windows, although some way from them. LADY CAROLINE *is standing by a neat flower bed, sniffing the flowers. There is a faint hum of a bee. She bends over a flower, the humming becomes louder, she jumps back, a bee erupts, buzzes noisily past her. Shot of her in close-up, looking startled. She turns, walks across the lawn, towards the windows.*

INT. LIVING-ROOM. DAY

The living-room, with the french windows that look over the lawn and the drive. LADY CAROLINE *enters. The room is empty, except for a chair by the window. No carpets. Full of sunlight. She walks across the room to a door on the left, opens it, calls up.*

LADY CAROLINE: Hu-bert. Hu-bert.

(*She waits a second, then turns to the door on the right, opens that, as if experimentally, and for the first time. There is a small passage opposite, with a door at the end, slightly open, with a large bolt opposite it. To her right the hall.* LADY CAROLINE *looks to the right, to the left, frowns at the door, then goes back into the living-room, walks to the chair. She opens her handbag, takes out a small silver flask, raises it to her lips, takes a swallow, shakes the flask, puts it back into the handbag, takes out a bag of*

*peppermints, pops a couple into her mouth. She sighs, looks
around the room, gets up and goes towards the door, right.*)

INT. BASEMENT ROOM

*The room, windowless, is lit by a naked bulb. On one wall there is a
ring and a bolt. There are a few boxes, pieces of wood, old tins, to the
right; and to the left there is a heavy door, padded with old felt.*
SIR HUBERT *and* MR GREATORIX *are standing under the light.* SIR
HUBERT *has his hat in his hand,* MR GREATORIX *has a sheaf of
papers, which he looks at.*

GREATORIX: I must say I can't smell anything, Sir Hubert.
(SIR HUBERT *sniffs.*)
And I can tell the damp straight away, it goes straight to my
nostrils like arthritis, I think it is.

SIR HUBERT: Come sir, a definite odour. (*Sniffs again.*) It's a
dog. I know a dog when I smell one.

GREATORIX: Now you mention it, Sir Hubert, the Kerneys did
have a dog, an alsatian, yes. Perhaps they gave it the run of
the basement.
(SIR HUBERT *points to the ring and the bolt on the wall.*)

SIR HUBERT: Not much of a run, I think. Kept the poor brute
chained. (*He turns, points to the door.*) And look at that stuff
on the door, so they needn't hear it when it's barking out for
them. There's a garden, isn't there?
(*Looks at* GREATORIX.)

GREATORIX: Oh yes, Sir Hubert, a particularly lovely one, as you
commented yourself.

SIR HUBERT: (*Almost to himself*) Can't say I like that. Can't say I
like it at all.
(GREATORIX *lowers his voice confidentially.*)

GREATORIX: I quite agree, Sir Hubert. Of course, strictly
between you and me and these four walls, Mr Kerney –
(*raises and lowers the papers to his mouth, in drinking
movements*) but I think I can promise you we can get the
smell out, Sir Hubert, if –

SIR HUBERT: (*Shakes his head*) We have an obligation when we take them on. (*Little pause.*) I'd like you to pass that on to these Kerneys, when you see them. Tell them they need freedom.

(GREATORIX *ducks his head in embarrassment.*)

GREATORIX: Oh, I will, Sir Hubert, I most certainly will. Of course, Greendene has a lovely smell in the summer, lovely from the garden –

(*He is interrupted by* LADY CAROLINE *pushing the door open. She should be seen to be still sucking on a peppermint.*)

LADY CAROLINE: Oh, here you are, I must say I've been looking all over for you, upstairs and outside, shouting at the top of my voice, and Hubert, I was nearly stung by a bee.

SIR HUBERT: (*In alarm*) But you're all right, my dear? (*Goes to her.*)

LADY CAROLINE: Yes, I am, but it gave me a nasty shock, it was a very big one. (*Looks around.*) What a horrid place.

GREATORIX: Just an old storeroom we think it was, Lady Caroline.

LADY CAROLINE: Ooooh, and what an odour.

SIR HUBERT: It was a prison, my dear, where these people Kerney kept their dog.

LADY CAROLINE: Well, why don't you come upstairs and talk there, it's quite fresh upstairs.

(*She makes for the door, followed by* SIR HUBERT. GREATORIX, *following* SIR HUBERT, *makes a cynical face to himself.*)

GREATORIX: I can see that you're fond of dogs.

INT. LIVING-ROOM. DAY

LADY CAROLINE *enters, talking, followed by* SIR HUBERT *and* MR GREATORIX.

LADY CAROLINE: . . . dearest little thing, and we still don't know what happened to him. The MacPhersons have written twice to say they haven't found him. And on the last night too. Of

course, Whitey was very intelligent, poodles are, they know when there's going to be a change, don't they. Hubert?
(SIR HUBERT, *an expression of pain on his face, nods.*)

SIR HUBERT: Almost certain that a snake got him.

GREATORIX: Well, I think I can assure you there aren't any snakes in Greendene. (*Chuckles, clears his throat.*) Now my own view, for what it's worth, is that the asking price is very reasonable, very. I'm given to understand that if Mr Kerney hadn't passed so unexpectedly, with an estate to be settled in Scotland, more could have been tried for. But that's only my own personal view.

SIR HUBERT: So this Kerney is dead, is he?

GREATORIX: Yes, most tragic and unexpected, although not really surprising, as I think I hinted (*to* LADY CAROLINE) downstairs to Sir Hubert, Mr Kerney had a little problem. (*He makes drinking movement.* LADY CAROLINE *glares back at him.*)

SIR HUBERT: (*Sharply*) May I ask how you intend to convey my remarks to him, sir, if this Kerney is dead?

GREATORIX: (*After a pause of recollection*) Ah, well I – his relatives would be most interested to hear. *Mrs* Kerney is still with us.

SIR HUBERT: A lady, sir? They're scarcely remarks to be passed on to a lady.
(GREATORIX *ducks his head.*)
Now, my dear, what do you think?

LADY CAROLINE: Well, will we be able to get a gardener, we'll need one with all the grass and those beds need a lot of work to keep them nice. You know how much I love gardening, Hubert –
(*He nods*) but even so it's a big house, I couldn't look after it by myself, could I? (*To* GREATORIX) We've heard the domestic problem is terrible now. In Kjiarna we shared two marvellous boys with the MacPhersons for the garden, and of course I didn't have to lift a finger around the house, but I still had to think of everything. It's quite a responsibility, dear, that's what I'm saying, a garden this size.

SIR HUBERT: (*Going to window*) But ah, my dear, it's an English

339

garden, and much more orderly by nature. Think what that means. I can hear the difference.

LADY CAROLINE: (*To* GREATORIX) We had wild parrots in Kjiarna, we think they were parrots, Hubert never really found out, but even so, Hubert, it's a lot to bite off by myself.

GREATORIX: Well now, I agree that's a very important point, Lady Caroline, but I think I can assure you on that. The Kerneys had a gardener, and a girl up from the village for the house. I think you'll find Greendene is the sort of house that runs itself once everything's arranged.

(*While* GREATORIX *is talking,* SIR HUBERT *has been looking out of the window, smiling. Then he stops smiling, squints.*)

EXT. GARDEN. DAY

Shot of the garden, serene but slightly out of focus.

INT. LIVING-ROOM. DAY

On SIR HUBERT's *face.*

SIR HUBERT: Do you have any Kibbobolas in the neighbourhood?

(*He turns to* GREATORIX, *stares at him intensely.*)

LADY CAROLINE: (*Laughs*) In Sussex, dear?

SIR HUBERT: (*Blinks, chuckles*) Habit, you know, habit.

(*He nods, smiles at* GREATORIX. *Turns back to the window, squints at the garden, now seen in normal shot.*)

Well, dear, if you're satisfied, I'll meet these Kerney's – Mrs Kerney's price. (*Smiles at* LADY CAROLINE.) For a special occasion, after all. (*Said very tenderly*).

GREATORIX: Well, I'm very happy. I think Mrs Kerney will be very happy indeed that it's passing into such – and if we're all agreed I can promise to expedite the matter very quickly indeed. As far as I'm concerned you can virtually call it your own as soon as the papers are signed. (*Stops, smiles.*) A special occasion, did you say, Sir Hubert?

SIR HUBERT: (*After a pause*) A wedding present. (*Smiles at* LADY CAROLINE.)

GREATORIX: Well, I'm sure your bride will be very happy here. (*He turns, bows to* LADY CAROLINE.)

LADY CAROLINE: Thank you very much, although really of course it's an anniversary. (*With a laugh.*)

GREATORIX: (*Laughing*) Ah! I thought so. Of course, of course.

SIR HUBERT: Our first anniversary.

LADY CAROLINE: They said in Kjiarna that he was so busy sentencing Kibbobola he hardly had time to notice English ladies, did you Hubert? (*Giggling.*)

SIR HUBERT: (*Very gravely*) I noticed *you*, my dear.
(*A long pause while he gives her a long, possessive smile. She giggles, takes a peppermint out of her bag, pops it into her mouth.*)

LADY CAROLINE: It took you five years to say so, though.

GREATORIX: (*Coughing*) I expect you've noticed some changes, since coming back. (*Shakes his head sadly.*)
(SIR HUBERT *turns back to look in the garden.*)

SIR HUBERT: None at all.

LADY CAROLINE: Oh, but Hubert, think of the clothes. In my day we wouldn't have been allowed on the beaches in those, some of them.

SIR HUBERT: Fashion, my dear. Fashion passes. But I look into this garden and I see the grass of the country, as it always was. The trees are English, as we remember them. And those are English birds, I know their sounds. If you had brought me (*Turns to* GREATORIX) a Sussex hedge-robin during a Kjiarna thunder, I would have known it for a hedge-robin, and would have attributed it to Sussex, sir, I think.

GREATORIX: Greendene's particularly fortunate in its birds, Mrs Kerney –

SIR HUBERT: (*Lifting a finger*) But bring to Sussex the son of the first Kibbobola I had dealings with, show me this young Kibbola in his suit and let me listen to his parrotings, and I

341

could tell you something about change, sir. (*Little pause.*) And his father from the bjunga would back me up. If you could understand him. (*Little pause.*) I have the father's voice inside me, just as I have the chirping of the hedge-robin inside me. I would recognize the father's son, suit or no suit, Oxford accent or no Oxford accent. Do you follow me, sir? I know a Kibbobola when I see one, sir, And he knows me, I think. (GREATORIX *nods, very solemnly.* SIR HUBERT *looks out of the window again.*)

EXT. GARDEN. DAY

It shifts out of focus, there is an indistinct dark figure in a far corner of the lawn.
Close-up of SIR HUBERT'*s face, staring, lips open.*

INT. COTTAGE. DAY

GREATORIX: (*Voice breaking in*) . . . can assure you you won't have that sort of problem around here, Sir Hubert.
(*His voice fades,* SIR HUBERT *blinks.*)

EXT. GARDEN

Shot of garden, indistinct black figure becomes more prominent, waving feathers, etc., then disappears.

INT. COTTAGE. DAY

LADY CAROLINE: (*Out of shot*) . . . miss them, whatever he says. I never heard them myself, just vaguely, but he's got such sharp ears, he says it comes from listening to so many Kibbobola lies. (*Giggles.*)

GREATORIX: Well, there's a famous old owl in the woods behind
    Picker's Dip.

SIR HUBERT: No. (*Shakes his head, turns into the room.*) I know an
    owl when I see one, sir.

INT. BAR IN A SOUTH KENSINGTON HOTEL

*Bar is of the kind that specializes in colonial retireds and well-off old
people: seedy but comfortable, although the bar itself demonstrates a
ghastly attempt to capture the modish. It is off a main hall that leads to
the stairs that go up to the first-floor rooms: the doorway is very large,
so that a section of the stairs and the hallway is visible. There is a bead
curtain, sometimes lifted back, sometimes hanging, instead of a door.
The bar itself consists of a counter, with a passage, and behind that
shelves on which the bottles are placed, and of course a large mirror. In
front of the bar are several high stools, and then a number of chairs
and tables scattered about. The effect is at once cramped and garish
(by the bar) and cavernous (the room as a whole) – brightly lit by the
bar, gloomy in the rest of the room.*

Open with a shot of SIR HUBERT *and* LADY CAROLINE *at the
entrance, talking, with the bar behind them and* CLAUD, *the barman,
indistinctly leaning on the counter, over a pad. There are one or two
people scattered about in the bar.*

SIR HUBERT: Now don't you worry your pretty little head about
    a thing, dear, I won't take any nonsense from Greatorix. I'll
    see to it myself. (*Takes out his watch, looks at it.*) But I'll have
    to hurry along, if I'm to catch Geoffrey at the Colonial
    Office. What will *you* do, my dear?

    (LADY CAROLINE *glances into the bar, and away.*)

LADY CAROLINE: Oh, I'll go upstairs and lie down, I've got my
    headache on again.

SIR HUBERT: You give yourself a rest then. I'll see you later.

LADY CAROLINE: Yes dear. Give my love to Geoffrey and tell him
    to come and see us as soon as he can.

    (*She turns and goes up the stairs, out of camera shot.*
    SIR HUBERT *smiles after her, wiggles his fingers in a sort of*

salute, turns. As he does so the bar and CLAUD *come into sharp focus.* CLAUD'*s face given in a sudden close-up. Then a close-up of* SIR HUBERT, *staring as if in shock. He blinks, turns away, looks back again.* CLAUD *is still watching, smiling. Then transfer to a shot of* SIR HUBERT *from* CLAUD'*s point of view, peering into the room. This shot should be both comic and sinister. Then* SIR HUBERT *disappears from sight.* CLAUD *makes an expression of wonder, looks down at the pad. He is doing a savage caricature of two old men at one of the bar's tables. Looks up again as* LADY CAROLINE, *peering down the hall, comes into view, she stands at the entrance for a second, then turns, comes in, walking very quickly.*)

CLAUD: Good evening, madame, and how are you this evening? (*Slipping the pad away.*)

LADY CAROLINE: Good evening, Claud, very well thank you, well, I'm not really, I've got a terrible headache, so I thought I'd better get myself something for it. (*Opens her handbag.*)

CLAUD: I'm very sorry to hear that, it's the heat, I expect. Aspirins? (*Slightly sardonically.*)

LADY CAROLINE: I don't know what it is, but I feel exhausted. No, not aspirins, thank you, (*takes the flask out of her bag, keeps her eyes off* CLAUD, *as if in embarrassment*) but perhaps you'd be kind enough to fill this up, it takes exactly a quarter of a bottle to the rim.

CLAUD: Certainly, madame. (*Little pause.*) With what? (*As* CLAUD *takes the flask.*)

LADY CAROLINE: Yes, gin, please. I think that would be best, it always seems to settle my head.
(*Watches* CLAUD *filling the flask, talks more confidently.*)
Yes. I'm sure you're right, it's the heat.
(*Pops a peppermint into her mouth, then as* CLAUD *comes back to the counter with the flask, holds the bag out.*)
Peppermint?

CLAUD: No, thank you. No. That'll be – um – twenty-five shillings, please.
(LADY CAROLINE *takes the flask. As she does so the shot changes,* CLAUD *and* LADY CAROLINE *are seen from the*

entrance, then a close-up of SIR HUBERT, *his face grim, standing by the curtains.* LADY CAROLINE'S *voice and* CLAUD'S *cannot quite be heard, but there is the sound of* CLAUD'S *laughter.* LADY CAROLINE *turns away from the bar.* SIR HUBERT *dodges away, out of sight. Shot of* LADY CAROLINE *coming across the bar, to the entrance, stuffing the flask out of sight. She turns up the stairs.* CLAUD *watches her go, drops some money into a box, smiles, then takes the pad out, and begins to draw.* SIR HUBERT *reappears at the entrance, stares at* CLAUD, *turns away a second before* CLAUD, *frowning, looks up towards him.*)

INT. LADY CAROLINE'S BEDROOM

It is small, with a single bed, a large wardrobe with a mirror inset in its door; a dresser covered with boxes of make-up, lipstick, etc., in disorder. There are sea-trunks at one end of the room, with the labels still on them, and hat-boxes. The wardrobe juts out from the wall and adds a few feet to the passage from the bedroom proper. There is a sink on the other side of the room.

LADY CAROLINE *is sitting at the dresser, putting on make-up. She has the flask, opened, to hand. A drawer in the dresser, at knee-level, is open and full of underclothes. She stops powdering her cheeks to take a sip from the flask.*

There is a knock on the door. LADY CAROLINE *putting the top on the flask and putting the flask under the underclothes, popping peppermints into her mouth, shutting the drawer with her knee – this done to give an impression of practised speed.*

LADY CAROLINE: Come in. Oh, hello dear.

> (*As* SIR HUBERT *comes into view, with only his middle part visible in the mirror.*)

> Didn't you go to see Geoffrey, then?

SIR HUBERT: No, I – no, I thought I'd leave it until tomorrow, probably too late, I expect I –

> (*Voice falters, puts his hand to his forehead.*)

LADY CAROLINE: (*Swinging around*) Hubert? Are you all right, my dear?

(SIR HUBERT *shaking his head as if to clear it, then smiling.*)

SIR HUBERT: Yes, yes, thank you, Petal, quite all right. I just remembered – Colonial Office bound to be closed. (*Shakes his head again.*) London is very tiring, one feels so dirty. (*Gets up, goes across to the sink, washes his hands. As he does so* LADY CAROLINE *breathes on the back of her hand, sniffs, then pops several peppermints into her mouth.*)
By the way, saw a chap downstairs, bore a striking resemblance to – ah –
(*Washes his hands a little more.*)
Kibbobola, to one of the Kibbobola.

LADY CAROLINE: Oh? Do you mean Colonel Whimpers, it's funny you should say that, *I* thought he had a touch of the tar –

SIR HUBERT: No, no, my dear, not Whimpers, certainly not. This was a – quite different, black (*turns off the tap*) downstairs.
(*There should be a shot of him staring in the mirror above the sink, watching* LADY CAROLINE.)
In the bar, I think.

LADY CAROLINE: Oh! Claud, you mean.
(SIR HUBERT *meets his own eyes in the mirror, then straightens, dries them on a towel, turns nonchalantly.*)

SIR HUBERT: Claud, my dear?

LADY CAROLINE: Well, isn't that his name, the one who works in the bar. I'm sure it is, and now you mention it I was downstairs getting some aspirins earlier and he does have a Kibbobola look about him. I mean so very black, but he comes from the West Indies I expect, or somewhere like that. They mostly do around here.

SIR HUBERT: (*Coming back*) And is he a pleasant fellow, do you think?

LADY CAROLINE: Well, really dear, I've hardly noticed, I mean as far as I know he is, why?

SIR HUBERT: Oh. (*Laughs.*) Just wondering, on account of his astonishing similarity to . . .
(*Comes over, stands behind her, puts his hands on her shoulders.*

346

A close-up of his face, a look of great pain on it. Then a shot of LADY CAROLINE, *from his position.*)
My dear, you're looking particularly lovely tonight. May I see you in your dress, my dear? You know how much I admire you in it.

LADY CAROLINE: (*Stands up*) Thank you, kind sir. (*Does a little curtsy.*)

SIR HUBERT: Has anyone else noticed it, Petal, so gay and (*looks at her in her dress*) so short and flirtatious, my dear.

LADY CAROLINE: As long as you notice it, that's all that matters to me. (*Gives him a smile.*)

SIR HUBERT: Oh come, my dear, how could anyone *not* have said something. Someone's been admiring you, the blushes are still on your cheeks. (*With a chuckle.*) Surely this – even this Kibbobola West Indian Claud barman fellow had a word to say? Your eyes are bright with compliments, Petal. They are, I think. I think they are.

LADY CAROLINE: (*Sucking on the peppermint*) They're bright with *your* compliments, you silly old judge. (*Touches him on the cheek.*)

SIR HUBERT: (*After a pause*) I love you very much, Petal, I love you with all my love.

LADY CAROLINE: And I love you back, Hubert, I do, I do.

SIR HUBERT: (*After a long pause*) And would you prove it to me, my dear?

LADY CAROLINE: (*Giggles*) Of course I would.
(SIR HUBERT *goes to the cupboard, takes out a long white evening dress.*)

SIR HUBERT: Would you wear this for me tonight. It served once, for a very important moment in my life, if I'm not mistaken.

LADY CAROLINE: Well, not quite dear, but one very like it, the only thing is, isn't it a little long, I mean I'll wear it if you really want me to –

SIR HUBERT: I do, Petal, I do. (*Close-up of his face.*) Please. (*Turns to the window, stares out.*)
(*Shot of* LADY CAROLINE *looking at him, then she begins to*

unfasten her dress. Cut back to SIR HUBERT, *concentrate on his face, licking his lips nervously, once or twice touching his forehead, then takes out his key-ring, in which are a few small keys, and jangles it. There should be the sounds too, of a dress being taken off, rustles, etc.*)

LADY CAROLINE: It means I've got to change my slip and everything, you wicked thing.

SIR HUBERT: (*Strained smile*) I'm sorry, my dear.
(*More rustling sounds.* SIR HUBERT *jangling the keys noisily, begins to hum, suddenly turns around, as if unable to help himself. Shot of his face, then cut to* LADY CAROLINE, *who is standing in the dress, touching at her hair.*)

LADY CAROLINE: Well, where are you going to take me?

SIR HUBERT: Well (*blinking, then*) beautiful, my Petal, how beautiful you look. (*Shakes his head.*) I thought we'd – er, we'd celebrate with a little dinner, a private dinner, of our own, celebrate the purchase of a home, my dear, just the two of us, have it brought up (*hesitates*) here.

LADY CAROLINE: Here? (*Looks around her room.*)

SIR HUBERT: Yes, my dear (*calmly*), so I can keep you to myself, you see. Now I'll just pop next door and change for you.
(*Cut to* LADY CAROLINE, *looking disappointed, watching him as he leaves the room, keys jangling.*)

INT. STAIRS. NEXT MORNING

Stairs that pass the bar.

SIR HUBERT *comes down, walking jauntily. Stops, stares. Cut to the bar entrance.* CLAUD *is coming out in street clothes, whistling, pad under his arm. Goes down the hall.* SIR HUBERT *takes a few more steps, stops again. Cut to* CLAUD *coming back, shaking his head to himself, goes into the bar.* SIR HUBERT *passes the bar, turns his head. Cut to* CLAUD, *who is standing with his hands on his hips, staring about him.* SIR HUBERT *watches him, then passes by.*

SLEEPING DOG

EXT. STREET

SIR HUBERT *walking along, people passing him, among them some Africans, he stares after them, stops once or twice when he sees Nigerians in full kit, etc., occasional shots of his face, his eyes darting about.*
He hails a taxi, gets in, shot from inside the taxi at various points. SIR HUBERT *staring out, catching black faces, his expression intent. Then settling back with a sigh. Taxi draws up outside the Colonial Office. Shot of* SIR HUBERT *getting out, paying the taxi driver, pausing to stare after an African, perhaps several together passing him. Then shot of him going up the stairs.*

INT. THE COLONIAL OFFICE

SIR HUBERT *walking along the corridors, being passed by and passing comfortable English figures in dark suits, and comfortable middle-aged women secretaries, etc.*
The walls should be white, there should be a sheen of whiteness about the faces, the walls.
SIR HUBERT'S *face becomes calm. He goes into a door, comes out again almost immediately accompanied by a* YOUNG MAN *in glasses, who conducts him into a room opposite.*

INT. WAITING-ROOM

Comfortable armchairs spread about, a sofa, a table with magazines, books, etc., on it.
The YOUNG MAN *holds the door open, and* SIR HUBERT *enters. There is another door opposite.*

SIR HUBERT: . . . unexpectedly, but I think Sir Geoffrey will know me, I think he will. After all, he has for forty years. (*He chuckles.*)

YOUNG MAN: I'll just go and hunt him up then, sir, if you don't mind a short wait.

(SIR HUBERT *goes and sits down, the* YOUNG MAN *closes the*

349

door. SIR HUBERT *picks up magazines, looks at the first one, which is* Drum *and stares at the cover, of three Africans shaking hands or something, puts it down quickly, picks up a newspaper, begins to glance through it, then straightens, reads very intensely. Shot of his face, shaking his head. Puts the newspaper down, stares straight ahead of him. Then the other door opens.* SIR HUBERT *stares at it, gets to his feet. Cut to a vague figure in feathers, a long gown, this very quick and confusing, then to a black smiling face. Cut to* SIR HUBERT, *his eyes wide, a clicking noise. He blinks, looks at the door. It is closed. The door behind him opens. Two Africans come in.* SIR HUBERT *stares at them, transfixed. They are smiling, coming forward with outstretched hands, a voice behind them:)*

SIR GEOFFREY GRAY: No introductions necessary. Hubert, you remember Mr Kwane and Mr Tjomuba, Sir Hubert's just left Kjiarna for ever, a sad day for everyone there, particularly the Kibobbola.

(*This as* SIR HUBERT'*s hand is being shaken by the Africans, then* SIR GEOFFREY *takes* SIR HUBERT'*s hand, shakes it warmly, looks into* SIR HUBERT'*s face.*)

Hubert, how are you? Very well, I'm sure. (*To the Africans*) Brought back a new bride, you know. It's wonderful to see you.

SIR HUBERT: It's – I –

(*He looks at the two Africans, then concentrates his gaze on* SIR GEOFFREY. *Seems to be pulling himself together.*)

Very well, thank you. Very well indeed, Geoffrey. I've just come to ask you around for a drink. Thought I'd drop in while I was passing (*chuckles*) the old place. Tomorrow evening, if you can.

(*He shifts his glance to the two Africans, then quickly away.*)

SIR GEOFFREY: I'd love to. I think we can negotiate a truce in our negotiations (*smiles at the two Africans*) for an evening, gentlemen? *Will* you give me leave?

FIRST AFRICAN: (*Smiles*) Of course.

SECOND AFRICAN: And we will consult our expert, while you consult Sir Hubert. (*He bows.*)

(SIR HUBERT *licks his lips, produces a strained smile*.)

SIR HUBERT: Talking of Kibbobola, Geoffrey, one of them just
put his, er, head through the door (*gestures to door*), gave me
quite a surprise, fine looking – didn't recognize him, though.

SIR GEOFFREY: A Kibbobola. Here?

SIR HUBERT: (*Smiles*) He looked a little lost, poor fellow.

SIR GEOFFREY: So he should. To my knowledge, the nearest
Kibbobola is ten thousand miles away, in Kjiarna.

SIR HUBERT: (*Drawing himself up*) I think I may say I know a
Kibbobola when I see one.

(*Shot of* SIR GEOFFREY *staring at him; then of the two Africans,
then a shot of* SIR HUBERT, *staring back at them*.)

I think I may say that.

EXT. COLONIAL OFFICE

SIR HUBERT *coming down the stairs of the Colonial Office, sees a
taxi, hails it. It stops. An African, accompanied by a middle-aged
white woman gets in.* SIR HUBERT *stops, stares after it, hails another
taxi, gets in.*

INT. BAR ENTRANCE. LUNCH-TIME

Shot from within to the entrance.

SIR HUBERT *passing, mopping his brow, stops, stares in. Puts his
handkerchief away, seems to be bracing himself. Cut to his position,
shot of bar interior, then of* CLAUD, *bending over the sink beneath the
shelves, washing glasses, looking up suddenly and seeing* SIR HUBERT
in the mirror standing silently, watching him. Turns.

CLAUD: (*Smiling*) Sir?

(SIR HUBERT *stares at* CLAUD.)

(*Wiping his hands on towel.*) Sir? What can I get you, sir?

SIR HUBERT: (*Smiling suddenly*) Good afternoon, Claud.

CLAUD: Good afternoon, sir. (*Slightly puzzled.*) What's your
pleasure, sir?

SIR HUBERT: My pleasure, Claud? (*Laughs.*) What would you
advise as my pleasure, Claud?

CLAUD: (*Embarrassed, laughs*) Well, sir, that depends on whether
you want a long cool one or a short strong one.

SIR HUBERT: Tell me, Claud (*Leans forward, smiling*), what's
your favourite pleasure?

CLAUD: (*Thinks, shrugs*) Rum and coke, with a slice of lemon.

SIR HUBERT: Then it's mine, Claud. Yes, with the lemon cut
from the underneath, Claud, with a touch of the flesh still
attached, if you please, Claud.

CLAUD: Yes, sir. Right away, sir.

(*He turns to the bottles. As he makes the drink, SIR HUBERT
watches him intently. When he cuts the lemon he looks in the
mirror, and sees SIR HUBERT's eyes fixed on him. He should
become noticeably self-conscious.*)

There we are, sir.

(SIR HUBERT *continues to stare at* CLAUD.)

Would you prefer it at a table, perhaps?

SIR HUBERT: No. I'd prefer it here (*places a hand on counter*)
please, Claud. Thank you.

CLAUD: You're welcome, sir.

(*He turns back to the glasses, continues to wash them, glancing
up occasionally in the mirror to see* SIR HUBERT *watching him.*)

SIR HUBERT: Claud.

CLAUD: Yes sir?

SIR HUBERT: Claud, how much is this rum and cocoa business,
Claud?

CLAUD: Four shillings, sir.

(SIR HUBERT *reaches into his wallet, takes out a pound note,
puts it on the counter.* CLAUD *picks it up, puts the change on a
saucer, puts it back on the counter.* SIR HUBERT *takes out all the
change – this registered by* CLAUD *– then as* CLAUD *goes back to
his glasses (with a slightly sardonic smile) puts some coins, one at
a time, back into the saucer.* CLAUD *watches this in the mirror.*)

SIR HUBERT: Claud, these are for you.

CLAUD: (*Turning*) Thank you, sir. Thank you very much.

(SIR HUBERT *pushes the saucer across the counter, nods at*

CLAUD *to take the money.* CLAUD *does, puts it in a box under the counter, but is evidently embarrassed.* SIR HUBERT *watches him.*)

SIR HUBERT: Tell me, Claud, where do you come from?

CLAUD: (*Tensing slightly*) Stepney Green, sir.

SIR HUBERT: Really, Claud? Didn't you come from somewhere before you came from Stepney Green. I think you did. I think so.

CLAUD: (*Coolly*): My family comes from Trinidad, but most of them live in Stepney Green.

SIR HUBERT: I see. From Trinidad to Stepney Green. And tell me, Claud, have you been anywhere else?

CLAUD: I was in New York for five years.

SIR HUBERT: Indeed, Trinidad. Stepney Green. New York. Quite the rover, I think, Claud. Quite the rover.

CLAUD: (*Dryly*) Yes, sir. Here today and gone tomorrow.

SIR HUBERT: Here today and gone tomorrow. And gone tomorrow.

(SIR HUBERT *nods, stares at* CLAUD, *chuckles.*)

Tell me, Claud, have you served any (*little pause*) beautiful ladies recently?

(*He smiles at* CLAUD *intensely. After a pause,* CLAUD *laughs in embarrassment.*)

CLAUD: No, sir. Not a one, sir.

(*After a long pause, during which he smiles at* CLAUD, SIR HUBERT *says:*)

SIR HUBERT: Not a one, Claud? Not a single solitary one, Claud?

(CLAUD *shakes his head, laughs.* SIR HUBERT *stares at him.* CLAUD *stops laughing.*)

Ah come, Claud, a rover like you, sir, with a roving eye, I think? Must have spotted *one* beautiful lady?

CLAUD: No, sir.

(*Sharply. They exchange stares,* CLAUD *looks uncomfortable, turns, goes down the bar, fiddles with some glasses.*)

SIR HUBERT: Claud.

CLAUD: (*Stiffening*) Sir?

SIR HUBERT: (*Patting the counter*) Claud.

CLAUD: (*Coming back*) Sir?

SIR HUBERT: (*Lowering his voice*) Tell me something, Claud, in the strictest confidence.

(CLAUD *nods suspiciously*.)

Do you like beautiful ladies, Claud? Ummm?

(*He raises a finger jovially*.)

CLAUD: (*after a pause, shrugs*) Of course, sir.

SIR HUBERT: I was sure you did, Claud, I was sure you did. I could tell at once. (*Wags his head reprovingly, then chuckles*.)

(CLAUD *stares at him, then begins to laugh, half in embarrassment*.)

And yet you say, I think you do, Claud, that you haven't seen one beautiful lady recently? (*Shakes his head*.) If you did, you'd know what to do, I think? (*Winks*.) You would, wouldn't you now?

CLAUD: Well, I hope so (*after a little pause*), sir.

(SIR HUBERT *leans over the bar, his face suddenly serious*.)

SIR HUBERT: Do you know me, Claud? Do you know me, sir?

(CLAUD *shakes his head, stares at him*.)

Come sir. (*Sharply*.) You know me. I . . .

(*He stops, as he sees in the mirror an elderly gentleman standing beside him, converts his voice into a chuckling one*.)

. . . I'm the man for a rum and cocoa thing, and I'll have another, Claud, if you please.

(*He swallows the drink in front of him down*.)

CLAUD *does him another one as* SIR HUBERT *turns, nods to the man beside him, who looks at him blankly, nods back. Then when* CLAUD *brings him his new drink stands uncertainly, then goes across the bar to a far table. Sits down. Watches as* CLAUD *serves the other man, then as* CLAUD *goes to the far end of the bar.* CLAUD *looks towards him. Shot of* SIR HUBERT *in the distance, staring at him. Shot of* CLAUD, *making a face to himself. Then smiling. Picks up the pad, props his chin in his hand, begins to draw, as if casually. Looks up once towards* SIR HUBERT, *who is still staring at him. Then down at the pad. He has begun a savage caricature of* SIR HUBERT. *Shot of the page, then of* CLAUD *looking towards* SIR HUBERT, *as if casually.* SIR

HUBERT *smiles at him, raises his glass in a sort of salute.* CLAUD *smiles back, bends over his pad, then as he hears footsteps clicking across the room, shuts the pad quickly.*)
(LADY CAROLINE *is approaching the counter.*)

CLAUD: Good evening, madame. Headache all cleared?
(LADY CAROLINE *glances quickly towards the entrance, stands so that she has her back to* SIR HUBERT.)

LADY CAROLINE: Yes, Claud, but something much worse has happened. I'm afraid, something really tragic. (*She takes flask out of handbag.*) I spilt it all over a new dress, every last drop of it.
(*As* CLAUD *takes the flask.*)
And it was completely ruined, it's so dreadful I don't know what I'll do, I can't go around smelling of gin, can I?
(*Sucks on a peppermint as* CLAUD *with a cynical smile fills the flask, then glances again towards the entrance, then back to* CLAUD. *There is a sudden shot of them from* SIR HUBERT'*s position,* LADY CAROLINE *leaning over the bar,* CLAUD *leaning towards her, as if they were holding hands. Then cut back to* CLAUD *handing over the flask.*)

CLAUD: There we are, madame. Be careful with this one, now.
(LADY CAROLINE *puts the flask in her bag, puts the money across the counter: cut back to* SIR HUBERT, *seeing* CLAUD *leaning towards* LADY CAROLINE *again. He rises from his chair, eyes fixed, mouth open, as* LADY CAROLINE *turns. Close up of* LADY CAROLINE'*s face as she sees* SIR HUBERT, *momentarily shocked, then she smiles, waves, comes towards him. Back to* SIR HUBERT, *watching* LADY CAROLINE *advance, with* CLAUD *watching behind.* LADY CAROLINE *is closing her bag as she comes.* SIR HUBERT *forces a smile on to his face, holds out a chair for* LADY CAROLINE.)

LADY CAROLINE: (*Sitting down laughing nervously*) I wondered where you'd got to, I didn't expect to find you in here. (*Touches her forehead.*) Oh, this head of mine, I've just been getting some more of Claud's aspirins.

SIR HUBERT: Have you, my dear? (*Smiles at her.*) And he satisfied you, I hope.

LADY CAROLINE: Yes, yes, I feel a little better already, although not much.

SIR HUBERT: (*After a pause*) He's as bright as a new penny, don't you think? Most unusual fellow. I've been having a chat with him.

LADY CAROLINE: With Claud? (*Pretending carelessness.*) Oh? What about?

SIR HUBERT: This and that. (*Little pause.*) I find him rather charming.

(*Looks towards* CLAUD, *who is staring towards them from over his pad.*)

I admit. Don't you?

LADY CAROLINE: Well, Hubert, I suppose so, he seems very nice, yes, for a – although he gets things muddled up, makes mistakes, not that it matters, of course, they're all like that.

SIR HUBERT: (*Stares at her intensely*) So you *do* remember him, this Claud of mine?

LADY CAROLINE: (*Laughs*) Of course I do, dear. It's you who didn't know who he was.

SIR HUBERT: (*Leaning across the table*) And do you think he remembers you, my dear?

(LADY CAROLINE *looks at him, nervously: opens her bag, takes out two peppermints and pops them into her mouth.*)

LADY CAROLINE: Well, that's a strange question, Hubert, he may get me confused with other people, or whatever he's been saying, I don't know what nonsense he's been – but I hope I'm not so dull – after all, it's not as if the hotel was crowded with, well, gay young things, is it? (*She touches her head and blinks.*) Oh.

SIR HUBERT: (*Studies her*) You need a drink, I think, my dear? (*Looks towards the counter.*)

(*Cut to* CLAUD, *who is bent over the sketch-book. He looks up,* SIR HUBERT *is signalling him, he goes around the counter, towards the table.* LADY CAROLINE *and* SIR HUBERT *watch him come,* LADY CAROLINE *apprehensively,* SIR HUBERT *with a fixed smile.*)

356

LADY CAROLINE: So you don't know me, Claud? (*Giggles apprehensively*.)

CLAUD: I beg your pardon, madame?

LADY CAROLINE: I should think you do know me, Claud. (*Licks her lips*.) After all those aspirins I've bought from you.

(CLAUD'*s eyes meet hers, they look at each other. Cut to* SIR HUBERT *watching them closely*.)

CLAUD: Oh yes, madame, for your headache. And how is it now?

LADY CAROLINE: (*In relieved excitement*) Oh ever so much better, thank you, Claud, although it never quite goes, it's always just there.

(*Little pause.* CLAUD *stands waiting.* SIR HUBERT *continues to watch them.* LADY CAROLINE *turns to* SIR HUBERT *and smiles*.)

I'd like a – what shall I have?

SIR HUBERT: Orange squash, my dear? You were always very fond of that in Kjiarna?

LADY CAROLINE: No, no, I don't think – no, something different.

SIR HUBERT: Why don't you ask Claud for a suggestion, my dear. He's full of helpful suggestions, aren't you Claud?

(*He stares up at* CLAUD.)

CLAUD: (*With slight irony*) Well, perhaps madame would like to try a gin?

LADY CAROLINE: Yes. That sounds *very* nice.

SIR HUBERT: There you are. You know all our pleasures, Claud, I think. I think you do. (*Chuckles*.) Eh, my dear?

(*As* CLAUD *goes off, stares at her, a little pause*.)

My dear (*puts his hand on hers*), have I said how, how very lovely you're looking this afternoon.

(*He stares into her face, close-up of* LADY CAROLINE'*s face, smiling at him*.)

(*Cut to Claud's sketch-pad. His pencil is just putting the finishing touches to a caricature of a spindly, naked* LADY CAROLINE, *sitting on a chair, with an arch smile on her face and a bottle of gin raised to her lips.* CLAUD *suddenly looks up.* SIR HUBERT *is standing opposite him;* LADY CAROLINE *beside him*.)

He shuts the book, gives a desperate smile.)

CLAUD: Sir?

(SIR HUBERT *takes out his wallet, extracts a pound note.*)

SIR HUBERT: There we are, Claud. And the change is for you.

CLAUD: Thank you, sir. Thank you very much. (*Awkwardly.*) If it's not too much, sir.

SIR HUBERT: Nonsense, Claud, nonsense. Tell me, though, what do you do exactly in that book of yours?

CLAUD: Book, sir?

SIR HUBERT: (*Dropping his hand on it*) Yes, Claud, this book (*wags his head, smiling*), I've been keeping my eye on you, you see.

CLAUD: (*Licks his lips, smiles*) Well, it's just a pad, sir, for writing notes in, doodling, while I'm waiting between orders.

(SIR HUBERT *fondles the book, as if tempted to open it.*)

SIR HUBERT: Is it, indeed? Is it? Notes and doodlings, eh? What sort of doodling? Faces, figures, telephone numbers of your conquests. Claud? Hah (*laughs, shakes his head*), appointments with your – dentist, Claud, although I can see *you* don't need a dentist (CLAUD *should be smiling fearfully, teeth on display*), and I expect you keep your important appointments in a more private place, don't you, Claud? (CLAUD *looks at* SIR HUBERT'*s hand, toying with the cover of the pad.*)

CLAUD: Well, sir, it's not – I don't have that many appointments, sir, no sir. (*Shakes his head.*) I wish I did.

LADY CAROLINE: Claud's far too clever to be caught like that, not like you dear, aren't you, Claud?

SIR HUBERT: Ah (*in a serious tone, staring at her, his hand still on the book*) but he wishes he did, my dear. He wishes he did. But, Claud, if wishes were horses, beggars would ride. You'll have to pass some of those notes around –

(*He picks up the book, as if unable to resist any longer.* CLAUD *starts forward.*)

Let's see what we can find.

LADY CAROLINE: Oh, you're embarrassing the poor boy, dear. (*She tries to take the book from him, with* CLAUD *grinning*

helplessly. SIR HUBERT *resists for a second.*)
It's not fair to pry into his personal life; I'm sure we've all got our little secrets.
(*She gets the book away from* SIR HUBERT.)
Haven't we, Claud?
(*She gives him a significant look.* SIR HUBERT *sees it.*)

CLAUD: (*Taking the book gratefully. To* SIR HUBERT, *who has been staring at him in loathing and fear, but who changes this to a smile*) Oh there's nothing there but bad drawings, that's my secret, that I'm a bad drawer, sir.

SIR HUBERT: (*After a pause, chuckles*) But if I know you, sir, and I think I do, you're capable of more badness than that. I think you are, Claud.
(*He moves away from the bar, with* LADY CAROLINE *beside him, chuckles.*)
I think you are.

CLAUD: (*Laughs*) Good afternoon, sir.
(*He takes up the pad, makes an expression of relief to himself.*)

EXT. GREENDENE. THE GARDEN

The black Rover parked in the drive. SIR HUBERT *and* LADY CAROLINE *are walking across the lawn to the french windows, which are open.*

INT. LIVING-ROOM

There are ladders around the wall, rolls of wallpaper, buckets, etc.; LADY CAROLINE *and* SIR HUBERT *enter,* SIR HUBERT *is smiling, jingling his key-ring, looks peaceful;* LADY CAROLINE *is sucking a peppermint.*

LADY CAROLINE: . . . see why, I mean if the men are taking the afternoon off, which is very nice for *them*, I must say, it's just depressing to see it all in this state, Hubert, it makes me despair, with so much on my plate as it is.

SIR HUBERT: But it is so peaceful, Petal, after the rush of London. There is always something to disturb – every time one goes out of the door I see something – (*shakes his head*) I thought it would help your head to spend a quiet afternoon out of that hotel.

LADY CAROLINE: (*Sharply*) What do you mean?

SIR HUBERT: (*Turning to her, sadly*) Nothing, my dear, nothing. I just wanted your company – it was selfish of me to drag you here. (*Little pause. He looks towards the drive as a small truck appears, then with a smile.*) Besides, I have a little surprise for you.

LADY CAROLINE: (*Sees the truck*) Oh. Oh Hubert, what is it?

SIR HUBERT: Ah. (*He lifts his key-ring, jangles it jovially.*) Ah, my dear, wait and see.
(*He waves to the truck, gestures towards the living-room, opens the window wider.*)

EXT.

The truck stops, a man gets out on the side closest to the window; the door on the other side opens; a figure in overalls, not clearly seen, gets out on that side. The two men go to the back, only one visible, open the door. One gets in, the man who is visible waits, a piano is pushed out. He grabs the end, swings it around towards the window, moves slowly, the other MAN *is behind the piano. It is carried towards the windows.*

INT. LIVING-ROOM

SIR HUBERT *and* LADY CAROLINE *watch it coming towards them, step aside to let it pass.*

LADY CAROLINE: (*Claps her hands*) Oh Hubert, you darling you.
(*She gives him a kiss on the cheek.* SIR HUBERT, *beaming, watches the two men deposit the piano in the centre of the room.*)

SIR HUBERT: I couldn't have a home, my dear, without your music in it.

(*The sentence falters, and his expression changes as he watches the* MAN *nearest him, hitherto not seen properly, straightening, and turning.*)

MAN: (*Momentarily seeming to be West Indian*) Is this all right for you, just here?

(*His face seen in close-up.*)

SIR HUBERT: (*Staring*) I – I –

LADY CAROLINE: Oh further back I think, please, if you wouldn't mind. (*She goes over to the piano.*) It's beautiful – where are you going, dear?

(SIR HUBERT *walks to the door, right.*)

SIR HUBERT: Just remembered something, my dear, downstairs, check up on the smell, won't be a minute.

(*He looks at the white mover, who is wiping his hands on a handkerchief, nods, smiles, hurries down.*)

LADY CAROLINE: Oh.

(*She looks puzzled, then turns to the two men.*)

Just a few feet, that's all, so that it doesn't take up the whole room.

INT. THE CELLAR

SIR HUBERT *enters, sits down on an old trunk, closes his eyes (he has left the doors open) rocks slightly. Then opens his eyes and stares straight ahead. Closes his eyes again. Presses his knees together, begins to rattle the keys up and down compulsively, the camera on his face. He opens his eyes, they widen in shock. Cut to the West Indian face at the door, smiling in. Then stepping into the room, rubbing his hands along his trousers.*

MAN: That's done then. All moved.

SIR HUBERT: Moved, eh. Moved.

(*He chuckles automatically, stares at the man.*)

MAN: The lady seems very pleased.

SIR HUBERT: Is she? I think she is. I think I can say that.

(*He nods and continues to stare.*)

MAN: We got it all square for her. She wants to get at it straight away from the look on her face.

(*He throws back his head and laughs.* SIR HUBERT *looks at him, appalled.*)

SIR HUBERT: Does she? Does she now? Does she?

MAN: Yes, well I just thought I'd tell you it was done.

(*He turns and makes for the door.*)

SIR HUBERT: Ah – ah – ah wait. (*He looks at him, then reaches into his pocket, takes out his wallet.*) Here's a little something . . . (*he hands over two pound notes*) . . . a little something for your trouble.

MAN: (*Grinning*) Thank *you* sir. No trouble, it was a pleasure, sir. (SIR HUBERT *stares at him fixedly, and somehow cutting him off.*)

SIR HUBERT: Goodbye.

MAN: (*Freezing*) Goodbye, sir. And thank you. (*Exits.*)

(SIR HUBERT *stands, staring at the door, sits down again, wipes his hand across his forehead. Then begins to sniff. Makes a face of disgust. Sniffs again. Suddenly the sound of the piano, playing 'Somewhere over the Rainbow'. He stands stock still, listening. The playing is very coarse and brash.* SIR HUBERT'*s face becomes calmer, he smiles, nods his head in time to the music, then goes to the door.*)

INT. LIVING-ROOM

LADY CAROLINE *is standing by the piano, pushing her flask back into her handbag, and taking out a couple of peppermints, as the door, right, opens, and* SIR HUBERT *enters. She pops the peppermints into her mouth, turns, smiles.*

LADY CAROLINE: Thank you, Hubert. Thank you so much, dear.

(*She smiles at him.* SIR HUBERT *walking across to her.*)

SIR HUBERT: I heard your tune downstairs. I could tell your touch, my dear, from the grave itself. (*Walks over and stares at her, very seriously.*) It carried me back, for a minute, to Kjiarna. (*Takes her hand and kisses it.*)

362

(LADY CAROLINE *smiles at him, her face slightly averted. Then they walk towards the windows.* SIR HUBERT *stops, stares out.*)

EXT.

The truck is backing down the drive, out of sight.

INT. COTTAGE.

LADY CAROLINE: Sometimes, you know, Hubert, sometimes – I know it's silly of me, but I can't help feeling everything was easier in Kjiarna, I mean I never got these headaches there, did I?
(*She looks at him.*)
SIR HUBERT: No my dear. No, you didn't.

EXT. THE LAWN

Shot of LADY CAROLINE *and* SIR HUBERT *walking across the lawn,* LADY CAROLINE *leaning on* SIR HUBERT's *arm. Then of* LADY CAROLINE *sitting beside him.*

EXT.

Shot of street from Sir Hubert's bedroom window.

INT. SIR HUBERT'S BEDROOM WITH SHOT OF STREET FROM THE WINDOW

He is sitting on the bed, fiddling with his keys, staring straight ahead. Suddenly he gets up, goes to a trunk, opens it. Takes out a revolver, looks at it, puts it back. Closes the trunk. Walks to the window, opens it, stares out. Ordinary street noises come up to him. He takes great

363

*gulps of air, listens to the roar of traffic, honking, voices rising, shuts
his eyes, these noises transform into jungle cries, shrill, like the cries
of the parrots in the first scene only confused.* SIR HUBERT *stares out,
jerks the window down. Puts his hands to his ears. Removes them,
slowly. Silence. Opens window again. Traffic noises which
transform again into the same cries and screechings. He slams the
window down, walks around the room, sits down on the bed,
jangling his keys, gets up, stares at himself in the mirror. Then goes
to the window. Draws the curtains, straightens his shoulders, goes to
the door.*

INT. LADY CAROLINE'S BEDROOM

*She is putting the finishing touches to her make-up as there is a knock
on the door, and* SIR HUBERT *enters. She gets up, does a little
curtsy.*

LADY CAROLINE: Where are we taking Geoffrey for this drink?
  Somewhere glamorous, I hope.
SIR HUBERT: (*Blinks*) Ah – well, I – perhaps we could have a
  quiet drink up – send down for something and have it –
LADY CAROLINE: No Hubert, I'm not having that, dear. We're
  not going to sit in a poky bedroom, if you won't take us out
  then the least we can do is use the hotel bar.
SIR HUBERT: The bar?
LADY CAROLINE: Can you imagine Geoffrey's face if we have
  him in the bedroom? I don't know why I bother to change
  for you, I really don't, and you know what an old woman
  he is about some things.

INT. BAR

CLAUD *is drawing in his pad – a thin, elderly face caricatured into
corrupt effeminacy, suggestions of eye make-up and lipstick and a
blouse and skirt. Switch from the drawing to* SIR GEOFFREY (*the
subject of the cartoon*) *listening very seriously at a far table,* LADY

CAROLINE *beside him, also listening. Drink in front of them.* SIR
HUBERT *not seen, but the first shot includes a glass of rum and coke
and with a slice of lemon in it.*

SIR HUBERT'S VOICE: I slept like a log all through it. Yes, like a
   log. (*Chuckles.*) I could hear this Kibbobola cavorting and
   cursing outside my window all night, but I just fitted my
   dreams around him, and slept like a log. (*Chuckles again.*)

SIR GEOFFREY: *That's* the way to rule an empire, *and* it confirms
   my favourite moral – never give cures to the native, it teaches
   them the disease.

LADY CAROLINE: They used to call him Lord Justice. (*Giggles.*)

SIR HUBERT: (*Out of shot*) Justice, justice. It's not only the
   Kibbobola that need justice.
   (*Little pause.* SIR GEOFFREY *looks at him curiously,* LADY
   CAROLINE *sips from her glass and attempts a serious expression.*)
   It's needed everywhere, I think. Yes, everywhere. For
   instance, this Meadle . . .
   (*camera shifts to his face, he is staring intensely*)
   in the newspapers the other morning.

SIR GEOFFREY: (*Politely*) Meadle?

SIR HUBERT: This Meadle . . . (*turns to* LADY CAROLINE,
   addresses the rest of this to her) was a lodger with a family in
   Willesden Green, two adults – husband and wife, naturally,
   my dear – and a daughter of ten. A daughter of ten. (*Pause.*)
   A daughter of ten. (*Pause.*) Meadle himself was in his early
   forties, or thereabout, and reading between the lines I should
   say he was definitely black. A West Indian, my dear. (*Long
   pause.*)

LADY CAROLINE: Hubert – you don't mean – how disgusting!

SIR GEOFFREY: (*Suavely*) Good heavens.

SIR HUBERT: (*Nodding*) The parents were suspicious, of course.
   Asked him to leave. He had the impertinence to become
   angry, actually angry, threatened the father, insulted the
   mother, grabbed a taxi from under the nose of. (*Stops,
   blinks.*) The daughter didn't understand, you see, how could
   the poor child understand? Innocent and ten years old, very
   gifted musically. (*Pause, smiles sinisterly.*) But her actions

became most mysterious after this Meadle's departure. They were forced to watch, to wait and watch. (*Long pause.*) They found the two-way radio under a floorboard in her bedroom.

SIR GEOFFREY: (*With real enthusiasm*) Good heavens!

LADY CAROLINE: (*Blinking, sipping*) A what, dear?

(SIR HUBERT *who has been staring over at the counter, where* CLAUD *is drawing busily.*)

SIR HUBERT: For transmitting messages to, and receiving messages from (*looking at* LADY CAROLINE) another person, my dear, also in possession of a two-way radio. They found his, this Meadle's, in the wardrobe of his new lodging room in Kilburn.

SIR GEOFFREY: How old did you say the girl was?

SIR HUBERT: Nine.

LADY CAROLINE: I thought you said ten.

SIR HUBERT: Going on ten, my dear, I think I said.

(*Stares over at* CLAUD *again.*)

You see, my dear, he was quite open about it. (*Swivelling his head back, staring sightlessly.*) He kept it in the wardrobe, and when he went to bed at night he could take it with him, rest in on the pillow, whisper into its ear, he could talk as softly as he liked and say anything out that was moving about in his head. *That* is the point, my dear. He could say it all in whispers, and it would stretch, so to speak, from Willesden to Kilburn. And she, this innocent child, the little lady, would have hers on the pillow beside her, and would listen to the whispers as if they were dreams, or as if they came from inside herself. And who could get hold of it? You can't track it down when it's under the floorboard or carrying itself through the night air, like the parrots at Kjiarna when Whitey vanished.

(*Stares towards* CLAUD *again, shot of* CLAUD *closing his pad as some elderly people advance into the bar.*)

Unless you watch for it, and wait, can you? Because he could be anywhere, this – this – this Meadle with his two-way set.

LADY CAROLINE: Hanging's too good for people like that. If you give them an inch. (*Nods.*)

SIR GEOFFREY: (*Staring at* SIR HUBERT *hard*) You read this in the newspaper.

SIR HUBERT: (*Blinking*) It was a short item.
(*Stares towards* CLAUD *again, then as* CLAUD *goes over to a very distant table, gets to his feet as* SIR GEOFFREY *says:*)

SIR GEOFFREY: There's the real danger of the technological –
(*Stops. Watches* SIR HUBERT *walking quickly to the counter, turns to* LADY CAROLINE, *who is also watching* SIR HUBERT.)
Caroline, is everything all right with Hubert?

LADY CAROLINE: Oh yes, I think so, why?

SIR GEOFFREY: Nothing, nothing, I was sure it was. Thought perhaps he might be a bit on edge – often happens when they come home for good, you know. I was hoping to get him interested in some troublesome Nigerians we've got swinging about the Office, but he didn't seem quite himself when he bumped into them.

LADY CAROLINE: Well, of course we've got so much on our plates at the moment, what with this new house, there's so much to do settling in, I can hardly face the thought of it sometimes. And another thing, I've had a perpetual head –
(*Cut to* SIR HUBERT, *who is at the bar, with his hand on Claud's pad. Moves his hand as* CLAUD *comes back. Smiles.*)

SIR HUBERT: Look after those good people first, Claud, I'm in no hurry.
(CLAUD *smiles, nods, goes to the shelves,* SIR HUBERT *watches him, his hand close to the pad. Cut back to* LADY CAROLINE *and* SIR GEOFFREY.)

LADY CAROLINE: . . . all over the place when he first got back, he even thought he saw one in the garden at Greendene, but it was just a mood, habit he called it, he hardly ever talks about them these days, he's too occupied with what he's found over here, mark you I wish there *were* a few Kibbobola about . . .
(*Shot of* CLAUD *passing with a tray of drinks, from the table; then cut to* SIR HUBERT *rustling through the pad, stopping at a page, close-up of his face, glaring down, then rips the page out and stuffs it into his pocket. Stands there humming, looks towards* CLAUD, *who is now coming back, takes out his key-ring*

and begins to jangle it innocently. Cut back to:)

LADY CAROLINE: . . . wonderful about the house after they'd
been broken in, I often wonder how we'll manage without
them, and very reliable, ah Hubert . . .

(*As* SIR HUBERT *comes back to the table, still jangling his
key-ring*) why ever did you rush off like that, dear, Geoffrey
thought there must be something wrong with you.

SIR HUBERT: (*Calmly sitting down*) Oh, I'm sorry, Geoffrey, just
ordering another round. (*There is a little pause. Very calmly.*)
That snake, I buried it in the garden, where it could be
watched. I had almost forgotten. It was a long time ago. I've
often wondered, my dear, whether those parrot things didn't
come at first to dig it up. I think they did, you know, I think
they did.

SIR GEOFFREY: Snake, Hubert?

LADY CAROLINE: Dear, what *are* you going on about?

SIR HUBERT: Wasn't I telling you about this Kibbobola, the one
who danced and cursed all night. (*Little pause.*) The one
whose hash I settled? (*Chuckles.*)

SIR GEOFFREY: Oh yes, of *course* you were. The cure and disease
witch-doctor chappie.

(LADY CAROLINE *nods contentedly.*)

SIR HUBERT: (*Smiling*) But I didn't tell you *how* I settled his hash
did – ah, and here's our Claud.

(*As* CLAUD *approaches with the tray, and drinks on it.*)
Geoffrey, let me introduce you properly to our good friend
Claud, who is indispensible to us. He comes from Trinidad
by way of Stepney Green.

(SIR GEOFFREY *embarrassed, but smiling smoothly.*)

SIR GEOFFREY: How do you do, Claud.

SIR HUBERT: Caroline and Claud are the greatest of friends,
aren't you, my dear? He has a special aspirin that clears
Caroline's head.

(LADY CAROLINE *giggles nervously.*)

SIR GEOFFREY: Really? I could do with some of those!

(*As* CLAUD *takes away the empty glass and puts a fresh drink in
front of him.*)

I was in Jamaica last winter, saw the finest cricket game of my life. Bottles over the pitch, transistors, umpire assaulted – now that's what I call sport. Do you play, Claud?

CLAUD: (*Serving* LADY CAROLINE) No, sir. I don't like cricket, sir.

SIR GEOFFREY: Oh? I thought it was in your bl— part of your tradition?

CLAUD: (*Serving* SIR HUBERT) No, sir. I was very bad at sports, sir. All of them.

SIR HUBERT: All of them, Claud? Come now, Claud, there must be some sport you excel at. (*Chuckles.*) Athletic chap like you, eh, Caroline? Wouldn't you think Claud would be a natural athlete?

CLAUD: No, sir.

SIR GEOFFREY: (*Looking at him closely*) I haven't seen you before somewhere, have I?

CLAUD: (*Staring at him impassively*) I sometimes go to the The Gay Fellow, sir, off Amble Street, in Kensington?

SIR GEOFFREY: The Gay (*embarrassed but smooth*) the Gay? No, no, I've never been there. I'm sure I haven't.

LADY CAROLINE: Oh but you have to be careful with Claud, according to Hubert he's got a roving instinct. (*She giggles, sips at her drink.*)

(*Shot of* SIR HUBERT'*s face, swinging around to stare at* LADY CAROLINE, *then swinging back to* CLAUD.)

SIR HUBERT: Well, how much do I owe you this time, Claud?

SIR GEOFFREY: Oh, do let me get these.

(*He seems slightly flustered, avoids looking at* CLAUD.)

My round, you know. Old tradition.

(CLAUD *looks at him, smiles.*)

SIR HUBERT: Oh certainly not. Certainly not. *I* will settle with Claud. Claud?

(*He takes out his wallet, with the sheet of drawing paper folded around it, takes the paper away, ostentatiously but casually, watching* CLAUD'*s face all the time.*)

Eh, Claud?

(*He puts the paper down in front of himself.*

CLAUD *smiles again at* SIR GEOFFREY, *who is still avoiding him.*)

CLAUD: Um, one scotch, one rum and coke, one large gin, eleven shillings, please, sir.

(SIR HUBERT *takes a pound out of his wallet, hands it to* CLAUD. *When* CLAUD'*s fingers are around it* SIR HUBERT *hangs on to the note.*)

SIR HUBERT: You wouldn't be cheating would you, Claud?

CLAUD: (*Shocked*) Sir?

(LADY CAROLINE *and* SIR GEOFFREY *look at him, and then at* SIR HUBERT. SIR HUBERT *releases the note. He should seem utterly confident of himself.*)

SIR HUBERT: Yourself, Claud, I mean. What about all those aspirins you've been getting from Claud, my dear, did he let you pay for them?

LADY CAROLINE: Of course I paid, Hubert, what an idea!

SIR HUBERT: Ah, well that's all right then. That's all right, Claud. You haven't been cheating yourself, you see. I was worried on your account.

(*He chuckles, nods at* CLAUD, *turns back to the table, taps the paper with his fingers casually.* CLAUD *takes change out of his pocket, puts it on the tray, holds it out to* SIR HUBERT, *who affects not to see.*)

Yes, I think the parrots opened the grave. One morning I noticed that the mud had been turned up (*to* SIR GEOFFREY) and the grave was empty. It's just come back to me.

(*As he says this* CLAUD *slips the change on a corner of the table and goes off. Cut to* SIR GEOFFREY *who glances furtively at* CLAUD'*s back.*)

SIR GEOFFREY: I've never been in Amble Street in my life. Why should that fellow say –

SIR HUBERT: Claud! (*He gets to his feet.*) Claud!

(CLAUD *stops. Close-up of his face, lips tightening in irritation, rolls his eyes, turns, goes back to the table.*)

I think you've forgotten something, Claud?

(*He puts his hand on the paper, then shifts his hand to the change.*)

CLAUD: Sir?

SIR HUBERT: The change, Claud.

CLAUD: (*After a little pause*) It's there, sir.

SIR HUBERT: (*Chuckles*) Exactly, Claud. And you've forgotten it,
I think.

> (CLAUD *hesitates, looks at* LADY CAROLINE, *then at* SIR
> GEOFFREY, *their eyes meet*, CLAUD *gives a little smile, then puts
> his hand down on the table and scoops the change on to the plate,
> missing the paper by a fraction of an inch.*)

CLAUD: Thank you, sir.

> (*He looks again at* SIR GEOFFREY, *with the same knowing
> smile.*)

SIR HUBERT: My pleasure, Claud. (*Chuckles after him.*)

> (LADY CAROLINE, *as* CLAUD *turns away, reaches over and
> picks up the paper*)

LADY CAROLINE: Hubert, is this something important? (*Begins to
unfold it.*)

SIR HUBERT: No, my dear, a surprise, you're not to –

> (SIR HUBERT *reaches over, snatches it from her hand, knocks
> over her drink, which spills over her lap.* LADY CAROLINE *cries
> out.*)

LADY CAROLINE: (*Pushing the chair back*) Hubert!

> (CLAUD *turns, hurries back.* SIR HUBERT *is stuffing the paper
> back into his pocket.*)

SIR HUBERT: I'm terribly sorry, my dear, a surprise, I don't want
you to see, I'm so – most clumsy –

LADY CAROLINE: I'll just smell of gin. (*Brushes futilely at the
splashes.*)

CLAUD: Allow me, madame.

> (CLAUD *bends down, mops at the hem of her dress, very rapidly
> and discreetly; cut to* SIR HUBERT *watching, with eyes staring,
> then cut back to* CLAUD's *hands, which seems to be travelling
> everywhere, a multiplicity of hands at Lady Caroline's hem,
> moving under the dress, etc.; cut back to* SIR HUBERT *gaping.*)
> No harm done, madame. (*Straightening.*) No harm done.
> (*He smiles down on* LADY CAROLINE, *close-up of his face, teeth,
> mouth open, in a sudden exaggeration of a smile.*)

371

INT. SIR HUBERT'S BEDROOM

SIR HUBERT *is sitting on his bed, fully clothed, but his head nodding, as if he had dozed off. The drawing of* LADY CAROLINE, *naked, is open beside him.*

SIR HUBERT: . . . anything to say, my Claud, why sentence – (*His voice slurs off, his eyes blink open, leaps to his feet.*) Let madness in and justice out?
(*Looks down at the drawing, rushes to the window, makes to open it, stops himself, looks out fearfully, comes back, goes to the trunk, opens it, takes out the revolver, puts it in his pocket, folds the drawing, puts it in his pocket, sits down on the edge of the bed, buries his face in his hands.*)
The devil. The devil.
(*He raises his face, there are tears trickling down it.*)

INT. THE BAR

CLAUD *is behind the counter, in his shirt sleeves, putting glasses away. He is whistling softly. There is a crashing noise behind him, he looks up, startled, sees* SIR HUBERT *in the mirror, seated on one of the stools. Turns.*

SIR HUBERT: Just clearing up, Claud? Putting it all straight for the morrow, eh?

CLAUD: Yes, sir.

SIR HUBERT: What about a last drink with me, Claud? (*Smiles ingratiatingly.*)

CLAUD: Well, sir (*hesitates*) the bar's closed, sir, by law. (*Looks at the clock.*)

SIR HUBERT: By law? In that case, I mustn't incite you to break it. That's a criminal offence. Did you know that, Claud?

CLAUD: (*Shakes his head, smiling*) No, sir.

SIR HUBERT: Of course you didn't. Why should you? It's my job to know about the law, and your job (*stops smiling*) and your job to help yourself to whatever will help *you*, eh Claud? And that's what I want to have a short word with you about. How

would you like to earn yourself five five-pound notes? To add
to those tips of yours?

CLAUD: Twenty-five pounds, sir?

SIR HUBERT: Mmmm?

> (*He tilts his head to one side, smiling. His hand in his jacket
> pocket.*)

CLAUD: Well, that sounds very interesting, sir.

SIR HUBERT: But I insist on one condition beforehand, and that
is complete discretion, Claud, complete discretion. You see,
I want you to assist me in a little surprise, one I've been
preparing for my lady wife. (*Chuckles.*) You know my lady
wife, I think?

> (*He stares at him.* CLAUD *nods, smiling.*)

Now what I have in – by the way, do you live with your
family, out in that Stepney Green of yours?

CLAUD: No, sir. I've got a room here, 22 in the basement
corridor. It goes with the job.

SIR HUBERT: Good. Excellent. I'll know where to get hold of
you, 22 in the basement, although we mustn't be seen
together, or the lady in question will know there's something
afoot. Now . . . (*Leans forward.*)

INT. LADY CAROLINE'S BEDROOM

*She is in her night-dress and night-gown. She goes to her handbag,
takes out the flask and peppermints, goes back to the bed.* LADY
CAROLINE *puts the flask under her pillow, the peppermints beside the
pillow, gets into bed with a book. Sighs.*

INT. BAR

SIR HUBERT *and* CLAUD *are still at the counter, their heads together.
Shot of them from the entrance first, the low murmur of their voices,
intimate-sounding, then close-up.*

SIR HUBERT: You're the expert, Claud, you're our barman.

When can you come and see the room for yourself?

CLAUD: (*Shrugs*) Any morning?

SIR HUBERT: Well, sir, and are you an early riser?

CLAUD: (*Shrugs*) When I have to be. (*Smiles.*)

SIR HUBERT: I thought not. The nights are not for sleeping in, I think, where you're concerned, eh Claud? Well, I've a little business to attend to tomorrow, a few purchases. (*Gestures.*) Meet me outside the Gloucester Road underground station at eleven sharp? How does that appeal to you?

CLAUD: (*Nods*) That's fine, sir.

SIR HUBERT: (*Looks at him, smiles*) Good, Claud, good. Very good. (*Little pause.*) Tell me, Claud, what do you do with all your tips? (SIR HUBERT *takes his hand out of his pocket.*) If I'm not being presumptuous, of course?

CLAUD: (*Hesitates*) Save them, sir.

SIR HUBERT: Do you, indeed? And what for, may I ask? Some special luxury, mmm? (*Wags his head, smiling.*)

CLAUD: No, sir. Well (*hesitates again*) it's to go to New York on.

SIR HUBERT: (*Raising a finger*) There you are, quite the rover, I think I said that as soon as I saw you. (*Wags his finger.*) Here today, gone tomorrow, now we see you, now we don't, eh Claud? Why New York, Claud?

CLAUD: Well, I've always wanted to go back, I've got a friend, he just went over, so I thought I would too. You know.

SIR HUBERT: (*Chuckling*) He, Claud?

CLAUD: (*Suddenly embarrassed, stiffens*) Yes, sir.

SIR HUBERT: Well, I don't know that it's a worthy cause, Claud, to contribute to your disappearance.

(*He laughs, begins to shake with laughter, gets off the stool as* CLAUD *smiles in embarrassment, touches him on the shoulder.*) See you tomorrow then, my dear Claud, see you tomorrow.

CLAUD: I'll be there, sir.

SIR HUBERT: And God bless, old Claud. God bless.

(*Touches his shoulder again, goes to the entrance. He turns, waggles his fingers,* CLAUD *nods, smiles.*)

INT. LADY CAROLINE'S ROOM

LADY CAROLINE *is lying in bed, with a breakfast tray on the table beside her, and her teeth in a glass. She is clearly only half-awake. There is a gentle knock on the door, she jerks upright, pops the teeth into her mouth, fixes her face in a smile.*

LADY CAROLINE: Come in, dear.

> (SIR HUBERT *enters, hat in hand, smiling.*)
>
> (*Shaking her head.*) I don't know how you do it. I really don't.
>
> (SIR HUBERT *stands over her tenderly.*)

SIR HUBERT: And I don't know how *you* do it, Petal, so beautiful so early.

> (*He bends, kisses her on the cheek.*)
>
> I thought I'd go over to Greendene for the day, put the finishing touches to this and that.

LADY CAROLINE: Oh. Do you want me to come with you, dear?

> (*Wearily.*)

SIR HUBERT: No, this is man's work, my work.

LADY CAROLINE: Oh. Well, Hubert, don't overdo it.

> (LADY CAROLINE *stares up at him, he stands smiling very gently down at her, she blinks, as if almost in tears.*)
>
> Oh, Hubert, I hope I don't let you down. It was much easier being a wife in Kjiarna, I mean I felt like a bride there, but I don't seem to know what to do in England, my head pounding, even when I wake up. I don't want to let you down, I don't.

SIR HUBERT: It's not your fault, my Petal. I've never thought it was your fault.

> (*He bends, kisses her on the forehead again.*)
>
> I'll make everything as it was in Kjiarna – I promise you that.
>
> (*Goes towards the door, turns, smiles, wags his fingers.*)

LADY CAROLINE: (*Emotionally*) Thank you, Hubert. Thank you for everything.

EXT. GREENDENE. THE GARDEN

SIR HUBERT *and* CLAUD *walking across the lawn, from the Rover.*
SIR HUBERT *is carrying a large bag in one hand, is holding* CLAUD's
arm by the other. Stops, to show CLAUD *a flower.* SIR HUBERT *and*
CLAUD *then move towards the living-room, the windows of which are*
shut. SIR HUBERT *takes out his key-ring, opens the windows, they*
step inside.

INT. LIVING-ROOM

The walls are papered and the floor is carpeted, but the only furniture
is the piano.
SIR HUBERT *ushers* CLAUD *in most solicitously, is replying to*
something CLAUD *has just said.*
SIR HUBERT: Ah, that's what I mean by expert, Claud. Expert.
    (*He smiles in complimentary bewilderment.*)
    Tell me, do you see yourself in white?
CLAUD: Sir?
SIR HUBERT: Oh, but not, of course, if you have some other
    preference. Fancy dress, feathers and wings, as far as I'm
    concerned.
    (*He chuckles. Throughout this scene* SIR HUBERT *is very*
    animated, talking more quickly than usual.)
CLAUD: (*Ironically*) Oh, I think white's more usual, sir.
SIR HUBERT: I suppose it is, yes, I suppose it *is* usual. (*Walks*
    towards him, smiling, then veers away to stand beside the
    piano.) She loves this instrument, Claud. (*Stares at him.*)
    She might play for us all, that would be a rare treat, I
    think. And you, of course, will pay her special attention,
    won't you? She has a generous nature, Claud, and she lets
    herself be deceived.
    (CLAUD *smiles and nods in embarrassment.*)
    As you know, yes, I think you do. She suffers from
    headaches, a perpetual headache, very frail, frailer even
    than she thinks. She was sad to leave Kjiarna, and so was

I. So we must make this a happy occasion. And you'll be here, Claud, and that'll make a difference. (*Little pause, smiles.*) An expert to keep her under control, eh? (*Chuckles now briskly.*) What were your plans again? Did you bring them with you?

CLAUD: Yes. (*Takes a piece of paper out of his pocket.*) If we have a still bar, we could put it alongside, here, or if the trolley bar, we could keep it in one half of the room –

(SIR HUBERT *listening to this inattentive, eager, smiles, looks past him, to the garden.*)

SIR HUBERT: Is that a robin? I think it was. Do *you* see a robin?

(CLAUD *puzzled, looks out of the windows.*)

CLAUD: A robin?

SIR HUBERT: (*Stands beside him*) In Kjiarna, Claud, we had a special kind of bird we were never able to identify. It cried out at night, its wings flapped noisily – (*he lowers the big bag he has been carrying to the ground, it clanks slightly*) but it was never to be seen during the day. Doubtless it slept during the day. It had an odd cry, unforgettable, Claud.

(*He turns to* CLAUD, *his face very close.*)

Heeee-eeeee, heeee-eeeee.

(CLAUD *takes a nervous step back.*)

Perhaps *you* know it, this parrot of ours?

(CLAUD *shakes his head.* SIR HUBERT *takes a step nearer, puts his hand on* CLAUD's *arm.*)

My wife has green fingers you know, Claud. Everything she touches grows. Even in Kjiarna, where the sun baked the soil barren or the rains washed it into a swamp, she managed to raise a flower or two, and a little bed of tomatoes, with the help of the MacPhersons' gardeners, whom we shared, so to speak. She made them water the tomatoes every day, cover them with glass, nursed them up. But here, you see, everything comes up by itself, if you watch it. Especially the weeds. That's the difference, Claud. It's very difficult to understand, at first, and you have to keep some things down. Especially the weeds, Claud, especially the weeds.

CLAUD: Yes, sir. (*Little pause.*) I'm not one for gardening, sir.

SIR HUBERT: I know. I know. (*Stares at him, chuckles*.) Tell me, Claud, do you like this room?

CLAUD: Yes, sir. (*Little pause*.) Yes, it's a beautiful room.

SIR HUBERT: (*Chuckles*) But not for the likes of you, eh, Claud? (*Stares at him*.) Come, I know you, sir, with your roving instincts, you wouldn't want a room like this. It's not in your blood, it it? Eh?

CLAUD: (*Ironically*) Perhaps it's not my tradition, sir, no. Not quite my style.

SIR HUBERT: No, you're quite right. (*Pause*.) In the summer there will be flowers. She'll put them in vases around the room. She'll choose them herself. And in the evenings she'll play the piano and sing. Her headaches will go, I think I can promise her that. Everything will be in its proper place, you see. Can you imagine what it will look like then, Claud, the civilization of it?

CLAUD: Yes, sir, I'd like to see it then.

SIR HUBERT: But you won't be able to, will you? Because you'll be in *your* proper place then, won't you? (*Laughs*.) With God's help, and if there is justice in the world.
(CLAUD *looks baffled*.)
New York, old Claud. New York. (*Whispers it*.)

CLAUD: Oh. Yes, sir. Well, it's kind of you to help me, sir.

SIR HUBERT: (*Raises a finger*) It's my duty. I see it as that. By the way, there's something I have to put right, downstairs. Would you be good enough to wait a moment?

CLAUD: Yes, sir.

SIR HUBERT: I'll be right back.
(*He goes to the door, right*.)
Oh, my – bits and pieces, would you be good enough . . .?
(CLAUD *picks up the bag, obviously finds it heavier than he expected, carries it to* SIR HUBERT, *who smiles at him*.)
By the way, Claud, I have a feeling that you're something of a musician yourself. Are you, Claud?

CLAUD: Well, I like to try sometimes, but not a proper one, sir.

SIR HUBERT: Please. (*Gestures to the piano*.) Please. While I'm gone, if you feel in the mood.

CLAUD: Thank you, sir.

SIR HUBERT: Because I shan't be here to judge, if the thought of that puts you off.

(*He smiles, goes out the door, right.* CLAUD *makes a silent, whistling noise, rolls his eyes, stares around the room.*)

INT. CELLAR

SIR HUBERT *enters, turns on light. Opens the bag, takes out padlocks, one big one for the door, five lengths of chain, a hygiene spray, and his revolver. Walks across to the ring, very quickly, the chains in his hand.*

INT. LIVING-ROOM

CLAUD *saunters over to the piano, touches a note very softly, frowns, plays a chord. Makes a face.*

INT. CELLAR

The chains are padlocked to the ring. SIR HUBERT *is pulling on them, they have padlocks in the end. He goes to the cellar door, where the large padlock has been fixed. Shuts it. Stands in the centre, raises his hands, cups them around his mouth, draws in a breath. Cut to:*

INT. LIVING-ROOM

CLAUD *plays a hideous discord, winces, laughs. Plays another, then raises his hands to play another, and cut to:*

SLEEPING DOG

INT. CELLAR

SIR HUBERT, *hands still cupped around his mouth.*
SIR HUBERT: Boy. Claud. Claud. Nigger. Blackie Black-ie.

INT. LIVING-ROOM

CLAUD *with his hands over his ears as another discord sounds. Then trails his fingers across the keys.*

INT. CELLAR

SIR HUBERT: Black-ie. (*A mighty bellow.*)

INT. LIVING-ROOM

CLAUD *engrossed, picking out a tune very softly. Stops once, as if listening to another sound, then goes on playing. The door, right, opens and* SIR HUBERT *enters softly, comes over and stands behind* CLAUD. CLAUD *stops, whirls around.*
SIR HUBERT: I knew you had the gift. I knew you had it.
    (*Smiles.*) Play a few more bars.
CLAUD: Well. (*Makes to get up.*)
SIR HUBERT: Please, Claud. (*Smiles.*)
CLAUD: It needs tuning, sir.
SIR HUBERT: Oh no, Claud, that won't do. (*He shakes his head, raises his finger, smiles.*) It's already passed that test, I think.
CLAUD: Well, sir, you listen to this and you'll know.
    (*He sits down, begins to play, very expertly, so that everything comes out flat.*
    SIR HUBERT *stands beside him, tapping his foot out of time to the music, and watching* CLAUD *as if hypnotized by him.* CLAUD *stops, throws his hands up as if in surrender, turns to* SIR HUBERT.)

You see, sir?

SIR HUBERT: I see that you've got the touch, Claud. That's what
I see. (*Long pause, then rubs his hands together.*) I wonder if
you could give me a hand with a little something I've rigged
up downstairs – another little surprise, but it needs a
finishing touch.

(CLAUD *gets up.*)

Thank you.

(*He leads the way to the door, right.*
The camera lingers on the room, full of sunlight.)

INT. CELLAR

SIR HUBERT *holds the door open for* CLAUD *to enter.* CLAUD *stops,*
sees the chains.

SIR HUBERT: Why do you sniff, Claud?

CLAUD: No, sir. I wasn't sniffing.

SIR HUBERT: (*Sniffing himself*) I thought you smelt something.

CLAUD: No, sir.

SIR HUBERT: Really? You don't? I do. (*Picks up the squirt gun,*
squirts.) It's below the earth-line, you see. A subterranean
smell. It doesn't rise. Of course it depends on the system's
development.

(*Chuckles, squirts again in the general direction of* CLAUD.)

That's where the danger of a bad smell is. Now to work. If
you could just pick up the ends of those chains there.

(CLAUD *looks at him, goes over to pick up the chains, looks at*
SIR HUBERT.)

Yes, and give them a pull, as hard as you can. I've been
doing it myself, but I'm probably not as powerful as you.

CLAUD: To pull them free, you mean?

SIR HUBERT: (*Nods*) Well, to see if you can.

(CLAUD *gives them a tug.*)

No, no, harder, Claud, all you've got.

(CLAUD *strains at the chains.*)

Now really savage. (*Pantomimes a savage jerk.*) Ah, excellent,

you see, deeply imbedded and quality chain, you couldn't
get them free in a month of Sundays, I think, Claud. Now, if
you'd just slip the third one, have you got it, the third one?
(CLAUD *extracts the third one, holds it out.*)
Yes, around your throat, Claud.
(*Bends down, away from* CLAUD, *who stands looking at him
with incomprehension, opens the trunk, takes out the revolver,
points it at* CLAUD, *then barks out.*)
Around your throat, sir. If you please, sir.
(CLAUD *stares at* SIR HUBERT, *makes a noise like a laugh.*)
Or die instead, Claud. I will honour you for that. (*His finger
squeezes.*)

CLAUD: Sir? Sir? (*Makes another noise like a laugh.*) Please?
(*Shakes his head.*)

SIR HUBERT: And I do honour you, Claud. You've chosen the
nobler course.
(*Close-up of the gun, then* CLAUD *staring at it. Then* CLAUD
tries to wrap the chain around his throat, has to kneel to do so.)
Slip the tongue of the padlock (*this said very smoothly*) into
the fourteenth link – that will do. Now attend to your
ankles please, Claud, with the extreme left and the extreme
right chains, Claud, and do them properly as I shall check,
you know.
(CLAUD *does them.*)
Excellent. Excellent. Now your right wrist with your left
hand, please, Claud, and tight, you know, very tight. There
won't be any second chances.
(CLAUD *does this. Then he stares up at* SIR HUBERT, *in terror
and pleading.*
SIR HUBERT *comes across and inspects him from closer to, then
holding the pistol close to* CLAUD'*s head, bends down and clicks
the other chain around* CLAUD'*s left wrist, and steps away.*
CLAUD *stares at him. He should be so chained that he is held
back, his hands not able to meet, and his legs in a kneeling
position.* SIR HUBERT *advances to him, goes through his coat
pockets, breathing heavily, takes out some keys, a drawing
pencil, a tube of pastilles (half eaten), a comb. Puts these things*

carefully into his own jacket pocket, plus a wallet. Then steps away, lowering the gun.)

Now Claud, there *you* are, sir, and here am I.

(*Raises the gun again, and squeezes the trigger. It clicks empty.*)

And do you think I shoot men down in cold blood, Claud, without giving them a chance of a hearing? Do you think that is my way, sir? Or that I need *this* to deal with you?

(*Opens the trunk, drops the gun in.*)

I do not, sir, I do not.

CLAUD: (*Shaking his head*) I don't understand. I don't understand.

SIR HUBERT: You know what I want, I think.

CLAUD: No. No, I don't. (*Little pause.*) I haven't any money, I haven't anything.

SIR HUBERT: (*Gazes at him in contempt*) Money! (*Pause.*) It is the *truth*, Claud, that I want from you. The truth, and nothing more, sir.

CLAUD: The truth? About what, sir?

SIR HUBERT: I think you know, Claud, I think you do.

CLAUD: Please, sir. I don't. I don't.

(SIR HUBERT *reaches into his breast pocket, takes out the folded drawing, unfolds it, shows it to* CLAUD.)

(*Staring at it in horror.*) I – I – I – I'm sorry, sir, I didn't mean anything by it. I didn't.

(SIR HUBERT *sitting down on the trunk, holding the drawing out.*)

SIR HUBERT: Tell me about it, Claud.

CLAUD: It's what I told you, sir, that's all. Doodlings. I do them all the time, nothing. I've got them all over my room, sir. I put them on the walls.

SIR HUBERT: Yes?

CLAUD: That's all. That's all, sir.

SIR HUBERT: All? But what do you do with them in your room? Do you laugh at them? Do you abuse them? Do you make jokes at them and whisper to them?

CLAUD: I – I don't even see them any more.

SIR HUBERT: You don't see them any more? After you have

undressed ladies, and drawn them down on paper, and laughed at them, you don't see them any more, Claud. My wife, sir. My *wife*.
(*Rises to his feet, stares down at* CLAUD, *then turns to the door, opens it, goes out.*)

CLAUD: (*Tugging against the chains*) Hey! Hey, sir! Sir!
(*The door opens,* SIR HUBERT *comes back in. He is smiling and composed.*)
What are you going to do with me, sir. (*Little pause.*) Please.

SIR HUBERT: Come, Claud, come look at you down on all fours. Do you call *that* dignity, whining like a dog?
(*Turns off light. There is the sound of the door shutting. Then the sound of the chains rattling.*)

CLAUD: Hey.

EXT. THE GARDEN

SIR HUBERT *walking back to his car, stops to examine a flower, then continues jauntily.*

INT. BAR

LADY CAROLINE *appears at the door, looks around, the bar is empty. She goes to the counter, takes out the flask, sits on a stool, puts the flask under her handbag. Puts a peppermint or two into her mouth, stares towards the entrance. Then glances impatiently around the bar.*

INT. CLAUD'S ROOM

The walls are covered with drawings, most of them cartoons, but above the single bed there is a line of sentimental sketches of a boy of about twenty-two. There is a wash-stand with a toothbrush and shaving kit, a case under the bed, the end just sticking out, a photograph of the boy on the bedside table. But first shot should be of

the cartoon of SIR GEOFFREY, *a hand reaching out, tearing it off.
Then the other cartoons being torn down, a hand shown. Then a long
shot of* SIR HUBERT *ripping the pictures down. Stops, looks around,
sees the case, heaves it out, and working very swiftly, begins to dump
the drawings in. Cut to:*

INT. BAR

LADY CAROLINE *gets off the stool, walks to the end of the counter,
peers behind it. Comes back, walks to the bar entrance, stares up and
down the hall, comes back. She comes back to the stool, looks very
irritable, puts another peppermint into her mouth.*

INT. CLAUD'S ROOM

SIR HUBERT *standing in the middle of Claud's room, the case in his
hand, looking around at the bare walls, etc., to make sure he has
missed nothing. He has the key of the room in his other hand. There is
a knock on the door. He stands stock still, the knock again.*
MAN'S VOICE: Claud, Claud.
> (*Another knock. Silence.* SIR HUBERT's *mouth is open, he is
> breathing heavily. Then he goes to the door, opens it, peers out.
> Steps outside.*)

INT. BAR

LADY CAROLINE *sitting on the stool, her expression tight with
irritation. She has the bag of peppermints open in front of her, her
fingers extracting them and popping them compulsively into her mouth.
Sudden shot of the bar entrance, several people passing, followed by*
SIR HUBERT, *carrying the suitcase. He gazes in, and steps quickly out
of sight just as* LADY CAROLINE *turns around. She turns back to the
counter.*
LADY CAROLINE: This is preposterous.

385

INT. SIR HUBERT'S BEDROOM

SIR HUBERT *shutting one of the large sea-trunks, goes to wash his hands at the sink. Dries them. Brushes at his clothes. Straightens his shoulders, goes towards the door.*

INT. BAR

LADY CAROLINE *at the counter, a large gin in front of her. She takes a sip from the gin, then opens her handbag and puts the flask in it. Her face is composed. She swallows down the rest of the gin, crams a few peppermints into her mouth, then gets up and goes to one of the tables. Sits down.* SIR HUBERT *appears at the entrance, walking slowly and blandly towards her. She sees him, smiles, gives a little wave. A girl in a black dress and an apron follows him, goes behind the bar. His eyes follow her, then go back to his wife. He smiles.*

SIR HUBERT: (*Kisses her on the cheek, sits down*) How's the head, my dear?
   (*Looks at her tenderly, puts his key-ring, now covered with keys, on the table.*)

LADY CAROLINE: It's no good complaining about it, I'm trying not to think about it, I've had a very trying evening, what with one thing and another, but what have you been up to, Hubert?

SIR HUBERT: Getting a few things into place, my dear. Putting the finishing touch to a little plan of mine.

LADY CAROLINE: Oh. Well, I ordered some curtains, I told the man I couldn't be expected to put them up myself, could I? And anyway they're coming along next week.
   (*As she talks, the girl in the apron comes to the table, stands beside* SIR HUBERT, *who looks up at her in surprise.*)

GIRL: Yes, sir?

SIR HUBERT: And where's our good friend, Claud?

GIRL: (*Shakes her head*) Not come in. (*Irish accent.*)

SIR HUBERT: Do you hear that, my dear? (*To the girl*) It looks as if our gone tomorrow Claud's gone today, eh?

GIRL: He's probably in trouble, Mr Tomkins says. And if he hasn't got an explanation he can clear his room up, and out.

SIR HUBERT: Ah, but he's a rover, you see. A real rover, if I know my Claud. And I think I do. I think so at least. A gin, my dear? (LADY CAROLINE *nods*.) And nothing for myself, thank you. (*As the* GIRL *goes off*.) What do you think of that, my dear?

LADY CAROLINE: Well, what do you expect, Hubert, they're always like that, even if they do laugh and get on with people, you should know that, I was here for a long time before – if I wanted anything, I'd just have had to sit twiddling my thumbs, for all Claud cared.

SIR HUBERT: (*Intensely*) And Claud doesn't care. Mark my words, dear, Claud never cared. (*Picks up the keys, and begins to jingle them*.) Never cared at all, you see.

EXT. GARDEN

SIR HUBERT *crossing it, carrying a large brown bag. Goes towards the french windows.*

INT. CELLAR

Complete darkness. Scuffling and chinking noises, a little, keening hum. Then CLAUD's *face leaps on to the screen. He blinks and sways his head from side to side, then stares up. The figure of* SIR HUBERT *comes into focus. He is smiling. He picks up the squirt-gun, squirts towards* CLAUD, *then all around the cellar.*

CLAUD: I'm so hungry. I'm so hungry.

SIR HUBERT: Come then, Claud. The truth.

CLAUD: Please, sir.

SIR HUBERT: The truth, Claud. Confess it.

CLAUD: (*Nods*) I confess. I did it. I confess. I confess, sir.

SIR HUBERT: You did it, did you, Claud? You confess to it, do you?

CLAUD: Yes, sir.

SIR HUBERT: (*After a pause*) What?

CLAUD: I – I – I did that drawing, sir. It was a wrong thing to do. I'm sorry for it. Very sorry, sir.

SIR HUBERT: And what else, Claud?

CLAUD: Nothing, sir. Nothing. That's all I've done wrong.

(SIR HUBERT *sits down on the trunk, crosses his legs*.)

SIR HUBERT: How else have you imagined my wife, Claud? What else have you done to her, in here?

(*Taps his forehead.*

CLAUD *shakes his head*.)

Never, Claud?

CLAUD: Never, sir, never. I swear. I swear.

SIR HUBERT: (*Smiles*) Tell me, Claud, do you find my wife an unattractive woman?

(CLAUD *looks at him, as if trying to read the correct answer on his face. Shakes his head*.)

No, sir. She is not. On the contrary. She is beautiful. Is she not?

(CLAUD *nods*.)

And when you had your little conversations with her, what were you thinking about?

CLAUD: (*Thinks*) About how much I respected her, sir.

SIR HUBERT: Do you think you can trick me? Those lips of yours, that hair, your skin? (*Laughs*.) I have spent a lifetime watching you, Claud. I have spent a lifetime sniffing at you. Your smell is everywhere, and I have learnt to interpret it. From the day I first set foot amongst you it came up to me, it filled my breathing, it gave me headaches at night, it caused me giddiness at important meetings. But I learnt about it, Claud, and learnt to endure it. And I know what it means, when I catch the faintest whiff of it.

(*Stands up, looks down at* CLAUD, *who is staring up in horror, and speaks whisperingly*.)

Did you take her at night, when I was asleep? Or did you notice me once staring from the wrong window? Did you laugh at me as I kept my watch? Slithering into the room, slithering. Here.

(*Touches* CLAUD's *forehead.*)
Here. Where the stink is.
(SIR HUBERT *straightens, turns away, puts his hands behind his back.*)
Well, there are no windows in this room, Claud, I think.

CLAUD: Please, please let me go. I'm so hungry. So hungry, sir.
(SIR HUBERT *turns around, looks down at him, blinks as if recognizing something, looks momentarily horrified.*)
I – I promise you, sir, I promise you, I never had anything to do with your wife, sir, never looked at her in that way. I didn't do anything, even in my mind I didn't. I never went to that place. I come from Stepney, sir, like I told you. I was brought up in Stepney, my father was a porter and my mother, she worked for some Jew people in Bethnal Green, she had lunch with them at their table, and I'm clean, sir, I have a bath every night.

SIR HUBERT: Clean, Claud? (*Laughs.*) This cellar is stinking with you.

CLAUD: (*Goes on*) I won't do it again, sir, ever, ever, if you let me go, I'll never do another drawing. Oh God, sir, please, I promise you, please.

SIR HUBERT: Just tell me the truth, Claud.

CLAUD: I never touched her. Ask her, sir, *ask* her.

SIR HUBERT: (*Stares at him in amazement*) Ask my *wife*?
(*Turns, goes out.*
CLAUD *begins to sob hysterically. The door opens and* SIR HUBERT *reappears, walking slowly. He is carrying a bowl in one hand of meat and in the other of water. He puts them on the floor, in front of* CLAUD, *who of course can't reach them. Goes out.* CLAUD *strains down at the food. The door opens.* SIR HUBERT's *hand appears, gropes for the light switch, darkness.*)

INT. LADY CAROLINE'S BEDROOM

LADY CAROLINE *is in her night-dress and dressing-gown, in bed, with her flask in her hand, peppermints beside her, reading. There is a*

knock on the door, she flicks the top of the flask, shoves it under the
pillow. Popping some peppermints into her mouth.

LADY CAROLINE: Is that you, dear?

> (SIR HUBERT *in his dressing-gown and pyjamas, enters, comes*
> *down and sits in the chair.*)

What is it, Hubert? Are you all right?

SIR HUBERT: (*Stares at her blankly*) I can't seem to sleep tonight.
(*Little pause.*) I went off for a minute, and then I had a dream.
(*Little pause, makes a mechanical chuckle.*) I thought I would
keep you company for a while. (*Little pause.*) Or perhaps try
one of those aspirins you get from our . . . (*Voice trails off.*)

LADY CAROLINE: I've used them all, my dear, I'm sorry, but you
know what my head has been. Have you tried closing your
eyes and humming to yourself, that's what I do.

SIR HUBERT: But I don't want to sleep if I'm going to have bad
dreams. (*Very intently.*) It's better to stay awake, I think.
(*Stares at her.*) It was about you, my dear.

LADY CAROLINE: (*Interested*) About me? What was it?

SIR HUBERT: You were in danger. Great danger. And I – I was
powerless to help you, I was bound and helpless, watching
you being –

> (*Shakes his head, unable to go on.*)

LADY CAROLINE: (*Eagerly*) What?

SIR HUBERT: I don't know. I woke up and went straight to the
window, but there was nothing there. (*Pause.*) Do you ever
have such dreams, my dear?

LADY CAROLINE: No. I have funny dreams, they don't mean
anything. When I was in Kjiarna I had dreams about being
back in Roehampton with Uncle Richie and now we're in
London I have dreams about having tea with Geraldine
MacPherson, but I certainly don't sleep as well as I used to in
Kjiarna, but that's not surprising with all this worry.

SIR HUBERT: You don't ever feel my dear – (*hesitates*) – as if
someone were trying to break in?

LADY CAROLINE: Break in what, dear, to my sleep you mean?

SIR HUBERT: Yes. Force his way in? You don't feel that, do you,
my dear?

LADY CAROLINE: No I don't, I'm sure I'd remember it if I did, what a funny idea, Hubert.

(SIR HUBERT *after a long pause, gets up, goes over, looks down at her. She stares up at him, smiling.*)

SIR HUBERT: I love you so much, my dear. So very much. (*Bends down, kisses her, she turns her mouth away so that he kisses her on the cheek. He exits.*)

(LADY CAROLINE *watches him, then reaches under the pillow.*)

INT. CELLAR

Light on.

CLAUD *is staring up, the two bowls out of his reach just below him.*

SIR HUBERT: (*Off screen*) There was resistance, of course?

CLAUD: Yes, sir. (*His voice very husky.*) But I was too strong, sir. And she was asleep, sir.

SIR HUBERT: Every last garment, I think.

(CLAUD *nods.*)

(SIR HUBERT *still off screen, his voice only just in control.*) And then, sir?

CLAUD: I forced myself.

SIR HUBERT: And?

CLAUD: (*Whispering*) I did it, sir.

(*He looks at* SIR HUBERT *beggingly. There is a long pause, then the camera swings to* SIR HUBERT *sitting on the trunk. A pad on his knee, a pen in hand.*)

SIR HUBERT: Let us go back to the scene in the bar, Claud, please.

CLAUD: I saw her there, sir, she was standing there, and I was behind it. It's my work, sir. I looked up and there she was.

SIR HUBERT: What did she want?

CLAUD: A – (*frowns, shakes his head*) – was it aspirins, sir?

SIR HUBERT: And how was she dressed?

CLAUD: In white, sir?

SIR HUBERT: (*Writing*) And she was –

CLAUD: Very beautiful, sir. Oh, very beautiful.

SIR HUBERT: (*Writing*) Which is why –

CLAUD: (*Nodding*) This is why I couldn't help myself, sir, because she was so beautiful, sir, there was such kindness and graciousness in her ladyship, sir, what could I do?

SIR HUBERT: Yes?

CLAUD: I leaned across the bar and I uttered some words, sir.

SIR HUBERT: The words, Claud?

CLAUD: (*Looks at him, slyly*) I can't remember the words, they rose up in me they came from something bad, but that's gone now, sir, and I can't remember the words, sir.

SIR HUBERT: The words, Claud, please.

CLAUD: I can't remember, honestly can't remember, please I can't, sir.

(SIR HUBERT *snaps the pad shut, puts his pen away, walks to the door.*)

Wait, wait, yes, I remember, yes, sir.

(SIR HUBERT *comes back, stares at him.*)

I was too ashamed to say them to you, sir.

(SIR HUBERT *sits down, opens his pad, waits.*)

Hello, baby.

(SIR HUBERT *writes.*)

How do you like this black boy here, baby?

(SIR HUBERT *writes.*)

And she was angry with me, sir, I could see she was disgusted with me for it, sir, like I am disgusted now, sir. She went away from me.

SIR HUBERT: But you brought her back, Claud, I think?

CLAUD: Yes, yes. No. She come back, sir, because she was so kind and gracious she had already forgiven me, and this time I didn't say anything. I had learnt my lesson, I kept my eyes from off of her and brought her the bottle of gin –

SIR HUBERT: (*Sharply*) The bottle of –?

CLAUD: As–pirin, not gin, I don't know why I say gin, sir. (*Shakes his head, laughs.*) And she took the aspirins sir and she went upstairs.

SIR HUBERT: (*Writing*) And how did you get into her room?

CLAUD: She forgot to lock the door, sir?

(SIR HUBERT *stares at him.*)

I picked the lock, sir. I'm very good at that.

SIR HUBERT: (*Writing*) And where was I, Claud?

CLAUD: You were in the next room, sir, watching for me from the window, sir.

SIR HUBERT: (*Writes*) And what did you do?

CLAUD: I – I undressed myself, sir.

(SIR HUBERT *nods, writes.*)

Then I climbed in, between the white sheets, sir, and I took her in my arms, your lady-wife, sir.

SIR HUBERT: She remained asleep, Claud, I think.

CLAUD: Yes, yes, she was asleep still. (*Little pause.*) And so was I, sir. Yes, I was, it was in a nightmare it happened, everything was asleep, I didn't know what I was doing, the black in me was moving me to everything, because of my lips and hair you explained to me, sir, and suddenly it was happening –

SIR HUBERT: (*Interrupting*) Keep to the facts, please, Claud. My wife was in a night-gown, of course?

CLAUD: Oh yes, sir. Very beautiful in her night-gown, sir, and gracious.

SIR HUBERT: Describe, it, please.

CLAUD: It was – it was transparent, sir.

SIR HUBERT: (*Writing*) Transparent. You could see through it, therefore?

CLAUD: No, sir. I kept my eyes sealed, sir.

SIR HUBERT: (*Very calmly*) And what did you do then, Claud?

(CLAUD *desperately thinking, close-up of his face.*)

CLAUD: I – I – did it, sir.

(SIR HUBERT *shuts his notebook, gets up, turns to the door.*)

Please, sir, there is more, sir, more.

SIR HUBERT: Lies, Claud. More lies, sir. My wife has never owned a transparent night-gown, she *would* not own such a thing. I trapped you there, I think, Claud. (*He goes to the door.*)

CLAUD: (*Screaming*) Yes, yes, I lie, yes. I wouldn't touch her, the old bag, I wouldn't touch the old bag, your lady wife, she makes me sick, filthy old white gin filth, makes me sick. She drinks.

(SIR HUBERT *walks on, out of the door, close-up of his face, set and deaf.* CLAUD *stares at the door, then* SIR HUBERT *comes back in, leaving door open, the keys jangling in his hand.*)

SIR HUBERT: You must be calmer, Claud. You make me forget my responsibility to you.

CLAUD: I'm sorry I said that, sir, your wife is so beautiful, so beautiful. (*Little pause.*)But it couldn't be me who did that to her, sir. Not your Claud. (*Little pause.*) I'm very queer, sir.

(SIR HUBERT *takes out his notebook.*)

SIR HUBERT: Yes, Claud?

CLAUD: I had a friend, sir, he left me. Ask them, they all know in The Gay Baron, Amble Street, South Kensington, sir. They'll tell you there. Find Micky, he'll tell you, he loves me, sir, he's in America now. Yes, he'll help me. (*Little pause.*) That cricketing gentlemen, sir, *he* knows. He knows me, I saw him in Amble Street, he knows me.

(SIR HUBERT *puts his pad away with a smile.*)

SIR HUBERT: We all know you, Claud. We all know you for what you are. And now you're beginning to know us a little better, sir, I think.

(*Bends down, unlocks Claud's chain around the neck, pushes the bowls close.* CLAUD *looks up at him.*)

Come now, my Claud, help yourself.

(*Goes to the trunk, sits down, watches with a smile. Goes out. Indicate time passing – about a week.*)

INT. LIVING-ROOM

LADY CAROLINE *enters, followed by* MR GREATORIX.

LADY CAROLINE: . . . you to say that, and I would have given you more notice, but *I'll* have to do the clearing up, won't I, and frankly, Mr Greatorix, I'm not up to it any more. I'm really not, and nor is Sir Hubert, he's got a great deal on his plate, you know. (*Looking around the room.*) Wherever he is.

MR GREATORIX: I think I can assure you, Lady Harriet, that we'll find someone to help you out. Perhaps he's upstairs.

LADY CAROLINE: If I know him, he'll be doing something he shouldn't be, he always takes on more than he can chew.
(*In on* SIR HUBERT, *smiling, seated on the trunk.*
(CLAUD *off screen, and in between gobbling noises.*)

CLAUD: Into her, sir, you know me, sir, grabbed hold of him and tore off the clothes he was in. White. Oh, she's beautiful, so scrawny white and beautiful, sir, I confess to it, me touch her for you if you wish, you know me, sir, I think, this one for black Claud, that one for sir. I think you know me sir, I can't help myself.

SIR HUBERT: There there, Claud, it's all right, sir, it 's all right, boy.

INT. LIVING-ROOM

LADY CAROLINE *is sitting on the piano stool.* MR GREATORIX *is standing by the door, left, which is open.*

MR GREATORIX: There'll be nothing for you to do but unpack your personals and have a nice hot bath. (*Little pause.*) I'd be happy to give you a lift back if you think you might have to wait. Or shall I try the cellar, first?

LADY CAROLINE: No, no, he'll turn up, well perhaps if you wouldn't mind, the only thing is, Mr Greatorix, is this person you have in mind reliable for the garden and the girl – can she be trusted?

MR GREATORIX: (*Ducking his head*) I'm sure you'll be satisfied with her, Lady Caroline, she's never been in trouble that I know of.

LADY CAROLINE: Oh dear! I don't know, I really don't. This gardener, now.

INT. CELLAR

In on CLAUD *who is staring up, nodding.*
SIR HUBERT: (*Off screen*) Should bring out the best in a man, if he's

a real man. That's what a crisis is for, sir, in a sense. They had to know who they were dealing with. So I strapped it over my handle-bars, the tail dangling over the crossbar, the head level with the bell, and pedalled along to the compound. He screeched, of course, and jabbered and capered about, but you could have knocked him over with a tjonker. (*Little pause.*) That night these parrots of ours started up, every tree in the garden, sir –

INT. LIVING-ROOM

MR GREATORIX *is standing by the window*, LADY CAROLINE *with him.*

MR GREATORIX: . . . again, Lady Caroline, unless you want to change your mind about that lift. Which would be *my* pleasure, of course.

LADY CAROLINE: No, I'll catch Sir Hubert at whatever he's up to – oh, you were kind enough to offer to peep into the cellar for me, I really can't bear it down there, the smell makes my head spin.

MR GREATORIX: Of course.

(*Ducks his head, goes to the door, right. Opens it, goes on down. Shot of* LADY CAROLINE *sitting down again, feeling in her handbag, pauses, takes out two peppermints which she pops into her mouth.*)

INT. THE DOOR BEFORE THE CELLAR

MR GREATORIX *approaches the door before the cellar which is slightly open.*

SIR HUBERT'S VOICE: . . . Kept an eye open all night, but how could I see any black bodies in all that darkness. That was it you see, devils to track in the dark, you've got to have them somewhere you can leave them without a spot of worry –

(MR GREATORIX *a close-up of his face, frowning, clears his throat slightly*.)

INT. LIVING-ROOM

LADY CAROLINE *is just stuffing the flask back into her bag. She looks up, looks very embarrassed.*

LADY CAROLINE: Oh. (*Laughs.*)

MR GREATORIX: Well, he *is* down there, Lady Caroline, but he seemed to be in the middle of a serious talk, so I didn't want to disturb him, I thought I'd just let you know where he was.

LADY CAROLINE: Oh, well thank you. Mr Greatorix, thank you very much. (*Gets up.*) How kind you are, well (*as* MR GREATORIX *goes towards the windows, accompanying him*) we'll see you soon with those persons you've got arranged to help me, then?

MR GREATORIX: Yes indeed, Lady Caroline. (*With a knowing smile just on display.*) Yes, I'm at your service, whenever you want me.

(*Steps out, into the garden.* LADY CAROLINE *turns, makes a worried face, puts peppermints into her mouth, closes her handbag, walks to the door, left. Stands at the door, calls.*)

LADY CAROLINE: Hubert! Hubert!

INT. CELLAR

SIR HUBERT *is standing pumping the hygiene spray around, there is a clinking of chains.*

SIR HUBERT: . . . A wash and brush up, Claud, and clean out this mess, which is a filthy job, let me tell you that, but it's my responsibility, it's always been my responsibility, and always will be, I think. But I'll keep you clean, Claud, whatever *you* may want . . .

INT. LIVING-ROOM

LADY CAROLINE *leaning through the door calling irritably.*
LADY CAROLINE: Hu-bert! Hu-bert!
  (*Disappears from view, her voice fading as she descends.*)
  Hubert! Hubert!

INT. LIVING-ROOM. EVENING

Open with a close-up of an African face, laughing, as much like
CLAUD's *as possible. Then distance away from him, to show him*
behind a table which has been made into a bar, and taking in the room
as a whole. It is fully furnished now, table, chairs, flowers
everywhere. The room is full of elderly people, most of them white, in
evening-suits, formal gowns, etc., with a few Africans. The windows
are open. There is conversation and laughter.
Include a shot of LADY CAROLINE *at the bar, talking to the barman*
animatedly. She has no glass in her hand.
Then cut to two beside the open window, their backs to it, and shift
from them to SIR HUBERT *and* SIR GEOFFREY, *standing directly in*
front of the open windows but facing into the living-room.

SIR HUBERT: . . . because someone has to tell them, hasn't he,
  what it's like to live over there, work amongst them and live
  for them? To show the feeling of the place and people, I
  think. I know them, you see – ah there you are, my dear,
  how's our Fred the barman shaping up? I saw you winding
  him around your little finger.
  (*He chuckles.* SIR GEOFFREY *smiles.*)
LADY CAROLINE: Oh, he seems very nice, but Hubert, dear, I
  thought I heard him a minute ago, howling.
SIR HUBERT: Sixth sense, my dear, sixth sense. You couldn't
  have heard him, you must have been listening for him in
  your mind.
SIR GEOFFREY: Sounds like a dog?
SIR HUBERT: (*As he and* LADY CAROLINE *smile at each other*) Most
  like, extremely like, Geoffrey.

LADY CAROLINE: A very hungry one, dear.

SIR GEOFFREY: Oh, what kind? And what's his name?

SIR HUBERT: A rather wild one, when I first got hold of him, to tell you the truth, I think he's a mixture of things, but almost exactly the opposite of poor little Whitey.

LADY CAROLINE: We call him Rover. He gets very upset sometimes, if Hubert hasn't been down to keep him calm, or if his meals aren't punctual, he throws himself against his chain and tries to break free, we're afraid he'll do something to his neck. (*Little pause.*) It's for his own good, you know.

SIR GEOFFREY: Ah, my favourite domestic moral. The dog's the master, the master's the servant.

SIR HUBERT: (*Shaking his head, chuckling.*) Oh, he is a great responsibility, feeding him, keeping him clean and healthy, but you know, once you take one on, Geoffrey. (*Shakes his head*).

LADY CAROLINE: (*Winsomely*) Can I go down and give him a snack, dear?

(*They exchange looks. Then* SIR HUBERT *smiles and nods,* LADY CAROLINE *goes through the crowds, to the door, right.*)

SIR HUBERT: (*Watching her*) He and Caroline didn't get on at first, there was some – (*smiles*) you should have seen her face when I brought them together, and his – jealousy, some jealousy about I think, but now she's got used to him, and he's got used to her, they're the greatest of friends, can hardly tear them apart. (*Shakes his head.*) Now where were we?

SIR GEOFFREY: I know where *I* was. I was in the middle of thinking that you're quite your old self again. (*Little pause.*) You seemed a wee bit on edge when you first got back.

SIR HUBERT: Was I? Perhaps I was. (*Gets up, turns to the window, looks out.*) Perhaps there was something missing, that I'd left behind and thought I'd never recover. It's peaceful here, after all. Listen to it, if you can hear it above the babel of human voices – the calm of England. It's a real sound, I tell you, Geoffrey, a real sound. I'd forgotten it, you see, how peaceful a home was. But there was the extra feeling, you know, of Kjiarna, that I'd got used to. I missed it. You have to have it sometimes, and to know that you've got it safe, where it can't get at you. Or if it's going to get at you, then to know where it comes from, what it looks like. (*Little pause.*) I found it here all right, in the end. I couldn't miss it, once I'd set myself to watch for it. Now I've got it pinned down, you see, got it straight in my mind and keep it under control. (*Turns, smiles.*) After all, I've kept it under control for thirty-five years. Do you know what I mean?

SIR GEOFFREY: (*After a pause*) More of you chaps come back mystics – poets, philosophers, saints – I suppose that's what happens to you, if you carry the experience of a whole continent around in you, the beaurocrats at home know what we owe to –

LADY CAROLINE: (*Coming between them*) He's asleep. I must have imagined it, dear, after all.

SIR HUBERT: But it was as well, to look, I think. (*Smiles at* LADY CAROLINE.) My dear, your hand is empty.

SIR GEOFFREY: What can I get you, Caroline?

LADY CAROLINE: Nothing, thank you, nothing.

SIR HUBERT: Well, my dear, in that case, what about a tune?

SIR GEOFFREY: Oh, yes please.

(LADY CAROLINE *smiles graciously, and goes off. The two men watch her, then* SIR HUBERT *turns to the window, looks out, smiling calmly.*)

INT./EXT.

The camera rests on SIR HUBERT'*s face, then retreats slowly to a long-distance view of the house. There should be, first of all, the laughter and talk of the party, then the sounds of a tranquil English night – a few bird noises, an owl – then unmistakably, although muted, the slightly off-key chords of* LADY CAROLINE *at the piano. Fade out.*